Lifting the Veil on The Lost Continent of Mu, Motherland of Men

By
Jack E. Churchward

This volume contains the entire contents of the original 1926 version of
The Lost Continent of Mu: Motherland of Men
and
Accumulated Research

OZARK
MOUNTAIN
PUBLISHING

PO Box 754, Huntsville, AR 72740
800-935-0045 or 479-738-2348 or fax 479-738-2448
www.ozarkmt.com

For permission, serialization, condensation, adaptions, or for our catalog of other publications, write to Ozark Mountain Publishing, Inc., P.O. Box 754, Huntsville, AR 72740, ATTN: Permissions Department.

Library of Congress Cataloging-in-Publication Data

Churchward, Jack, 1957 -

Lifting the Veil on the Lost Continent of Mu, the Motherland of Men, by Jack Churchward

New information on the lost continent of Mu.

1. Mu 2. James Churchward 3. Lost Continent

I. Churchward, Jack, 1957- II. Mu III. Title

Library of Congress Catalog Card Number: 2011928011

ISBN: 978-1-886940-17-8

Cover Art and Layout: www.noir33.com

Book set in: Baskerville Oldface, Times New Roman

Book Design: Julia Degan

Published by:

PO Box 754, Huntsville, AR 72740

800-935-0045 or 479-738-2348 or fax 479-738-2448

www.ozarkmt.com

Printed in the United States of America

Lifting the Veil on
The Lost Continent of Mu: Motherland of Men

Table of Contents

This work is dedicated to:

The memory of a dear, late friend,
Christopher Cromie

and

Helen & Robert Sarver
for all you do to help

Preface

The purpose of this volume is to examine the underlying evidence that James Churchward presents in the 1926 "The Lost Continent of Mu: Motherland of Men." The pursuit of identifying his sources and by extension, his research materials, is the ultimate aim. In addition to creating possible avenues of future investigation, the current work can be evaluated as one volume of the many that he authored.

Except for autobiographical information, I have examined the presented material and provided amplifying information in the form of Notes. Where further detail is required, Appendices have been created. A thorough treatment of James' biography "My Friend Churchey and His Lost Sunken Continent of Mu" in addition to new research will paint a more complete picture of James Churchward. It would be unfair to link his personal life to his theories. Therefore, those assertions by James of personal experience shall go unchallenged, unexamined and discussed elsewhere.

In addition to an index and notes, this work also contains Appendices to discuss topics in more depth than the notes. Persons of Interest mentioned are contained in their own appendix with:
   a. A short biography,
   b. Quotes and/or text attributed to them,
   c. A quotation of the original source document (if applicable or available,)*
   d. Further references in his scrapbooks or elsewhere, and
   e. A list of works that the Person of Interest has published and/or written.

The Quoted Works mentioned in the text are also assigned their own appendix with:
   a. A brief description of the work
   b. Name of the author and cross-reference to the appropriate page in the Persons of Interest appendix,
   c. The relevant passage from the text,
   d. A quotation from the original source (if applicable or available.)*

* Please note that the "Quotations from the original source" have been handled as follows:
The quotes supplied as the 'original,' have not always been drawn from the source document. In some instances, this researcher was unable to find the quoted text in the original documents perhaps due to the differences in translation or other reasons. Digging into James' scrapbooks and other volumes he was purported to have, equivalent passages were substituted when found. Some of the books are easily identified – such as the LePlongeon books that Percy Tate Griffith mentions in his biography of James or those authored by his brother Dr. Albert Churchward. The inclusion of excerpts from these works does not imply or certify that these excerpts are the primary source of the quoted passage. As a regular broadcaster on WNYC – James had access to the best libraries in New York City on which to base his research.

To save a few trees, the text from the original has been compressed and as many complete pages as possible are placed on a single page. The original page delineation will remain distinct. Footnotes from the original will use normal type and the newly added notes will be enclosed in parentheses and reference an entry in the "Notes" section for each chapter. Also note that the original text is in a different font "Baskerville Old Face" and any new material is done in "Times New Roman."

Lastly, there are texts promulgated to cause division, inspire contempt for others, and/or set an agenda. This is not one of them. As a researcher, I undertook this work to learn more about the theories and underlying evidence. Rationally and without prejudice I gathered evidence and have presented it here. I neither categorically commend nor condemn the works, the authors, or any of their other theories – the evidence is simply presented. If after reading some material contained herein deemed insensitive or even offensive, please be aware of the period in which it was created. The reader is assumed to have free will to either accept or reject any assumptions, comments, remark or evidence and form their own opinions on the veracity of the data. Actually, it is required.

Jack E. Churchward
Clearwater, Florida

The Lost Continent of Mu

the Motherland of Men

By
James Churchward

Originally published:
New York
William Edwin Rudge
1926

Page iii

PREFACE

All matters of science in this work are based on the translations of certain ancient Naacal(2) tablets which I discovered in India many years ago. These tablets were written either in Burma or in Mu, the lost continent, and their extreme age is attested by the fact that legendary history says that the Naacals left Burma more than 15,000 years ago.

Some of the subjects embodied in these tablets are: An account of the creation of the earth; Life and its origin; the origin and workings of the Forces.

With the aid of the high priest of the temple I deciphered and translated these tablets, which unfortunately were only fragments of the various subjects. I spent many years proving, as far as possible by experimentation, that the facts set forth were true. This work represents over fifty years of investigation and research and embodies what I have found written on these ancient and intensely interesting tablets.

The gist of them indubitably establishes to my own satisfaction that at one time the earth had an incalculably ancient civilization which was, in many respects, superior to our own, and far in advance of us in some important essentials that the modern world is just beginning to have cognizance of. These tablets, with other ancient records,

Page iv

bear witness to the amazing fact that the civilizations of India, Babylonia, Persia, Egypt and Yucatan were but the dying embers of this great past civilization.

I desire here to express my appreciation and thanks for the courtesies and contributions received for the benefit of this book from: The British Museum, London; *The Dearborn Independent*, Dearborn, Michigan; *The American Weekly*, New York; and *The World*, New York.

The Lost Continent of Mu, Motherland of Men
Dedication and Preface Notes

(1) Dr. George L. Tanzer is discussed in the Persons of Interest Appendix beginning on page 53.

(2) The "*Nacaal Tablets*" are discussed in the Written Works Appendix beginning on page 29.

CONTENTS

1
Alpha - The Beginning

The Garden of Eden was not in Asia but on a now sunken continent in the Pacific Ocean. The biblical story of creation-the epic of the seven days and seven nights came first not from the peoples of the Nile or of the Euphrates Valley but from this now submerged continent, Mu-the Motherland of Man.

These assertions can be proved by the complex records which I discovered upon long-forgotten sacred tablets in India,(1) together with records from other countries. They tell of this strange country of 64,000,000 inhabitants, who, 50,000 years ago, had developed a civilization superior in many respects to our own. They described, among other things, the creation of man in the mysterious land of Mu.

By comparing this writing with records of other ancient civilizations, as revealed in written documents, prehistoric ruins and geological phenomena, I found that all these centers of civilization had drawn their culture from a common source-Mu. We may, therefore, be sure that the biblical story of the

---

Page 2

creation as we know it today has evolved from the impressive account gathered from those ancient tablets which relate the history of Mu-history 500 centuries old.

The manner in which this original story of the creation came to light forms a tale that takes us back more than fifty years.

It was a famine time in India. I was assisting in relief work the high priest of a college temple. Although I did not know it at first, he was exceedingly interested in archaeology and the records of the ancients, and had a greater knowledge of those subjects than any other living man.

When he saw one day that I was trying to decipher a peculiar bas-relief, he took an interest in me that brought about one of the truest friendships I have known. He showed me how to solve the puzzle of these peculiar inscriptions and offered to give me lessons which would fit me for still more difficult work.

For more than two years I studied diligently a dead language which my priestly friend believed to be the original tongue of mankind. He informed me that this language was understood by only two other high priests in India. A great difficulty arose from the fact that many of the apparently simple inscriptions had hidden meanings which had been designed especially for the Holy Brothers -the Naacals (2)-a priestly brotherhood, who were sent from the motherland to the colonies to teach the sacred writings, religion and the sciences.

One day, when he was in a talkative mood, he told me that there were a number of ancient tablets in the secret archives of the temple. What they consisted of he did not know, for he had seen only the chatties which contained them. Although he was in a position to examine the writings he had never done so, as they were sacred records not to be touched.

In discussing these secret writings he added something that sent my curiosity up to a new high point. He had already mentioned the legendary motherland of man-the mysterious land of Mu. Now he amazed me by the admission that these precious tablets were believed by many to have been written by the Naacals, either in Burma or in the vanished motherland itself. I became impatient to see them when I learned that the writings were only fragments of a vast collection that had been taken from one of the seven Rishi (sacred) cities of India. The bulk of them was believed to have been lost. Still, however, there remained this opportunity to see what I might of the ancient fragments of antiquity that lay dust-laden in the dark.

Day after day I attempted to discover some method by which I could obtain access to these hidden treasures, but my friend, although extremely courteous, was adamant in his refusal to let me see them.

"My son," he would say, with a touch of sadness in his voice, "I would that I could satisfy your desire, but that may not be. They are sacred relics that must not be taken out of their containers. I dare not grant your wish."

"But think-they may not be packed properly and may break and crumble in their boxes," I urged. "We should at least look at them to see if they are safe."

But this argument was of no avail.

Six months passed. Curiosity or anxiety about their condition had won the contest over my priestly friend, for one

evening on the table in front of him two of the ancient tablets were lying on a cloth.

I examined the long-hidden tablets with curiosity. They were apparently of sun-burnt clay and extremely dusty. With great care I cleaned them and then set to work deciphering the characters that were in the same dead language that I had been studying with my friend.

Fortune was with me that evening, for these two precious forms of clay revealed facts of such import that we both realized that here indeed were the genuine records of Mu. The history, however, broke off abruptly at a most interesting point at the bottom of the second tablet. Not even the high priest could restrain his curiosity to see the rest.

"It is impossible for us to leave off here, my son," he said " will get the next tablets out tomorrow."
Fortunately, the next tablets that he procured were not of the same series, but had to do with an entirely different subject, and in order to find the consecutive tablets all had to be brought out. It was well, for many of the tablets had been so badly packed that they were broken. These we restored with cement. When I repacked them, I wrapped each tablet in tissue paper and cotton wool.

"My son," said the priest, "I feel that a sacred warning was sent to me through your voice to safeguard these relics."

Months of intense concentration in translating the tablets followed, but the reward justified the effort. The writings described in detail the creation of the earth and of man, and the place where he first appeared-Mu.

Realizing that I had unearthed secrets that were of

Page 5

great importance in the elucidation of that eternal problem, Man, I sought the other lost tablets, but without success. I carried letters of introduction to high priests of temples throughout India, but in every instance I was received with coldness and suspicion.

"I have not seen any such tablets," each would declare, and doubtless they were telling the truth. Like my friend, they had probably only looked at the containers.

Once in Burma, I visited an ancient Buddhist temple in my search for the missing records.

"From where do you come?" asked the high priest, looking at me with veiled suspicion.

"From India," I replied.

"Then go back to India and ask the thieves who stole them from us to show them to you." And, spitting on the ground at my feet, he turned and walked away.

These rebuffs disheartened me somewhat, but I had already obtained so much valuable information from the tablets that I determined to study the writings of all the old civilizations and compare them with the legends of Mu.

This I did, and found that the civilizations of the early Greeks, the Chaldeans, the Babylonians, the Persians, the Egyptians and the Hindus had been definitely preceded by the civilization of Mu.

Continuing my researches, I discovered that this lost continent had extended from somewhere north of Hawaii to the south as far as the Fijis and Easter Island, and was undoubtedly the original habitat of man. I learned that in this beautiful country there had lived a people that colonized the earth, and that this land of smiling plenty had

---

Page 6

been obliterated by terrific earthquakes and submersion 12,000 years ago, and had vanished in a vortex of fire and water.

Also I learned an original story of the creation of the world. It was on the continent of Mu that man first came into being.

I have traced this same story from Mu to India (3), where colonizers from the vanished continent had settled; from India into Egypt (4); from Egypt to the temple of Sanai (5), where Moses copied it; and from Moses to the faulty translations of Ezra 800 years later (6). The plausibility of this will be apparent even to those who have not studied the subject carefully, when they see the close resemblance between the story of the creation as we know it and the tradition that originated in Mu.

Before commencing to relate the writings on the tablets I will give a page of the vignettes found on them, with their decipherings and translations:

NAACAL TABLETS

Vignette la. Fine, straight, horizontal lines. Symbol for space.

Vignette 1b. Symbolizes the Seven-headed Serpent moving in space. The surrounding circle is the universe.

Vignette 2. Wavy horizontal lines. Symbol for earthly waters.

Vignette 3. The circle is a picture of the sun. The sun was the collective symbol of all the attributes of the deity.

Vignette 4. Fine vertical lines from the sun symbolizing his forces which are affinitive to the earth's light force,

Some of the interesting symbols and vignettes found on the Naacal tablets which, being set in movement, gives light upon the earth.

Vignette 5. Vertical wavy lines from the sun symbolize the sun's forces which are affinitive to the earth's heat force; they meet and the earth's heat force becomes active.

Vignette 6a, Vertical dotted lines from the sun symbolize his forces which are affinitive to the earth's life force.

Vignette 6b. Symbolizes the sun's affinitive forces striking the earth's life force in cosmic eggs, which are in the water, and bringing them into life.

Vignette 6c. Symbolizes the sun's affinitive forces striking the earth's life force in cosmic eggs, which are on the land, and hatching them into life.

Vignette 7. This is the geometrical symbol that was assigned by the ancients to Mu. It is also the hieratic letter M and reads: "Moo, Ma, mother, land, field, country" and "mouth."

Vignette 8. The Tau was the symbol of resurrection in Mu. It is a picture of the constellation, the Southern Cross. The Tau also symbolizes "bringing forth," "emerge," etc.

Vignette 9. The lotus flower was the floral symbol of Mu. Tradition says that the lotus was the first flower to appear upon the earth, and for that reason it was adopted as the symbolical flower of the motherland.

Vignette 10. Three was the symbolic numeral adopted to represent Mu. This was because the continent consisted of three separate areas of land divided from each other by narrow channels or seas.

Vignette 11. Keh—the leaping deer—is frequently found

---

in the Naacal tablets; it is the symbol of "first man." This animal was selected to symbolize the first man because of its leaping power. Man came on earth fully and perfectly developed; he "leaped" upon the earth in his first and original form without going through nature's development of life. In other words, he was a special creation.

Vignette 12. This was the ancient symbol for fire in Mu. The lines began thick at the bottom and wave and taper to a fine point.

Vignette 13. This vignette appears on a tablet describing the raising of the mountains and the formation of gas belts. Therefore, we see where the Egyptians obtained their symbol of fire; also the scarab. The Naacals from India carried them to Egypt. The Egyptian fire symbol is only a modification of the Naga. The Egyptians put a handle on the Naga and turned it into a sword. It is not hard to find the reason for the Egyptian change or modification. In their hieroglyphics they wanted to depict two forms of fire: the fires of the underneath and actual flames. This they did to record the destruction of the motherland, which they say "sank into a fiery abyss" and "was enveloped in flames as she went down." This symbol is shown in our chapter on the Egyptian sacred book, the Book of the Dead.**(7)**

Vignette 14. I consider this one of the most interesting of all those found on the Naacal tablets. It depicts man's advent on earth in the land of Mu. I will first dissect it by showing separately each symbol: A is the lotus, the symbolical flower of Mu.

Page 10

B Three pieces of foliage, giving Mu's numeral.

C The hieratic letter M, Mu's alphabetical symbol.

D The Tau symbol of resurrection, "emerging," "coming forth," and "to appear." The head of the Tau, being the hieratical letter M, also means land; so land is emerged.

E is the water symbol. The emerged land is surrounded by water.

F is Keh—the first man.

This vignette three times tells the name of the land, Mu, by the symbols A, B and C. Man, symbol F, is in the act of appearing on earth, leaping in the exuberance of his spirits.

This vignette was the cause of my world search for information regarding Mu.

I found that the tablets included several subjects and that it required a series of tablets to explain each subject. Each series ran from two tablets, the shortest, to sixteen, the longest. Fortunately for us, we found two tablets that were keys to the various symbols and hieroglyphics. I arranged the tablets as follows:

Series 1. A description of the creation down to and including the advent of man.

Series 2. The raising of the mountains by the "fires of the underneath" (gases) ; and provisions for the disposal of future gases.

Series 3. The origin and workings of the great forces throughout the universe.

Series 4. The origin and workings of the earth's great primary force, showing two divisions and differentiating between the two.

Page 11

Series 5. The origin and workings of the earth's great atomic force—a subdivision of one of the two principal divisions.

Series 6. The origin of the force that creates and sustains life, with its workings. A subdivision of one of the two principal divisions.

Series 7. The origin of life, showing what life is, the changes in the forms of life—imperative as the earth developed.

Series 8. The creation of man, showing what man is and in what way he differs from all other creations.

Series 9. The advent of man upon earth and where he first appeared, which was called in the tablets "the Motherland of Man." Unquestionably these were only the commencement of a long series—probably the early history of Mu.

Series 10. This series consisted of two tablets, but each was double the size of the others—possibly larger. They served as a key to the writings and vignettes on the other tablets.

It was the first two tablets of this series which started the work that ended in the translation of all. However, had we not possessed the key, our chances for deciphering the rest of the tablets would have been exceedingly small. Without the key, I do not believe that we could have deciphered one-half of the writings. Our work was made simpler by the old priest's amazing knowledge of the past. If he only grasped the first line of secret writing he knew what the rest of the tablet contained. He told me that it was believed that certain other temples had many such records that had been saved when the ancient cities were destroyed.

Page 12

Taking them in the foregoing order, the tablets start by saying:

"Originally, the universe was only a soul or spirit. Everything was without life—calm, silent, soundless. Void and dark was the immensity of space. Only the Supreme Spirit, the great Self-existing Power, the Creator, the Seven-headed Serpent, moved within the abyss of darkness.

"The desire came to Him to create worlds and He created worlds; and the desire came to Him to create the earth, with living things upon it, and He created the earth and all therein. And this is the manner of the creation of the earth, with all the living things upon it:—

"The seven superlative intellects of the Seven-headed Serpent gave seven commands." (I shall use the Naacal esoteric meanings as they are the most intelligible to the reader. The demotic are all symbolical and not easily understood.)

The first intellectual command was:

" 'Let the gases which are without form and scattered through space be brought together, and out of them let the earth be formed.' The gases then assembled themselves into the form of a whirling mass."

The second command was:

" 'Let the gases solidify to form the earth' Then the gases solidified; volumes were left on the outside, out of which water and the atmosphere were to be formed; and volumes were enveloped within the new world. Darkness prevailed and there was no sound, for as yet neither the atmosphere nor the waters were formed."

The third command was:

Page 13

" 'Let the outside gases be separated and let them form the atmosphere and the waters' And the gases were separated; one part went to form the waters, and the waters settled upon the earth and covered its face so that no land appeared anywhere. The gases that did not form the waters formed the atmosphere, and:

"*The light was contained in the atmosphere.*

"And the shafts of the sun met the shafts of the light in the atmosphere and gave birth to light. Then there was light upon the face of the earth; and (Fig. 4):

"*The heat was also contained in the atmosphere.*

"And the shafts of the sun met the shafts of the heat in the atmosphere and gave it life. Then there was heat to warm the face of the earth." (Fig. 5.)

The fourth command was:

" 'Let the gases that are within the earth raise the land above the face of the waters.' Then the fires of the under-earth lifted the land on which the waters rested until it appeared above the face of the waters, and this was the dry land."

The fifth command was:

" 'Let life come forth in the waters.' And the shafts of the sun met the shafts of the earth in the mud of the waters and there formed cosmic eggs (life germs) out of particles of the mud. Out of these cosmic eggs came forth life as commanded." (Fig. 6*b.*)

The sixth command was:

" 'Let life come forth upon the land.' And the shafts of the sun met the shafts of the earth in the dust of the land, and out of it formed cosmic eggs; and from these cosmic

Narayana, The Seven Headed Serpent. The symbol of the Creator and Creation

Nara means the Divine One; Yana – creator of all things; Naacals – seven superlative intellects; Vendanta – seven mental planes

(8)

Page 14

Page 15

eggs life came forth upon the earth as was commanded." (Fig. 6c.) And when all this was done, the seventh intellect said: "Let us make man after our own fashion, and let us endow him with powers to rule this earth."

"Then Narayana,(8) the Seven-headed Intellect, the Creator of all things throughout the universe, created man, and placed within his body a living, imperishable spirit, and man became *like* Narayana in intellectual power. Then was creation complete."

The seven commands are, without doubt, also indicative of seven periods of time. A period of time is not measured by any particular number of years. It may mean a day, a year, or millions of years. Thus these tablets do not assign any particular length of time to creation. It may have taken millions or tens of millions of years to accomplish what was recorded in the tablets. It is merely stated that the earth was created in seven periods of time, not in seven days, as recorded in the biblical legend.

The general resemblance of the opening part of the Naacal record, as regards the story of the creation, to the account as found in the Bible is remarkable, and it is also remarkable how great are the divergences thereafter. Legends of the creation are prevalent among peoples throughout the world, and in all instances I have found so much of the material identical that the only conclusion to be drawn is that they are of common origin and their genesis was in Mu.

The seventh command was the hardest of all to translate. The actual deciphering was easy, but we found it impossible to find modern words that would convey identically the same meanings as the ancient. For instance,

Page 16

"soul" or "spirit" were the nearest words we could find to represent what was put into the body of man. The word "living" may or may not be exactly what was intended in the original. The word "imperishable" is, without doubt, absolutely correct. But what does the phrase "after our own fashion" actually mean? Certainly not "in our own image." It, in some way, refers to mentality and mystic powers, and this is substantiated by the words: "endow him with powers to rule the earth."

The Bible uses a good symbolical example when it refers to "the breath of God." At any rate, it is clear that the meaning is *special powers received from God*, and may therefore be looked upon as a part of God, as a leaf is a part of the tree. Man came from God and must return whence he came.

The Naacal tablets were exceedingly difficult to decipher, there being so many vignettes and tableaux and so very little hieratic writing. Some of the parts were also so worn and obliterated that we could make nothing of them. Words also appeared for which we could find no equivalent in modern languages.

At the commencement of our studies my priestly friend informed me that it would be impossible to decipher ancient tablets and inscriptions without a knowledge of what he called the Naga-Maya language; as all of the ancient writings that have to do with Mu are in this language ; and, all Naacal writings have an esoteric or hidden meaning, known only to the Naacals and to those whom they taught. To this hidden language he held the key, and, after he had taught me its use, it proved a sesame that unlocked for me many strange doors.

Page 17

For more than two years I studied this ancient language, with intermittent decipherings to test my progress.

My old Hindu friend and teacher remarked when we had completed our task: "My son, we have got the general meaning but not the perfect detail." I must candidly admit that without this dear old gentle friend the tablets could never have been deciphered by me, I was totally incompetent.

I find the reflection of the teachings of these tablets, or other similar ones, in the old Hindu literature; also in old literature other than Hindu. As an example:

HINDU : *The Manava Dharma Sastra*, Book 2, sloka 74:

"In the beginning only existed the Infinite called Adite."

Book l, sloka 8: "This germ became an egg."

Book l, sloka 10: "The visible universe in the beginning was only darkness."

Book l, sloka 9: "He first produced the waters and in them deposited an egg."(9)

Rig Veda, sec. 3, 1. 2, v. 4, pp. 316-317 (2000-2500 B.C.): "In this egg was reproduced the intellect of the Supreme Being *under the form of Buddha*, through whose union with the goddess Maya, the good mother of all the gods and man . . ." (This corresponds with Adam and Eve 1,700 years later.) Page 3: "Other than Him nothing existed; darkness there was." Page 4: "He who measures out *the light in the air*."(10)

Aitareya-A'ram-'ya, slokas 4 to 8: "Originally this universe was only a soul, nothing active or inactive existed. The thought came to Him, "I wish to create worlds," and so He created the worlds, the light, the mortal beings, *the atmosphere that contains the light*, the earth that is perishable, and the lower depths, that of the waters."(11)

Page 18

Yucatan—Nahuatl: "The particles of *atmosphere* on being hit by the divine arrows became animated. Heat, which determines the movement of matter, *was developed in it.*"

There is no question whatever, and both written and legendary history say, that these books were written from ancient temple records, and that the Naacals wrote the temple histories, and taught religion and science.

In southern India the temples have libraries of ancient writings, but none, apparently, go back beyond the Sanskrit. I worked over several of these with high priests and they were all in Sanskrit and on religious subjects. As none of them contained any facts of historical value, I was not sufficiently interested to continue their study.

There are considerable variations of the legend of the creation in different sections of the world, which no doubt is due to the manner in which it has been handed down to generation after generation. Startling as it may appear, the most scientific version, and the one above all others except the Naacal that can be sustained by geological research, is the version found among the semi-savages and cannibalistic races of the South Sea Islands, especially the Marquesans.

The Hindu, Chaldean, Egyptian, Maya and the Greek in later times, describing the creation, eliminated the scientific sections and recorded, by the use of symbols the facts without the whys and wherefores. The reason for this is well told by Clement of Alexandria,(12) who said:

"The Egyptians neither entrusted their mysteries to every one nor degraded their secrets of divine matters by disclosing them to the profane; reserving them for the heir apparent to the throne, and to such of the priests who excelled in virtue and wisdom." In other words, the esoteric meanings were not given out publicly.

It is a certainty that the Egyptian legend of the creation, from which Moses (13) wrote the biblical account, came from India when the Naacals went to Egypt as missionaries to teach the seven sacred inspired writings, religion and the sciences. Therefore the dramatic story that is taught in Sunday schools throughout the Christian world today originated in the lost continent of Mu.

Chapter 1: Alpha—The Beginning Notes

(1) Material of an autobiographical nature is not covered in these notes. This is explained in the Preface.

(2) Nacaals/Nacaals Tablets are discussed in the Written Works Appendix beginning on page A2—26.

(3) Tracing the story from Mu to India is discussed on pages 59-60; see "VALMIKI. *Ramayana*. Vol. I Page 342. — "The Maya adepts, the Naacals…""

(4) Tracing the story from India to Egypt is discussed on pages 59-60; see #(3)

(5) Tracing the story from Egypt to Mount Sanai is discussed on pages 59-60. See #(3)

(6) Tracing the story of the faulty translation is discussed on pages 285-286

(7) The "*Egyptian Book of the Dead*" is discussed in the Written Works Appendix beginning on page A2—10.

(8) "Narayana" is mentioned in Le Plongeon's book: *Sacred Mysteries of the Mayas and Quiches*; (1886), page 109-110:
"We read in the *Manava-dharma-sastra* that the visible universe in the beginning was nothing but darkness. Then the great, self-existing Power dispelled that darkness, and appeared in all His splendor. He first produced the waters; and on them moved Narayana the divine spirit."; The same passage is also contained on page 256 of "*Queen Moo & The Egyptian Sphinx*"; Le Plongeon, Augustus; 1896.

(9) The "*Manava Dharma Sastra*" is discussed in the Written Works Appendix beginning on page A2—20.

(10) The "*Rig Veda*" is discussed in the Written Works Appendix beginning on page A2—29.

(11) The "*Aitareya-A'ram-'ya*" is discussed in the Written Works Appendix beginning on page A2—3.

(12) Clement of Alexandria [Titus Flavius Clemens] (150-215) was born in Athens and moved to Alexandria where he taught and practiced Christianity. He was forced to flee to Cappadocia (modern-day Turkey).
The quotation on pages 18-9 is from the Stromata, or Miscellanies Book V Chapter VII.
Excerpt from "Signs and Symbols of Primordial Man" (1912) provides this text:
> Clement of Alexandria tells us that "the Egyptians neither entrusted their mysteries to everyone, nor degraded the secrets of divine matters by disclosing them to the profanes, reserving them for the heir-apparent to the throne, and for such of the priests as excelled in virtue and wisdom."
> Albert Churchward, "Signs and Symbols of Primordial Man" (1912), page 10-11

(13) Moses is discussed in the Persons of Interest Appendix beginning on page A1—28.

2
The Lost Continent

The record of the destruction of Mu, the Motherland of Man, is a strange one indeed. From it we learn how the mystery of the white races in the South Sea Islands may be solved and how a great civilization flourished in mid-Pacific and then was completely obliterated in almost a single night. A few decades ago scientists would have been very doubtful about the possibility of the former existence in the Pacific Ocean of a huge continent such as Mu. But since then, records have come to light and comparisons have been made which prove that such a land did at one time exist. The proofs are of several types.

First, as I have already explained in the opening chapter, there are the sacred tablets found in an Indian temple and deciphered with the aid of a learned priest. These tablets gave me the first hint about Mu and sent me on a world-wide search. They had been written by the Naacals, either in Burma or in the motherland. They told how the Naacals had originally come from the motherland, the land in the center of the Pacific. They also told the story of the creation of man and his advent in this land. Rec-

ords of later date written in Mayax, Egypt and India tell and describe the destruction of this land of Mu, when the earth's crust was broken up by earthquakes and then sank into a fiery abyss. Then the waters of the Pacific rolled in over her, leaving only water where a mighty civilization
had existed.

Second, there is confirmation of Mu in other ancient manuscripts, including such a classic as the Hindu epic Ramayana **(1)**, written by the sage and historian, Valmiki **(2)**, from the dictation of Narana **(3)**, the high priest of the Rishi temple at Ayhodia, who read the ancient temple records to him. In one place Valmiki mentions the Naacals as "coming to Burma from the land of their birth in the East," that is, in the direction of the Pacific Ocean. Other documents confirming the story of the sacred tablets and Valmiki are: The Troano Manuscript **(4)**, now in the British Museum. This is an ancient Maya book written in Yucatan. It speaks of the "Land of Mu" using the same symbols for Mu that we find in India, Burma and Egypt. Another reference is the Codex Cortesianus **(5)**, a Maya book of about the same age as the Troano Manuscript. Then there is the Lhasa record **(6)**, with hundreds of others from Egypt, Greece, Central America, Mexico, and the cliff writings in our western states. **(7)**

Third, there are existing ruins which, by their location and the symbols with which they are decorated, tell of the lost continent of Mu, the motherland of man.
On some of the South Sea Islands, notably Easter, Mangaia, Tonga-tabu, Panape, and the Ladrone or Mariana Islands, there stand today remains of old stone temples and lithic remains which take us back to the time of Mu. **(8)**

Page 22

At Uxmal in Yucatan, a ruined temple bears inscriptions commemorative of the "Lands of the West, whence we came"(9); and the striking Mexican pyramid southwest of Mexico City, according to its inscriptions, was raised as a monument to the destruction of these same "Lands of the West."(10)

Fourth, there is the universality of certain old symbols and customs as discovered in Egypt, Burma, India, Japan, China, South Sea Islands, Central America, South America and some of the North American Indian tribes and other seats of ancient civilizations. These symbols and customs are so identical as to make it certain that they came from one source only—Mu. With this background, then, we can follow the tale of the destruction of Mu.

We find that this continent was a vast stretch of rolling country, extending from north of Hawaii, down towards the south. A line between Easter Island and the Fijis formed its southern boundary. It was over 5,000 miles from east to west, and over 3,000 miles from north to south. The continent consisted of three areas of land, divided from each other by narrow channels or seas.

Basing my description on the records shown in Chapters IV and V, I will try to picture her as she was.

(11) Back, far back, into very remote times — many, many thousands of years ago, and yet, on the very edge of what we call historical times—there was a great continent in the middle of the Pacific Ocean where now "we find only water and the sky," 1 and groups of small islands, which are today called the South Sea Islands.

1 Lhasa Record.

Page 23

It was a "beautiful"2 tropical country with "vast plains."3 The valleys and plains were covered with rich grazing grasses and tilled fields, while the "low rolling "hill-lands"4 were shaded by luxuriant growths of tropical vegetation. No mountains or mountain ranges stretched themselves through this earthly paradise to give an irregular, jagged, yet soft and graceful sky line. Mountains had not yet been forced up from the bowels of the earth.

This great rich land was intersected and watered by many broad, slow-running streams and rivers, which wound their sinuous ways in fantastic curves and bends around the wooded hills and through the fertile plains. Luxuriant vegetation covered the whole land with a soft, pleasing, restful mantle of green. Bright and fragrant flowers on tree and shrub added coloring and finish to the landscape. Tall fronded palms fringed the ocean's shores and lined the banks of the rivers for many a mile inland. Great feathery ferns spread their long arms out from the river banks. In valley places where the land was low, the rivers broadened out into shallow lakes, around whose shores myriads of sacred "lotus flowers"5 dotted the glistening surface of the water, like varicolored jewels in settings of emerald green.

Over the cool rivers, gaudy-winged butterflies hovered in the shade of the trees, rising and falling in fairy-like movements, as if better to view their painted beauty in nature's mirror. Darting hither and thither from flower to

2. Easter Island Tablet.
3. Greek Record.
4. Troano Manuscript.
5. Various Records.

Page 24

flower, tiny hummingbirds made their short flights, glistening like living jewels in the rays of the sun.6

Little feathered songsters in bush and tree vied with each other in their sweet lays.7

The chirpings of lively crickets filled the air, while above all other sounds came those of the locust as he industriously "ground his scissors," telling the whole world all was well with him.

Roaming through the primeval forests were herds of "mighty mastodons and elephants" napping their big ears to drive oft annoying insects." 8

All this great continent was teeming with gay and happy life over which "64,000,000 human beings" reigned supreme." 9 All this life was rejoicing in its luxuriant home.

Broad "smooth roads" ran in all directions "like a spider's web." These roads were laid with smooth stones, so perfectly matched that grasses could not grow between them. 10

At the time of our narrative, the 64,000,000 people were made up of "ten tribes" or "peoples," each one distinct from the other, but all under one government." 11

Many generations before, the people had selected a king and added the prefix Ra to his name. He then became the hieratical head and emperor under the name "Ra Mu."12

The empire received the name "Empire of the Sun."

6. S. A. Record.
7. Easter Island Tablet.
8. Indian and Maya Records.
9. Troano Manuscript.
10. Easter Island Tablet.
11. Troano Manuscript.
12. Lhasa Record and others.

Page 25

All followed the same religion, a worship of the Deity through symbols. All believed in the immortality of the soul, which soul eventually returned to the "great source" from whence it came.13

Their reverence for the Deity was so great that they never spoke His name, and in prayer and supplication always addressed Him through a symbol. "Ra the Sun" was used as the collective symbol for all His attributes."14

As high priest, Ra Mu was the representative of the Deity in religious teachings. It was thoroughly taught and understood that Ra Mu was not to be worshipped, as he was only representative.

At this time the people of Mu were very highly civilized and enlightened. *There was no savagery on the face of the earth, nor had there ever been,* for all the peoples on earth were children of Mu and were under the suzerainty of the motherland.

The dominant race in the land of Mu was a *white race* exceedingly handsome people, with clear white or olive skins, large, soft, dark eyes and straight black hair. Besides this white race, there were people of other races, people with yellow, brown or black skins. They, however, did not dominate.15 These ancient people of Mu were great navigators and sailors who took their ships all over the world "from the eastern to the western oceans and from the northern to the southern seas. They were also learned architects, building great temples and palaces

13. Lhasa Record and many others.
14. Maya and others.
15. Troano Manuscript, Codex Cortesianus and others.

Page 26

of stone."16 They carved and set up great monoliths of stone as monuments.

In the land of Mu there were *seven* great or principal cities, the seats of religion, science and learning.17 There were many other large cities, towns and villages scattered throughout the *three* lands.

Many cities were built at or near the mouths of the great rivers, these being the seats of trade and commerce, from which ships passed to and from all parts of the world. The land of Mu was the mother and the center of the earth's civilization, learning, trade and commerce; all other countries throughout the world were her colonies or colonial empires.

According to records, inscriptions and traditions, man's advent on earth was in the land of Mu and on this account the name "land of Kui" (12) was added to that of Mu.18 Great carved stone temples without roofs, sometimes called "transparent" temples, adorned the cities. These temples were roofless to permit the rays of Ra to fall on the heads of those in supplication and prayer, a symbol of acknowledgment by the deity. "The wealthy classes adorned themselves in fine raiment with many jewels and precious stones. They lived in imposing palaces attended by many servants. 19

Colonies had been started in all parts of the earth.

Being great navigators, their ships were constantly car-

16. Valmiki.
17. Lhasa Record.
18. Troano Manuscript and inscriptions.
19. Lhasa Record.

Page 27

rying passengers and merchandise to and from the various colonies.20

During cool evenings might be seen ships on pleasure bent, filled with gorgeously dressed, jewel-bedecked men and women. The long sweeps with which these ships were supplied gave a musical rhythm to the song and laughter of the merry passengers.

While thus this great land was at its zenith, while it was the center of the earth's civilization, learning, trade and commerce, and while great stone temples were being erected, and huge statues and monoliths were being set up,21 the land of Mu received a rude shock; a fearful visitation overtook her. Rumblings from the bowels of the earth, followed by earthquakes and volcanic outbursts, shook up the *southern* parts of the land of Mu.22

Along the southern shores of the continent great cataclysmic waves from the ocean rolled in over the land, and many a fair city went down to destruction. The volcanoes belched out their fire, smoke and lava. The country being flat, the lava did not run, but piled up, forming cones which subsequently became igneous rocks, and are to be seen today on some of the southern islands.23 Eventually the volcanic workings ceased. The volcanoes died out, and have ever since remained silent.

After the cessation of these volcanic workings, the people of the land of Mu gradually overcame their fright.

20. Valmiki.
21. Remains on the islands.
22. Easter and other islands
23. Easter and other islands.

The Destruction of Mu
"Temples and palaces came crashing to the ground"
Page 28

Page 29
The ruined cities were rebuilt and trade and commerce were resumed.

Many generations after this visitation, and when the phenomenon had become past history, Mu again became the victim of earthquakes. "*The whole continent* heaved and rolled like the ocean's waves. The land trembled and shook like the leaves of a tree in a storm. Temples and palaces came crashing to the ground and monuments and statues were overturned. The cities became heaps of ruins."[24]

As the land rose and fell, quivered and shook, the fires of the underneath burst forth, piercing the clouds in roaring flames *three miles in diameter.* [25] There they were met by lightning shafts which filled the heavens. A thick black pall of smoke overshadowed the land. "Huge cataclysmic waves rolled in over the shores [26] and extended themselves over the plains." Cities and all things living went down to destruction before them. "Agonizing cries of the multitude filled the air. The people sought refuge in their temples and citadels only to be driven out by fire and smoke, and the women and the men in their shining garments and precious stones cried: 'Mu save us!' "[27]

As the setting sun showed himself on the horizon beneath the pall of smoke that overhung the whole land, he was like a ball of fire, red and angry looking. When he had sunk below the horizon, darkness intense prevailed relieved only by lightning flashes.

24. Troano Manuscript, Codex Cortesianus and Lhasa Record.
25. Hawaii, Niuafou and others.
26. Greek Record.
27. Lhasa Record.

Page 30
"During the night[28] the land was torn asunder and rent to pieces. With thunderous roarings the doomed land sank." Down, down, down, she went, into the mouth of hell—"a tank of fire." As the broken land fell into that great abyss of fire, "Flames shot up around and enveloped her."[29] The fires claimed their victim. "Mu and her 64,000,000 people (13) were sacrificed."[30]

As Mu sank into that gulf of fire another force claimed her—*fifty millions of square miles of water.* From all sides huge waves or walls of water came rolling in over her. They met where once was the center of the land. Here they seethed and boiled.

Poor Mu, the motherland of man, with all her proud cities, temples and palaces, with all her arts, sciences and learning, was now a dream of the past. The deathly blanket of water was her burial shroud. In this manner was the continent of Mu destroyed. This catastrophe was the first step in the destruction of the earth's *first great civilization.*

For nearly 13,000 years the destruction of this great civilization cast a heavy pall of darkness over the greater part of the earth. The pall is being lifted, but many spots yet remain covered by it.
When the continent was rent asunder and went down, for geological reasons which I shall hereafter explain, ridges and points of land here and there remained out of water. These ridges and points were thus made islands and groups of islands, but were very jagged and broken up

28. Codex Cortesianus and Troano Manuscript.
29. Egyptian.
30. Troano Manuscript.

Page 31

by the volcanic workings which had occurred beneath them.

All these ridges and points were covered to their capacity with humanity that had escaped from the sinking land-their land, the motherland of man—which now formed the bed of seething, steaming, muddy waters around them

Having swallowed up the land with all thereon, the waters rested as if satisfied with their grim work of destruction, and this is the *Pacific* Ocean. Was ever a name more ironically applied to anything on earth?

On these islands, in the midst of the boiling sea the remnants of Mu's population huddled, waiting for the terrific quakes to abate. They had seen their temples and palaces, their ships and their roads go crashing down, to be swallowed by the ocean. Nearly the entire population had been engulfed by this catastrophe. The few that remained alive, all that were left of the motherland of man, the ruler of the world, discovered that they were destitute. They had nothing—no tools, no clothing, no shelter; little land and no food. Around them hissed and seethed the boiling waters that had rushed into the center of the fiery pit when the continent sank; above them dense clouds of steam, smoke and ashes cut off the friendly light, and they were in an impenetrable darkness. In their ears still rang the despairing shrieks of their comrades who had perished in chaos when the seemingly solid ground had given way beneath their feet. It was a scene of horror for the survivors, who found themselves facing death by starvation and exposure. Few were able to survive the dreadful ordeal and most of them perished miserably.

Only small islands were left. Some of them we know

Page 32

today as the South Sea Islands, and some of their inhabitants can claim, as remote ancestors, the people of ancient Mu.

After a period of days the atmosphere was somewhat cleared of the smoke and sulphurous fumes that had turned the place into an inferno. The sun broke through the veil of clouds and looked down upon a scene of death and desolation. The newly formed islands might be seen thronged with appalled men and women—those who were lucky or unlucky enough to be still alive. They must have been pitiful looking beings, these survivors of the world's greatest catastrophe *since* the flood of biblical fame. One can picture some wringing their hands in despair while others huddled together, dumb and motionless, reason gone. staring with unseeing eyes at the spot where a continent had been.

Where now was their once fair land? It lay deep beneath the waters of the Pacific Ocean. Where man once reigned supreme was now the abode of fishes and the haunt of uncanny, creeping things. Seaweeds would grow where flowers had once raised their faces to the sun, and the coral insects would build their reefs on the spots where man's busy hands had once reared palaces. Out of the tens of millions of human beings that had once swarmed the streets of the vanished cities, only a pitiful handful remained on the newly formed islands that were otherwise barren of all life.

As these wretched beings gazed out over the vast desert of seething water, let us try to re-create, if we can, their feelings of horror and despair. Everything was gone. All was lost! What remained for them? Nothing except slow

Page 33

starvation. They were crowded and huddled together on tiny specks of land in the midst of an immense ocean, thousands of miles from the mainland, without boats, ships or food.

Under such circumstances it may easily be imagined what happened. Many of them, of course, were hopelessly insane, driven mad by the sheer horror of it all; others prayed for death to relieve them from a strain that was intolerable. To exist, one thing alone was left to them: *to go down into the lowest depths of savagery and for a time at least, live upon one another.*

Skins of animals, if any were left, and the leaves of coarse foliage must, in future, be their only dress. Stones, spears and arrows must be their weapons of defense and offense. Their cutting tools must be fashioned from flints and shells. But the primary question was where to get food? No doubt many of them died from exposure, fright and hunger, and as these died, their bodies became the food of the survivors. In this manner, *began the first cannibalism and savagery.*(14) Thus these survivors of the highest civilization descended to the lowest savagery which has continued on through the ages to the present time. Were they to blame for their fall? This is a question for each reader to answer for himself.

One may readily imagine the loathing and repugnance that these cultured beings must have had for such food, and we may feel comforted in believing that many died before they could force themselves to partake of it. Gradually, however, as generation followed generation through the long procession of years, these poor islanders sank lower and lower until even traditions of their past, which

---

Page 34

at first were religiously kept and handed down to posterity, became dim and at last forgotten. Their former greatness was erased from their minds as completely as the treacherous waters of the Pacific had wiped away their motherland, but, although this past is forgotten by the islanders, marks have remained among them for future identification, thus carrying out an unvarying law.

I have previously mentioned that a veil of darkness was cast over mankind by the destruction of Mu, but I mean this in a comparative sense only. The colonial empires, for a time, carried on the civilization of the motherland, but without her aid they gradually declined, then flickered out, and from their ashes the new and present civilization has arisen.

(15)

Chapter 2: The Lost Continent Notes

(1) The "*Ramayana*" is discussed in the Written Works Appendix beginning on page A2—29.

(2) Valmiki is discussed in the Persons of Interest Appendix beginning on page A1—52.

(3) According to tradition, Naranda is a nomadic Devarishi that visited Valmiki when he was meditating. Naranda told Valmiki the story of Rama and Valmiki penned the Ramayana.

(4) The "*Troano Manuscript*" is discussed in the Written Works Appendix beginning on page A2—34.

(5) The "*Codex Cortesianus*" is discussed in the Written Works Appendix beginning on page A2—7.

(6) The "*Lhasa Record*" is discussed in the Written Works Appendix beginning on page A2—16.

(7) This is a broad, general statement. Some specific documents that are included in the 'hundreds of others' are addressed in subsequent chapters, however, a list of the hundreds is not included in the text. Cliff writings are treated in Chapter 10; "North America's Place Among the Ancient Civilizations."

(8) Further discussion of the stone temples and lithic remains begin on page 63 under the heading 'The Great Stone Remains of the Pacific Islands' in Chapter 4.

(9) See page 58 for further description of the Temple and its writings.

(10) See page 58 for further description of the pyramid and its writings.

(11) Beginning of extensive narrative using multiple sources for small fragments of sentences. While a good example of literary prose and the use of adjectives, it causes difficulties if the reader is required to analyze and compare the narrative and original documents. The table below provides the cross-reference between the sources and the Printed Works Appendix.

Footnote #	Name	Written Works Appendix page
1	Lhasa Record	
2	Easter Island tablet	
3	Greek Record	?
4	Troano Manuscript	
5	Various Records	?
6	S.A. Record	?
7	Easter Island Tablet	
8	Indian and Maya Records	
9	Troano Manuscript	
10	Easter Island Tablet	
11	Troano Manuscript	
12	Lhasa Record and others	
13	Lhasa Record and many others	
14	Maya and others	?
15	Troano Manuscript, Codex Cortesianus	Pages 8, 38

Footnote #	Name	Written Works Appendix page
16	Valmiki *	Page 32
17	Lhasa Record	Page 18
18	Troano manuscript and inscriptions	Page 38
19	Lhasa Record	Page 18
20	Valmiki *	Page 32
21	Remains on the islands	-
22	Easter and other islands	Page 35
23	Easter and other islands	Page 35
24	Troano manuscript, Codex Cortesianus and Lhasa Record	Pages 8, 18, 38
25	Hawaii, Niuafou and others	?
26	Greek Record	?
27	Lhasa Record	Page 18
28	Codex Cortesianus, Troano Manuscript	Pages 8, 38
29	Egyptian	?
30	Troano Manuscript	Page 38

* Valmiki is the purported author of the *Ramayana* and page references are for that document.

(12) Khui-Land is mentioned on page 241 in "*The Origin and Evolution of the Human Race*"; Albert Churchward; 1921; Also, 'Kui' is mentioned on page 34 of "*Sacred Mysteries Among the Mayas and the Quiches*"; Le Plongeon, Augustus; 1886.

(13) Reference to numbers killed in the cataclysm are contained on page xviii of the Preface of "*Queen Moo and the Egyptian Sphinx*"; Augustus le Plongeon; 1900.

(14) See Chapter 14 "Origins of Savagery."

(15) Similar to Plate II page xlii "*Queen Moo and the Egyptian Sphinx*"; Augustus le Plongeon; 1900. Also similar to Plate III of "The Origin & Evolution of Religion" page 72, Albert Churchward; 1924.

3
The Land of Man's Advent on Earth

Page 35

In the land of Mu we have unquestionably found where man made his advent upon the earth. Various records conclusively prove that the land of Mu was the biblical Garden of Eden. The records show that the land of Mu lay to the west of America and to the east of Asia, and therefore in the Pacific Ocean.

Data that I have examined also show that the motherland was in the Pacific Ocean, because much of this data consists of the actual remains of this vanished continent. On parts that were not submerged there still remain vestiges of temples, traditions, statuary and sacred symbols, and the written evidence and inscriptions show that these mute mementoes of a vanished race originated in Mu. The authenticity of these remains is corroborated in every possible manner—by written records, by inscriptions, by customs, by language and, finally, by traditions.

I have established by this indisputable evidence the place where there was a prehistoric civilization. Much of this evidence is concretely furnished by stone temples, stone monuments, stone statuary, cut and dressed stone

Page 36

THE GEOGRAPHICAL POSITION OF MU

The Geographical Position of Mu

Page 37

waiting shipment, and the quarries from which the stone came. In these quarries unfinished statuary has been found, and as these discoveries have been made in the South Sea Islands, it demonstrates beyond the shadow of a doubt that these islands were once parts of the submerged continent of Mu.

The records and data based on the supposed age of the Troano Manuscript (1) show that the land of Mu was in existence up to the very edge of historical times. The land of Mu was in existence up to within 12,000 to 12,500 years ago. Taking the islands upon which remains and traditions have been found, I have sketched a map showing where Mu was situated in the Pacific Ocean. There is nothing upon which to base either a western or a northern coast line. From various records it would seem that this continent was made up of three separate lands, divided from each other by narrow seas or channels, but where or how these divisions were made by nature there is nothing to show, except, possibly, an Egyptian hieroglyphic which represents three long, narrow lands running from east to west.

For various reasons, the principal one being colonization, I think the land ran much farther north than has been shown. I have given Easter Island as the southeast corner, Tonga-tabu as about the southwestern corner, the Ladrones as the northwestern corner, Hawaii in the north, and no defined northeastern corner. As will be seen, I have made many large bays and estuaries, because records show that the land was low, without mountains. As the land was so low and rolling, with immense plains, it would naturally have a coast line similar to the one I have drawn.

Page 38

Both the Troano Manuscript and the Codex Cortesianus (2) refer to the land of Mu as the land of hills of earth or "ridges of earth." The Greek record refers to it as "plains." I feel convinced that all three of these records are correct, because up to the time that the continent vanished beneath the Pacific, there were no mountains. The volcanic work-

MAP OF MU
The Lands of the West from the Egyptian Book of the Dead (3)

ings which sent Mu down beneath the waves were preparatory to mountain raising.

Frederick O'Brien, (4) who has written most interestingly of the South Sea Islands, says:

"Darwin's theory is that these islands are the tops of a submerged continent, or land bridge, which stretches its crippled body along the floor of the Pacific Ocean for thousands of leagues. A lost land, whose epic awaits the singer; a mystery perhaps forever to be unsolved. "There are great monuments, graven objects, hieroglyphs, customs and language; island people with suggestive legends, all perhaps remnants of a migration from Asia or Africa a hundred thousand years ago.

"Here, three centuries ago, they were discovered by the peoples of the great world, and, rudely encountering a civilization they did not build, they are dying here: with their passing vanishes the last living link with our prehistoric past, and I was to see it before it disappeared forever."

Where we find specks of land out of water with incontrovertible evidences of continental resources, we are made doubly certain that these specks are parts or remains of a continent. These bits of land are, as I have already said, little islands peopled by savages. They are thousands of miles away from any mainland, and it is therefore the strongest possible proof, stronger than any record, inscription or tradition, that back in prehistoric times there was a continent and that the continent was peopled by highly civilized human beings.

The ancient records and remains found on these South Sea Islands show us that man was created a civilized being but untutored and uncultured. He was created with a knowledge of his own soul and he believed in and worshipped the Deity. It is revealed by the presence of certain figures used as sacred symbols that man, generally, was at that time in an undeveloped intellectual state and the simplicity of the first sacred symbols was necessary in order to convey ordinary subjects to his mind that he might grasp them more fully. When, however, we first get in touch with man, thousands upon thousands of years after his advent upon earth, we find that in spite of his original

---

lack of intellectual development he was then in a highly enlightened and civilized state—and that was more than 50,000 years ago!

Certain archaeologists have, in their writings, touched the subject of the land of Mu and the Lands of the West; but, as they took no pains to verify various records that came before them, but simply made deductions, and, as these deductions have seen their way into print, it is time that readers who are interested in the early appearance of man on earth should be informed of certain positive facts based upon my own careful investigations.

Schliemann, (5) on apparently two records only, the Troano Manuscript and the Lhasa Record (6), asserts that Atlantis was the land of Mu. These records *do not* state that Mu and Atlantis were identical; it is mere surmise on the part of Schliemann. Other records which he might have consulted would have told him plainly that the land of Mu lay to the west of America and not to the east, the location of Atlantis. However, both Atlantis and the land of Mu were destroyed by volcanic eruptions and submerged. Science has proved that beyond the shadow of a doubt.

Le Plongeon (7) advanced the theory that Central America was the Lands of the West and therefore the land of Mu, basing his deductions on the contour of the land around the Caribbean Sea, but forgetting entirely that all records establish the fact that the Lands of the West were destroyed and submerged, while Central America to this day is, of course, unsubmerged. This is as plausible as saying that a certain man is dead while he is arguing some point with you.

Possibly some of these errors arose from the fact that

Page 41

certain records were *read in Europe* that were *written in America*, and the readers, without thinking, based their calculations from Europe instead of from America. This would be in keeping with the reference to Atlantis made by the old Greek philosopher **(8)**: "The Land beyond the Sea—the Saturnian Continent." The Saturnian Continent, by the way, was one of the ancient names for Atlantis.

The exact difference between the records is—the Lands of the West *from America* and the Land beyond the Sea *from Europe.* Evidently the writer of the Greek record wished to avoid mistakes, because he qualified his statement about the Land *beyond* the Sea by designating it clearly as the *Saturnian* Continent, which was Atlantis. Surely this is plain enough to satisfy the most exacting!

The Troano Manuscript places the sinking of the land of Mu as having occurred approximately 12,500 years ago. (I think 12,000 is nearer correct). However, the figures must all be approximate only because the exact age of the Troano Manuscript is not known.

Sanches **(9)**, high priest of the temple of Sais, told Solon **(10)** that Atlantis sank 11,500 years ago and that the passage-way to the Lands of the West was blocked on account of the sinking of this great country, and the destruction of the intervening country beyond Atlantis by cataclysms, which made that country impassable. This clearly eliminates the possibility that Atlantis may have been the land of Mu or the Lands of the West.

Those who have hitherto written about the land of Mu have ignored the most important records connected with this prehistoric continent, namely, the remains on the

Page 42

THE LAST MAGNETIC CATACLYSM. THE BIBLICAL "FLOOD"
AND THE GEOLOGICAL MYTH, THE GLACIAL PERIOD

The last magnetic cataclysm. The Biblical "Flood"
and the geological myth, the glacial period

Page 43

South Sea Islands and the inscriptions on the walls of the Temple of Sacred Mysteries at Uxmal (11), Yucatan, to which may be added the astounding traditions that are to be found among the South Sea Islanders.

From the remains found on the South Sea Islands backed by records and traditions, it is shown that the South Sea Islanders, in spite of their present savage and semi-savage state, were not always in that condition; it is clearly established that they are the descendants of highly civilized and enlightened forefathers. Looking at their present condition it is self-evident that far back, in the prehistoric past, some great calamity overtook their ancestors.

In their anxiety to sustain their monkey theories, scientists have tried to prove that man did not appear upon the face of the earth until the early Pleistocene Time, but a pin-prick can dissipate this scientific bubble. The remains of man have been found in the gravel beds of Europe which were made by the settling waters of the last great Magnetic Cataclysm, the geological Glacial Period, an occurrence that marked the end of the Pliocene. The den men of Nebraska were also wiped out by this same cataclysm. (12)

Niven's (13) upper city was built before the mountains were raised at the beginning of the Pleistocene; his lowest city was built tens of thousands of years before this and goes far back into the Tertiary Era. (Page 122.) This is also corroborated by the cut on Capital Hill in Smyrna, Asia Minor. (Page 120.)

Would it help modern man to know the trials and tribulations that were endured by prehistoric man? It might, and then again—it might not.

Page 44

Scientists have always tried to maintain the theory that the white races originated in Asia, yet they have not a vestige of proof to sustain it—not a single record of any description. Their deductions are only surmises. I will undertake to show in this book where they originated and trace them to Europe.

One of the most startling discoveries, due to Frederick O'Brien, is that the natives of the Polynesian groups of South Sea Islands are a *white* race. Further, they are an exceedingly handsome people, a link that joins perfectly the white races of the earth.

Records show us, as I have established, that man undoubtedly made his advent on this earth in the land of Mu, and the Polynesian Islands are jagged remains of the ill-fated continent that went down in a maelstrom of destruction. Records also show us that Mexico and Central America were colonized and settled by people from the land of Mu. Traditions also establish the fact that these first colonizers from Mu were blond-whites, that these blond-white people were driven from the land by another white race of more swarthy complexion—brunettes: that the blond-white people sailed in their ships to a far-off land in the direction of the rising sun—east—and there settled, in the northern part of Europe—Scandinavia of today. It is also made plain by these same records that southern Europe, Asia Minor, and northern Africa were colonized and settled by the brunette race by way of Mayax, Central America and Atlantis.

I will quote, with his permission, some passages from Frederick O'Brien's fascinating book, "White Shadows in the South Seas."(14) The passages referred to are as follows:

Page 45

"Over this land bridge, mayhap, ventured the Caucasian people—*the dominant blood in Polynesia today*—and when the continent fell from the sight of sun and stars, save in those spots now mountainous islands like Tahiti and the Marquesas, the survivors were isolated for untold ages.

"Here in these islands the brothers of our long-forgotten ancestors have lived and bred since the Stone Age, cut off from the main stream of mankind's development. Here they have kept the childhood customs of our white race, savage and wild, amid their primitive and savage life."

It is evident from the foregoing that O'Brien based these paragraphs on the theory that the white race originated in Asia. It is an accepted theory and O'Brien cannot be blamed for the error.

On page 112 of his book, O'Brien writes:

"My savage friends with their clear features, their large, straight eyes and clear olive skins, still show the traces of their Caucasian blood. Their forefathers and mine might have hunted the great winged lizards together through primeval wilderness, until, driven by who knows what urge of wanderlust or necessity, certain tribes set out in that drive through Europe and Asia towards America, that ended at last when a continent sank beneath their feet in the South Seas."

Let us now leave the white Polynesians and visit one of the brown races found farther west, in the group of South Sea Islands called Micronesia. We find the brown, as well as the white races of the South Sea Islands, are today splendid specimens of physical manhood. They resemble

---

Page 46

the finest of the old Greek bronze statues. The Fijians, a brown race, are said to be the most skilled of the South Sea Islanders.

The accompanying picture is one from a brown race, Arawali, a native of Arorai Island of the Gilbert group, which lies about 4,000 miles southwest of Hawaii.

The picture shows a young lady with an extremely well shaped and well developed head, of pleasing countenance and gentle expression. It has been said of her that "she is a very gentle, lovable woman, but quick-tempered and slightly jealous, but very dignified notwithstanding her wretched surroundings. She is the daughter of the King of Arorai Island."

Arawali's head and face belong to the representative of a high type of civilization, although her dress is that of a savage. Poor Arawali! She is one of a tribe of cannibals, but, strangely enough, she herself has never tasted "long-pig," the euphemistic name applied to human flesh by the natives. In her hand she carries a fan, the ornamentation of which is the royal escutcheon of Mu—the Empire of the Sun.

No ancient record has ever been found that mentions savagery as existing on any spot of the earth's surface prior to the destruction of Mu. Then why did such magnificent specimens of man as the forefathers of the South Sea Islanders become degraded cannibals ? Our story of the great calamity that overtook the first race of man answers this question.

Loaned from the Collection of the American Weekly Section of the New York Sunday American

PRINCESS ARAWALI OF ARORAI ISLAND, GILBERT GROUP, CARRYING FAN, THE ORNAMENTATION OF WHICH IS THE ROYAL ESCUTCHEON OF MU—THE EMPIRE OF THE SUN

Loaned from the collection of the American Weekly Standard Section of the New York Sunday American
Princess Arawali of the Arorai Island, Gilbert Group, carrying fan the ornamentation of which is the Royal Escutcheon of Mu – The Empire of the Sun

Page 47

Page 48

Courtesy Bernice P. Bishop Museum, Honolulu
Agingan, Saipan, Mariana Islands

Page 49

The fan carried by the Princess Arawali

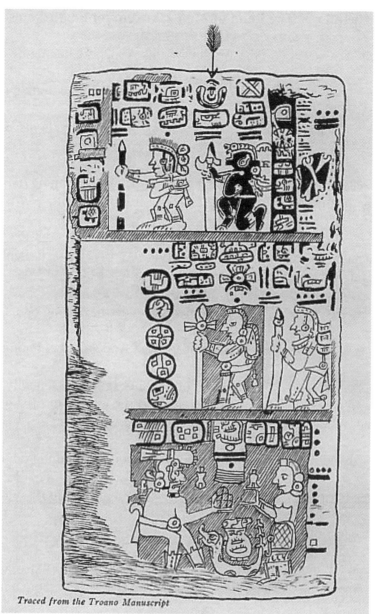

Traced from the Troano Manuscript

Traced from the Troano Manuscript
Troano Manuscript recounting the Destruction of Mu
The arrow points to the Maya hieroglyphic for the Land of Mu (15)
Page 50

Chapter 3: The Land of Man's Advent on Earth Notes

(1) The *"Troano Manuscript"* is discussed in the Written Works Appendix beginning on page A2—34.

(2) The *"Codex Cortesianus"* is discussed in the Written Works Appendix beginning on page A2—7.

(3) The source of this drawing has not been found. The *"Book of the Dead"* is discussed in the Written Works Appendix beginning on page A2—10.

(4) O'Brien, Frederick is discussed in the Persons of Interest Appendix beginning on page 38. The text quoted is from "White Shadows in the Pacific" (1919), which is discussed in the Written Works Appendix beginning on page A2—36.

(5) Reference to Schliemann is to the self-identified grandson of Heinrich Schliemann, Paul. Paul S. is discussed in the Persons of Interest Appendix beginning on page A1—45.

(6) The *"Lhasa Record"* is discussed in the Written Works Appendix beginning on page A2—16.

(7) Le Plongeon, Augustus is discussed in the Persons of Interest Appendix beginning on page A1—22.

(8) The 'old Greek Philosopher' is unidentified in this volume, but Ignatius Donnelly in the 1882 "Atlantis: The Antediluvian World" refers to Berosus with this moniker. Also see entries in the Persons of Interest Appendix for both the "old Greek philosopher" and Berosus.

(9) Sanches (Sonchis) is discussed in the Persons of Interest Appendix beginning on page A1—46.

(10) Solon is discussed in the Persons of Interest Appendix beginning on page A1—46.

(11) See page 58 for further description of the Temple and its writings.

(12) The 'Den-men of Nebraska" are discussed in length on pages 197-200. Also an untitled article in one of James' scrapbooks has the same name written across the top. The article is without a named source.

(13) William Niven is discussed in the Persons of Interest Appendix beginning on page A1—33.

(14) O'Brien, Frederick is discussed in the Persons of Interest Appendix beginning on page 38. The text quoted is from "White Shadows in the Pacific" (1919), which is discussed in the Written Works Appendix beginning on page A2—36.

(15) Similar to Plate LIV page 147 of *"Queen Moo & The Egyptian Sphinx"*; Le Plongeon, Augustus; 1896

Page 51

The records referring to the land of Mu are many and various. Among the written records are some that tell us man made his advent on earth in the land of Mu—the Naacal tablets for instance.

Other records give us the geographical position of this lost continent.

The American written records, which are many, tell us that the land of Mu lay to the *west* of America. The Asiatic records all say Mu, the motherland, lay to the *east* of Asia—"towards the rising sun." Therefore the motherland of man, being between America and Asia, lay in the Pacific Ocean, and here we find on the islands stone remains of her great cities and temples, and also, a white race.

I will first take the American written records, commencing with the Troano Manuscript **(1)**, an ancient Maya book written in Yucatan. Its age has been estimated to be from 1,500 to 5,000 years old. I think it is between 1,500 and 3,000 years old. I base this on the form of its writing.

I herewith present several extracts from the Troano

Page 52

Manuscript that will conclusively prove the correctness of my contention regarding Mu:

Extract i. "In the year 6 Kan, on the 11 Muluc, in the month of Zac, there occurred terrific earthquakes which continued until the 13 Chuen without interruption. *The country of the hills of earth—the land of Mu* was sacrificed. Being twice upheaved, it disappeared during the night, being constantly shaken by the fires of the underneath. Being confined, these caused the land to rise and to sink several times in *various places.* At last the surface gave way and the ten countries (or tribes) were torn asunder and scattered. They sank with their 64,000,000 inhabitants 8,060 years before the writing of this book." **(2)**

Geologically, it will be positively shown that the description "the country of the hills of earth" is absolutely correct and accounts for the quarries that are to be found on Easter Island.

Extract 2. "The birthplace of the sacred mysteries. Mu—the Lands of the West. *That land of Kui,* **(3)** *The motherland of the gods*" **(4)**

1. Is one of the letters M in the hieratical alphabet of Mu and is her alphabetical symbol; thus we have Mu.
2. Is one of the letters T in the hieratical alphabet, and often used as the word "the" in the spoken language.
3. Is the universal geographical symbol for the Lands of the West.

The characters being in block designate the past tense; thus, "Mu was the Lands of the West."

Page 53

1. That.
2. Land of Kui or Kui Land.
3. Lands of the West.
The Lands of the West were the Land of Kui.

This extract is the most important passage known referring to the Motherland of Man, for it has already been shown that the geographical name of the Motherland of Man was the Lands of the West. and as the Troano Manuscript was written in America, it also shows that the Lands of the West lay to the *west of America*. Many records will be brought forward confirming the fact that the Motherland of Man lay to the west of America.

"That land of Kui" means the land of departed souls. The Egyptian *Ka* with its extended meaning comes out of the Maya *Kui*.

In ancient times "god" did not mean the Deity. It referred to the soul of a departed one. Thus, the Motherland of the gods, mentioned in the manuscript, means, by extension, the Motherland of Man.
Sir Gardner Wilkinson (5), the great Egyptologist, in his book, "Manners and Customs,"(6) Volume III, page 70 says:

"Kui-Land or the Land of Kui, according to the Maya language, was the birthplace of the goddess Maya, the mother of the gods—and of man."
Extract 2, by the way, is corroborated many times in the Egyptian Book of the Dead.

Page 54

Plate from the Codex Cortesianus

Plate from the Codex Cortesianus
National Museum, Madrid, Spain
Page 55

Page 56

Codex Cortesianus (7).—The Codex Cortesianus is another of the old Maya books that escaped the eyes of the fanatical Bishop Landa.(8) This book is now in the National Museum of Madrid, Spain. The characters, figures and writings would indicate that it is about the same age as the Troano Manuscript. The language of the Codex Cortesianus, however, is much more symbolical than that of the Troano Manuscript. Here are some extracts from it, bearing on our subject:

"By his strong arm Homen caused the earth to tremble after sunset and during the night *Mu, the country of the hills of earthy was submerged.*"

"Mu, the life of the basin (seas), was submerged by Homen during the night."

"The place of the dead *ruler* is now lifeless, it moves no more, after having *twice* jumped from its foundations: the king of the deep, while forcing his way out, has shaken it up and down, has killed it, has submerged it."

"Twice Mu jumped from her foundations; it was then *sacrificed by fire.* It *burst* while being shaken up and down violently by earthquakes. By kicking it, the wizard that makes all things move like a mass of worms, *sacrificed* it that very night." (9)

It is self-evident that both the Codex Cortesianus and the Troano Manuscript were written from the same temple record. The Codex Cortesianus gives the land its hieratical name only, while the Troano Manuscript gives both its hieratical and geographical names.

The Lhasa Record (10)—This record was discovered by Schliemann (11) in the old Buddhist Temple of Lhasa, Tibet. Schliemann deciphered and translated it. It very evi-

Page 57

dently does not come from the same original record as do the Troano Manuscript and the Codex Cortesianus. It is more modern and is not written in Maya characters.

Here is an interesting extract from the Lhasa Record:

"When the star of Bal fell on the place where now is only the sky and the sea, the seven cities with their golden gates and transparent temples, quivered and shook like the leaves in a storm; and, behold, a flood of fire and smoke arose from the palaces. Agonies and cries of the multitude filled the air. They sought refuge in their temples and citadels, and the wise Mu—*the Hieratic Ra Mu*—arose and said to them: did I not predict all this? And the women and the men in their precious stones and shining garments lamented 'Mu, save us!' and Mu replied: You shall all die together with your servants and your riches, and from your ashes new nations shall arise. If they forget they are superior not because of what they put on but what they put out the same will befall them.' Flames and smoke choked the words of Mu: the land and its inhabitants were torn to pieces and swallowed up by the depths."

Bal is a Maya word meaning "Lord of the Fields." "Transparent temples" is, without doubt, a mis-translation. These temples were not built of glass or any other transparent substance. They were *open* or *roofless* temples so constructed that the rays of Ra—the sun—could fall upon the heads of those who were in prayer and supplication within the temple, like the Parsee temples of today.

Le Plongeon *(12)* found records in Yucatan stating that "the Hieratic head of the Land of Mu prophesied its destruction, and that some, heeding the prophesy, left and went to the colonies where they were saved."

Page 58

Le Plongeon's death occurred many years before Schliemann published the Lhasa Record.

Uxmal Temple.—This temple is situated at Uxmal, Yucatan, and has been named by Le Plongeon "The Temple of Sacred Mysteries." On its walls there is an important inscription which reads: "This edifice is a commemorative monument dedicated to the memory of Mu—*the Lands of the West—That Land of Kui—the birthplace of our sacred mysteries.*

This temple is built facing west, where the Motherland once stood.

The inscription quoted is a full corroboration of the second extract from the Troano Manuscript, and confirms other records which state that the Motherland lay to the *west* of America. Further, and this is most important, it tells us that the religious teachings of this temple came from there. So that whatever we find here we know *originated* in Mu, the Lands of the West. With this information, we can trace the Egyptian religion and learning back to its source.

Mexican Pyramid.—This pyramid is at Xochicalo, to the southwest of Mexico City. There is an inscription on it which Le Plongeon has translated as follows: "This pyramid is a commemorative monument raised to perpetuate the destruction of *The Lands of the West* among coming generations."

Akab-Dzib.—In the city of Chichen Itza, there is a slab which forms the lintel of the door of the inner chamber at the southern end of the building called Akab-Dzib. (13) Here we have "the awful, the tenebrous record." This slab

Page 59

is a description of *The Lands of the West* being shaken to her foundations by earthquakes and then engulfed

Maya Beliefs.-The Mayas of Yucatan regarded the *West* as the region of darkness, the place where the souls of the dead *returned to the bosoms of their ancestors*," as shown in Codex Cortesianus.

Greece—A few references to the Motherland of Man are to be found among the writings of the old Greek philosophers.

In the year 403 B.C., during the archonship of Euclid, the Greek grammarians rearranged the Athenian alphabet in its present form. The Greek alphabet today is composed of Maya vocables forming an epic that relates the destruction of Mu. The translation of the Greek alphabet is as follows:

The Greek Alphabet

The alphabet of the Greeks is an epic composed of Kara-Maya vocables, and is a commemorative memorial to their forefathers who lost their lives at the destruction of Mu.

In Plato's (14) "Timeus Critias" (15) we find this reference to the lost continent : "The Land of Mu had ten peoples"

Proclus (16) wrote: "The Lands of the West had ten peoples."

Here we find two of the old Greek philosophers writing about the Motherland of Man. One uses its hieratical name while the other uses its geographical name, but both assert that there were ten separate peoples.

VALMIKI. (17) *Ramayana.* Vol. I Page 342. (18) — "The Maya adepts, the Naacals, starting from *the land of their birth in the east,* as missionaries of religion and learning went first to Burma and there taught the Nagas. From

Page 60

Burma they went to the Deccan in India, whence they carried their religion and learning to Babylonia and to Egypt."

Burma.—At Angkor Thom, Cambodia, may be seen conventional beasts that have been called by archaeologists "lions." All are placed facing the *east*, looking toward the place where the Motherland once stood. That these beasts refer to her there can be no question, as they are saying "Mu." This is shown by their conventional mouths, elongated squares, one of the forms of the letter M in the hieratic alphabet of Mu, and, one of her symbols.

Plutarch. (19) *Life of Solon.* (20)—"Sanches, (21) the High Priest of Sai's, told Solon [600 B. C.] (22), also Psenophis, a priest of Heliopolis, that 9,000 years before, the relations of the Egyptians with the inhabitants of the *Lands of the West* had been interrupted because of cataclysms destroying the *intervening* country, and—the mud that had made the sea impassable since the *destruction of Atlantis by earthquakes and submersion.*"

It is here shown beyond controversy that the Lands of the West were to the west of America, because America was the "intervening lands" that prevented travel to them when she was made impassable by cataclysms. Again it is clearly shown that neither Atlantis nor the intervening country was the Lands of the West, nor was Atlantis the intervening land, because the intervening land was made impassable only, while Atlantis was submerged.

I will now make a survey of the South Sea Islands and note the stone remains found on them, also the extraordi-

---

Page 61

nary and astounding legends found among the savages and semi-savages on these islands.

In going out on the Pacific Ocean from America we shall be traveling west—from America. The reader will note that out on the Pacific Ocean we are West-of Yucatan; remembering this, it will enable him to appreciate certain records that hereafter appear.

Among the tiny specks of land forming the Polynesian and other groups, we shall find links that joined, in prehistoric times, the civilization of America with the civilizations of Southern and Eastern Asia, and, eventually, the various civilizations throughout the world. Although the journey is a long one, it will be interesting and full of astounding surprises. Where we shall look for the remains an ancient civilization, and where we shall find it, will be on islands that within the memory of living man were inhabited by cannibalistic savages, many of which are cannibalistic to this day.

Yet these cannibals, as I have already shown, are the descendants of highly civilized peoples. The forefathers of the present Polynesians, who are now savages and semi-savages, were once the center of the earth's civilization.

VALMIKI. *Ramayana.* Vol. I. Page 353.— "The Mayas were mighty navigators, whose ships traveled from the Western to the Eastern oceans, and from the Southern to the Northern seas in ages so remote that the sun had not yet risen above the horizon.

"That likewise, being learned architects, they built great cities and palaces."

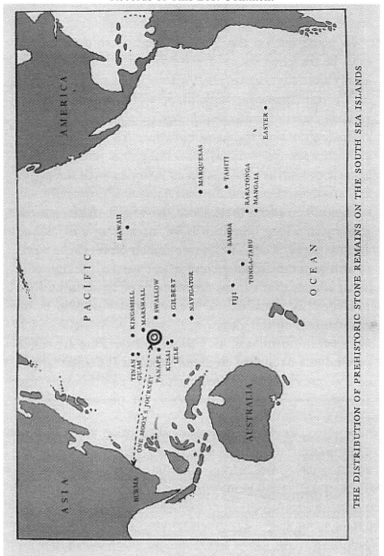

The distribution of Prehistoric Stone remains on the South Sea Islands
Page 62

The Great Stone Remains of the Pacific Islands

Throughout the whole length and breadth of the Pacific Ocean are scattered groups of small islands. On scores of them are the remains of a great civilization. There are great stone temples, cyclopean stone walls, stone-lined canals, stone-paved roads and immense stone monoliths and statuary—works that required continental resources and workmen of skill. Yet we now find them not on a great continent, but on tiny specks of land inhabited by savages and semi-savages.

These great ruins appeal alike to both layman and scientist as being the work of a great past civilization that existed ages ago, about which we know nothing.

In attempting to enumerate and describe these remains I have undertaken a monumental work, for they are so many, and so scattered, that it is hard to tell where to begin or how to end. It would require many volumes to describe them all, instead of a few pages, so that I can give only a mere glance to that which deserves a long and detailed study. My description will be popular, not technical.

On many of the islands the remains are so overgrown with vegetation and covered up with soil, that it is difficult to find them. I do not believe that one-half of the stone remains on the South Sea Islands are visible; they are covered up, they are overgrown mounds.

Another difficulty the explorer has to contend with is the savage inhabitants; they all appear to have a superstitious dread of going near any of the great ruins. They believe them to be haunted by ghosts and evil spirits, which

they call *mauli* so that it is next to impossible to get any of them to guide you to these ruins or even to tell you where they are. A good way to discover their whereabouts, however, is to have a native show you over the island; but, go your own way and do not follow him. Simply take him along to tell you the best road home. If you are approaching a ruin he will try to make you go in an opposite direction. Should you persist in going on, when you get near the ruin, he will run away and leave you. Then you will know you are close to the object of your search.

I will make my start with the remains on Easter Island. They are better known than any of the others.

EASTER ISLAND. (23)— Easter Island is situated at the southeastern extremity of Polynesia, 2,100 miles from the coast of South America. Its greatest length is 13 miles and its greatest width 7 miles.

On this little island, all told, there are at present 555 carved stones, colossal statues, as well as other examples of the art of a great prehistoric race.

W. J. Thomson (24), whom I believe to be the best authority on what is found on Easter Island, says:

"The largest image is in one of the quarries in an unfinished condition and measures 70 feet in height; the smallest was one found in a cave, and was about 3 feet long. The majority of them are from 15 to 18 feet high. It is supposed these images represent distinguished personages, and are intended as monuments to their memory."

The tops of some of these towering stones are capped with huge *spheres*, which show *red* in the distance. Many of these spheres were carved from the red igneous rock forming the sides of the now silent volcanoes. One of

Easter Island Statuary
Page 65

Page 66

these spheres, which is carved out of a red sandstone, measures 12 feet in diameter. It is to be seen at the quarry at Terrai Hills.

Besides the statuary on Easter Island there are several immense platform-like accumulations of cut and dressed stone.

These piles are about 30 feet high and from 200 to 300 feet in length. They are awaiting shipment to some other part of the continent for the building of temples and palaces.

Near the extinct volcanoes Rana Roraka and Rana Rao are the remains of what was once a large stone temple. As the fallen stones lie, they outline a structure of about 100 feet long and 20 feet wide.

Walls are still standing 5' feet high and 5 feet thick. Some of the stones of this structure have carved upon them figures which were the sacred symbols used in the first religion of man.

W. J. Thomson: "There are in existence about 7 tablets, all that are left of a vast number, bearing the written story of Easter Island."

Thomson, with the aid of an old native, the only one on the island that knew the meaning of the glyphs on these tablets, deciphered and translated some of them. Herewith is Thomson's translation of two:

Tablet l. "When this island was first created and became known to our forefathers, the land was crossed with roads beautifully paved with flat stones. These stones were laid together so nicely that no rough edges were exposed. Coffee [mistranslation] trees were growing close together along the borders of the roads. They met over-

Page 67

Easter Island Tablet
(25)

Page 68

head and their branches were laced together like muscles.

"Heke was the builder of the roads, and it was he who sat in the place of honor, where the roads branched away in every direction.

"In that happy land, that beautiful land where Romaha formerly lived with his beloved Hangarva.

"Turaki used to listen to the voices of the birds and feed them.

"In that beautiful land governed the gods from Heaven, who lived in the waters when it was cold.

"There the black and white pointed spider would have mounted to heaven, but he was held back by the bitterness of the cold."

Remains of these roads are to be seen on Easter and many other of the South Sea Islands.

Tablet 2, entitled "The Great King": "What power has the Great King on land? He has the power to make the plants grow and to change the color of the sky.

"All hail the power of The Great King who makes us lenient to the young plants, to admire the different colors of the sky and to behold the clouds that rise.

"All hail the power of The Great King who enables us to appreciate the blessings of bright stars, the lowering clouds, the gentle dew, the falling rain and the light of the sun and the moon.

"What power has The Great King on land?

"He has the power to populate the earth to create both kings and subjects.

"All hail to the power of The Great King, who hath created the human beings, given authority to kings, and created loyal subjects.(26)

Page 69

"What power has The Great King"?

"He has the power to create the lobsters, white bait, eels, ape-fish and everything in the sea.

"What power has The Great King over the seas ?

"He hath the power to create the mighty fish that swim in deep water.

"All hail the power of The Great King who enables us to withstand the attacks of the maggots, flies, worms, fleas and all manner of insects."

A legend tells the following:

"*This little island had once been a part of a great continent of land,* crossed with many roads, beautifully paved with flat stones. The roads were cunningly constructed to represent the plan of the web of the gray and black pointed spider, and no man could discover the beginning or the end thereof."

Pictured slabs from houses on Easter Island **(27)**

Page 70

W. J. Thomson: "At the south end of the island there are from 80 to 100 stone houses, built in a regular line against a terrace of rock or earth, which in some cases form the back walls of the building. The walls of these peculiar houses average 5' feet in thickness and 4 1/2 feet in height.

They are 4 1/2 feet broad and 13 feet long.

"The doorways are tiny affairs, not more than 20 inches high and 19 inches wide. The walls are formed by layers of irregular stones. These latter are often painted red, white and black, showing birds, faces and figures.

"Near the houses the rocks on the banks of the sea-cliff are carved in strange shapes, resembling human faces, tortoises, birds, fishes and mythical animals."

The history of Easter Island since the white man discovered it forms one long scene of tragedies.

*Cook group.—*The Cook group of islands lies directly south of Hawaii about 40 degrees. It is also about half way between Tahiti and Fiji, but south of a direct line. I shall note two islands of this group.

*Raratonga Island (28).—*On this island there is a small section of the road referred to in the Easter Island tablet and legend.

*Mangaia Island. (29)—*This is the southernmost island of the Cook group and about half the size of Easter Island. On it are remains similar to those on Easter Island. As there are no quarries, or evidences of their being chisled on this island, it is presumable that they were brought here.

*Tonga-Tabu.—*Tonga-tabu is a coral atol belonging to the Tonga group. There is not a particle of natural stone upon it, nothing but corals. Here on this patch of coral we find an immense stone monument, set up in the form of

Page 71

Stone arch on Tonga-Tabu **(30)**

Page 72

an arch. It consists of two huge uprights weighing about 70 tons each, which are bound together at the top with another stone weighing about 25 tons. **(30)**

There being no native stone on the island and the nearest available stone being over 200 miles away, it leaves open a wide field for speculation as to what sort of ships the ancients had to carry such enormous weights, how they landed them from the ships, and what contrivances they had to set them up in place, as we now find them, after they had been safely landed.

The Gilbert and Marshall groups.—On several of the islands composing these two groups are found tall, slender pyramids built of stone. **(31)**

The natives use the sacred symbols of the Motherland as ornamentations without knowing how they obtained the designs, or their meanings. I have shown a very prominent ornamentation from Arorai Island—the fan of Princess Arawali with the royal escutcheon of Mu.

The Caroline group. **(32)**—As regards prehistoric remains, nowhere throughout the Pacific Ocean are there to be found such astounding ruins as on the Caroline Islands. An added interest is that they lie "one moon's journey towards the rising sun (from Burma)," where according to the Naacal Tablets and Valmiki, the Motherland of Man once stood, the spot whence came the first settlers in Burma and India.

Panape. **(33)**—On Panape stands what I consider to be the most important ruin in the South Sea Islands. It consists of the ruins of a great temple, a structure 300 feet long by 60 feet wide, with walls still standing (in 1874) 30 feet high, and at the ground 5 feet in thickness.

Page 73

On the walls are the remains of carvings of many of the sacred symbols of the Motherland.

This temple is connected with canals and earthworks, and has vaults, passages and platforms. The whole is built of basaltic stone.

Below the pavements of the great quadrangle, on opposite sides, are two passages or gateways, each about 10 feet square. These are pierced through the outer wall with passageways leading down to the canal. Within the great quadrangle is a central pyramidal chamber, unquestionably the holy of holies.

According to the natives, many generations ago this temple was occupied, for a time, by the shipwrecked crew of a Spanish buccaneer. Relics of these outlaws are still being found in one of the vaults which they used as a storehouse.

The natives cannot be induced to go near this ruin, because they say it is haunted by ghosts and evil spirits, which they call *mauli.*

Other ruins also are on Panape, some of which are close to the seashore, others are on tops of mounds or hills, and some are to be found on cleared spaces towards the center of the island, but all command views of the ocean. On one of these cleared spaces there is a ruinous heap of stones covering between 5 and 6 acres; it is situated on a sort of tableland. Around it appears to have been a ditch or a canal.

At the corners, which were at the cardinal points, the ruins assume tall mounds, indicating by the various distribution of these mounds that the building was square.

To my mind the various ruins on Panape are the ruins

of one of the Motherland's capital cities, one of the Seven Sacred Cities. It is impossible to estimate the population, but it must have been very large—a hundred thousand at least.

Swallow Island (34) 12° east of Panape.—On this small island is a pyramid of similar construction to that which will be found on Guam and Tinian.

On the west side of this island is a vast quadrangular enclosure of stone, containing several mounds. Probably if the coverings of guano and soil were removed edifices of some kind would be found.

Kusai Island, (35) southeast corner of the group.—On this and the surrounding islands are found similar ruins to Panape, but not nearly so extensive.

On the south side of the harbor of this island are several canals lined with stone. They cross each other at right angles. Between their intersections are artificially made islands, which originally had buildings on them, One tower still remaining is about 35 feet high.

Native traditions of this island say: "The people who once lived here were very powerful. They had large vessels in which they made voyages far distant, east and west, taking many moons to complete a voyage." Does this not entirely agree with Valmiki when he says, "The Mayas were mighty navigators, whose ships passed from the eastern to the western oceans and from the southern to northern seas"?

Lele Island (36) is separated from Kusai Island by a very narrow channel. On this island is a conical hill surrounded by a wall 18 or 20 feet high and of enormous thickness. The whole of this island presents a series of

cyclopean enclosures and lines of great walls. Some of the enclosures are parallelograms 200 by 100 feet in extent. There is a very large one between 300 and 400 feet in length and over 150 feet wide.

The walls generally are 12 feet thick, and within are vaults, artificial caverns and secret passageways.

The natives of this corner of the Carolines were extremely hostile to the white man and were cannibals of the worst description in 1874. Possibly they have been tamed down a bit since then.

Kingsmill Islands.—On *Tapiteau Island* (37) of this group are found the same tall, slender pyramids of stone as are found in the Gilbert and Marshall groups.

Navigator Islands.—On these islands are found great stone structures. On one of the islands there remarkable structure on the top of a 1,500-foot hill, and near the edge of a precipice which has a sheer drop of 500 feet. The structure is a platform built of huge blocks of igneous stone. It is 150 feet in diameter and 20 feet high. On one side of this structure is the precipice and on the other a ditch, which originally might have been 18 or 20 feet deep.

Ladrone, OR Mariana Group (Guam). (38)—The relics on these islands are of a character of their own. They consist principally of solid stone, truncated pyramidal columns, usually about 20 feet high, including the hemispherical stone or capital, and ten feet square at their bases. Some are capped with a stone hemispherical in shape, in other cases these stones lie on the ground as if they had been shaken off by some seismic disturbance. On the Island of Tinian they are arranged in columns.

Courtesy Bernice P. Bishop Museum, Honolulu
HOUSE OF TAGA. TINIAN ISLAND, MARIANA GROUP

Courtesy of Bernice P. Bishop Museum, Honolulu
House of Taga, Tinian Island, Mariana Group

Courtesy Bernice P. Bishop Museum, Honolulu
LATTE. HINAPSAN ISLAND, MARIANA GROUP

Courtesy of Bernice P. Bishop Museum, Honolulu
Latte, Hinapsan Island, Mariana Group

Courtesy of Bernice P. Bishop Museum, Honolulu
House of Taga. Tinian Island, Mariana Group

Page 77

Page 78

Extract from article by Larrin Tarr Gill: **(39)** "Three of the latter have fallen with their tasa still intact; three are completely shattered and the capitals of two lie as though shaken from their supports by some violent shudder of the earth. Shaped like truncated *pyramids* and capped by *hemispherical* stones, the pillars are 18 feet in circumference at the base, 11 feet high, and taper at the top to a little over 15 feet around, on which the capitals stand 5 feet high and 6 feet thick. Hewn from rough, hard, *sedimentary* rock, each monument weighs close to 30 tons and the two parallel lines of columns, which originally stood 7 feet apart formed a ground plan almost 54. feet long by 10 1/2 wide.

HAWAII. **(40)**—"About 30 miles from Hilo there is a great ruin on a hill called Kukii. There are no stones on this hill except those which have been carried there.

"The summit was leveled and squared, and the building laid out according to the cardinal points and the floor paved. Two square blocks of stone in an upright position, about 15 or 16 feet apart, range exactly east and west.

"The upperpart of the hill was terraced, and the terraces had been faced with hewn stone. The stones were perfect squares, the smallest three feet in diameter, while others were larger. Every stone was faced and polished on all sides, so that they could perfectly fit together. There is still about 30 feet of facing left on the lower terrace partly in position.

"On the western side there was a stairway running from the base to the top of the hill, a height of nearly 300 feet.

"On Kona is another ruin."

THE MARQUESAS. **(41)**—There are several noteworthy ruins

Page 79

on the Marquesan Islands. Apparently no one has ever felt inclined to make an examination of them. I believe the fact that they are there has never been published.

The foregoing is a long list of Titanic stone remains, and yet I have not enumerated one-half of what are to be found on the South Sea Islands. From this evidence can be formed only one conclusion to the logical mind, and that is: *At one time in the earth's history there was a great continent of land in the Pacific Ocean which embraced all of the groups of islands where prehistoric remains are to be found. This great continent had an exceedingly high civilization.*

That continent was Mu, the motherland of man. That her name was Mu and her geographical position are attested by the records of India, Uighur, Egypt, Mayax, Peru and of the cliff dwellers of North America.

These cyclopean remains are her pathetic withered fingers that refused to go down with her broken back and mangled body. They are her "footprints on the sands of time."

NEW ZEALAND. **(42)**—The Maoris, the natives of New Zealand, are rich in legends and traditions of the dim past.

Many of the ancient sacred symbols are also found among them. The most prominent of all is the Tat or Totem Pillars, which they erect at the entrance of their villages. In using the name Tat I am using the Egyptian. These pillars were used by the Mayas, Incas, Atlantians, Egyptians, Chaldeans, and other ancient peoples. The meaning of the Tat or Totem Pillar is given in my section on the ancient Sacred Symbols.

AUSTRALIA. **(43)**—Australia appears to be particularly bare

Page 80

of ancient records, legends and traditions, which is not to be wondered at if my geological deductions about Australia are correct.

Geometrical figures have been found rudely carved on some of the boomerangs of the Northern tribes. The bushmen of Northern Australia are probably the lowest type of humanity on earth, lower than the ordinary forest beasts.

This sketch is a reproduction of an Australian cave painting which, without doubt, antedates their low savagery.

There are three remarkable objects in this painting: the first is Ra - the Sun - and the second is the numeral 3, symbol of Mu, shown twice, and the third is an axe.

When the English first settled in Australia, axes of any description were unknown to the savage natives.

A SAMPLE OF THE ART OF PREHISTORIC MAN
Hands, Feet and Weapons Printed in Colors on the Walls of an Australian Cave

A SAMPLE OF THE ART OF PREHISTORIC MAN
Hands, Feet and Weapons Printed in Colors on the Walls of an Australian Cave

Page 81

I have never heard of any legends or traditions having been found among the native Australians.

After deciphering and translating the symbols found carved on the stones of the ancient Polynesian remains of the temples and statuary, and in the quarries among the unfinished work, I felt at the time that among the South Sea Islands, and especially in the division called Polynesia, traditions might be found that would prove of the greatest value in connecting the past civilization of the South Sea Islands with a civilization of a later date, of which we have at least some fragmentary records.

The great stone monuments found among the South Sea Islands have always been a puzzle to ethnologists. All have been convinced that a great civilization once existed among the South Sea Islands, and then, "the shadow of time that was, became darkness; the new day, the beginning, as civilization now calls it, dawned there-after"

While I have been able to decipher and explain the meanings of the symbols found among the South Sea Islands, it has fallen to the lot of Frederick O'Brien **(44)** to have the honor of bringing the world in close touch and sympathy with the Islanders and their traditions and thus drawing back the veil of darkness which has for so many thousands of years overshadowed a great race.

I will now take extracts from O'Brien's "Mystic Isles of the South Seas," **(45)** capping each legend with the corresponding biblical legend.

Page 21—"The great god Ra of the Polynesians."

In Ra we have a connecting link between the Polynesians and our known ancients. Ra was the symbol of the

---

Page 82

Sun, and the Sun was the collective symbol of the Deity among the Mayas, Quiches, Incas, Hindus, Chaldeans, Babylonians, Assyrians, Egyptians, etc.

Easter Island (Pages 64-66)—"Huge stone gods that had been thrown down. Some were 37 feet high, and had red stone crowns ten feet in diameter."

The Easter Island Statuary were not meant as gods. They were statues to be set up elsewhere in memory of some important personage who had passed away.

This view is also taken by Thomson, the Easter Island authority.

Red Circles, Red Discs and Red Spheres have been, from the beginning, universally throughout the world, and among all peoples, a sacred symbol. It was a picture of and represented the Sun, which, in the mother tongue, was called Ra.

As Ra was the symbol or representative of the Great God among the Polynesians, including the people of Easter Island, and, as red spheres are one of the pictures or representatives of Ra, it leaves no question for doubt. As to the meaning of the great red spheres and the statuary itself, the red spheres in conjunction with the statues correspond with what we see today in our Christian burial grounds—a figure associated with the Christian Cross. The Easter Islanders possessed a complicated religion of the pantheistic character having a triune Godhead.

The Marquesas.—Among the Marquesas and other groups of Polynesian Islands O'Brien has found descendants of the original white race from which the Aryans sprang.

Although today these white Polynesians are savages

Page 83

and semi-savages, they are, unquestionably, our distant cousins, having come down from the original white stock. The Marquesans are today one of the handsomest races on earth.

The Marquesans and other white Polynesians clear up one of the great mysteries connected with early man, and form an unbreakable link which completes the chain, showing from where and how the whole earth was peopled.

O'Brien's deductions that they came down from the original white race seems to be more than confirmed by records and traditions found in various parts of the earth : Mexico, Central America, India and Egypt.

There are traditions in Central America and Mexico stating that the first people who inhabited those countries were a white race.*31 The Mayas of Mayax, those who built the great edifices whose ruins now dot the land, were a white race. Temple inscriptions in Yucatan say they came there from lands that lay to the west of America. Polynesia lies to the west of America.

The Guatemalan tradition also shows the White Race advancing to the east from America.

Hindu records tell us that the central parts of India (the Deccan) were first colonized by a white race called Mayas, who came to India via Burma, and that their motherland was one moon's journey towards the rising sun, East of Burma. Polynesia lies to the east of Burma. It is thus shown that those coming to America came from the west, and those coming to India, came from the east. This is conclusive evidence that the original home of the

*31. See Guatemalan tradition quoted on page 247.

Page 84

white race was a land that lay geographically between America and Asia.

O'Brien has adorned his writings with many interesting and astounding traditions which he found among the South Sea Islanders. I will quote some of them:

The Creation.—"The Marquesans said that in the beginning there was no light, life or sound in the world, that a boundless night called Po enveloped everything over which Tanaoa (darkness) and Mutu-hei (silence) reigned supreme.

'Then the god of light separated from Tanaoa (darkness), fought him and drove him away and confined him to the night. Then the god Ono (sound) was evolved from Atea (light) and banished silence. From all this struggle was born Atauana (dawn). Atea (light) married Atauana (dawn) and they created earth, animals and man."

This is not the cosmogony of savages or semi-savages, yet in Polynesia we find it among those who fifty years ago were cannibals. O'Brien seems to think that there are among them today some that are not adverse to the taste of "long pig."

Among these people I find a tradition of the Creation, corresponding in all material details with that of the ancients throughout the world:

" Polynesian Researches." Ellis. Vol. I. Page 100. (46) - "In the Sandwich Islands (Hawaii) there is a tradition that in the beginning there was nothing but water, when a big bird descended from on high and laid an egg in the sea; the egg burst and Hawaii came forth."

This is the cosmogony of all the ancients. All say water

Page 85

covered the face of the earth, and that life started from a cosmic egg laid in the sea.

Samoa: The Samoans have a tradition that: "In the beginning the whole earth was covered with water."

THE Flood.—O'Brien says in "Mystic Isles of the South Seas":

"In most of Polynesia there are legends of a universal flood from which but few escaped."

Adam And Eve.—"The Polynesians had very fixed ideas upon the origin of the universe and man."

In *Hawaii:* "Taaroa made man out of red earth Araea and breathed into his nostrils. He made woman from a man's bones and called her Ivi." (In the Polynesian language Ivi is pronounced Eve-y.)

Cain And Abel.—A Tonga tradition states that "the son of the first man killed his brother."

New Zealand: A tradition of the Maoris, the natives of New Zealand, states "that the son of the first man killed his brother."

Tower of Babel.—"In Fiji is still shown the site where a vast tower was built because the Fijians were curious and wanted to peep into the moon to discover if it was inhabited.

POLYNESIAN COSMOGONY.—*Tahiti:* "Taaroa, whose name was spelt differently in separate archipelagos, was the father of Tahitian cosmogony. His wife was Hina - the earth, and his son Oro was the ruler of the world, Tane the Hualine god was a brother of Oro and his equal."

This corresponds with the cosmogony of the most ancient namely a Trinity or a Triune Godhead.

Page 86

Mystic Forces: During the time of the earth's first civilization, many abstruse sciences were known which today are not known. They have been lost between the two civilizations.

The adepts of the ancients could walk through fire without being scorched, as related in the Bible **(47)** and Popol Vuh. **(48)**

O'Brien gives a thrilling account of a Tahitian adept walking bare-footed on red-hot stones, without being burnt. The same thing has been shown in Hawaii and I have personally seen it done in the Fiji Islands.

A few years since a report was made that in Samoa the blind were made to see through their flesh. The report was sneered at by scientists, and the public generally looked upon it as a newspaper story, a traveler's lie.

The following from the *New York World*, reporting from Paris the accomplishment of the same phenomenon, answer, I think, the scientific sneers that were handed out when the report came from the savages of Samoa. This article is as follows:

"Not only have you eyes in the back of your head, but your body is simply covered with them, and they can all be used if trained properly.

"This conclusion is reached by several scientists here who have witnessed experiments by Jules Remain **(49)**, writer of a book on the subject. They contend, with M. Remain, that just beneath the skin are 'ocelles'— microscopic organs united to the central nervous system—and that these are dormant eyes.

"M. Remain, it is claimed, has succeeded in training a number of persons to use these eyes effectively. They can distinguish colors and read while heavily blindfolded.

Page 87

Some can see with cheeks and fingers, some with their noses. One subject was able to distinguish a hat four yards away.

"These results, it is asserted, are accomplished after the subject has been placed in a state of great mental concentration not allied to hypnotism.

"While the first experiment is not apt to show much result, second tests have shown in some subjects an ability to 'read' playing cards blindfolded after three hours of concentration. The ability of the subject, it is said, improves with each succeeding test."

Thus it is now demonstrated that the blind can be made to see through the skin, but the Samoan practised it thousands of years ago.

The foregoing traditions and legends are astounding, and at first glance must stagger one, for here among savages who have been shut off from the outside world up to within 300 years and most of them within 200 years, we are met with the fact that they have among themselves legends and traditions about the creation and the early history of man that are identical with the legends and traditions found in the Bible.

THE GREEK ALPHABET

The Alphabet of the Greeks is an epic composed of Kara Maya vocables, and is a commemorative memorial to their forefathers who lost their lives at the destruction of Mu.

THE GREEK ALPHABET
AND ITS ESOTERIC MEANINGS

Greek	*Kara Maya.* English meanings.
Alpha	*Al*, heavy; *páa*, break; *ha*, water
Beta	*Be*, walk; *ta*, where, place, plain, ground
Gamma	*Kam*, receive; *ma*, mother, earth
Delta	*Tel*, deep, bottom; *ta*, where, etc.
Epsilon	*Ep*, obstruct; *zil*, make edges; *onom*, whirlwind
Zeta	*Ze*, strike; *ta*, where, ground, etc.
Eta	*Et*, with; *ha*, water
Theta	*Thetheha*, extend; *ha*, water
Iota	*Io*, all that which lives and moves; *ta*, where, ground, etc.
Kappa	*Ka*, sediment, obstruction; *páa*, break, obstruct
Lambda	*Lam*, submerge; *be*, go, walk; *ta*, where, ground, etc.
Mu	*Mu*, Mu
Ni	*Ni*, point, summit, peak
Xi	*Xi*, to rise, to appear over
Omikron	*Om*, whirl; *ik*, wind; *le*, place; *on*, circular
Pi	*Pi*, to place little by little
Rho	*La*, until; *ho*, come
Sigma	*Zi*, cold; *ik*, wind; *ma*, earth, mother, etc.
Tau	*Ta*, where; *u*, bottom, valley, abyss, etc.
Upsilon	*U*, abyss, etc.; *pa*, tank; *zi*, cold; *le*, place; *on*, circular
Phi	*Pe*, come, etc.; *hi*, mud, clay
Chi	*Chi*, mouth opening
Psi	*Pe*, come, out, etc.; *zi*, vapor
Omega	*O*, there; *mec*, whirl; *ka*, sediments

Greek	*Kara Maya*	Free Reading
Alpha	*Al-páa-ha*	Heavily break the waters
Beta	*be-ta*	extending over the plains
Gamma	*kam-ma*	they cover the lands
Delta	*tel-ta*	in low places, where
Epsilon	*ep-zil-on-om*	there are obstructions, shores form and whirlpools
Zeta	*ze-ta*	strike the earth
Eta	*et-ha*	with water.
Theta	*thetheha-ha*	The waters spread
Iota	*io-ta*	on all that lives and moves
Kappa	*ka-páa*	obstructions give way and
Lambda	*lam-be-ta*	submerged is the land of
Mu	*Mu*	Mu.
Ni	*ni*	Peaks only
Xi	*xi*	appear above the waters
Omikron	*om-ik-le-on*	whirlwinds blow around
Pi	*pi*	and little by little
Rho	*la-ho*	until there comes
Sigma	*zi-ik-ma*	cold air. Before
Tau	*ta-u*	where valleys existed, are
Upsilon	*u-pa-zi-le-on*	now abysses, cold depths. In circular places
Phi	*pe-hi*	mud formed.
Chi	*chi*	A mouth
Psi	*pe-zi*	opens, vapors
Omega	*o-mec-ka*	come forth and volcanic sediments.

STRAIGHT READING

Heavily break the waters over the plains. They cover the low places. Where there are obstructions shores form. The earth is struck with water; the waters spread on all that lives and moves, the foundations give way and *submerged is the land of Mu*. The peaks only appear above the water, whirlwinds blow around until gradually comes cold air. Before where existed valleys are great depths, cold tanks. In circular places mud banks formed. A mouth opens, out of which vapors pour forth and volcanic sediments.

The Greek Alphabet written in the Hieratic Characters of Mu

This is written to read from left to right. The ancients generally wrote to read from right to left, when the writing was in horizontal lines.

GREEK CROSS   MU'S ESCUTCHEON
ORIGIN OF THE GREEK CROSS

The Greek Cross as it is known has always been an enigma and a puzzle to scientists on account of its being found in so many inscriptions which are unreadable to our archaeologists. It appears in inscriptions in Yucatan and Central America especially.

Winter **(52)**, in his work "Guatemala," **(53)** page 15:6, says: "The mysterious symbol of the Greek cross, which has also been found on the stones of Quirigua and Copan, has been the cause of much speculation among scholars." No one, apparently, can solve this simple problem.

The Greek cross, Fig. 1, was the central figure of the Royal Escutcheon of Mu—the Empire of the Sun. The hieroglyph is a phrase in the mother tongue of Mu, reading U'luumil (pronounced *Oo-loo'-oom'-il*). Translated into English it is: "the land of, the country of," and by extension, "the Empire of" or "the Kingdom of." So that in all of the inscriptions where it appears, it represents one of the foregoing phrases, depending on what comes before and what comes after it.

The Greek cross confirms the accuracy of my deciphering of the Greek alphabet; the Greek alphabet confirms the accuracy of my deciphering of the cross; and the two confirm the existence of Mu—the Empire of the Sun - and that she was the Motherland of the Greeks.

Chapter 4: Records of This Lost Continent Notes

(1) The "*Troano Manuscript*" is discussed in the Written Works Appendix beginning on page A2—34.

(2) Passage same as page 147 of "*Queen Moo & The Egyptian Sphinx*"; Le Plongeon, Augustus; 1896

(3) Khui-Land is mentioned on page 241 in "*The Origin and Evolution of the Human Race*"; Albert Churchward; 1921; Also, 'Kui' is mentioned on page 34 of "*Sacred Mysteries Among the Mayas and the Quiches*"; Le Plongeon, Augustus; 1886.

(4) Passage same as page 34 of "*Sacred Mysteries Among the Mayas and the Quiches*"; Le Plongeon, Augustus; 1886

(5) Sir John Gardner Wilkinson (1797-1875). Compare the text on page 53 to the following:
> "Sir Gardner Wilkinson, Manners and Customs of Ancient Egyptians, vol. iii, p. 70. "Kui Land," according to the Maya language the "land of the gods," the birthplace of the Goddess Maya, "the mother of the gods" and of men, the feminine energy of Brahma by whose union with Brahma all things were produced."
> Augustus Le Plongeon, "Queen Moo and the Egyptian Sphinx" (1896), Introduction page lxiv Footnote 1

(6) Ibid.;

(7) The "*Codex Cortesianus*" is discussed in the Written Works Appendix beginning on page A2—7.

(8) Bishop Landa [De Landa Calderon, Diego (1524-1579)] was a Bishop of Yucatan and leaves a mixed legacy with regards to the Yucatan. On one hand he destroyed most of the printed works that fell under his control, but due to his efforts to catalog the Mayan alphabet, the meaning was finally deciphered. Augustus Le Plongeon, "Queen Moo and the Egyptian Sphinx" (1896) Appendix 1 Note i contains a biography of Diego de Landa

(9) Same as page 148 of "*Queen Moo & The Egyptian Sphinx*"; Le Plongeon, Augustus; 1896

(10) The "*Lhasa Record*" is discussed in the Written Works Appendix beginning on page A2—16.

(11) Reference to Schliemann is to the self-identified grandson of Heinrich Schliemann, Paul. Paul S. is discussed in the Persons of Interest Appendix beginning on page A1—45.

(12) Le Plongeon, Augustus is discussed in the Persons of Interest Appendix beginning on page A1—22.

(13) Akab-Dzib is discussed on page 92 of "*Sacred Mysteries Among the Mayas and the Quiches*"; Le Plongeon, Augustus; 1886.

(14) Plato is discussed in the Persons of Interest Appendix beginning on page A1—41.

(15) The "*Timeus Critias*" is discussed in the Written Works Appendix beginning on page A2—34.

(16) Proclus is discussed in the Persons of Interest Appendix beginning on page A1—44.

(17) Valmiki is discussed in the Persons of Interest Appendix beginning on page A1—52.

(18) The "*Ramayana*" is discussed in the Written Works Appendix beginning on page A2—29.

(19) Plutarch is discussed in the Persons of Interest Appendix beginning on page A1—27.

(20) The "*Life of Solon*" is discussed in the Written Works Appendix beginning on page A2—19.

(21) Sanches (Sonchis) is discussed in the Persons of Interest Appendix beginning on page A1—46.

(22) Solon is discussed in the Persons of Interest Appendix beginning on page A1—46.

(23) Easter Island. Archaeological evidence indicates that human habitation started about 300 A.D.

(24) Thomson, William Juddah is discussed in the Persons of Interest Appendix beginning on page A1—48.

(25) The source is Plate XXXVI of "*TE PITO TE HENUA, OR EASTER ISLAND*"; William J. Thompson; From the Report of the National Museum, 1888-'89, pages 447-552 (with plates XII-LX). WASHINGTON: GOVERNMENT PRINTING OFFICE. 1891. See discussion in the Written Works Appendix beginning on page A2—31.

(26) The source "*TE PITO TE HENUA, OR EASTER ISLAND*"; William J. Thompson; From the Report of the National Museum, 1888-'89, pages 447-552 (with plates XII-LX). WASHINGTON: GOVERNMENT PRINTING OFFICE. 1891. See discussion in the Written Works Appendix beginning on page A2—31.

(27) Ibid; Plate XXIII. See discussion in the Written Works Appendix beginning on page A2—31.

(28) Raratonga (Cook Islands), archaeological evidence indicates a human presence dating back at least to 300 B.C.E. Seafaring peoples came from Samoa and Tonga and colonized the Cook Islands.

(29) Mangaia (Cook Islands) archaeological evidence indicates a human presence dating back at least to 300 B.C.E. Seafaring peoples came from Samoa and Tonga and colonized the Cook Islands.

(30) The island is now known as Tongatapu. The megalithic gate from Tongatapu, illustrated by Churchward and shown on page 71 is known as Ha'amonga 'a Maui (Burden of Maui). The structure was bult in the early 13th century by King Tu'i Tonga Tu'itātu as a gateway to his royal compound, Heketa.

(31-32) Gilbert, Marshall, and Caroline Groups. The Gilbert Islands are today part of the nation of Kiribati and archaeological evidence dates human habitation to 1000 B.C.E. The Marshall Islands are their own nation and archaeological evidence indicates human habitation to 1000 B.C.E. The Caroline Islands are now divided between the Federated States of Micronesia and Palau and archaeological evidence indicates human habitation starting about 2000 B.C.E.

(33) Panape (Pohnpei) Known today as Pohnpei, and part of the Federated States of Micronesia, carbon dating on the structures of Nan Modal has placed construction beginning in 1200 A.D, however evidence of occupation exists from 200 B.C.

(34) Swallow Island. Part of the Solomon Islands, there is evidence that this area was colonized at least 30,000 years ago.

(35) Kusai Island is located in the Federated States of Micronesia and formerly part of the Caroline Islands. Archaeological evidence indicates human habitation starting about 2000 B.C.E.

(36) Lele Island is located in the Federated States of Micronesia and formerly part of the Caroline Islands. Archaeological evidence indicates human habitation starting about 2000 B.C.E.

(37) Kingsmill Islands (Tapiteau Island), are part of the Gilbert Islands that are today part of the nation of Kiribati and archaeological evidence dates human habitation to 1000 B.C.E.

(38) Ladrone or Mariana Group (Guam) are today known as the Commonwealth of the Northern Mariana Islands. Archaeological evidence indicates human habitation starting about 2000 B.C.E.

(39) Larin Tarr Gill was an American author that wrote about the people of the South Seas and Pacific Islands. She was affiliated with the Bernice Bishop Museum in Hawaii.

(40) Hawaii is part of the United States of America and archaeological evidence indicates human habitation beginning in 400 A.D.

(41) Marquesas are part of French Polynesia today and archaeological evidence indicates human habitation dating from 300 A. D.

(42) New Zealand. Archaeological evidence indicates that human habitation started around 100 A.D.

(43) Australia. Archaeological evidence indicates that human habitation began 50,000 years ago.

(44) O'Brien, Frederick is discussed in the Persons of Interest Appendix beginning on page A1—34.

(45) "*Mystic Isles of the South Seas*" is discussed in the Written Works Appendix beginning on page A2—21.

(46) "*Polynesian Researches: During a Residence of Nearly Eight Years in the Society and Sandwich Islands (1839)*" by the Rev. William Ellis (1794-1872). Compare text on page 84 to

Excerpt from "Queen Moo and the Egyptian Sphinx" (1896) provides this text:
> "Ellis in his "Polynesian Researches" says: "In the Sandwich Islands there is a tradition that in the beginning there was nothing but water, when a big bird descended from on high and laid an egg in the sea. That egg burst and Hawaii came forth."
> Footnote on entry at bottom of page says: "Ellis, Polynesian Researches, vol I., chap. V., p. 100
> Augustus Le Plongeon, "Queen Moo and the Egyptian Sphinx" (1896), page 74

(47) The *Bible* is discussed in the Written Works Appendix beginning on page A2—4.

(48) "*Popol Vuh*" is discussed in the Written Works Appendix beginning on page A2—28.

(49) No biographical data on Jules Remain has been uncovered.

(50-51) A similar table is shown on page 151-153 of "*Queen Moo & The Egyptian Sphinx*"; Le Plongeon, Augustus; 1896 (reproduced below)

GREEK ALPHABET.	MAYA VOCABLES WITH THEIR ENGLISH MEANING.			
ALPHA.	**Al** Heavy ;	**páa** break ;	**ha.** water.	
BETA.	**Be** Walk ;	**ta.** place.		
GAMMA.	**Kam** Receive ;	**ma.** earth.		
DELTA.	**Tel** Depth ; bottom ;	**ta.** where.		
EPSILON.	**Ep** Obstruct ;	**zil** make edges ;	**on-om.** whirlpool ; to whirl.	
ZETA.	**Ze** Strike ;	**ta.** place ; ground.		
ETA.	**Et** With ;	**ha.** water.		
THETA.	**Thetheah** Extend ;	**ha.** water.		
IOTA.	**Io** All that which lives and moves ;	**ta.** earth.		
KAPPA.	**Ka** Sediment ;	**páa.** break ; open.		
LAMBDA.	**Lam** Submerge ;	**be** go ; walk ;	**ta.** where ; place.	
MU.	**Mu.** Mu.			
NI.	**Ni.** Point ; summit.			
XI.	**Xi.** Rise over ; appear over.			
OMIKRON.	**Om** Whirlpool ; whirl ;	**ik** wind ;	**le** place ;	**on.** circular.
PI.	**Pi.** To place by little and little.			
RHO.	**La** Until ;	**ho.** come.		

The Lost Continent of Mu, Motherland of Men

GREEK ALPHABET.	MAYA VOCABLES WITH THEIR ENGLISH MEANING.				
SIGMA.	**Zi** Cold;	**ik** wind;	**ma.** before.		
TAU.	**Ta** Where;	**u.** basin; valley.			
UPSILON.	**U** Abyss:	**pa** tank;	**zi** cold; frozen;	**le** place;	**on.** circular.
PHI.	**Pe** Come; form;	**hi.** clay.			
CHI.	**Chi.** Mouth; aperture.				
PSI.	**Pe** Come out;	**zi.** vapor.			
OMEGA.	**O** There;	**mec** whirl;	**ka.** sediments.		

FREELY TRANSLATED.

ALPHA.	Heavily break—*the*—waters
BETA.	extending—*over the*—plains.
GAMMA.	*They*—cover—*the*—land
DELTA.	*in low places where*
EPSILON.	*there are*—obstructions, shores form and whirlpools
ZETA.	strike—*the*—earth
ETA.	with water.
THETA.	*The*—water spreads
IOTA.	*on* all that lives and moves.
KAPPA.	Sediments give way.
LAMBDA.	Submerged is—*the*—land
MU.	*of* Mu.
NI.	The peaks—*only*
XI.	appear above—*the water.*
OMIKRON.	Whirlwinds blow around
PI.	by little and little,
RHO.	until comes

SIGMA.	cold air. Before
TAU.	where—*existed*—valleys,
UPSILON.	*now*, abysses, frozen tanks. In circular places
PHI.	clay—formed.
CHI.	*A*—mouth
PSI.	opens; vapors
OMEGA.	come forth—and *volcanic* sediments.

(52) Winter, Nevin Otto (1869-1936) wrote several books on South America and was a lawyer that practiced in Toledo, Ohio.

(53) "*Guatemala*" is discussed in the Written Works Appendix beginning on page A2—15.

5
The Egyptian Sacred Volume
Book of the Dead

PER-M-HRU

Page 92

In the preceding chapter I have referred to the Egyptian Book of the Dead (1). It contains many records that prove that the Motherland of Man, the submerged continent of Mu, was, indeed, the original habitat of the race of men, and that other countries were merely orbits for bodies that moved about a center of attraction, which was the highly civilized continent of Mu, colonizer of the worlds that lay beyond its immediate ken; consequently it does not appear to me to be out of place to say a few words about the Book of the Dead at this point.

The Book of the Dead is the common name by which this sacred volume is known. In Egyptian hieroglyphics the name is written: *Per-m-hru*. According to Egyptologists, *per* means "coming forth," *hru* means "day" and *m* is a preposition meaning "from."

Page 93

But Egyptologists are not all in accord on the exact meaning of the title of this book. Dr. Pleyte (2) in his "Chapitres Supplementaires du Livre des Morts," (3) says the name should be read, "going forth from the day." Brugsch Bey (4) in his "Steinschrift und Bibelwort," (5) page 257, maintains that the correct meaning is, "Book of the outgoing by day." Lefebure (6), Maspero (7) and Renouf (8) say the reading is, "Coming forth by day "

While these great Egyptologists are in dispute, who shall say which is correct? The only way the problem can be solved, it appears to me, is to show what the book actually refers to, and what it actually means; for, all the writings composing it are symbolical, and it is therefore necessary to know what they symbolize. This has not been shown by any Egyptologist up to the present time.

The Book of the Dead is a sacred commemorative memorial, dedicated to the multitudes of people who lost their lives at the destruction of Mu, the forefathers of the Egyptians and all mankind. These are the "dead" referred to. This feeling of love and devotion to the Motherland, this feeling of love and respect for forefathers is the origin of "ancestor worship," so common throughout the world in past and present ages. Have we not a reflection of it among ourselves? Do we not lay flowers on the graves of those who have passed away?

I entirely disagree with all Egyptologists on the meaning of *Per-m-hru*. *Per* means "gone forth"; *hru* means the day and *m* means Mu.

The letter *m*, which Egyptologists term a preposition is nothing of the kind; it is a symbol, the symbolic letter and also the name of Mu; therefore: *Per-m-hru* reads,

Page 94

"Mu has gone forth from the day." This is in accord with what I have previously said: The Book of the Dead is a sacred commemorative memorial to the 64,000,000 people who lost their lives at the destruction of Mu."

My many years of study in the Orient with some of the most capable of Oriental scholars have enabled me to read many of the esoteric meanings appearing in the Book of the Dead; for it must be remembered that there is a very close connection between the ancient learning of India and that of Egypt. *Upper* Egypt was colonized and settled by Mayas from India, and when their settlement Maioo was firmly established, a party of Naacals left India and went to Egypt, to establish the teachings of the "Seven Sacred Inspired Writings," religion and the sciences; thus it is seen that the teachings I received in India, to an extent, applied also to Egypt.

At what date the Book of the Dead was first formed is unknown; apparently, however, the first copies contained only a few chapters, which were subsequently added to until it assumed the proportions in which we now find it. In this respect it has been a duplication of the Hindu book, Maha-bharatta, (9) which commenced small and grew large with time.

Every chapter in the Book of the Dead either directly or indirectly refers to Mu, and the book is permeated with symbols wich were assigned to Mu before the foot of man trod the soil of Egypt.

As already stated, Mu was first torn to pieces by earthquakes and then sank through the flames of the underneath into a fiery abyss or caldron.

I will now take a few vignettes from the Book of the

Dead, decipher and translate them, to show the connection between the Book of the Dead and Mu, the Motherland.

Vignette l. This is an Egyptian compound symbol or vignette describing the destruction of Mu. Found in the Book of the Dead.

1. Is the Egyptian symbol for flames of fire.

2. Is the hieratic letter M of the Motherland and her alphabetical and geometrical symbol, and one of the most commonly used symbols for her.

3. Is an ancient symbol, depicting an abyss, a tank or a pit.

4. Is this tank or abyss filled with fire.

Thus the vignette reads: "Mu has gone down into an abyss of fire, and, as she sank, flames of fire shot up around her and enveloped her." This is told by flames being set all around Fig. 2—Mu.

One of the most prominent symbols, on account of its being so oft repeated, is a conventional altar, over which is a set sun, and above the sun a dead closed lotus.

This compound symbol is found scores of times among the vignettes of the Book of the Dead, and a notable fact

---

is that the lotus is invariably depicted as dead and closed. throughout the book.

I will decipher and translate this little vignette:

1. Is the Egyptian conventional form of an altar.

2. Is the sacred lotus flower, the sacred floral symbol of Mu.

3. Is the sun without rays, symbolizing that the sun has set, gone down beyond the horizon. Being placed *below* Mu, the lotus, it symbolizes that the sun has dropped below the horizon of Mu. The sun has forever set on dead Mu. All is darkness. Mu is in "the region of darkness." Before the submersion of Mu her common geographical symbol was a three-pointed figure (Fig. 4), reading, "The Lands of the West," the three areas of land which composed the Motherland.

After Mu was submerged, her geographical location was called "the region of darkness," and in this condition she was symbolized by placing a sun without rays over the center point (Fig. 6). Occasionally the center point was cut out altogether and a rayless sun substituted (Fig. 5).

THE VIGNETTE OF CHAPTER 81

In the Book of the Dead, Egyptologists have described this vignette as "a head peeping out of a lotus flower."

Page 97

The last line of the eighty-first chapter reads: "I am a pure Lotus sprung out of the Field of the Sun."

The deciphering of this vignette is:

The head represents an Egyptian and Egyptians, as shown by the head-dress.

The head has arisen out of a lotus.

The lotus is shown as dead and closed.

In this vignette the lotus is dead Mu.

Translated it reads:

"The Egyptians came from Mu, a land which is dead and exists no more."

The last line is the crux of the whole chapter.

"I am a pure Lotus" means: "I am a pure descendant from the people of Mu."

"Sprung from the Field of the Sun" corroborates the lotus. "The Field of the Sun" also means the Empire of the Sun, the imperial name of Mu.

Mu in the tongue of the Motherland meant: "mother, land, field, country, empire" and "mouth."

A free reading of this vignette would be: "I am an Egyptian of pure descent; my forefathers came from the motherland Mu, the Empire of the Sun, which is now dead and gone."

Space will not permit me to decipher more vignettes from the Book of the Dead. A large volume could be filled with them.

I will make one more note, which is all Egyptian, but only partially from the Book of the Dead.

All ancient peoples, including the Egyptians, believed in the reincarnation of the soul. Our old Oriental tablets showed us that the ancients understood the origin and the

---

Page 98

workings of all the forces: they knew that when a force had done its allotted duty, that which had been assigned to it by nature, it became exhausted, *but not dead,* force cannot die any more than an element can die. An exhausted force is drawn back to the source of generation for regeneration, then to be passed into nature's storehouse, there to await the next call from nature. This is what the old tablets tell us.

Man's soul is the greatest force connected with the earth except that of the Deity. The soul of man was incarnated in the land of Mu, the Lands of the West. When man's body sleeps its last sleep and decomposes, his soul does not die with the body, but, the ancients believed, returns to the place of incarnation, Mu, there to await reincarnation.

From the time of Menes, when Upper and Lower Egypt became one kingdom, down to about 2700 B. C., there were two religious cults in Egypt, known as the *West* cult and the *East* cult. The belief of the Lower Egyptians was that the soul traveled *west* to reach the place of reincarnation. The Upper Egyptians claimed that the soul must travel *east* to reach a celestial paradise. Both cults claimed that the soul must travel back over the same road, to the place of reincarnation, by which their forefathers came to Egypt.

When looking at the foregoing and reading the speculations of professional Egyptologists concerning these diametric cults, one is tempted to smile, for I have failed to find a single Egyptian authority who explains the origin and cause of these two cults, which at one time existed in

Page 99

Egypt; yet the problem is easy to answer, as the following will prove:

Lower Egypt was settled from the motherland via Mayax and Atlantis, both of which lay to the *west* of Egypt; therefore to reach the place of reincarnation from *Lower Egypt* and to travel back over the same road by which their fathers came, the soul had to travel back to the west.

The Upper Egyptians came to Egypt from the Motherland by way of Burma and India. Both of these countries lie to the east of Egypt; so that for the souls of the *Upper Egyptians* to arrive at the place of reincarnation and to travel back over the same road by which their fathers came, they had to travel back to the *east.* So it is seen that both cults were right, although it took them many hundreds of years to find it out.

Donald A. Mackenzie: (10) "The fusion of the two ancient Egyptian cults, that of Osiris, which originally believed in a paradise in the *west* and that of the *sun-worshippers* who believed in a celestial paradise in the east.

"Osiris, an ancient deified *king* was identified with the gods of the *western* cult."

"The early conflict between the two cults is echoed in the mortuary texts, dating back till about 2700 B. C."

Like all Egyptologists, Mackenzie is sadly deficient in symbolology. All fail to differentiate between the symbol and what it represents. They fail to remember that the ancients used a special symbol for every attribute of the Deity, and that the sun was the collective symbol of all the attributes of the Deity, and therefore represented the Diety Himself.

Page 100

The Upper Egyptians were *not* sun-worshippers, as stated by Mackenzie. Ra, the sun, was their collective symbol for the Deity. Temples were dedicated to Ra as *representing* the Divinity, just as the cross today represents Christ. (11)

A symbol is an intimate reminder, mentally concentrating and bringing in closer touch with the eyes of the mind, bringing in closer touch and mental view the object addressed. With the use of symbols many encroaching outside thoughts are driven away. A symbol permits of greater concentration.

Mackenzie asserts that Osiris was an ancient king. What people he reigned over Mackenzie does not say, but by inference it would be the Egyptians; if so, he is wrong again, because when Thoth (12) started the first Lower Egyptian colony at Sais, he taught the Osirian religion, as various papyri show, and that was 16,000 years ago. From two different sources I find it stated that Osiris lived in Atlantis 18,000 or 20,000 years ago, and that he was a great religious teacher—a master.

The two Egyptian cults form another convincing proof that the advent of man on earth was on Mu, and that Mu was situated in the Pacific. The geographical position is thus positively established as east of Burma and west of Mayax and therefore in the Pacific Ocean.

The destruction of the Motherland was also commemorated in their religious ceremonies. The advancement of the novice through the second degree was by symbolically submerging him in a tank of fire to remind him of the fate that befell his forefathers in the beloved Motherland, and also to hint where his soul must go for reincarnation. This

Page 101

is reflected in the Book of the Dead, Chapter 22, where it says: "I come, I do that which my heart wishes on the day of the *Fire* when I extinguish the flames as soon as they appear."

Before closing my section on records, I think it advisable to show corresponding records from all areas surrounding the Pacific Ocean. This will help readers to fuly grasp the situation and the facts.

I will first take the symbol, the Royal Escutcheon of Mu, the Empire of the Sun—a sun with eight rays.

The particular design here given was found on the dress of a Kooteney Indian living in British Columbia. The border of the dress of another Kooteney Indian was composed of a continuation of one of the symbols of "Mu submerged." See page 139. The garment with the sun symbol was black, the sun is in pale yellow, the points of the rays in pale indigo blue and the intervening space between the sun and the points of its rays a pale reddish pink.

Among the Indians of the northwestern section of North America are found the now famous totem pillars, the original meaning of which I give on page 159.

On page 49 I showed a picture of the Royal Escutcheon of Mu painted on the fan of one of the savages of the Gilbert Islands, 7,000 miles from British Columbia.

Page 102

On page 79 I noted the totem poles of the Maoris of New Zealand, 12,000 miles from the Kooteney Indians.

On page 174 I will show symbols among the Nevada cliff writings that referred to Mu, also in New Mexico, and again in Niven's "Mexican Buried Cities," page 208 and in "Yucatan," page 237.

A great impenetrable forest of dense tangled tropical jungle growth covers the southern half of Yucatan and extends far into Guatemala, which is half covered by it. It extends into Chiapas and Tabasco, and stretches into Honduras. This great forest is not primeval, for once the land was densely populated with great cities and highly cultivated fields. Throughout this now impenetrable wilderness are ruins, great imposing ruins, in every part of the forest, and, if we can believe the tales of the Indians, Copan and Quirigua, (13) which are on the outer edge of this tangled jungle, are only samples of still greater ruins hidden away in the depths of these forests, and lying beyond the present reach of the white man.

Personally I believe the tales of the Indians to be true, for they talked about these ruins with superstitious awe, which lent credence to their tales. Beyond the tales of the Indians, we have Egyptian records confirming them.

This great forest is a part of "the country beyond," which was made a ruin and "impassable" with the loss of "nearly all the people," by great "cataclysmic floods which rolled over the land."

This civilization was wiped out and their cities wrecked between 11,500 and 11,750 years ago, when the gas belts, which run under and around this area, were being forged,

A Central American Obelisk
Quirigua

with the attendant mountain raising, a little while before the submersion of Atlantis.

For the Egyptians to say the country was impassable, after such devastating phenomena, is certainly a mild way of describing the conditions.

At Copan in Honduras, Quirigua in Guatemala, Opico and Cirraca-Mecallo (14) in Salvador, there are vast prehistoric ruins. Among each of these ruins there are symbols referring to Mu.

At Quirigua there are some notable stelai or obelisks, 13 in number, which have symbolical human figures carved upon them, each wearing a triple crown, thus showing their allegiance to the Motherland.

Each of these stelai has a different totem symbol, showing that they refer to various dynasties of kings. Each of the ancient dynasties had a different totem, such as the Elephant, Tiger and Serpent.

I will next take the great monolith at Tiahuanaco (15), on the shores of Lake Titicaca, South America, which I show on page 162, with its decipherings and translation. Thus it is shown that a continuous string of records exists from end to end of the western parts of "North, Central and South America, all telling us that Mu was their Motherland.

I have noted symbols among the savages of the South Sea Islands and on the stones of the ruins among these specks of land, then I went from the South Pacific to New Zealand, so that nothing remains but Asia to complete the circuit around the ocean. Burma and India are full of records about Mu, as I have heretofore prominently shown, corresponding in all details with those of America.

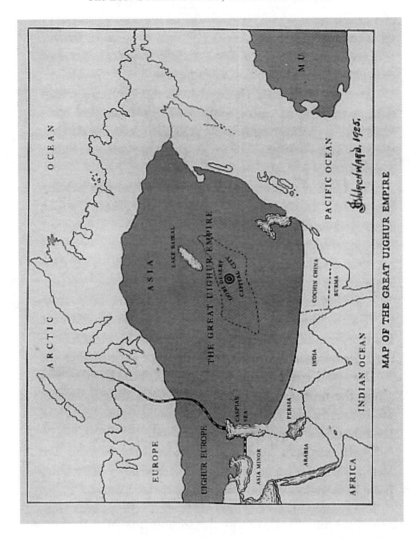

Map of the Great Uighur Empire

Page 105

Page 106

I think the Uighur **(16)** records will be all that is necessary to convince the most skeptical mind that it is clearly proven by symbols alone that Mu was the motherland of man; but, as an old Hindu saying goes:

"It is easier to snatch a pearl from the teeth of a crocodile, or to twist an angry, venomous serpent around one's head like a garland of flowers, without incurring danger, than to make an Ignorant or an obstinate person change his mind."

The Uighur was the principal colonial empire belonging to Mu at the time of the biblical "Flood," which destroyed its eastern half.

Chinese legends tell that the Uighurs were at the height of their civilization about 17,000 years ago. This date agrees with geological phenomena.

The Uighur Empire stretched its powerful arms from the Pacific Ocean across Central Asia and into Eastern Europe from the Caspian Sea on. This was before the British Isles became separated from the continent of Europe.

The southern boundary of the Uighur Empire was along the northern boundaries of Cochin China, Burma, India and Persia, and this was before the Himalayas and the other Asiaitic mountains were raised.

Their northern boundary extended into Siberia, but how far there is no record to tell. Remains of their cities have been found in the southern parts of Siberia.

Eventually the Uighurs extended themselves into Europe around the western and northern shores of the Caspian Sea, as related in a very ancient Hindu record; from here they continued on through Central Europe to its western boundary, Ireland.

Page 107

They settled in northern Spain, northern France, and far down into the Balkan region. The late archaeological discoveries in Moravia are Uighur remains, and the evidences on which ethnologists have based their theories that man originated in Asia, have been marks left by the advancing Uighurs in Europe.

The history of the Uighurs is the history of the Aryans.

Ethnologists have classed certain white races as Aryans which are not Aryans at all, but belong to a totally different line of colonization.

The capital city of the Uighurs was where the ruins of Khara Khoto **(17)** now stand in the Gobi Desert. At the time of the Uighur Empire the Gobi Desert was an exceedingly fertile area of land.

The Uighurs had reached a high state of civilization and culture: they knew astrology, mining, the textile industries, architecture, mathematics, agriculture, writing, reading, medicine, etc. They were experts in decorative art on silk, metals and wood, and they made statues of gold, silver, bronze and clay; and this was before the history of Egypt commenced.

About one-half of the Uighur Empire was destroyed before Mu went down, the other half subsequent to Mu's submersion.

Professor Kozloff **(18)** unearthed a tomb 50 feet below the surface at Khara Khoto **(19)** and in it found wonderful treasures, which he photographed, not being allowed to disturb or take anything away. Through the courtesy and kindness of the *Sunday American* I have obtained the loan of some of these pictures, two of which I here reproduce with their decipherings, as they are symbolical. I

Loaned from the Collection of the American Weekly Section of the New York Sunday American.
An Uighur Queen and her consort (20)

Page 108

SCEPTER CARRIED BY A MONARCH OF THE UIGHURS
Of later date than that shown in the hand of the Queen. Both show the trident

SCEPTER CARRIED BY A MONARCH OF THE UIGHURS (21)
Of later date than that shown in the hand of the Queen. Both show the trident

think I am safe in believing that these pictures represent a time between 16,000 and 18,000 years ago.

These pictures are symbolical, the various symbols telling who they are, and what they are. In the original they are paintings on silk and represent a queen and her consort in a sitting posture. I will now pick out the symbols of the Queen. On her head is a three-pointed crown with a disc in the center with three sets of rays emanating from it. Behind her body is a large disc, the sun. At the back of her head is a smaller disc, an inferior sun. The large disc symbolizes Mu, the small disc the Uighur Colonial Empire. The crown on her head, a sun with rays on one half only, shows the escutcheon of a colonial empire. In her left hand she carries a scepter, the ends of which are in the form of a trident—three points—the Motherland's numeral.

Her seat is a full-blown sacred lotus, the floral symbol of the Motherland, so that she is depicted as sitting in the lap of and being upheld by Mu, the Motherland. Her consort does not carry a scepter, nor has he a sun with rays, but in its place a sphere. His crown also shows the Motherland's numeral.

Kozloff had pictures of various scepters. This illustra-

tion is of a different pattern to the one held in the queen's hand, and of later date, but symbolically reads the same, the ends being divided into three giving the numeral of the Motherland.

Thus we see the symbols of Asia, America, South Sea Islands and New Zealand all agreeing in the tale they tell. Could anything be more definite or convincing—unless we could get our old forefathers to rise from their graves, and tell us by word of mouth what happened to them in the land of Mu?

(22)

Chapter 5: The Egyptian Sacred Volume, Book of the Dead Notes

(1) The *Egyptian Book of the Dead* is discussed in the Written Works Appendix beginning on page A2—10.

(2) Dr. Willem Pleyte (1836-1903) was a Dutch Egyptologist.

(3) "*The Chapitres Supplementaires du Livre des Morts*" (English: "*The Additional Chapters of the Book of Deaths*")

(4) Brugsch-Bey, Heinrich Karl (1827-1894) was a German Egyptologist.

(5) "*Steinschrift und Bibelwort* " (English: "*Stone writing and Bible word*").

(6) Lefebure, Eugene (1838-1908) was a French Egyptologist.

(7) Maspero, Gaston (1846-1916) was a French Egyptologist.

(8) Renouf, Sir Peter le Page (1822-1897) was a British Egyptologist.

(9) The "*Maha-baratta*" is discussed in the Written Works Appendix beginning on page A2—20.

(10) Mackenzie, Donald A. is discussed in the Persons of Interest Appendix beginning on page A1—26.

(11) Jesus Christ is discussed in the Persons of Interest Appendix beginning on page A1—5.

(12) Thoth is discussed in the Persons of Interest Appendix beginning on page A1—51.

(13) Copan (Guatemala) was originally settled about 159 A.D. with the large monuments and hieroglyphic texts being constructed between 435 to 822 A.D. Quirigua (Guatemala) was originally settled about 200 A.D. with the large monuments and hieroglyphic texts being constructed between 550 to 850 A.D.

(14) Opico (El Salvador) has been dated to 900 B.C. with population moving abruptly in A.D. 250 due to a volcano eruption. References to Cirraca-Mecallo remain to be uncovered.

(15) Tiahuanaco [Tiwanaku] (Peru) was founded in 200 B.C. and grew into a regional power between 600 and 800 A.D. and collapsed in 1000 A.D.

(16) The historical Uighur Empire existed from 744 AD to 840 AD in what is now modern day Mongolia. For further references see:
Sinor, Peter, Editor; The Cambridge History of Early Inner Asia; Cambridge University Press; 1994; Chapter 12 pages 317-342.
Barthold, W.; Turkestan Down to the Mongol Invasion; Munishiram Manoharlil Publishers Pvt Ltd; 1992
Grousset, Rene; The Empire of the Steppes a History of Central Asia; Rutgers University Press; 1997
One mention of the ancient Uighur Empire is referenced in note # 16 from James Churchward's scrapbooks.
Other references:
Childress, David Hatcher; "Lost Cities of China, Central Asia & India"; Adventures Unlimited Press; 1989 pages 350-354. Note, this is a circular reference in that Childress quotes James Churchward as an authority. As further proof, he states that the "Book of Manu says: The Uigers had settlements on the northern and eastern shores of the Caspian Sea." Also, "Max Mueller once wrote 'The first Caucasians were a small company from the mountains of Central Asia.'"

(17) Khara Khoto is not a unknown dead ancient city. As mentioned in *"The Desert Road to Turkestan"* (Lattimore, Owen; Kodansha Press; 1995), Khara Khoto, the "Black City" in Mongolian, was known in Marco Polo's time as Etsina (Edsina) and was inhabited by Tangut peoples (page 192.) Peter Hopkirk in *"Foreign Devils on the Silk Road"* (Hopkirk; University of Massachusetts Press; 1980) recounts how the city was conquered and subsequently destroyed in the 14th century (pages 200-201) by a Chinese army after rerouting the Edsin Gol river.

(18) Kozloff, Piotr Kumich is discussed in the Persons of Interest Appendix beginning on page A1—20.

(19) Contained within James Churchward's scrapbooks is an article with the handwritten title, "Khara Khota Kosloff" which mentions the tomb and provides additional details. The source nor date is on the article. The text is reproduced below:

Moscow.

One of the most picturesque and important of archaeological discoveries of the century has been made by Professor P. K. Kozloff, of Moscow, under the sand-covered ruins of Khara Khoto, in the Gobi Desert of Mongolia.

Khara Khoto, or the Black City, was the capital both of Genghis Khan and Kubla Khan, two of the great Mongol conquerors, who during their lives swept with their hordes over Asia and a good part of Europe. It was of Kubla Khan that the English poet, Coleridge, wrote that strange and haunting verse of his, beginning:

"In Xanadu did Kubla Khan
A stately pleasure-dome decree
Where Alph, the sacred river, ran
Through caverns, measureless to man
Down to a sunless sea."

Digging down through half-a-hundred feet of shifting sand, Professor Kozloff has unearthed there the tombs of what appear to be the legendary Seven Kings of ancient Tartary - certainly the oldest kings that ever ruled any civilization. At this depth the tools of his men struck brick and fossilized black wood. Cutting through this an opening large enough to let a man go through, they lowered Kozloff into the black depths.

As the explorer reached the bottom of the secret chamber his flash revealed one of the most astonishing sites ever seen by an archaeologist - stranger than the scene that met the eyes of the finders of old Pharaoh Tutankhamen's tomb.

He was in a great vaulted chamber. In the center of the chamber was a long table of fossilized wood.

And on seven thrones, each facing the west, sat seven mummies, each dressed in gorgeous robes and with heavy gold masks over their faces. On the table were large bowls of jade, whose cups showed that the had once held some crimson liquid. Another bowl was at the feet of each mummy and each one held in his hand a golden cup of white sand. Set in each throne was a silver tablet in the ancient Uighur, but of such a remote period that they have not been as yet deciphered. They probably contain the names of the kings, the dates of their rule and other particulars.

Around the necks of the mummies were necklaces, upon which were strung miniature models of weapons of war and domestic utensils - little golden javelins, swords, etc., and little golden pots and (missing)

(missing) utter dryness of the place, so far beneath the dry desert, ad preserved all the fabrics and wood. In high chests decorated with weird designs of flowers and animals of unknown type were found pictures and writings painted upon heavy silk, and a great number of thin silver plates bearing characters in the same ancient Uighur writing.

The whole chamber, indeed, was a tremendous treasure trove of the greatest historical importance. Once the writings can be read there is little doubt that they will reveal details of a lost civilization of which only the legends of China, India and Persia speak vaguely, legends of an unknown superior race which existed in the region of the Gobi when the rest of the world was merged in barbarism and whose cities were built centuries before the Pyramids.

"The writings in the tomb," commented Dr. Lao Chin, the Chinese archaeologist associated with the Kozloff expedition, "are the books of a golden age. In the secret chambers of the old Tao temples are to be found fragments of the same kind of writing, but no one has been able to decipher them. Once a great white race inhabited what is now the Gobi. China, India and the Mediterranean countries were then inhabited only by barbarians. These men of the Gobi sent out expeditions to colonize the wilds of a savage earth. Some of them came to China and, mixing with the best of the yellow savages, became the Chinese race. Others went to Egypt, India, and Greece and northern Europe and did the same thing there. They probably even got as far as America and were the founders of that lost civilization which was old before the Aztecs came down and fond its ruined cities."

Professor Kozloff places the date of the burial of these last seven kings at between 8,000 and 6,000 B.C. The seven kings would seem to include a complete dynasty. According to the legends they ruled the whole of Mongolia and central Asia, all the Altai and Himalayan regions, and the territories now covered with a moving sand, barren of cultivation and inhabited by various nomadic tribes. The legends tell that the Gobi Desert and the highlands between the Siberian and Tibetan mountains formed at that time a cultivated land of fertile fields, forest, lakes and rivers, filled with delicious fish. Magnificently constructed highways and roads connected the various cities and towns with each other. There were well-built cities, huge temples and public institutions, elaborate private houses and palaces of the rulers.

"I could distinctly see the dried up beds of rivers, canals, and lakes and what might have been rich orchards and active life."

The first excavation under the various ruins of Khara Khoto gave evidence merely of the time of Genghis and Kubla Khans and the last days of its existence. At the time of Genghis Khan Khara Khoto was already a militaristic decadent city, greatly shrunk from its former glory. Its predominant religion of this late period was Buddhism, and its life was altogether commercial. The merchants of the West and the East came there to exchange their goods. The West brought here all its merchandise and received here gold and silver, whereas the East brought raw materials, silk and hides.

Great workshops of domestic implements and utensils of agriculture and hunting indicate that the people were not warriors or savages. Even paper money of the time of Genghis Khan was discovered in large bulks, with which the Tartar ruler paid his troops and officers. Heaps upon heaps of old Mongolian and Tartar manuscripts, pictures, garments and weapons were found in one of the burial chambers of the Black Palace and among them the first autographic documents written by Genghis Khan.

The real treasures were found far below the surface ruins, in the remains of a much more ancient city, which had preceded the other by thousands of years.

Gold was evidently the easiest and most abundant metal of the Gobi Desert, in those days. It had no more value with the ancient Uighurs than our iron and copper. Horseshoes made of gold, appears and shovels were of silver.

Historical records say of the Uighurs that they first came to power about 7000

(break in text)

Professor Kozloff then undertook his expedition to the dead city with a special guide of Prince Tsazak.

In less than a month's journey with a caravan Kozloff's expedition arrived at the mountain range that overlooked the desolate valley with its black ruins, which at some places rose to more than fifty feet high in the air and of which he writes:

"A feeling of awe overcame us on seeing the most overwhelming ruins, perhaps the oldest metropolis of the world. All the impenetrable region. With its desolation and loneliness, lay before our eyes.

Without which the venture would mean little. By presenting his friendly Mongolian Prince with a phonograph and records of the chants of lamas and songs of the shepherds, the latter became unusually friendly and said that if he could present similar marvelous objects to a number of other princes and the lamas he might get permission for the excavation of Kara Khoto.

But with the condition that he should not take away the dead, or anything that belonged to them, but see and copy everything he wished, and cover again the place with sand.

Professor Kozloff had heard frequently during his previous expeditions of the ruins of a dead city located in the province of Alashan, in the Gobi Desert, but all his efforts to secure full information of it accurate locality from the native Mongols remained fruitless. It was only through his long friendship with a Mongolian Prince, Baldyn Tsazak, near Urga, that he obtained the following allegoric description:

"My Dear Brother - What I shall tell you is a secret that only the ruling Khans of the Gobi Desert can know. Khara Khoto - the Black City - lies aside from all the present caravan routes, over a thousand miles south of Urga, near the picturesque like of Soho Nor. The ruins are only visible to the initiated. The strangers can never see it. The phantoms of the dead are guarding its unknown treasures. Some few bandits have tried to dig under its ruins and sell things to foreigners, but only a few have gotten away alive. Our tradition does not permit digging in the soil, and there is a penalty of death for anyone who digs up the graves of our buried ancestors."

For a long time Kozloff could not secure permission from the authorities and the inhabitants to make an expedition to Khara Khoto and start an excavation,

[break in text]

There is a good reason to believe that the various prevailing images of Buddhas, Boddhisatvas and gods and goddesses of China and India are largely copies of the ancient saints and rulers of the Uighurs as are also many of those used in the Tibetan lamaseries to-day.

[break in text]

The Uighurs, as the race was called, reached a high degree of culture: they knew astrology, mining, textile industry, architecture, mathematics, agriculture, writing and reading, medicine and Magianism. They had excellent training in decorative arts on silk, metal, and wood, and they made statues of gold and silver and wood, clay and bronze.

[break in text]

B.C. Somewhere from the south of Mongolia, from the present day province of Alashan of China, rose this white and strong nation. The origin of the Uighurs is problematic. But it is known that they ruled all the border lands of China, India and Mongolia, spread gradually northward, and eventually controlled all the more or less advanced nomadic tribes.

The greatest power of the Uighurs extended from 6000 B.C. till the rise of the new Chinese, Indian, and Persian empires. The Chinese annals of 500 B.C. describe them as being a light-haired and blue-eyed people. It was the rise of the new militant tribes, such as the Kirghiz, the Tartars of the Altai mountains, the Uriankhai and the newly formulated Mongolian races - mountaineers - that ultimately conquered the Uighurs.

Khara Khoto, as well as their other surviving old cities of Mongolia, were ultimately occupied by the hordes of Genghis Khan and Kubla Khan, and are since then buried in the sand.

About the same time as Professor Kozloff's discovery of the tombs of the Tartar kings, Professor Adrianoff excavated an ancient Uighur burial place in the Minusinsk district of Siberia, which borders on Mongolia. He found fifteen bodies mummified men on horseback, will all the equipments, buried there about 3000 B.C. On sinking a shaft down the mound he came upon a rotten beam of timber; four or five yards deeper he found mummified bodies in huge stone trunks or chests, sitting in their national garb and their faces covered with silver masks. A few yards deeper he found skulls of a dozen men and their bones in disorder. Here he found strange metallic discs of gold-bronze, the use of which is unexplainable.

A few years before Kozloff's excavation of Khara Khoto, Professor Le Coq excavated another dead city, Khotcho, in Chinese Turkestan, a thousand or more miles directly west from Khara Khoto, and discovered a vast amount of manuscripts of a latter period, mostly written in Uighur script, although the language in that case is either Persian, Chinese or Hindoo. What was the reason of those scholars or priests writing their sacred books not in Chinese or Sanskrit letters, whch were at that time fully developed? The Uighur script was evidently more scholarly or appropriate to express their ideas, as the Latin was for the Gothic period, or as the Slavonic script is still used by the Russian Greek Church.

The seven buried Tartar kings seem to include a complete dynasty, covering the periods of 8000 to 7000 before our time. The astronomical charts indicate clearly the position of the constellations of that time, which closely corroborate the counting of time from the other evidence.

What new and amazing light will be shed upon the history of the world when the copies of the writings upon those strange silver plates in the tomb of the Seven Kings are at last deciphered?

(20) These figures look the same as paintings of Bodhisattvas from Dunhuang.

(21) The 'scepter' is known as a Vajra (Tibetan: Dorje) and is an element of a Vajrayana Buddhist's ritual items. Symbolically it represents a lightning bolt. Half a Vajra forms the handle of the ritual bell. Also, a picture of a 'sceptre' is in one of his scrapbooks and is provided below.

A Painting of a Goddess of the Vanished Race, Photographed by Professor Kozloff in the Tomb of the Seven Kings.

the Tartars of the Altai Mountains, the

A Golden Scepter of One of the Ancient Kings Found in the Secret Tomb.

A few years before Kozloff's excav

(22) Drawing similar to Figure 1 on page 65 of "*Sacred Mysteries Among the Mayas and the Quiches*"; Le Plongeon, Augustus; 1886; Upside down from figure 2c on page 127 of "*Origin and Evolution of Religion*", Albert Churchward, 1924.

6
Mu, the Empire of the Sun

Page 111

Many students of the ancient have noted the fact that the ancient kings and emperors assumed the title, "Son of the Sun." They have, however, entirely failed to give the reason for these ancient monarchs assuming this title, except that in many instances it is asserted that they claimed to be sons of the celestial orb.

(1)

To find the actual reason for the assumption of this title we must go back to the earth's first empire or kingdom, the Empire of the Sun. This empire was formed in the Motherland of man, and a royal emblem or escutcheon was devised for it.

THE ROYAL ESCUTCHEON OF MU

The Royal Escutcheon of Mu, the Empire of the Sun, was in no way a haphazard device, for every line in it has a particular meaning, as the deciphering and translation show:

A. The form of the shield in a conventional letter M, one of the letters in Mu's hieratic alphabet. It was her symbolical letter: besides, the letter was her actual name, as the letter M was pronounced Mu and Moo in the language of Mu.

B. This hieroglyphic is the central figure in the escutcheon and reads: U-luumil—pronounced Oo-loo-oom-il, which, translated, is: "The Empire of—"

C. The circle inclosing the glyph is a picture of the sun, so that this compound glyph reads: "The Empire of the Sun." Then prefix the shield and it is: "Mu, the Empire of the Sun."

D. The sun has eight rays, symbolizing the eight cardinal points, thus saying that the whole earth was dominated by her.

E. The circle enclosing the rays is a symbol of the universe. This universe as applied to man—man's universe, the earth. It is thus shown again that her rays, her influence, fall on all mankind.

Thus, the Royal Escutcheon of Mu tells us that all mankind on earth was under her rule. Mu was mistress of the whole earth, and this is confirmed by the Codex Cortesianus, where Mu is referred to as *The Ruler.*

Traditions say that when Mu was turned into an empire the Hieratic Head was selected to be the king or

emperor. The Hieratic Head represented the Deity in religious teachings. The sun, called Ra, was the collective and highest symbol of the Deity. The sun was therefore the symbol of "the King of Kings."

When elected to be the king, the Hieratic Head assumed the title of Ra—the sun—Ra being the king's symbol. To this title was added the name of the land Mu, so that the king's full title was Ra Mu, or Sun Mu. Then a new name was added to the land and it was called The Empire of the Sun.

When the Empire of the Sun began is unknown. Empires and kingdoms which were under her suzerainty are traced back for more than 35,000 years, so that the commencement of the Empire of the Sun antedates 35,000 years ago by a long time; how long no one can say. It might have been only a thousand years and again it might have been tens of thousands of years. Nothing in the shape of an old record, writing or tradition has ever turned up to give us the slightest clue on this point.

Apparently, as the various colonies of the Motherland became large and sufficiently able to govern themselves, they were turned into empires or kingdoms, but under the control of the Motherland, so that the whole world was a great family under one control.

When a colony was turned into a kingdom or empire, the first king was one of the royal family of the Motherland, or possibly, in some instances, an appointee. When appointed, the new king assumed the title of Son of the Sun. This was not intended to imply that he was the Son of the celestial orb, but the Son of the Sun Dynasty of the Empire of the Sun, or Son of the Empire of the Sun.

Symbols in ancient writings and inscriptions referring to Mu

Page 115

The emblem of the new king was still the sun, but in order to show that he was a subject of the Motherland, or a part of it, only one-half of the orb was shown above the horizon, with rays ascending from it.

Valmiki (2), the ancient Hindu historian, speaking of the works of the Mayas in India, says: "Before the sun rose above the horizon," meaning before the Hindu colony was turned into an empire.

When the Maya colony of the Deccan, India, was turned into a kingdom, the first king was called Ra Ma. His emblem was the rising sun, with only one-half of it showing above the horizon. He assumed the title Son of the Sun.

The present Maharajah of Udipoor (3) is said to be a direct descendant of Ra Ma. If so, his forefathers were kings more than 30,000 years ago. Unquestionably his is the oldest royal family on earth.

The rising sun is the emblem of various nations today, among them being the Japanese, the Persians and some of the Central American republics.

Page 116

To differentiate between the rising sun and the setting sun, the ancients were accustomed to depict the rising sun with rays and the setting sun as a plain disc or orb without rays.

After the Empire of the Sun came to its untimely end, the sun whenever shown in connection with the Motherland, always appears as the setting sun.

Symbols Representing Mu Used in Ancient Writings

A. Is a Maya vignette, telling of the submersion of Mu, the Lands of the West.

DECIPHERING AND TRANSLATION

Fig. 1. The three points on the top of the glyph are Mu's symbolical numeral, therefore the writings below refer to Mu.

Fig. 2. The three-pointed crown is the Imperial crown of Mu—the Empire of the Sun.

Fig. 3. Is the sun without rays, therefore Mu is in the region of darkness.

Fig. 4. This symbol shows Mu submerged and in darkness, "peaks or points only appear."

Fig. 5. This is the ancient symbol for an abyss, tank or depth.

Fig. 6. These symbolize the other two Lands of the West which were carried with Mu down into the "tank of fire."

Free Reading.—"Mu, the Empire of the Sun, has fallen into an abyss; she is in the region of darkness, where the sun never shines upon her. The other Lands of the West

---

Page 117

were blotted out with her. Her crown no longer rules the earth." The form of the hieroglyphic itself is a conventional abyss.

B. Is hieratic writing reading, "Mu, Lands of the West."

C. Is the Motherland's numeral, three—assigned to Mu as her numeral symbol.

D. Is the hieratic letter M of the Motherland's alphabet. It is also a geometrical figure. It was Mu's symbol, both alphabetical and geometrical.

E. Is a three-pointed geometrical figure, and was the symbol used for Mu, showing her geographical position.

F. Is a symbol for Mu after her submersion.

G. Is the same. Sometimes one is used, sometimes the other.

H. Is the lotus flower in conventional form, the floral symbol for Mu.

I. Is a Maya vignette telling of the submersion of the Lands of the West.

K. Is another form of the lotus symbolizing Mu.

L. Is the lotus, closed and dead, symbolizing that Mu no longer exists.

M. Is a lotus bud, used as ornamentation.

N. Is a Maya vignette telling of the submersion of the land of Kui. **(4)**

O. Is an hieratic writing reading, "Land of Kui."

P. Is an Egyptian vignette symbolizing the destruction of Mu.

Chapter 6: Mu, The Empire of the Sun Notes

(1) The central symbol is similar to page xlvi of the introduction of "*Queen Moo & The Egyptian Sphinx*"; Le Plongeon, Augustus; 1896. LePlongeon's interpretation is that 'the escutcheon scarcely needs explanation. It is easily read U-luumil kin, the "Land of the Sun."'

(2) Valmiki is discussed in the Persons of Interest Appendix beginning on page A1—52.

(3) A picture of the Maharaja of Udipoor is contained in James Churchward's scrapbooks. It has additional written text.

DESCENDANT OF RAMA, AND POSSESSOR OF THE BLUEST BLOOD IN INDIA: THE MAHARAJAH OF UDAIPUR. DRAWINGS BY A. HUGH FISHER.

(4) Khui-Land is mentioned on page 241 in "*The Origin and Evolution of the Human Race*"; Albert Churchward; 1921; Also, 'Kui' is mentioned on page 34 of "*Sacred Mysteries Among the Mayas and the Quiches*"; Le Plongeon, Augustus; 1886.

7
Age of Mu's Civilization

Page 118

I have made the assertion that the civilization of Mu dates back to more than 50,000 years ago. Now let us see on what foundation I base such a date.

Le Plongeon (1) found in the center of the mausoleum of Cay, the high priest and eldest son of King Can, at Chichen Itza, Yucatan, a carving of a serpent having twelve heads, with an inscription saying that this serpent was a symbol of the twelve Maya dynasties that had reigned over Mayax previous to the Can dynasty, and that their combined reigns covered a period of 18,000 years. (2)

The last King Can lived 16,000 years ago, as proved by the Troano Manuscript. (3) Add 16,000 to 18,000 years and we find that kings reigned over Mayax 34,000 years ago.

The length of the Can dynasty is not known. There were, however, at least six kings, and there might have been a dozen or more, so that an approximate time of 35,000 years may be reasonably accepted as the time when the first Mayax king reigned.

Page 119

Mayax was one of Mu's colonial empires and had advanced to that status from a mere settlement. Such a radical step takes time, so that Mu's civilization must necessarily be much older than 35,000 years.

These twelve dynasties of kings reigning 18,000 years are confirmed in the Chinese book "Tchi." (4)

Japan also has a record stating that twelve dynasties of kings reigned 18,000 years ago, and an old Hindu tablet refers to twelve dynasties of kings whose combined reigns aggregated 18,000 years, and the same fact is mentioned in an acient Hindu manuscript.

In addition to these records, there are numerous legends both in India and China, which refer to twelve dynasties of kings whose combined reigns aggregated 18,000 years.

Not one of these records, however, except the Chichen Itza inscription, gives the slightest idea where these kings reigned.

Manetho, (5) the Egyptian priest-historian, in one of his papyri, writes: "The reign of the Sages of Atlantis was 13,900 years."

Atlantis was submerged 11,500 years ago. Now let us add 11,500 to 13,900 and we find that Atlantis was governed by kings 25,000 years ago. The first king of Atlantis commenced his reign 25,400 years ago, and the first king of Mayax 34,000 years ago. Time between the two - 8,500 years. Granting the same time to have elapsed between the first emperor of Mu and the first king of Mayax, we can, figure approximately that Mu was at the height of her magnificence 50,000 or more years ago.

The scientific world may possibly say that the foregoing is merely speculative, so let us bring geology in to

Page 120

help us, and, to quote John Tyndall's favorite expression, "clinch the point."

When were the mountains that succeeded the great magnetic cataclysm raised? If we believe the myths of geology, we should say hundreds of thousands of years ago, and some of them millions of years ago.

Now I am going to show you *seven* civilizations that were in existence *before* the mountains were raised, some of them thousands upon thousands of years before a single mountain appeared upon the face of the earth. So, according to geology, these civilizations which came out of Mu would date her civilization back hundreds of thousands of years. However, they do not, and geology, as usual, is wrong.

In the Capital Hill, Smyrna, Asia Minor, 500 feet above the level of the sea, are to be seen the remains of three prehistoric civilizations, one above the other, with a stratum of sand, gravel and boulders intervening between each civilization. These civilizations are not lying horizontally, but at an angle of 45 degrees, as shown in the accompanying picture.

Were it not for the fact that the civilizations are at an angle, following the angle of the mountain, our scientists might assert that they were built on top of the hill and had not been raised. Their angle, however, proves beyond all controversy that they existed before the mountains were raised. What are the ages of these civilizations? I leave it to the scientific world to say; also the age of these mountains in Asia Minor.

Twenty-nine miles north of Mexico City, Niven **(6)** has discovered three civilizations, buried one beneath the other,

Page 121

The Road-Cut, Capital Hill, Smyrna, Asia Minor
Three civilizations, 500 feet above sea level, existed before the mountains were raised.

with strata of sand, gravel and boulders between each. These cities are more than 1,000 feet above sea level, with mountains of from 1,000 to 15,000 feet in altitude intervening between them and the sea. I have traced the boulders to a formation on the west coast of Mexico, and the lowest mountain between the cities and the source of the boulders is 5,000 feet in height.

Did the ocean raise waves that were more than 5,000 feet in height in ancient times, when multitudes throngd the streets of these cities, so that these boulders could be formed and hurled along to their final resting place? Or, did Mexico borrow a glacier for the occasion in order that these boulders might be deposited where they now lie?

However, nothing of this sort happened down in Mexico. These cities were built before the mountains were raised, and, as is shown by tablets coming from them which I have deciphered and translated, they were Mu's colonies.

Geologically, the lowest city dates far back into the Tertiary Era and was in existence more than 50,000 years ago as a colony of Mu. Pictures and details of this archaeological discovery will be found in Chapter 11, page 223.

The last example is Tiahuanaco **(7)** on Lake Titicaca in the Andes. Irrefutable evidences are present in and around this ancient city, which prove that when it was built, the ground on which it stands was just above sea level. Now, however, it is 15,000 feet above the sea.

These facts are conclusive proofs that the civilization of Mu dates back more than 50,000 years.

Chapter 7: Age of Mu's Civilization Notes

(1) Le Plongeon, Augustus is discussed in the Persons of Interest Appendix beginning on page A1—22.

(2) Le Plongeon's observations are related on page 96 of "*Sacred Mysteries Among the Mayas and the Quiches*"; Le Plongeon, Augustus; 1886

(3) The "*Troano Manuscript*" is discussed in the Written Works Appendix beginning on page A2—34.

(4) See page 96 of "*Sacred Mysteries Among the Mayas and the Quiches*"; Le Plongeon, Augustus; 1886. "Of these rulers we again find a dim tradition in China in the Tchi, also called che-cull-tse - the twelve children of the emperor of Heaven, Tien-Hoang, who had the body of a serpent. Each of these Tchi are said to have lived eighteen thousand years, and to have reigned in times anterior to Ti-hoang, sovereign of the country in the middle of the land.

(5) Manetho of Sebennytos (3rd century BCE) Egyptian Priest Historian.

(6) William Niven is discussed in the Persons of Interest Appendix beginning on page A1—33.

(7) Tiahuanaco [Tiwanaku] (Peru) was founded in 200 B.C. and grew into a regional power between 600 and 800 A.D. and collapsed in 1000 A.D.

8
Simple Symbols

Page 123

The minds of primitive man, generally, were in such an uncultured state that they could not be brought to understand the meanings of such words, for instance, as "infinite," "everlasting", "almighty," without some special form of teaching. To enable man to grasp and understand such meanings he was first taught that there was a Deity and a heaven hereafter; that he had an everlasting soul which did not die; that the Deity had many attributes and was all-powerful and everlasting. Then symbols such as primitive man could understand were selected to represent each attribute of the Deity and heaven. Thus was laid the foundation of the many pantheons, with their various symbolic meanings that have crept into and permeated all religions down to and including the modern Christian religion.

The most primitive forms of symbols were lines and simple geometrical figures. At first these symbols were few in number, but as time went on the number increased, also their intricacy, until we reach the period of the Egyptians, when they had become so numerous and so complex

Page 124

that not more than one-half of the Egyptian priesthood understood them all.

Hermes Trismegistrus (1) in his writings said: "Oh, Egypt! Egypt! of all thy religion, fables only will remain, which thy disciples will understand as little as they do thy religion. Words cut into stone alone will remain telling of thy pious deeds. The Sythians, or the dwellers by the Indus, or some other barbarians will inhabit thy fair land."

Moses (2) fathered the doctrine of monotheism, as an outgrowth of the Osirian religion, yet he continued the use of many of the original symbols in his teachings. In fact, some of these symbols are to be seen today in Jewish synagogues.

Christ's (3) teachings were always in parables. He distinctly stated that he preached in parables because it was the only way the people could be brought to understand. Parables are phraseological symbols.

Max Muller (4) writes: "As soon as we know aught of the thoughts and feelings of primitive man, we find him in possession of a religion. A religion of faith or worship, of morality or ecstatic vision; a religion of fear and hope, or of surmise, or reverence of the Great God through *various symbols*."

When primitive man used a symbol it did not mean the object in sight, *but what it represented in his mind*.

This primitive and ancient custom remains very dear to us: we still use symbols, as, for instance, the cross symbolizing Christ.

The symbols on the walls of the Temple of Sacred Mysteries at Uxmal, Yucatan, are most valuable as applying

Page 125

to this work, as an inscription on the temple walls tells us that they came from the fountain-head - the Lands of the West, the Motherland of Man. Therefore we may safely say that these symbols are exact duplicates of the symbols first used in the religious teachings of man, a statement that is further confirmed by the fact that many of them are to be found carved on the stones of the South

Sea Island ruins. These symbols connect mankind throughout the world with the Motherland of Man—"That Land of Kui" (5) - Mu.

As before stated, among the fallen ruins on some of the South Sea Islands will be found many of these symbols. I have no doubt that if the walls were still standing intact all would be found on them, as these temples and ruins were on the land of man's first earthly domain.

It must be fully appreciated by the reader that the complex cosmogonic figures could only have come into existence after man's mind had been sufficiently educated to understand them. Probably thousands upon thousands of years elapsed between the time when primitive man was first taught that the circle represented infinity, and the time when the intricate and complex cosmogonic diagrams were intelligible to his more enlightened mind. Thus we find, however, that tens of thousands of years ago man was so advanced intellectually that he could master these intricate symbolic problems.

These sacred symbols have been found among all peoples throughout the world. By this I do not mean to imply all have been found among savage as well as civilized human beings, but I do mean that *some* of them are found everywhere, even among savages and semi-savages.

Page 126

The wide scope of these symbols and their common meanings prove them to have been of common origin. Records in Yucatan show that they came from the land of Mu. Egyptian records show that they originated in the Lands of the West, and Hindu records show that they came from the Motherland in the East.

Therefore I think that I have established clearly in the mind of the reader this one salient and dominant fact: The land of Mu, the Lands of the West, that land of Kui and the biblical Garden of Eden are one and the same.

I will now review a number of these ancient symbols, commencing with a group which were the first symbols used in man's religious teachings.

Fig. 1*a on Page* 127. *The Circle.*—The circle was one of the first three symbols used in man's religious teachings. It was looked upon as the most sacred of all symbols. It was a picture of the sun, called Ra, and the collective symbol of all the attributes of the Deity. Ra, the sun, was looked upon as the *symbol only* and not the Deity Himself. The Deity was worshipped and the symbol was merely used to represent him.

The Deity was treated with such reverence that His name was never spoken. The Hindus and the Mayas spoke of the Deity as The Nameless. The circle has no beginning nor has it an end. What more perfect symbol could have been devised or selected to teach an uncultured mind the meaning of infinity and the everlasting?

Evidently the reason for selecting the sun as the emblem of the Deity was because it was the most powerful object that came within the sight and reasoning power of primitive man. It well represents the All-Powerful.

Page 127

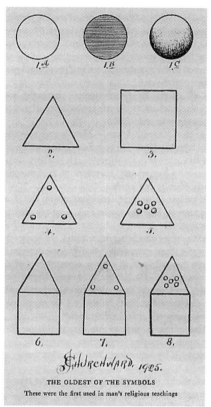

The Oldest of the Symbols
These were the first used in man's religious teachings.

Page 128

The circle is found on the stones of the Polynesian ruins and on the walls of the Temple of Sacred Mysteries.

Fig. 1c. Red Spheres. - The red spheres found on Easter Island statuary were representative of the sun and were used in ancient times as we us the cross today in connection with the dead.

In all of the Egyptian symbols connected with the Deity the heads of the figures are crowned with a red disc representing the sun. 1*b.*

Egyptian Papyrus Anana. (6)- Here is an interesting quotation from the Egyptian papyrus, Anana, which is dated 1320 B. C:

"Eternity has no end, therefore no beginning; consequently eternity is a *circle.*

"If we live on we must continue forever, and if we continue forever, like the circle and eternity, man had no beginning.

"Man comes into being many times, yet knows nothing of his past lives; except occasionally some day-dream or a thought carries him back to some circumstance of a previous incarnation. He cannot, however, determine in his mind when or where the circumstance occurred, only that it is something familiar. In the end, however, all of his various pasts will reveal themselves."

"The spirits or souls of one incarnation possibly may meet again in another incarnation, and may be drawn together as if by a magnet, but for what cause neither knows."

Christ said: "Except ye be born again ye cannot enter the kingdom of heaven."

Fig. 2. The Equilateral Triangle - The origin and

Page 129

meanings of the equilateral triangle are exremely interesting. The equilateral triangle is one of the first three symbols designed for the religious teaching of early man. It dates back more than 50,000 years. It was designed to symbolize both a Trinity and Heaven.

Its origin came out of the geographical makeup of the Motherland, which consisted of three separate areas of land, which were geographically called the Lands of the West. Apparently they were supposed to have been emerged at different times, one following the other. To explain this to the then undeveloped minds of the greater part of men, it was taught to him that three separate attributes of the Creator were instrumental in the emerging of the three lands, but only one Creator was involved.

The equilateral triangle was selected as a visible figure through which man could see and understand the conception of a *Triune God.* These three attributes formed the *first Trinity* and were the original conception of a *Trinity.* A conception which has come down to us through all these eons of time, it can never die, although from age to age its vestments have been changed, and it has been known under different names and guises among different peoples.

In connection with its symbolizing the Trinity it was used to symbolize Heaven. As the Triangle symbolized the Triune Godhead, and God's house was Heaven, it naturally followed that where God was, that was Heaven.

The conception of a Triune Godhead has come down to us from our forefathers of more than 50,000 years ago, and today, among many, it is held sacred.

Fig. 3. The Four-Sided Square. - The Four-Sided Square is the third of what are believed to be the three old-

Page 130

est symbols that were used in the teaching of religion to primitive man. It symbolized the earth. The four corners represented the four cardinal points—North, South, East and West. At each corner a keeper was assigned. This conception has also been brought down to us from early man, for are we not guilty of saying occasionally "the four corners of the earth"?

All of these sacred symbols are found carved on the stones of South Sea Island ruins; also on the walls of the Temple of Sacred Mysteries at Uxmal, Yucatan.

This completes the list of the simple sacred symbols. The others are compound symbols, with one or more of the foregoing three as the foundation. As we move down through time they become more complex and complicated, ending with the well-known Cosmogonic Diagrams, which symbolize the whole of the religious conceptions as they stood at the time.

Fig, 4. Triangle with Three Stars.—The equilateral triangle with three stars within the triangle symbolizes heaven with the Triune Godhead within.

Various peoples had various names for the Triune Godhead according to their language.

Fig. 5, Triangle with Five Stars.—The equilateral triangle with five stars within the triangle is simply an extension of the triangle with three stars. Five stars symbolize a full Godhead of five members. I have been able to find but one mention of the five names of the full Godhead, and the attributes they represented, and that was in the Egyptian. The symbol, however, is quite common among all ancient peoples, and in many instances its meaning is given without including the names.

Page 131

Fig. 6. Triangle Above the Square.—This is a compound symbol made up of Figs. 2 and 3 and symbolizes "Heaven above earth," a very old conception, but one that still remains with us. Above did not refer to altitude; it meant perfection. The perfection of Heaven was above that of the earth.

Fig. 7. The Triangle Above the Square with Three Stars.—This cut is a compound of Cuts 3 and 4. It is found at the end of the north room of the Temple of Sacred Mysteries. This was the room of initiation.

Fig. 8. The Triangle Above the Square with Five Stars. - This is a compound of Cuts 3 and 5. It is found on the end of the south room of the Temple of Sacred Mysteries. This was the room where the initiate was raised. From the room of raising, the initiate passed on to the central room, where he became a master or adept. In the north room he was initiated into the mysteries of the Triune Godhead and in the south room he was taught the mysteries of the full Godhead of Five.

THE TAU

(7)

The Tau.—The Tau is not only one of the most interesting, but one of the most ancient symbols. It is found in the earliest writings of the Motherland. It symbolizes

The Tau from a Maya Manuscript **(8)**

THE TAU FROM A MAYA MANUSCRIPT

RETURN OF THE RAINY SEASON, FROM THE TROANO MANUSCRIPT

Return of the rainy season, from the Troano Manuscript **(9)**

Page 133

resurrection, a springing into life, and in the ancient writings of Mu is used to symbolize the emersion of land.

The Tau is a picture of the constellation Southern Cross. The reason for its adoption as the symbol of resurrection was that when the Southern Cross appeared at a certain angle in the heavens over Mu, it brought the long looked-for rain. With the rain seeds in the ground sprang into life, drooping foliage revived and sent forth fresh shoots, upon which there were flowers and fruit; then it became a time of plenty and rejoicing in Mu—new life had been resurrected.

The Tau is very prominent in the old Maya writings and is generally depicted as a tree with two branches upon which there are flowers and fruit.

This Vignette (8) (Page 132) is from a Maya manuscript in the British Museum—No. 9,789—and represents the arrival of the rain in Yucatan. The two figures are allegorical, representing the divisions of Mayax. It is also a prominent symbol in the ancient writings of the Hindus, Chinese, Chaldeans, Incas, Quiches, Egyptians and other ancient peoples.

Tau is a word of the Motherland, meaning resurrection. It played an important part in ancient religions. Altars in temples, on which were made offerings of fruit and flowers, were shaped like the Tau, and, quite frequently the double triangle (Page 134) was associated with it, a double triangle being carved under each branch of the Tau. The double triangle is the symbol for an offering.

This symbol is one whose name has never been changed. It was Tau in the Motherland and it is Tau with us today.

Page 134

Ancient Sacred Symbols

Page 135

I now come to a series of symbols that followed those shown on Page 127. As will be seen, some did not originate in the Motherland, although the conceptions came from that source.

Figs. 9a, 9b, 9c and 10. The Eight Roads to Heaven. - It would appear that almost every ancient people had their own idea as to how the Eight Roads to Heaven should be symbolized. From the Hindu we learn that the eight roads were: Right belief, right speech, right living, right adoration of God, right thought, right action, right exertions and right meditations.

Fig. 9a comes from Central America; 9b, Egypt; 9c, is Oriental, and 10 is from the Pueblo Indians.

Fig. 11. The Ka. This symbol appears on a cornice above the lintel to the entrance of the Holy of Holies of the Temple of Sacred Mysteries at Uxmal. On this cornice it is many times repeated.

These emblems of mortality were used in the ancient religious ceremonies to impress upon the adept what will be his end and the end of us all, and to fix firmly in his mind the necessity of living a life that will bring no terrors when the soul releases itself from the mortal body to pass on into the world beyond.

The Egyptian was a reflex of the Maya, so that from Egypt we can get the original ceremonies. In the Temple of the Great Pyramid there was found a sarcophagus with the emblems of mortality arranged alongside it. The adept was placed in the sarcophagus to remind him of what he must eventually come to, and when he emerged from the sarcophagus he was reminded that after his soul left his mortal body, another life awaited him.

Page 136

Fig. 12. Double Triangles. - A pair of double triangles bound together at their bases was the ancient symbol for an offering.

Fig. 10. - This symbol, beyond showing eight roads to Heaven, is a cosmic diagram. The center is a square - the symbol for the earth. The extension of the sides of the square forms eight arms - the eight roads to Heaven. Towards the end of each pair of the arms are triangles - the symbol of Heaven.

Fig. 20.—This is a Pueblo Indian symbol and the only one I have ever found of this particular design. The outside triangle symbolizes heaven, the three small triangles at the base symbolize the Triune Godhead, and the diamond above, the full Godhead.

After deciphering it I asked the chief if I was right. He told me I was as far as I had gone, but that I had omitted something. The three inner triangles have three points which gives the Motherland's numeral, which indicates that the origin of this symbol and the people who use it was in Mu.

Fig. 21.—This is one of the most astounding symbols I have found among the North American Indians—two pairs of equilateral triangles interlaced, and placed one pair within the other. This is the central figure of the *Sri Santara* **(10)**—the cosmic diagram of the Hindus—and conveys identically the same meaning to the Pueblo Indian as it does to the Hindu.

Fig. 16.—Taking their learning and religious conceptions from the Uighurs, the Chinese have replaced the equilateral triangle with the figure Y. The Chinese at the time of Confucius **(11)** had "The Great Term," "The Great

Page 137

Unit," the great "Y." "The Y has neither body nor shape, all that has a body and shape was made by that which has no shape. The Great Term or The Great Unit comprehends Three: One is three and three are one."

Fig. 17. Two Triangles Interlaced Within a Circle. - This is one of the most ancient of compound symbols, originating at an early date in the Motherland. It is the most wonderful and far-reaching of all the sacred symbols and gives proof of the great and advanced civilization of man more than 50,000 years ago. This figure will be deciphered in the following chapter.

(12)

Page 138

HIERATIC LETTERS FROM VARIOUS ANCIENT ALPHABETS

Hieratic Letters from various ancient alphabets

A few simple symbols used in ancient writings

Page 139

Chapter 8: Simple Symbols Notes

(1) Hermes Trismegistrus (Greek for "Hermes the thrice-greatest") has been credited as the author of numerous texts. The quoted material is from the "Asclepian Dialogue", which some scholars believe to have been written by Apuleius (123-170 A.D.) Other scholars insist that the Corpus Hermes Trismegistrus plays a large role in Hermetic teachings.

(2) Moses is discussed in the Persons of Interest Appendix beginning on page A1—28.

(3) Jesus Christ is discussed in the Persons of Interest Appendix beginning on page A1—5.

(4) Muller, Frederick Max is discussed in the Persons of Interest Appendix beginning on page A1—31.

(5) Khui-Land is mentioned on page 241 in "*The Origin and Evolution of the Human Race*"; Albert Churchward; 1921; Also, 'Kui' is mentioned on page 34 of "*Sacred Mysteries Among the Mayas and the Quiches*"; Le Plongeon, Augustus; 1886.

(6) *Egyptian Papyrus Anana* is discussed in the Written Works Appendix beginning on page A2—27. Anana (Anani) is discussed in the Persons of Interest Appendix beginning on page A1—3.

(7) The Tau symbol is discussed on pages 130-132 of "*Sacred Mysteries Among the Mayas and the Quiches*"; Le Plongeon, Augustus; 1886.

(8) Similar to drawing on page 134 of "*Sacred Mysteries Among the Mayas and the Quiches*"; Le Plongeon, Augustus; 1886. Caption reads "From a Mexican M.S, in British Museum (add. M.S. b.m. 9789)." *The Maya Manuscript # 9789* is discussed in the Written Works Appendix beginning on page A2—6.

(9) Similar to drawing on page 116 of "*Sacred Mysteries Among the Mayas and the Quiches*"; Le Plongeon, Augustus; 1886. Adjoining footnote translates the picture as follows: "The Master of the basin of water turns it: abundant fluid submerges the land." A similar picture is also contained in figure 11 on page 106 of "*Origin and Evolution of Religion*", Albert Churchward, 1924. The picture is captioned, "The Maya God Chaic, Horus of Egypt, and Tlaloc of the Mexicans. Samin (Asima as the Samaritans called him) is the Phoenician name of Horus as "the pourer down of rain."

(10) The *Sri Santara* is discussed in the Written Works Appendix beginning on page A2—31.

(11) Confucius is discussed in the Persons of Interest Appendix beginning on page A1—7.

(12) Similar to Plate V page LX of "*Queen Moo & The Egyptian Sphinx*"; Le Plongeon, Augustus; 1896

9
Symbols

Page 140

VIGNETTES, TABLEAUX AND DIAGRAMS

THE Cosmic Diagram of the land of Mu was the first book ever written by man. I have traced this diagram back to more than 35,000 years ago. Just how long it had been in use before that, no one can say or even estimate.

All of the ancient nations copied the Motherland's diagram-the Mayas of Yucatan, the Naga-Mayas of India, the Babylonians, the Assyrians, the Egyptians and the Pueblo Indians of southwestern North America.

Only one retained its simple character with its original meanings: the Yucatan Mayas. The rest, except the Pueblos, added figures and introduced dogmas. They gave some of the original figures different meanings, so that the simple and beautiful symbol of the Motherland became sadly distorted. This was brought about by the unscrupulous Egyptian priesthood. They first invented the devil, then they had to find an abode for him, so they invented hell. Five thousand years ago the devil and hell were unknown. The priesthood of India, seeing the effects on the people of these inventions, were quick to follow Set with Siva.

The First Book Ever Written
The cosmic diagram of the Land of Mu. Over 35,000 years old.
(1)

Page 141

Page 142

In Mu the novice was taught to learn this book thoroughly and to repeat it as his belief in God and the hereafter. Just as children are taught their Bibles today, so was the child of this lost continent instructed in this book in ancient times.

In deciphering this cosmic diagram it will be seen that there is a central circle enclosed within two interlaced equilateral triangles. They form one single figure, having but one meaning. These two triangles are enclosed within an outer circle, which leaves twelve divisions between the two circles. Again, this outer circle is enclosed within twelve scallops. Falling from the main figure and downward is a ribbon that has eight divisions.

The central circle is a picture of the sun, Ra, who is the collective symbol of the Deity, and as the Deity is in Heaven, the Deity and Heaven are symbolized by this circle.

The twelve divisions formed by the two interlaced triangles, between the two circles, symbolize the twelve gates to Heaven. Each gate symbolizes a virtue, so that the soul must possess the twelve virtues in order to enter the gates of Heaven.

The outer circle symbolizes the intermediate world, the world beyond, the Amenti of the Egyptians. The twelve scallops surrounding the intermediate world symbolize twelve temptations. The soul must prove that it has overcome the twelve earthly temptations before it can enter the twelve gates of the world beyond.

The ribbon falling downward symbolizes that the soul must ascend in order to reach Heaven. The ancient meaning of the word "ascend" as used here did not signify

Page 143

rising to an altitude. It meant to rise to a higher level towards perfection. The ribbon has eight divisions. These signify the eight roads that man must traverse before his soul may enter the world beyond.

I have given a description of what the eight roads to Heaven are in the previous chapter.

What the twelve temptations and the twelve virtues were I was never able to discover collectively. This ancient religious belief of the people of Mu, freely given in modern language, would read:

"I believe there are eight roads which I must travel in order to reach Heaven. After having traveled the eight roads (mentioning them), I arrive at the twelve gates leading to the world beyond. Here I must prove that I have overcome the twelve earthly temptations (mentioning them). I shall then pass through into the world beyond and reach the gates of Heaven. There I must show that I learned and practised the twelve virtues on earth (mentioning them). Then I am taken through the gates of Heaven to the throne of glory, where sits the Heavenly King."

Have we today among all our sects and religions any that is purer and more simple than this of the lost people of the Motherland of Man?

FIGURES WITH MANY ARMS.-During the years that followed the translation of the tablets, we found the solution of many characters which we could not read in the tablets themselves. When deciphering old symbolical figures, which writers and archaeologists call "grotesque gods" and "grotesque goddesses," also bas-reliefs, we found the undeciphered symbols mixed in such a way in

Page 144

these carvings that their meanings became perfectly apparent. Chandler (2) and others have written: "Some grotesque Hindu goddess." The following is a specimen of these "grotesque gods" with the decipherings and translations of it, by which it will be seen that the figure is a tableau, *depicting the advent of man in the land of Mu.*

In India, especially, one is constantly finding carvings and paintings of the figure of a man having more than one pair of arms. These figures are found on temple walls, in illustrations in old Hindu manuscripts, and are extensively used at the present time in Hindu native jewelry.

All sorts of names are applied by writers to these figures. On one occasion I came across the following description: "These figures are grotesque idols and are worshipped by the poor, wretched, uneducated, unenlightened Hindu idolators." Fanatics who write that sort of stuff would without compunction, destroy these precious, I might say sacred, relics *of the earth's first civilization.*

These figures are not idols. They are sacred symbols of the Great Creator and Creation. They are of a very intricate design and character, the sort that one meets with occasionally when studying the first writings of man. They symbolize the Infinite, the Creator as having seven great or principal forces, attributes, powers, desires, commands or intellects. I have found each of these words used in various ancient writings, such as: "The Serpent with seven heads, which are intellects or powers." "The Serpent covered with feathers, whose seven commands brought the world into existence and created man to govern it."

The many-armed figures to which I refer undoubtedly

Page 145

originated in the Motherland, although I first found them among the ancient Brahmins. It is a well-known fact in India that the Brahmins obtained their cosmogony, science and arts of civilization from the Nagas. The Mayas in India, first called Nagas and afterwards Danavas, came to India from the Motherland many thousands of years before the Aryans became known in India. The Brahmins and the Nagas also used the Seven-Headed Serpent to symbolize the Creator. The figure of a man instead of the figure of the serpent appears to have been used, especially for depicting special creations.

I have selected a carving of one of these figures which appears in the Temple caves of Ajanta near Bombay, to decipher and translate. It is especially interesting from the fact that it symbolizes the raising of the Motherland above the waters, making it fruitful and productive, with man about to appear upon it. The central figure is in the form of a man, having seven points, the numeral of creation. In this instance a higher type of symbol is used-man, instead of the serpent. It was repeatedly said that man was a special creation and endowed with powers to govern the earth. This tallies in many respects with the tableau I am about to decipher.

The central figure wears the ancient sacred crown, a crown of pearls, which was assigned to the Deity, showing him to be a king. He is placed in the midst of creation, therefore he is the king of creation. In the upper left hand he carries a fruit and in the right hand the royal lotus, the symbolic flower of the Motherland, thus denoting that the Motherland is habitable.

The figure is shown standing in water. Two distinct

Symbolic Carving

Page 146

Page 147

symbols tell us this. First, the horizontal, irregular lines across his legs and the lower part of his body. Second, the single-headed serpent held in the lower right hand. Below the hand holding the serpent's head the body of the serpent becomes a pod from which seeds are seen rolling down. These symbolize nature's germs or the cosmic eggs of the ancients. These seeds or eggs have yet to break forth into life. Life still lies dormant in them. In time the Vital Force brings these seeds into life. The first of nature's life is thus depicted as coming forth in the waters. That is why the ancients called the sea "the Mother of Life," and this ancient conception has been proved to be correct by the tales of the early Paleozoic rocks.

Thus far it has been shown how nature's life appears and is created; it also shows that a habitable land exists above the waters. What is this land? At the lower left-hand corner is seen a deer in the act of leaping to the land. The deer, as we have shown, was the ancient symbol for first man. Therefore, this tableau is describing the Motherland, with man *about* to appear upon it.

The tableau is careful in differentiating between nature's creations and the special creation of man, for nature's creations are shown as seeds to be developed and brought into life, while man is shown as appearing fully developed without having to go through any evolutionary changes. It shows that man was not considered to be of nature's making.

This beautiful symbol does not look much like an idol when one understands it. It is a symbol confirming our biblical teachings, only this symbol originated tens of thousands of years before Egypt was peopled. It is not

Page 148

only wrong but wicked for religious fanatics to express opinions on subjects about which they know nothing.

This deciphering, by the way, is not complete, on account of the mutilated condition of the lower left hand. This mutilation makes it impossible to tell what it was supposed to depict.

THE SEVEN-HEADED SERPENT,-This is one of the most interesting of all the ancient symbols. Its origin was in the Motherland and it symbolizes the Creator and Creation and is very far-reaching in its esoteric meanings. In various writings it will be found under different names, but in each instance the seven heads are referred to. I have been unable to discover its original name in the Motherland, but in Hindu works I find it called both Caisha and Narayana. (3) In the Yucatan Maya it is called Ah-ac-chapat, (4) and today in Cambodia the name for it is Naga. This last appellation, however, is a modern christening, for it gives to the serpent the name of the people.

The Seven-headed Serpent permeates all ancient writings because it symbolizes the Creator and Creation. Whenever and wherever we see it, we know it says: "I am the symbol of the Deity, the Creator. Looking at me compels you to think of Him. I am the vehicle which carries your thoughts to God."

At Angkor Thom in Cambodia, which is a part of ancient Burma, there are the remains of a magnificent temple that may be classed among the architectural wonders of the world. The Seven-headed Serpent appears in many places among these ruins, but the principal one is the approach to the temple. On either side of this approach are carved Seven-headed Serpents, their heads upraised

Loaned from the Collection of the New York American, Weekly Section

THE GREAT SEVEN-HEADED SERPENT OF ANGKOR, CAMBODIA

Loaned from the Collection of the New York American
The Great Seven-Headed Serpent of Angkor, Cambodia

Page 149

Page 150

from eight to ten feet. Their tails end at the temple walls.

These two Seven-headed Serpents have been an enigma to the many archaeologists who have examined them, and all have placed themselves on record in saying that the builders of this temple were serpent-worshippers-all except one. A lady who does not claim to be an archaeologist, Helen Churchill Candee, (5) in her fascinating book of travel, "Angkor the Magnificent," (6) felt the heart-beat of truth about these magnificent conceptions. She writes: "It is Naga. It is like nothing else. The form is the result of centuries of legend and belief, the tangible evidence of past religion and story. It is not the fantastic creation of artist or architect, but the symbol of a demigod. His attributes, his history, are matters to dig out of inscriptions."

Madam Candee is absolutely right and all the others are wrong. These serpents are symbols, but she did not

CARVINGS ON THE GREAT SEVEN-HEADED SERPENT

CARVINGS ON THE GREAT SEVEN-HEADED SERPENT

AT ANGKOR THOM

Central Figure—Lotus flower.
First Circle—Picture of Sun surrounded by rays.
Rays divided into three sections. Symbolical numeral of the Land of Mu.

AT ANGKOR VAT

Outer Circle—The Sun.
3 Inner Circles—Mu's numeral; also colonies and colonial empires.
Central Figure—The Royal Lotus, the symbolical flower of the Land of Mu, the Motherland.

Page 151

carry her symbol high enough. Instead of symbolizing a demigod, they are symbols of the Great Creator of all worlds.

In front of their necks, and also at the back, are delicately carved symbols of the Motherland, which are indistinctly shown in the beautiful picture kindly supplied to me by the *American Weekly*. I have, however, separate sketches of these symbols which I made many years ago before the French got possession of Angkor. Then it was a hard, dangerous journey to get to Angkor from the coast, and I had some quite thrilling experiences; but that is the usual thing with all explorers-it is what is bound to happen.

With the *Sunday American's* picture I am giving cuts of two of these carvings, with the deciphering and translations.

How did the Seven-headed Serpent get the name of Naga in Cambodia? I can see only one possible way-the design came to Burma from the Motherland tens of thousands of years ago, brought there by the Nagas. The Nagas were wiped out by a cataclysm, a new people occupied their land when it became habitable again. They gave the name to the serpent, calling it after the people who first brought it.

And while we are at Angkor, let us consider another carving. There are conventional beasts there called by archaeologists "lions." That they are conventional and symbolical is shown by the shape of their mouths, an elongated square - one of the symbols given to Mu. These beasts are carved in a rising position, with their faces looking towards the east, the direction of the burial ground of

Page 152

Mu. From end to end in Angkor one meets the constant cry from the stones, "Mu, Mu the Motherland!"

The illustration shows Ganesha. He has been called a lot of bad names by those who did not know who he was. The Hindus, however, knew who this god was and adorned his likeness with flowers, for Ganesha was the symbol of the god who cared for the fields and crops and whose ancient name was "Lord of the Lands and Crops."

This symbol came from the land of Mu. I do not know what his name was in the Motherland, but should judge it was either Ra-Ma (God of the Lands) or Ra-Mana (Lord of the Field and Crops). The Yucatan PPeu dynasty of kings adopted him as their symbol, claiming they were the lords and owners of the land.

GANESHA, THE LORD OF THE FIELDS AND CROPS
Ganesha the elephant. The symbol of that attribute of the Deity which cares for the fields, gardens and crops

In Yucatan, on the buildings erected during the PPeu dynasty, elephants' heads are found carved in prominent parts of the structures. (7) In ancient times it was always usual to carve the symbol of the reigning kings on all palaces and governmental buildings.

Page 153

A NAGA-HINDU KNIFE.- I have in my possession an extremely ancient knife, which I believe to be the oldest knife in the world and is said to have been worn at one time by an ancient Naga king. As I have stated elsewhere, the Nagas were Mayas, who came to India from the Motherland by way of Burma. They settled in the Deccan and eventually turned this settlement into a colonial empire known as the Naga Empire. Their capital city was on the spot where the city of Nagpur now stands.

It is not known when the Naga Empire ended. Legends point to about 5,000 years ago. There are innumerable Hindu records, legends and traditions. Valmiki (8) does say, however, that it was the *First Hindu Colonial Empire* of the Motherland.

A careful examination shows that the present blade of this knife is not the blade originally fitted to the handle. The blade now attached is not of steel at all, but of hard iron. It is riveted to the handle by a hardened copper rivet. To make the blade fit the sheath, an overlaying ring is put on the blade, close to the handle. Everything points to the probability that the original blade was of either bronze or tempered copper and that it was thick enough at the handle to fit the sheath without the ring. The handle of the knife and the scabbard are of silver, richly carved with symbols, hieroglyphics and Maya tracings.

Apart from the interest that may be taken in the age of the knife, there remains a greater interest in the hieroglyphics and symbols which are carved upon the handle and scabbard. One symbol opens up an immense field for research work.

The symbols which appear on the handle of the blade,

A Hindu Naga Knife

Page 154

SYMBOLS ON THE HANDLE AND SHEATH OF THE KNIFE

front and back, are conventional tableaux, telling us who the people were that wore this knife and whence they came.

Fig. 1 - I will first take the symbol on the front of the handle. This is a tableau both symbolical and conventional. That it refers to the Motherland is plainly told by the many times that the number *three* is repeated- three being the symbolical number of the Motherland.

The face depicted is a conventional face, in which two elongated squares form the mouth and the nose. This symbol reads "Mu, the Motherland." I can prove this statement because it is substantiated in the tableau. First,

---

in the crown and plumes which adorn the head. The headdress is composed of three-three times repeated. Second, with an ancient water jar with a bud of the royal lotus on either side, thus denoting that the land stood in the midst of water and that it was the land of the royal lotus-Mu. On each side of this triple figure is a conventional plume which makes the main three. Each of these plumes is trifurcated so as to produce *three* points.

On each side of the conventional nose is the hieratic letter "k," which is used to denote the four cardinal points thus: North, South, East and West. These are conventional eyes looking east and west in the direction of the two main lines of colonization, as will be shown in the next tableau.

The cheeks are arched to symbolize the horizon. On both horizons are seen three suns appearing as semispheres without rays. The sun appearing on the horizon without rays symbolized a colony; with rays, a colonial empire.

The lower part of the figure is put there to balance the whole and give an artistic effect. At each side of this tableau is engraved a *fully open* royal lotus, thus emphasizing the fact that Mu-the Motherland-is indicated.

From the foregoing it seems evident that this knife was of the date of the Naga colonial days.

Fig. 2 - On the back of the handle is a tableau showing the Motherland standing in water, with two fish jumping along on top of the water, one traveling east, the other west. This symbol shows that India was separated from the Motherland by water and that the Nagas crossed the ocean to get to India. Their mode of travel is amusingly and very effectively told by the fish being out of water

Page 157

and neither flying nor swimming but hopping along the surface. Berosus, (9) the ancient Chaldean priest and historian, spoke of the Akkad-Mayas as being half fish and half man.

The rest of the handle is carved in artistic Maya patterns.

Fig. 3-The scabbard commences with five bands of very pronounced Maya traceries. Below these bands is a tableau, a compound hieroglyphic which no doubt will be astounding to all students of archaeology. It is most amazing to me to find it in India. The central figure in this tableau is a scarab rising through rays of glory. Beneath is the symbol of earth, or mother earth-the hieratic letter M-which is shown to be productive by the conventional leaves drooping from each end of the symbol. Beneath the surface of the earth are two young scarabs still unborn to light. On each side of the risen scarab is the symbol of first man, Keh, the deer, both in the act of adoration. This shows first man in adoration of the scarab beetle.

What does a scarab beetle symbolize ?

This is the first time I have come across the scarab in India, either in writings or carvings. The scarab has hitherto been looked upon as being a purely Egyptian symbol. It was selected by the Egyptians as the symbol of the Creator, who was called Kephera. On the headdress of Kephera, the scarab always surmounts it.

Anani, (10) the king's scribe and companion of Seti II, in one of his beautifully illustrated papyri, gives the following reason why the Egyptians selected the scarab to symbolize the Creative God:

"The scarab rolls up little balls of mud with its feet

Page 158

and in these balls deposits its eggs, there to hatch out. The Egyptians think this a perfect example of *the Creator rolling the world around and causing it to produce life.*"

This italicized sentence would be startling to the modern scientist if he understood anything about the origin and workings of The Forces, because here it is shown that the Egyptians, 3,000 or 3,500 years ago understood the origin and workings of the Great Forces, which I shall hereafter explain from the Hindu translations. Anani carries us back 3,500 years only, but the carvings on this knife's scabbard will carry us back to a time before the Egyptians came to Egypt.

The symbol on the front of the handle tells us that this handle and scabbard were made when the Nagas were only a colony in India.

Now I shall try to fix an approximate date of the Naga colony in India before it became a colonial empire.

One very prominent figure in the Naga or Maya Empire in India was Prince Maya. (11) The time of Prince Maya is doubtful. Although I have come across many records about him, not a single one even estimates the date when he lived; but according to traditions, and these traditions are as plentiful as leaves on a tree, Prince Maya lived 15,000 to 20,000 years ago.

In Ramayana, (12) we find this reference to him: "In olden times there was a prince of the Nagas whose name was Maya."

Prince Maya was the author of the *Sourya Siddhanta,* (13) the most ancient treatise on astronomy in India. Its age has been variously estimated at from 10,000 to 22,000 years.

Page 159

At the time of Prince Maya, the Nagas were an empire. When the handle and sheath of this knife were made, the Nagas were a colony antedating the Empire. That they were only a colony is clearly shown by the suns without rays on the horizon. This proves the extreme antiquity of the handle and sheath.

PILLARS

Pillars as sacred emblems are, without doubt, of extremely ancient origin. It is my firm belief that they date back to the first temple that was erected for the worship of God.

TAT PILLAR
Papyrus Ani B.C. 1500. British Museum

Pillars in ancient times were placed in the porches or entrances to temples. The oldest record of their use as such comes from Niven's "Mexican Buried Cities." **(14)**

In Egyptian mythology, pillars were placed at the entrance to Amenti. Above on this page I give a cut taken

Page 160

from the Papyrus of Ani, showing one of the two pillars at the entrance to Amenti. The Egyptians called them Tat Pillars, but they are more commonly known throughout the world as Totem Pillars.

As the Egyptians got them from the Mayas, I will give the Egyptian conceptions concerning them.

One pillar is called Tat, which means "in strength." The other pillar is called Tattu, which means "to establish." When combined, these two words mean: "In strength this place is established forever." (15)

The Tat in Egyptian is considered a figure of stability. It also represents four corners and is equal to a square. Two Tats form the entrance to Tattu. Tattu is the gateway to the region where the mortal soul is blended with an immortal spirit and "established in the mysteries of Amenti forever."

In the porch, or entrance to King Solomon's Temple, two special pillars were erected (I Kings, Chapter 7, 21st and 22d verses): (16) "And he set up the pillars in the porch of the temple; and he set up the right pillar, and called the name thereof Jachin; and he set up the left pillar, and called the name thereof Boaz."

In Hebrew the word *jachin* means "to establish," and the word *boaz* means "in strength."

At the entrance of King Solomon's temple and also at the entrance of the Judgment Hall of Osiris, two pillars were erected, standing perpendicularly. In each case the two pillars have identically the same name, language considered, and with identically the same meaning. Also the ornamentations on the pillars, down to the lily work, were identically the same, showing that King Solomon made a

---

Page 161

complete copy of the pillars at the entrance to Amenti for his own temple in Jerusalem.

Pillars are erected by the Maoris of New Zealand at the entrances to their villages, and similar pillars are used by the Indians of the Northwest.

Plato (17) informs us, speaking of Atlantis: "There the people gathered every fifth year and sixth year alternately, and with sacrifices of bulls, swore to observe the sacred inscriptions carved on the pillars of the temple."

Java is one of the large islands of the Malay Archipelago, and in writing of it, Forbes (18) says:

"In Java is a tribe called the Karangs, supposed to be descendants of the aborigines of the island, whose old men and youths, four times a year, repair secretly in procession to a sacred grove in a dense forest, the old men to worship, the youths to see and learn the mysteries of their forefathers. In this grove are the ruins of terraces laid out in quadrilateral enclosures, the boundaries of which are marked by blocks of stone, or fixed in the ground. Here and there on the terraces are prominent monuments, *erect pillars*, and, especially noteworthy, a pillar *erect within a square*. Here these despised and secluded people follow the rites and customs that have been handed down to them through their forefathers from vastly remote ages (12,000 to 13,000 years), repeating with superstitious awe a litany which they do not understand or comprehend, This very litany is found in the Egyptian Book of the Dead."

I have emphasized a *pillar erect within a square* because that, too, is found in the Book of the Dead.

The Great Monolith at Tiahuanaco **(19)**

HEAD-DRESS OF AN INCA HIGH PRIEST, PERU

HEAD-DRESS OF AN INCA PRIEST, PERU

THE GREAT MONOLITH AT TIAHUANACO, PERU (20)

This immense stone has been one of the great wonders and enigmas to all archaeologists who have ever looked upon it or its picture. To the archaeologist it is one of the wonders of the world. Perched up on the shores of Lake Titicaca, 13,500 feet above the level of the Pacific Ocean, it rests as a part of a ruin of a temple.

Much has been written about this stone, and the concensus of opinion among the various writers is: "If it could only be deciphered and read, what a wonderful tale it might possibly tell about the ancient past!" This stone does tell a wonderful tale, for it takes its readers back 16,000 years, when Mu, the Motherland, still held her proud sway throughout the earth, before she sank into that fiery abyss to be mourned by mankind for many thousands of years. It tells about the times when the first settlements were being made in Egypt on the Nile Delta under Thoth - the dawn of Egyptian history.

At the time the temple was built with its magnificently carved stones, the Andes Mountains did not exist; they had not yet been thrown up through the plains of western South America. It was the raising of these mountains that destroyed the country, most of the people and this temple, in doing which this great monolith was fractured into two pieces.

Many writers, I find, assign this stone to the work of the Incas. The Incas did not come to Peru for about 15,000 years after this temple was built. When the Incas (Quiches) arrived in Peru, the Andes Mountains had been in existence many thousands of years.

It is a wonderful old stone, for although a hieratic alphabet had been used for a long time, not a letter appears on it. This carving follows along the lines of the first forms of writings ever used-a combination of symbols forming a picture, the picture forming a writing. It is most unusual to find a carving of this date without hieratic writings forming a part of it; yet, without these writings the picture is as easy to read as a present-day printed book. All that is needed is a knowledge of the meaning of symbols.

The excellence of this stone shows great mechanical skill and artistry.

Now, with the aid of the symbols of the Motherland and those specially used in her colonial empires I will decipher it and read it to you.

On looking at the picture of the carving the most prominent object which strikes the eye is a conventional head of a human being; and the most striking point of this head is the number of times the numeral *three* is woven into it. Three, as previously stated, was the numeral assigned to Mu. I will now dissect the head.

It consists of *three* superimposed layers forming an escutcheon, the uppermost of which is sculptured so as to represent the human face. Above are *three* feathers forming a plume, and beneath a *triple* throne, which the figure surmounts. On each cheek there are *three* dots. The breast plate, if it can be so called, contains *three* oblong squares ⬜ which is one of the symbols for Mu (the geometrical and alphabetical symbol).

The scepter at its end is adorned with *three* macaws' heads. The shape of the mouth is also conventional, an

Page 166

oblong square [⬚]. Here nine times it says Mu. The head is surrounded by rays divided into groups of four. This makes a complete circle of rays, and is a part of the symbol reading, "Mu, the Empire of the Sun." The termination of each ray is ⊙. Ahau-King of Kings; thus saying: "The Emperor of the Empire of the Sun was the king over all of the earthly kings."

The macaws' heads at the end of the scepter are a colonial symbol, the totem of Queen Moo of Mayax, and, being attached to the scepter, designate that Mayax was a vassal state or colonial empire. On the rays of the upper angles are leopards' heads, also appearing on each side of the escutcheon. The leopard was the totem of Prince Coh, the brother husband of Queen Moo. At the lower angles are serpents' heads, the symbol of the Can dynasty. Thus the central figure tells us that Queen Moo with her husband Coh of the Can family are reigning in Mayax, and that Mayax was one of Mu's colonial empires.

On the lower band are sculptured seventeen small heads over each head and on either side are the symbols for land. The definite meaning of this I cannot state. It may mean that Mu has seventeen colonies; again this may not be the actual meaning.

Above this band are three bands of winged figures. Those in the middle row have macaw heads, indicating their allegiance to Queen Moo. The figures in the other two rows have human heads, but wear on their crowns Queen Moo's totem, showing that they recognize her as their sovereign.

All these figures are ornamented with twelve serpents,

Page 167

symbolizing the twelve Maya dynasties who ruled over Mayax.

The whole picture combined shows that the inhabitants of this land, where this temple was built, were vassals to or a sub-colony of Mayax at the time Queen Moo and her husband Coh were reigning in Mayax.

Queen Moo visited the Maya colony at Sais on the Nile Delta during the first century of its existence and there met Thoth, **(21)** its founder, according to the Troano Manuscript. **(22)** The Nile colony was started 16,000 years ago;

ONE OF THE SYMBOLIC STONES, ANARAJAPOORA, CEYLON, CALLED BY ARCHAEOLOGISTS "MOON STONES"

therefore this great monolith of Tiahuanaco was carved just 16,000 years ago.

CARVED STONE AT ANARAJAPOORA, CEYLON

On account of the shape of this stone, which is a half sphere, it has been called by archaeologists who have visited Anarajapoora, "the Anarajapoora Moon Stone." There are several of them and they are placed at the foot of the steps leading into the temple.

That this is a symbolical stone, telling who the Cinga-

Page 168

lese were and whence and how they came to Ceylon, has been overlooked by all the archaeologists, yet the writings are quite plain and distinct.

The center of the stone is carved as a conventional but elaborate lotus in full bloom. This, of course, is the symbol of the Motherland, the land of Mu. It was adopted as such, so Oriental traditions say, because it was the first flower to adorn the earth's surface. There is every reason for believing that these traditions told the truth and that the lotus was the first flower to appear on earth.

Carved on the stone is a series of half-circles, one of the symbols of a colony of the Motherland. On account of the bad condition of the outside band beyond the animals, I am unable to say whether it was an ordinary colony or a colonial empire.

Beyond the lotus is an ornamental band. This has no symbolical significance, unless it symbolizes water. It is also too indistinct to warrant any definite conclusions.

The next band consists of a procession of ducks, indicating the manner in which the colonists came to Ceylon. Like ducks they came on the surface of the water; that is, they came in their boats.

Outside of the procession of ducks is a band which, without doubt, is ornamental only, carved there as an artistic dividing line between the procession of ducks and a procession of animals. This procession of animals is divided into sets of three, the symbolic numeral of the Motherland.

Freely read, the symbols on this stone say:

"These people who came to Ceylon came there from a colony of Mu, in their boats, the road being across the

---

Page 169

ocean; and their forefathers came to that colony from the Motherland."

Anarajapoora was not an old city, about 2,200 years only, but before it was built, Ceylon had been occupied by a warlike race for at least 10,000 years, as recorded by Valmiki, the Hindu sage and historian.

(23)

Chapter 9: Symbols Notes

(1) Same as Plate XVII on page 17 of "*Queen Moo & The Egyptian Sphinx*"; Le Plongeon, Augustus; 1896; Same as drawing on page 25 of "*The Signs and Symbols of Primordial Man, being an explanation of the Evolution of Religious Doctrines from the Eschatology of the Ancient Egyptians*", Albert Churchward, 1910. Captioned: "from Mexico".

(2) Information concerning this Chandler has yet to have been discovered.

(3) "Narayana" is mentioned in Le Plongeon's book: *Sacred Mysteries of the Mayas and Quiches*; (1886), page 109-110:
"We read in the *Manava-dharma-sastra* that the visible universe in the beginning was nothing but darkness. Then the great, self-existing Power dispelled that darkness, and appeared in all His splendor. He first produced the waters; and on them moved Narayana the divine spirit."; The same passage is also contained on page 256 of "*Queen Moo & The Egyptian Sphinx*"; Le Plongeon, Augustus; 1896.

(4) Ah-ac-chapat is discussed on page 66 of "*Sacred Mysteries Among the Mayas and the Quiches*"; Le Plongeon, Augustus; 1886.

(5) Candee, Helen Churchill (1858-1949) was an American author and socialite. In addition to writing about interior decorating (and being established as one of the first professional decorators in Washington D.C.), she is also known for her writings about her travels in Asia. She is also known as a survivor of the sinking of the RMS Titanic in 1912.

(6) *Angkor the Magnificent* was written in 1924 and the author, Helen C. Candee was honored by the French government and the King of Cambodia.

(7) Representations of Mastadons are mentioned on page 93 of "*Sacred Mysteries Among the Mayas and the Quiches*"; Le Plongeon, Augustus; 1886. Also, James wrote an article entitled "Synopsis of the Earliest History of Central America and Yucatan" contained in his scrapbooks, but undated and not sourced. In the article he discusses the PPeu dynasty. The entire text is contained in footnote 4 of Chapter 11.

(8) Valmiki is discussed in the Persons of Interest Appendix beginning on page A1—52.

(9) Berosus is discussed in the Persons of Interest Appendix beginning on page A1—4.

(10) Anani is discussed in the Persons of Interest Appendix beginning on page A1—3.

(11) Prince Maya is discussed in the Persons of Interest Appendix beginning on page A1—43.

(12) *Ramayana* is discussed in the Written Works Appendix beginning on page A2—29.

(13) *Sourya Siddhanta* is discussed in the Written Works Appendix beginning on page A2—30.

(14) *Mexican Buried Cities* is discussed in Chapter 11. William Niven is discussed in the Persons of Interest Appendix beginning on page A1—33.

(15) See page 121 in "*Arcana of Freemasonry*"; Albert Churchward; 1915

(16) This Biblical quotation (1Kings Chap 7) is discussed in the Written Works Appendix beginning on page A2—4.

(17) Plato is discussed in the Persons of Interest Appendix beginning on page A1—41.

(18) Forbes is discussed in the Persons of Interest Appendix beginning on page A1—12.

(19) A similar image on the last page of "*Sacred Mysteries Among the Mayas and the Quiches*"; Le Plongeon, Augustus; 1886. Captioned as "GATE AT TIHIHANACO"

(20) Much of this discussion is the same as pages 102-107 "*Sacred Mysteries Among the Mayas and the Quiches*"; Le Plongeon, Augustus; 1886.

(21) Thoth is discussed in the Persons of Interest Appendix beginning on page A1—51.

(22) The *Troano Manuscript* is discussed in the Written Works Appendix beginning on page A2—34.

(23) Similar drawing as figure B on page 115 "*Sacred Mysteries Among the Mayas and the Quiches*"; Le Plongeon, Augustus; 1886. Similar drawing as on page 47 of "*Queen Moo & The Egyptian Sphinx*"; Le Plongeon, Augustus; 1896

10
North America's Place Among the Ancient Civilizations

TWO of the most interesting questions of the day, both to scientist and layman, are these: Where did man first appear upon the earth? At what date did he appear - how far back?

The first of these questions I can answer and give all reasonable proofs, which consist of written documents, inscriptions on historic ruins, traditions, and geological phenomena.

The second question cannot now be answered, and probably never will be, because the records and proofs which were once written now lie in the bed of one of our deepest oceans. There is a possibility, however, that in unearthing the ruins of ancient Hindu Rishi city temples, there may be found complete copies of "The Seven Sacred Inspired Writings of Mu." The seventh writing, or chapter, tells the tale and gives the history of man from his advent upon earth.

We have a biblical statement that says man first appeared on earth in the Garden of Eden, but where the Garden of Eden was, no two authorities agree. I main-

Page 171

tain that the biblical Garden of Eden was the Egyptian Lands of the West, the Maya's Land of Kui, **(1)** and the Hindu's Motherland. The hieratical name for all of these was the Land of Mu.

Now I shall follow ancient man around the world and, by the *written records* which he has left behind in *every country*, show beyond controversy the geographical position of Mu. I shall make the start from the United States of North America, because North America and eastern Asia were the two countries where man made his first settlements away from the Motherland.

In their excitement over the discovery of a few old human bones, such as the Neanderthal, Piltdown, and Heidelberg man, scientists, in both Europe and America, have completely ignored and cast aside the remains of ancient man in North America. That the European remains were those of idiots and degenerates is obvious from the abnormal shapes of their skulls. Doubtless they were outcasts from civilized communities. From Valmiki, **(2)** Druidical works, **(3)** the Popol Vuh **(4)** and other ancient writings we learn that such characters were driven into the forests, there to live and die like the beasts. It would appear from many ancient writings that the usual method of disposing of bodies was by cremation, consequently there remained no trace of those whose bones had been consumed by fire.

The mere bones of man do not show the degree of civilization which he has attained, or the manner in which he lived-*but his works do.*

The remains of ancient man's bones found in North America are few, but his works are many.

All of the scientists who became excited over the dis-

Page 172

covery of ancient bones in Europe agree that they are of the Pleistocene Time, or subsequent to the geological Glacial Period.

North Americans were highly civilized and were experts in the arts and sciences tens of thousands of years before these idiots and degenerates of Europe existed.

A scientific boom was given to Egypt, by way of change, by the assertion that Egypt was the mother of civilization, whereas there are numerous ancient documents telling us that the soil of Egypt was first trod by colonists from America and India, and that these colonists "brought the learning and civilization of the Motherland with them." Many of these documents were written by the ancient Egyptians themselves. As Schliemann has shown, the great civilization of Egypt declined with the loss of the support furnished by the Motherland.

Now the evolution craze has a firm grip upon our scientists, a theory which is impossible and untenable in the face of "The Sacred and Inspired Writings of Mu," These writings tell us what life is, how it originated and the forces which govern it. Although written more than 50,000 years ago, these writings inform us as to the nature of the force which our scientists call the electron; its origin, how it works, what it does and its final disposition.

There are the remains of highly civilized men in North America which date far back into the Tertiary Era and antedate the geological Glacial Period tens of thousands of years.

The "Sacred Mysteries" of Egypt tell us what the so-called Glacial Period was, what caused it, and give a scientific description of everything concerning it.

Page 173

Many of the North American remains of man date back to a time before our great western mountain ranges raised their imposing heads above the level of the plains.

In our western states there are traceable *four* civilizations of human beings who occupied the land before the Cliff Dwellers and the present red Indians.

It is quite possible that the actual Cliff Dwellers and the red Indians may be races that have descended from remnants that were saved during the raising of the mountains. The four civilizations are shown by their different forms of writings and the remains of their houses. These writings are on boulders and cliffs and give to us an imperishable history of the race that inscribed them. True, it is a fragmentary history, but it is sufficient to tell us whence they came, how they came, and of their religion and accomplishments.

The keys by which these writings may be read come from the Motherland and they consist of a hieratic alphabet and a system of symbols or picture writing. The pictures form an alphabet of words instead of letters, and they are quite easy to read with the aid of the keys and a knowledge of the language in which they are written. Following are a few of the most prominent of the ancient civilizations in North America:

OREGON.-In Oregon, at a place called Fossil Lake, the remains of a very ancient civilization have been found. Fossil Lake is the dried-out bed of what was once an ancient sheet of water. From the remains of the prehistoric animals found there, it has been proved that this lake existed in the Mesozoic Age.

Fossil Lake stands in the midst of the great Oregon

Page 174

SYMBOLS FOUND AMONG THE CLIFF-DWELLERS' WRITINGS

Page 175

Desert, which was once a fertile plain, but was made waterless by the raising of the mountains, which diverted the surface water. Around the dried-up bed of the lake the fossils of ancient animals have been unearthed. In the lower strata the bones of dinosaurs and other Mesozoic animals have been found. In the upper strata the bones of mastodons and other mammal life of the Pleistocene Time have been found. Among the bones of the mastodons have been found arrow and spear heads made of volcanic glass.

NEVADA.- (5) Some of the most valuable data relative to ancient man in North America have been discovered through the work of archaeologists in this state.

Hundreds, yes thousands, of writings have been found on the rocks and cliffs of our western states, involving thousands of symbols, hieratic letters and vignettes. I have selected a few from Nevada, sufficient to fill a page, as much as I can give in this curtailed work.

Symbol

A. This is one of the symbols of Mu, The Empire of the Sun. A sun in mid-heaven surrounded with rays.

B. This is the symbol for the rising sun, and was so used by all ancient peoples.

C. This is the symbol of the sun at its meridian commonly used by all ancient peoples.

D. This is the sun shown as gone down beyond the horizon, set. Usually it is depicted as a plain circle without rays. In this case it is a black disc, which says it is referring to something that has forever, passed away from the sun's rays.

Page 176

E. This symbolizes Mu forever in darkness. Mu's name is given by her numeral, three, placed on the top of the black disc.

F. This is a vignette saying that Mu lies across the ocean in the direction of the setting sun.

The serpent is Can, symbolic of the ocean Canab, the great waters. The semi-circle above the serpent is a picture of the western horizon. Here again Mu's name is given by her symbolic numeral three. She is shown by three feathers on the horizon.

G[1]. This is a hieroglyphic reading, *U-lummil*, "The Empire of -." This is the central figure on the royal escutcheon of Mu.

II[1]. This is a bud of a lotus, the royal and sacred flower of the Motherland.

G[2]. A single-headed, unadorned serpent, the symbol of the waters among all ancient peoples.

H[2]. Another symbol used for water, in place of the serpent.

I. The ancients sometimes used a plain cross instead of the usual symbol, the four-sided square. Both show four cardinal points.

K. This is the first letter in the hieratic alphabet of the Motherland, pronounced *ah*. It is also the numeral one, pronounced *hun*. Its meaning was extended to cover King Ahau, the King of Kings.

L. This is the letter *n* in the hieratic alphabet.

M. This is the symbol for an abyss, a valley or hole.

N. This is the letter *x* in the hieratic alphabet.

O. This is the letter *u* in the hieratic alphabet, reversed.

P. Pages might be written about this symbol of the serpent and the tree. It came into existence, however, after the submersion of Mu.

Q. This symbol has both plain and esoteric meanings. It symbolizes creation, also the numeral nine.

R. This is an Uighur-Maya religious symbol.

S. This is the Uighur hieratic letter *h*.

T. Is this a feather or shrub? I don't know.

U. This is the ancient symbol for a hundred.

V. This is a symbol for mountains, not very old.

W. This is an interesting symbol, as it is a map of the western coast line of North, Central and South America.

X. This picture has no symbolical significance. Such hands are found painted on cave walls throughout the world.

Y. This cross reads and refers to the active and passive elements in nature. It also has an esoteric meaning.

Z. I doubt if this symbol means anything beyond artistic effect.

AA. This is the picture of a skin of an animal.

BB. Similar heads are found in Egypt and elsewhere. The horns are adorned, showing that the animal is intended for some function or ceremony. It is not a very ancient symbol.

CC. A three-pointed figure symbolizing multitudes. It is generally found with the points pointing downwards.

DD.A guide-post telling the traveler the direction and length of his journey.

These cliff writings prove that the writers came from the Motherland and that they were intimately connected with the Mayas of Mexico and Central America, as their language is a branch of the Maya.

GROUND PLAN OF A TEMPLE AT GRAPEVINE CANYON, NEVADA

ANOTHER WRITING IN GRAPEVINE CANYON, NEVADA

Page 179

PAINTING. GRAPEVINE CANYON, NEVADA

1. Is the ground plan of a temple.

2. Is the symbol for submersion. Having gone down with myriads of inhabitants.

3. Is the symbol for the sun having set forever on the land or lands submerged, and includes the sunset, the life cross and submersion.

The details in this ground plan (1) say: "This temple is erected to the memory of Mu, the Motherland of Man, which has been submerged with myriads of souls."

The central figure (4) represents a shrine or holy of holies. Within this shrine is *m* reversed-*m*, Mu, Motherland, showing to whom it is dedicated and that she is no more. She is dead.

On either side of the central figure are three taus- T - the symbol of resurrection. This is a common way of referring to the Motherland all over the world.

On the moon stones of Anarajapoora, Ceylon, the symbolical animals are in groups of three. On the great monolith of Tiahuanaco, Peru, the thrones are in groups of three. On the heads of the figures in Central America are three crowns-and so on, ad infinitum.

The three devisions about the shrine represent the three rooms, where the devotee receives his three degrees in religious knowledge. This is the usual construction of ancient temples. The three rooms are confirmed by the treble figure (5) at the entrance. This is the shape of the ends of all the rooms, representing heaven and earth. In the room itself the degree is shown by the number of stars within the triangle.

Page 180

At the right of this temple is the glyph (2). This is a compound symbol and reads "land or lands submerged." 2*a* is a symbol meaning multitudes. Thus the glyph shows multitudes of souls submerged.

At the left is another compound symbol-(3); *a* is the sun, *b* lands submerged. Translated, it reads, "the sun shines no more on these lands which are submerged." Therefore, the whole tableau says: "Mu, with myriads of souls, has been submerged. The sun shines no more upon her. She is in darkness. She is dead."

The second stone is adjacent to the previous one. It represents a sacrificial scene: 1. The animal on the altar. 2. The fires to consume it. 3. The symbol of submerged Mu.

I have included this drawing to corroborate the previous one and furnish additional proof that the temple was dedicated to Mu and that Mu had been submerged.

There were no burnt sacrifices previous to the destruction of the Motherland. Burnt sacrifices were introduced as a religious ceremony, to commemorate Mu and her people being consumed by fire as she sank into the fiery abyss.

GOLD GULCH, BEATTY, NEVADA

This rock is one of nature's freaks that was utilized by man many thousands of years ago as a guide to travelers, and a commemorative monument to Mu.

Roughly, the stone resembles the squat and bent figure of a man in a posture of grief and mourning. He is heavily cloaked in the ancient Manchu style, with arms folded across the knees. On the top is a weather-worn stone, which represents the head of the figure. In place of eyes are pecked and painted two symbols, both very pronounced

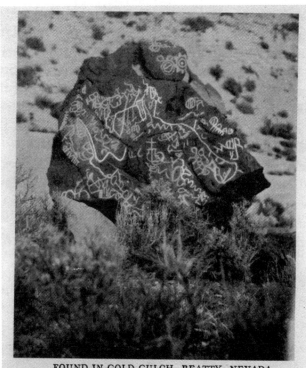

FOUND IN GOLD GULCH, BEATTY, NEVADA

FOUND IN GOLD GULCH, BEATTY, NEVADA

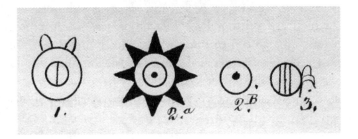

Page 181

Page 182

as to meaning: 1 reads, *chi-pe-zi*, which, translated, means "A mouth opened, fires came forth with vapors, the land gave way and went down."

2*a*. This is the escutcheon of the Empire of the Sun, the land of Mu. A sun with eight rays. Instead of the center being a symbol reading, "The Empire of-," this has in its place: 2*b*, "Ahau, the King, the Great King, the Great Ruler."

Freely read, the writings on this face say: "A mouth opened, volcanic fires and vapors came forth, the land gave way, and Mu, the Great Ruler, the Empire of the Sun, sank into that abyss of fire."

On the left arm of the figure, the first symbol is (3) *the-*

CLIFF DWELLERS' GUIDEPOST

the-ha, which, translated, reads: "Toward water, or in the direction of water."

From the main symbol are shown streams joining each other. The characters on this picture are all Uighur-Maya. These people may have been Mongols.

This is a guide-post, nothing more, telling the way to

Page 183

water. It is a crudely drawn ancient, conventional face looking in the direction of water. The first water to be found in this vicinity, by the way, is a spring, pond or lake, and farther on, a river. The ground is intersected with trails, and the figure shows which road to take to the pond or spring.

The first settlers in the United States made their settlements along the southwestern states. These settlements were wiped out by cataclysms at the same time that contemporary settlements in Mexico were also destroyed. These were of a very early date, probably during Pliocene times.

A second civilization, and probably a third, followed them. These were destroyed by cataclysms and by the raising of the great ranges of mountains. The raising of these mountains, by the way, made deserts of many fertile lands in Colorado, Arizona and Nevada. The Cliff Dwellers were the last colonizers to arrive from the land of Mu. When the first settlements were made in the southwestern states, it was *before* the mountains were raised. When the Cliff Dwellers entered America, the mountains probably *had been* raised, for we find their houses in the cliffs of the mountains.

The Cliff Dwellers spoke the Yucatan-Maya language, as is shown by their use of the Maya hieratic alphabet, which I have found in Nevada. One would judge, from the points where we find the remains of the Cliff Dwellers in Colorado, that the mouth of the Colorado River was their port of entry into America.

It is quite apparent that, after reaching their objective point from the Motherland, which was the mouth of the

Page 184

COLORADO RIVER AND TRIBUTARIES
The gateway of the Cliff Dwellers into the United States

Page 185

Colorado River, they proceeded to work up the river and inland. From remains of them found in various states, it is shown that they did not confine themselves to the main river, but worked out on all of its branches and smaller tributaries, some even going beyond the water route by trails on land, such as the old Zuñi trail. Generally, however, they seemed to choose water routes in preference to land routes.

Working inland from the Colorado River's mouth, they would first pass through Arizona, which state is full of their remains. Their old homes and remains show that they worked out on the Gila, Little Colorado and Grand Rivers. In New Mexico their remains are also very abundant.

After passing through Arizona, up the Colorado River, they wound their way into Utah. Utah is rich in their remains. Branches of the Colorado continue into Nevada and Wyoming and in both states there are remains of these ancient people.

Leaving the main river and working out on the branches, the Grand, San Juan, White and Yampa Rivers, the Cliff Dwellers would, naturally, enter Colorado, a state which is extremely rich in their remains.

Basing calculations on these not only possible but probable routes, the great figures which are pecked and painted on the rocks, in peculiar positions, with extraordinary hands and feet, were unquestionably guide-posts; a dumb language, guiding and telling the traveler about the journey ahead of him. I know this is true, because I have deciphered and translated some of them.

All of the regions surrounding the Colorado River are

Page 186

PAINTING OF MASTODON IN HAVA SUPAI CANYON, ARIZONA

literally filled with the works of the old Cliff Dwellers. These remains consist of cliff houses, rock paintings, rock writings and various utensils and instruments. The fact that these works are only found in the vicinity of the Colorado River and its tributaries, is the strongest sort of evidence that the Colorado River was the gateway through which the Cliff Dwellers entered America, and possibly their predecessors as well.

At what time the Cliff Dwellers came to America is problematical. There is no positive evidence, nor, in fact, is there anything to give us any intimation. They or their ancestors, however, were here before the mountains were raised, which would fix their date at 12,500 years ago.

ARIZONA. (6) -Dr. Walter Hough (7) of the Smithsonian Institution made an examination of the petrified forests of Arizona and reported that he had found the remains of four distinct peoples there. (8) This find corresponds with my own discoveries in our western and southwestern states,

Page 187

as well as Mexico. Three of Hough's civilizations existed before the mountains were raised.

The accompanying illustration is a copy of an ancient rock picture found in the Hava Supai Canyon, Arizona. It is more than 12,000 years old and shows that man was living in Arizona contemporaneously with the mastodon.

NEW MEXICO. (9) -The ancient history of New Mexico is the ancient history of the Pueblo Indians, whose past constitutes one of the most fascinating tales ever told about the ancient men of North America. The Pueblo Indians, when they first came to America, were a very highly civilized and enlightened people. Their traditions and the data found among them prove this fact. They have the oldest records and traditions of any North Americans who came to this continent from the Motherland.

In our western and southwestern states are many ancient ruined cities and structures - rock pictures, rock writings, pottery and traditions. Our famous scientists and archaeologists have been particularly bashful about telling us anything about the people who occupied this land before the present inhabitants. The most that they tell us is that these writings are from 3,000 to 5,000 years old.

It is from the Hopi and Zuñi Pueblos that the most information is to be obtained. To me these tribes are the most interesting of all the North American Indians living today. Possibly this is because I know them better than any of the others. Their connection with the Motherland is perfectly established, and their traditions also tell us that they originally came to America from Mu. All of their religious inspirations are traceable back to the first

Page 188

religion of man, and their sacred symbols are virtually those of Mu.

I have a Pueblo ceremonial blanket, the ornamentations of which are sacred symbols derived from the Motherland.

Their traditions are interesting and far-reaching. An extremely fascinating tradition of theirs is about the creation of the first man and woman-the Adam and Eve of the Bible. It is most valuable by reason of the fact that the language of the Motherland is found in the esoteric meanings of some of the words.

The Zuñis and the Hopis have two special gods who are supposed to shape the destinies of mankind. These gods are held sacred, but are not worshipped. In other words, they are comparable to our saints. The names of these two gods are *Ahaiinta* and *Matsailema*. These were the *first children of the God of the Sun.*

This sentence will bear careful analysis. The Hopi Indians have differentiated between the Sun, the collective symbol of God, and God Himself. They point out that the first man and the first woman were the children of God Himself and not the children of His symbol the Sun.

I have found in ancient writings, especially in those of the Hindus and Egyptians, passages where the sun is called the father of life, and the waters, the mother of life, but in each instance they are speaking about nature's products and not the special creation called man. They also speak of the sun's forces working on the earth's affinitive forces.

The Hopi Indians hold that man and woman were the children of God, the Great God *who rules the sun,* therefore, they are not the offspring of nature. A further cor-

Page 189

roboration of this lies in the esoteric meanings of the names of man and woman. Their names are composed of vocables of the mother tongue, and, like all ancient religious writings, have a hidden meaning. For instance: *Ahaiinta* is composed of the Motherland words *A-hai-in-la*, and *Matsailema* is composed of *Ma-tsai-le-ma*. Conjoined, they read: "God created the first man and the first woman to occupy the earth. These first children of God were the parents of all mankind."

The language of the Pueblo Indians contains many words of the mother tongue, as I have pointed out, and many others find their roots in the same source. Another legend reads as follows:

"Their forefathers came to America in their ships from across the sea in the direction of the setting sun."

Thus it is shown that they came to America from the west, in ships, not over the much abused and much imposed upon Bering land bridge.

When the Pueblos first came to America they were in a very highly civilized state, which is corroborated by their wonderful knowledge of geology, their cultivated language, and their use of the sacred symbols of the Motherland.

A peculiar coincidence that I discovered among the Pueblo Indians was this: they had *Seven Sacred Cities* of Cibola. This is a pure copy of the Motherland and a custom that prevailed among her colonial empires. For instance, the Motherland had seven sacred cities of religion and the sciences; Atlantis had the same, and India had her seven Rishi, or sacred cities.

Lieutenant Cushing **(10)** lived among the Hopi Indians for

Page 190

a long time while he translated what has been called the Zuñi Myths, which are myths only because the people into whose hands they have passed have failed to understand them. These Pueblo traditions have been handed down orally from father to son for thousands of years, but a tradition is actual history, not a myth.

I will take some extracts from Lieutenant Cushing's translations, which, added to my own personal knowledge of the Pueblos, makes interesting reading.

For example, a Zuñi tradition says: "Once the earth was covered with water, no land appeared anywhere." Is this a myth? Not at all, for it has been corroborated by the sacred writings of the Motherland and by geology.

Another Zuñi tradition says: "Just before man appeared upon the earth, the ground was so soft and watery man could not have walked upon it, his feet would sink into the ground, therefore he could not live upon it." A description of what sort of footwear a man must have had to enable him to pass over the soft, watery ground without sinking into it, is very amusing.

Although geological works do not mention this kind of ground as having been in the world at any time, yet that such was the case is clearly shown by the shape and character of the feet of the early Tertiary animals, who had long, spreading toes like the feet of our present-day wading birds who frequent the muddy shores of rivers, ponds and lakes.

Another so-called Zuñi myth-The ancient Zuñis, thousands upon thousands of years ago, had a perfect knowledge of the great reptilian monstrosities that frequented

Page 191

the earth from the Carboniferous Age down to the end of the Cretaceous Period. These traditions say:

"They were monsters and animals of prey; they were provided with claws and terrible teeth. A mountain lion is but a mole in comparison to them. Then Those Above said to these animals: 'Ye shall all be changed into stone, that ye be not evil to men, but that ye may be a great good to them. Thus have we changed ye into everlasting stone."

"Thus was the surface of the earth hardened and many of all sorts of beasts turned into stone. Thus, too, it happens *that we find them throughout the world*. Their forms are sometimes large (in shape), like themselves; sometimes they are shriveled and distorted out of shape, and we often see among the rocks many beasts that no longer live, which show us that all was different in the days of the new."

I think Cushing hardly caught the exact translations in the words I have italicised. My changes, however, in no way alter the meanings.

The foregoing has been passed along as another Zuñi myth. Yet, in order to prove that it is not a myth, one has only to stroll through one of our museums in order to see on every side the truth of the Zuñi tradition. Go to the Museum of Natural History in New York and look at the fossil of the crested trachodont, or visit the United States National Museum at Washington and gaze at the complete and perfect skeleton of the Jurassic dinosaur, Stegosaurus, crushed and flattened.

There may be readers who will say that these have nothing to do with the Pueblos and that they do not prove

Page 192

ROCK CARVING, HAVA SUPAI CANYON, ARIZONA (11)
Reptile Tyrannosaurus. Hopi legend refers to the great reptiles.

Page 193

that the tradition is not a myth. For the benefit of such doubters let us consider the Hava Supai Canyon in Arizona. There, drawn and carved on a rock, is a picture of the most terrible carnivorous dinosaur that ever existed on earth, the grewsome Tyrannosaurus of the late Cretaceous Period. This picture was probably drawn more than 12,000 years ago.

It is only within the last hundred years that this form of reptile was known to our scientists. Cuvier found a part of a skeleton and out of it made a reproduction-a great lizard walking on all four legs. I think I am correct in saying that it is actually only within the last fifty years that the true form of the Tyrannosaurus became known, although it had been faithfully depicted in rock drawings by ancient man thousands of years ago.

The Zuñis also have various traditions about the "Flood." I quote herewith the tradition about this catastrophe, as published by G. W. James: (12)

"In the long, long ago, the Zuñis were very wicked, and in spite of the continued warnings of Those Above, they persisted in their evil doings until the Shadow people determined to destroy them from the face of the earth. Accordingly the *two* great water sources of the world were opened: the reservoir of the *above* from which all rains descend, and the reservoir of the *below* from which all springs, creeks and rivers receive their flow.

"The very plugs were withdrawn and the rain poured down and the floods arose, until the Zuñis knew the wrath of the gods was falling upon them. Hastily they fled to the summit of *Tai-yo-al-la-ne* (Thunder Mountain), where the younger ones of the wicked and profane laughed

---

Page 194

at the fears of the others, and openly scoffed at the idea that even the floods of heaven and of the underworld beneath could ever rise so high as to reach them."

"But slowly the water arose; higher and higher it came, until even the scoffers were silenced, and dumb dread filled their souls. In vain the priests of the various brotherhoods danced, sang, prayed and made big smoke, made medicine and offered gifts. The anger of Those Above would not be turned away. At last the Chief of the Priests went away to a quiet part of the mountain summit, where he could meditate and pray and more especially intercede for the people. He finally came back and said that Those Above could have their anger turned away from them only in one way. The choicest of the young men and the fairest and sweetest of the young maidens must be sacrificed, and then, with appropriate ceremonies be flung into the waters. Thus could the wrath of the gods be appeased and their anger turned away.

"Sadly the people listened and then discussed as to who should be offered as the needful sacrifice. A youth was found as handsome as a young god, athletic, healthful, radiant, fine featured and beloved by all. Then while no one dared to whisper it, the thought went through the minds of all that the only maiden worthy was the beloved and only daughter of their revered *Cacique*. When he looked up to see whom the people had chosen, there was no maiden there. Tears sprang into his eyes. Calling his sweet daughter to him he said a few words to which she reverently bowed her head. Taking her stand beside the youth, those present knew that the sacrifice would be complete. Carefully robing them both in their finest ceremo-

Page 195

nial costumes, placing suitable decorations in their hair, around their arms, and in their hands, the young pair were made ready. Then, slowly and quietly, but increasing in volume and agony, the death wail was sung, after which the Cacique blessed them both; and, invoking the pardon of Those Above, to be gained at so great a cost, he flung them headlong into the seething waters.

"It was done not a moment too soon, for already the throng were standing on a small piece of high land left on the mesa-top with the waters completely surrounding them.

"In less than an hour the waters had gained their height and began to subside. Days and weeks passed, however, before the valley was dry and the chastened people could return to their homes.

"Not long after this one of the youths who had been foremost in wickedness happened to look up towards Taigoallane and there saw two figures standing out clear and plain on the mesa-top. Calling to his people, they were soon gazing in wonderment and awe at the sight, knowing that Those Above had given this to them as a sign. This was confirmed when the Cacique solemnly assured them that these were the heavenly made images of their loved ones given as a sacrifice. The outer, larger one, was the youth, and the inner and smaller one was the maiden."

As a matter of fact, there are six of these shafts on Thunder Mountain, two large ones and four small ones. James, after thanking his Zuñi narrator, pointed out this fact to him, whereupon the Zuñi replied:

"Ah! the youth and the maiden cried out to Those Above that they were lonesome, so the gods married them,

Page 196

and by and by four children came, two boys and two girls, to make them happy."

In this tradition it will be noted that the word *cacique* is used to designate the head or principal of the tribe. *Cacique* is a Quiche-Maya word, meaning the principal head. In Peru, the Quiches, who originally came there from Central America, are now known as Quichuas, and their word for principal or head is *cacique*. It is the same in Venezuela among the descendants of the Kara-Mayas from Central America.

The Zuñi tradition of the flood is a particularly valuable piece of geological information from the fact that it proves that the waters of the last magnetic cataclysm extended far beyond the geological drift line in America. Various Pueblo traditions, their language, their sacred symbols and other evidences *prove that the Pueblo Indians originally came to America from Mu.* As I have already shown, Mu was submerged some 12,000 years ago. Therefore, as these Pueblo Indians came directly from Mu, then they must have been in America at least 12,000 years.

The Pueblos have many of the Quiche-Maya words in their language, in addition to which many of their original conceptions are identical with those of the Quiches, proving that either in the Motherland, or on their first arrival in America, they were geographically in close proximity.

The Pueblos have been little influenced, if at all, by the white people of today, and live now as their ancestors did for many centuries, preserving with great care not only the purity of their language, which they teach their chil-

Page 197

dren to speak correctly, but also their customs, traditions and ancient rites and ceremonies.

Another connection with the Quiche-Mayas and the far-distant past is their prominent symbol, the bearded serpent Quetzalcoatl found principally in the Parjarito Park region.

In confirmation of the foregoing, Professor E. L. Hewitt (13) of the Las Vegas University reports that he has found in the homes of an ancient people, fossil remains of the mastodon and sabre-tooth tiger; also utensils made out of *live*, not fossil ivory, thus corroborating the Hava Supai Canyon picture.

COLORADO DESERT. - In the Colorado Desert there are some famous remains of a great past civilization. These remains have been a puzzle to scientists, but they merely substantiate the old tale of ancient man and his original habitat. The Colorado Desert, like the Oregon and most other deserts, was once fertile land made waterless by the raising of the mountains. It is conclusively proved, however, that the people who lived where the Colorado Desert now stands, lived there before the western mountain ranges were raised.

NEBRASKA. - Professor R. W. Gilder (14) of Omaha, Nebraska, has made one of the most remarkable and one of the most valuable archaeological discoveries (15) ever made in any part of the world. His discovery shows uncontrovertibly that man was living in North America, in a highly civilized state, back in the Tertiary Era.

Gilder has discovered a civilization that was wiped out by the waters of the last magnetic cataclysm, which was the biblical "Flood" and the geological Glacial Period.

Page 198

GILDER'S DISCOVERIES, NEBRASKA
1. Pipe – glazed clay; 2. Fishhook – bone; 3. Clay head; 4. Pink soapstone head;
5. Ornamental shell; 6. Comb – elk-horn

Page 199

Gilder reports that: "the familiar buffalo wallows of the west were never made by buffaloes; they are, instead, the entrances to ruins of underground dwellings, in which, thousands of years ago, lived a race which has vanished from the earth. There is no indication of who the people were or *how they were wiped out.*"

Among the ruins of these long-filled burrows Gilder has found various works of art of the vanished race.

Fig. 1. Is a glazed clay pipe.

Fig. 2. Is a fish-hook made of bone.

Fig. 3. Is a clay face with prominently sloping eyes.

Fig. 4. Is a small pink soapstone head. Gilder says of this: "The pink head is Egyptian in every feature. It is delicately carved and highly polished. It is Egyptian in head-dress, having even the rectangular ear-guards worn by the Egyptians. It is more than Egyptian; it resembles the face of Rameses II himself, if the marble busts in Oriental museums today are images of the Egyptian king."

Fig. 5. Is an ornament made of shell.

Fig. 6. Is a comb made of elk-horn.

"The floors of these underground burrows are strewn with charred sticks, reeds, coarse grasses and corncobs. In the floor of every cave is found a cache, where most of the domestic utensils and other valuables were kept hidden. Sometimes there are several in the same cave. The mouths of the caches are always found plugged with layers of burnt clay. On top of this is a layer of ashes. Beneath all, the cavity widens like a jug or bottle, often the size of a hogshead."

These artificial caves were filled in with the soil and

Page 200

drift torn up by the waves of the cataclysm as they rolled down over the plains. In time this filling packed and left a hollow at the entrance, which has been called a "buffalo wallow."

Gilder's civilization was wiped out by the last magnetic cataclysm. Therefore it was a *Tertiary Era civilization.*

KENTUCKY.-In Kentucky are found the remains of a civilization that was contemporaneous with Gilder's Nebraska civilization.

At Blue Lick Springs, Kentucky, several years ago, an excavation was being made. Twelve feet below the surface of the ground the workmen came across the bones of a mastodon; further down, they found a stratum of gravel, and underneath the gravel, a stone pavement. The stones forming this pavement had been quarried. Their upper surfaces had been cut and dressed, while their lower sides were in the rough.

The mastodon found in this excavation belonged to the Pleistocene Period, as it lay above the gravel. The gravel was formed by the waters of the last magnetic cataclysm, and the stone pavement, being below the gravel, shows that this civilization, like Gilder's, was a *Tertiary Era civilization.*

George W. Ranck, (16) the Kentucky historian, in his "History of Lexington," (17) wrote:

"The city now known as Lexington, Kentucky, is built of the dust of a dead metropolis of a lost race, of whose name, and language, and history not a vestige is left. Even the bare fact of the existence of such a city, and such a people, on the site of the present Lexington, would never have been known but for the rapidly decaying remnants of ruins found by early pioneers and adventurers to the 'Elkhorn lands.' But that these remains of a great city and a mighty people did exist, there can be not the shadow of a doubt.

"Who, then, were these mysterious beings? From whence did they come? What were the forms of their religion and government? These are questions that will probably never be solved by mortal man, but that they lived and flourished centuries before the Indian, who can doubt? Here they erected their Cyclopean temples and cities, with no vision of the red men who would come after them, and chase the deer and the buffalo over their leveled and grass-covered walls. Here they lived, and labored, and died, before Columbus had planted the standard of old Spain upon the shores of a new world; while Gaul, and Britain, and Germany were occupied by roving tribes of barbarians, and, it may be, long before imperial Rome had reached the height of her glory and splendor. But they had no literature and when they died they were utterly forgotten. They may have been a great people, but it is all the same to those who came if they were or not, for their greatness was never recorded. They trusted in the mighty works of their hands, and now, indeed, are they a dead nation and a lost race."

True, the mighty works of their hands, so far as buildings are concerned, "are one with Nineveh and Tyre," but their hands left other records upon the imperishable rocks, and it is by these records that we may identify them as colonizers from Mu, the Motherland.

Therefore, by the foregoing facts that I have recorded

CLIFF WRITINGS, NEVADA

CLIFF DWELLERS' GUIDE-POSTS IN THREE FORMS OF WRITING

Fig. 1. *Arizona.* Directions about an overland trail. Fig. 2. **(18)** *New Mexico.* Directions, land trail. Different language to Fig. 1. Fig. 3. **(19)** *Utah.* Directions, land and water route to a settlement. Not the same people as either 1 or 2.

about discoveries in North America, we have positive proofs that the *whole of western North America was peopled by highly civilized races during the latter part of the Tertiary Era and before the geological Glacial Period.*

Hundreds of rock writings, confirmed by many legends, also tell us that *these first civilizations of North America came from a country called Mu, and that "Mu lay to the west of America, beyond the horizon of the great water."*

This is positive because the Nebraskan and Kentucky civilizations have now been shown *to have existed during the Pliocene Period.* Oregon, Nevada, Utah, Colorado, Arizona and New Mexico show us civilizations that existed *before the mountains were raised.* As these civilizations antedate the mountains, they also went back into the *Tertiary Period.* How far back into the Tertiary Era these civilizations went is not known, as no date has so far come to light to tell us. This remains an open question.

Those ancient dwellers in our western states known as Cliff Dwellers were represented by several distinct tribes and it is possible that, instead of being merely tribes, they were distinct nationalities. I surmise this from their rock writings and rock paintings, which show that different tongues were spoken. The writings are also in varying forms of symbols and alphabets.

A close examination discloses the fact that some of the rock writings and pictures that have been assigned to the Cliff Dwellers of North America are thousands of years older than others which appear within a stone's throw of them. These very ancient writings and pictures were executed before the mountains were raised, which is proved by the fact that some of the rocks on which they are writ-

---

ten are fractured and displaced. In some instances the fracture divides the writing, and in others, characters are found that have been split in two, one part appearing on one side of the fracture and the remainder on the other. This indicates that the rock was fractured and displaced as the ground was being elevated. Other writings clearly reveal that they were written *after* the land was elevated.

It is impossible to give a detailed account of the rock writings and rock pictures of North America in this volume. I have, therefore, been compelled to confine myself to a few that cover two important points: First, those that give an approximate date of the civilization; and, second, those that tell us the origin of the people, where they came from, and how they came to America.

It is quite doubtful if all those classed as Cliff Dwellers actually belonged with that people; that is, certain writings assigned to the Cliff Dwellers were probably written by people who were not Cliff Dwellers at all.

That the Cliff Dwellers came from Mu is absolutely and undeniably certain, for everyone of their pictures that are used as guide-posts contains a reference to Mu. In fact, the rock writings and pictures of the Cliff Dwellers, except those drawn for artistic effect, are permeated with references to Mu, both before and after her submersion. In addition to this, they invariably used the symbols that were in vogue in the Motherland.

Among the rock writings I have found four different branches of the Maya language that were in use; also the evidence that these ancient Americans used three differently arranged alphabets.

Chapter 10: North America's Place Among the Ancient Civilizations Notes

(1) Khui-Land is mentioned on page 241 in "*The Origin and Evolution of the Human Race*"; Albert Churchward; 1921; Also, 'Kui' is mentioned on page 34 of "*Sacred Mysteries Among the Mayas and the Quiches*"; Le Plongeon, Augustus; 1886.

(2) Valmiki is discussed in the Persons of Interest Appendix beginning on page A1—52.

(3) *Druidical Works* covers an unknown number of unnamed manuscripts.

(4) The *Popol Vuh* is discussed in the Written Works Appendix beginning on page A2—28.

(5) An article entitled, "Ancient Relics in Nevada Caves" is contained in James Churchward's scrapbooks. See below.

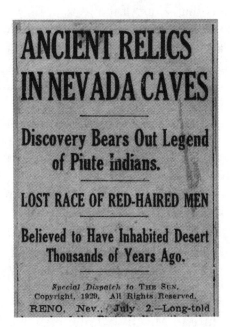

(6) Other pictures of Hava Supai Canyon are contained in James Churchward's scrapbooks. See image on next page. Also see footnote # 11

The "Ibex" Pictograph from the Hava Supai Canyon, Which Is Also Under Dispute, Since the Ibex Has Not Been Supposed by Science Ever to Have Lived in America.

(7) Hough, Walter is discussed in the Persons of Interest Appendix beginning on page A1—19.

(8) An article entitled "Mysterious Relics of An Unknown Race Found in Arizona" (American Weekly, October 16, 1927) is contained in James Churchward's scrapbooks. The article describes the findings of Page and Sykes that explored in the Tortolita Mountains, some 30 miles northwest of Tucson, Arizona.

(9) An picture captioned "Picture Rocks Near Otaivi Canyon, New Mexilo" is contained in James Churchward's scrapbooks. See below:

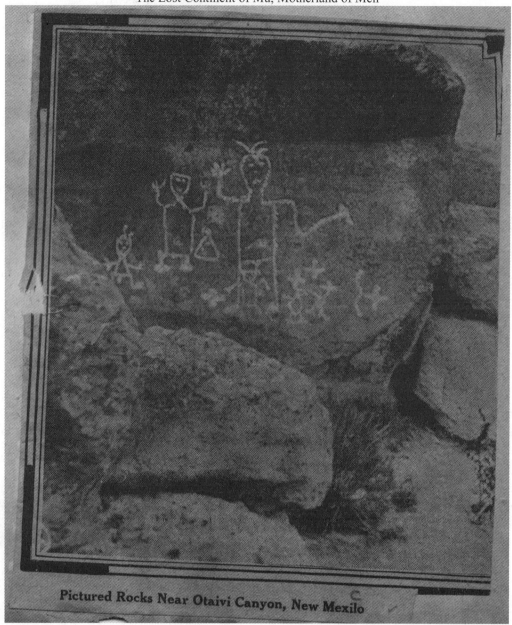

Pictured Rocks Near Otaivi Canyon, New Mexilo

(10) Cushing, Frank Hamilton is discussed in the Persons of Interest Appendix beginning on page A1—8.

(11) A picture captioned "Pictograph of the dinosaur found on very ancient red sandstone cliff in the canon of Hava Supai, Arizona" is contained in James Churchward's scrapbooks. See below.

Pictograph of the dinosaur found on very ancient red sandstone cliff in the canon of the Hava Supai, Arizona.

"To sum up, the dinosaur pictograph might be anything—probably a picture of a sitting lizard or kangaroo rat. The ibex pictures are probably as good a likeness as the artist could chisel out of desert varnish of the close-curled horns of a mountain sheep."

(12) James, George Wharton (1858-1923) was a prolific author and wrote about the American Southwest.

(13) Hewitt, Edgar Lee is discussed in the Persons of Interest Appendix beginning on page A1—18.

(14) Gilder, Robert Fletcher is discussed in the Persons of Interest Appendix beginning on page A1—12.

(15) An article entitled, "Den Men of Nebraska" is contained in James Churchward's scrapbooks. The text is reproduced below.

Den Men of Nebraska
Americans who lived in Underground Prairie Homes
Professor Robert W. Gilder, archaeologist for the University of Nebraska, has made the curious discovery that the familiar "buffalo wallows" of the West were never made by buffaloes. They are, instead, the ruins of underground dwellings in which thousands of years ago lived a race which vanished other thousands of years ago.

The "wallows" were thought to be what their name indicates even by the Indians, thus proving that the red men themselves knew nothing of the race that made the dens.

The modern Indian were just as much surprised as the whites when they discovered what Professor Gilder was taking out of the old indentations. The archaeologist would point to one of the wallows and then tell his little audience just what he would find in it. This he was enabled to do so by reason of the curious similarity in the arrangement of and the things found in the dens. The Indians were appalled, however, by what they thought his uncanny foresight, and now they call him "Man-Who-Sees-Through-the-Ground."

This curious people were skilled in the art of making pottery and in turning out realistic heads and figurines in clay and stone. All their underground houses and caves were built in the shape of squares. These rectangles, oddly enough, do not square like many primeval dwellings, with the points of the compass, but with the North Star, which is a few degrees off due north. The majority of the caves have their entrances at the south, and some have inclines fifty feet long leading down to the door.

This mysterious people dwelt by the millions on the prairies. Professor Gilder has uncovered near the west bank of the Missouri River, near Omaha, what appears to have been a metropolis of the race. Ethnologists who have examined the relics have found no resemblance with either the pre-Columbian Indians or with the mound builders.

There is no clue to indicate who these people were or how they were wiped out. Nor is it clear what conditions forced a whole race to live in burrows beneath the ground.

However, among the ruins, of the long-filled burrows Professor Gilder has found a little carved head of pink soapstone.

The little pink head is Egyptian in every feature. It is delicately carved and highly polished. It is Egyptian in headdress, having even the rectangular earguard worn by the Egyptians. It is more than Egyptian. It resembles the face of Rameses II himself. If the marble busts in Oriental museums to-day are images of the Egyptian king and the mummy unearthed the sands of Egypt in 1881 and now reposing in the Boulak Museum in Cairo is really his corpse.

Another clay image has the pronouncedly sloping eyes peculiar to Chinese.

Geologists have furnished some assistance to the archaeologists in determining the probable age of the ruins. It takes years for black soil to accumulate where it is not washed in. This soil accumulates from decaying grasses. Darwin once made an experiment in the accretion of soil, and computed that but little over an inch collected in a hundred years.

How many centuries, then, may have gone while these two or three feet of black soil have gathered on the sunken roofs of the fallen cave homes!

At least a thousand years before Christ, say the geologists, our cavemen dropped into oblivion and their homes had begun to decay.

In uncovering something over thirty of these homes professor Gilda has established the general character of the caves and their contents. The floor is strewn with charred sticks, reeds, coarse grasses and charred corncobs. In the floor of every cave is found a cache where most of the domestic utensils and the other valuables are hidden. It is this cache that the archaeologist always seeks. Sometimes there are several in the same cave. The mouth of the cache is always found plugged with a layer of burnt clay. On top of this is a layer of ashes. Beneath all, the cavity widens like a jug or a bottle, often to the size of a hogshead.

(16) Ranck, George W. (1841-1900) was an American author and Kentucky historian.

(17) *History of Lexington* is about the history of Lexington, Kentucky and was first published in 1883.

(18) Same as footnote 9.

(19) A picture captioned "Cliff Writings in Yellow jacket Canyon, Utah," is contained in James Churchward's scrapbooks. See image on next page.

Cliff Writings in Yellow Jacket Canyon, Utah,

Page 206

OUR first step on leaving the United States will be to pass into Mexico by crossing the Rio Grande.

In Mexico our first stop will be about 29 miles north of Mexico City. There we shall find a wonderful treasure.

One of the most remarkable, and, without doubt, one of the most valuable geological and archaeological discoveries ever made has been achieved by William Niven, mineralogist of Mexico, who recorded it some years ago; but like all other American discoveries, it was apparently not considered in the slightest way by the scientific world.

Niven's most wonderful discovery has a twofold significance; for, in addition to enlightening the world about prehistoric man, and dating his civilization far back into the Tertiary Era, thousands of years before the majestic ranges of mountains raised their imposing peaks above the plains, it also gives a clue as to when the great gas belts were formed and mountains raised.

It shows that highly civilized races struggled through the most appalling and terrific volcanic workings the earth has ever known.

Page 207

It shows that man was in existence and in a highly civilized state tens of thousands of years before the geological Glacial Period, and the European Pleistocene ape-man. It also adds links to a chain of evidence which shows that the earth's civilization can be divided into two parts or periods:

BEFORE AND AFTER

Before and after what ? The future will disclose. Niven's discovery being so valuable geologically and archaeologically, I cannot do better than to give his own wording about these ruins:

"Over an area of about 200 square miles in the Valley of Mexico, from Texcoco to Haluepantla, there are hundreds, yes thousands, of clay pits.

"After serving the City of Mexico as sources for building material for more than 300 years, these pits have enabled me to make an extensive examination of a vast ruin. Recently my efforts have been rewarded with some remarkable and startling discoveries, which seem to open up a new field for archaeological research on this continent.

"My operations have been confined to an area some 20 miles long by 10 miles wide, in the northwestern portion of the great valley. There I have found traces of two civilizations and three well preserved concrete floors or pavements, each one at some time underlying a large city. These pavements are at depths of from 6 to 25 feet from the surface. Above the first there is a deposit of small boulders, pebbles and sand covered with a foot-thick coating of the rich soil of the valley. The great age of this upper or younger floor must be plain, when every layman

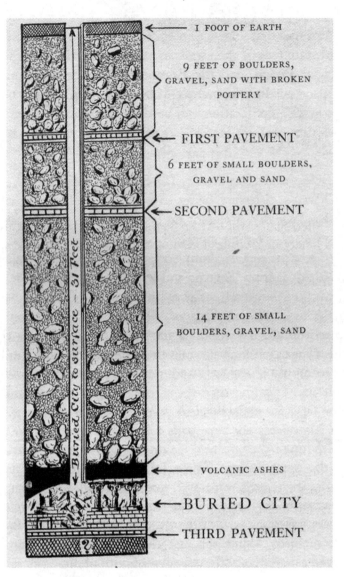

NIVEN'S MEXICAN BURIED CITIES
Now 7,000 feet above the level of the sea. Mountains of 5,000 feet higher
intervening

Page 208

**CONVENTIONAL SKETCH, PRESENT CONDITIONS SURROUNDING
NIVEN'S MEXICAN BURIED CITIES**

stops to consider the number of years required to deposit one foot of earth on a level plain. Everywhere in this deposit of boulders, pebbles and sand above the first floor I found fragments of broken pottery, small clay figures, diorite beads, spear and arrow heads, spindle whorls and other artefacts, mostly broken.

"The second concrete floor is from 4 to 6 feet below the first, the difference in distance between the two being accounted for by the broken condition of the lower pavement, due probably, to seismic disturbances. In the intervening space between the two pavements, one and two, I have failed to find a single piece of pottery, or any other trace to indicate that people had once lived there.

"Underneath the second pavement, however, came the great find of my many years' work in Mexican archaeology. First I came upon a well-defined layer of ashes from two to three feet in thickness, and since proved by analysis to be of volcanic origin. Just below the ashes I found traces of innumerable buildings, large, but regular in size, and appearing uniformly in more than 100 clay pits, which I have examined during my recent investigations.

"All of these houses are badly ruined, crushed and filled with ashes and debris. In the past week's work I found a wooden door, the wood of which had petrified and turned to stone. The door was arched with a semicircular lintel, made by bending the trunk of a tree about five inches in diameter or thickness. This is the first curved arch ever found in the ruins of Mexico; and, as the walls of the house were laid of stone, bound together with a white cement, harder than the stone itself, this wooden arch must have been put in as an ornament. Cutting through

the door, I came into a room about 30 feet square, filled with almost pure volcanic ash, apparently about the only room strong enough to withstand the terrible weight of soil, ashes and stone above it. The roof, which had been of concrete and stone, and flat, had caved in, but around the lower edges of the room great flat fragments of this roof had formed arches, little caves in the ashes, in which were preserved many of the artefacts of the dead race shown in the accompanying illustrations. With the artefacts were bones, numberless bones of human beings, which crumbled to the touch like slaked lime.

"Above their tomb the waters of a great flood had raged, wiping out another civilization. Flood and the crashing boulders had not disturbed the sleep of this mighty race.

"The doorway was over six feet deep, and on the floor, thirteen feet from the door, I came upon a complete goldsmith's outfit. It consists of a terra-cotta chimney 25 inches in height, tapering upwards from a round furnace 15 inches in diameter. On the floor around the furnace, to which still adhered bits of pure gold, I found more than 200 models, which had once been baked clay, but which had been transformed into stone. All of these were duplications carved on figures and 'idols which I found later in the same house. Evidently this had been the house of a prosperous goldsmith and jeweler of the better class in this ruined city.

"Some of the models or patterns were less than one-twentieth of an inch in thickness, and were used for the manufacture of the gold, silver and copper dress, head, breast, arm and ankle ornaments which the statuettes

Page 212

show the people to have worn in those days. Each model was thickly coated with iron oxide, bright and yellow, probably put on there to prevent the molten metals adhering to the patterns while in the casting pot. Later on a thin gold plate made for the breast, and ornaments with characters unlike any found in Palenque or Mitla rewarded my search, and I have since found several of these results of the labors of the goldsmith. The work is fine, beautifully polished, and shows a height of civilization fully as great, if not greater, than that possessed by the Aztecs when the Spaniards under Hernando Cortez first invaded Mexico.

"But what struck me most as the remarkable feature of the room was the mural decorations.

"Evidently there had once been a slight partition through the center, while from the rear walls the dim outline of the door appeared to lead into another room, which is now so complete a ruin that I doubt that anything other than bones will be found in it.

"In the front part of the present room, however, the goldsmith evidently had his workshop, while in the back was the entrance to his residence. Here are wall paintings done in red, blue, yellow, green and black, which compare favorably with the best photographs I have ever seen of Greek, Etruscan or Egyptian works of the same kind.

"The ground color of the wall was a pale blue, while six inches down from the fourteen-foot ceiling a frieze painted in dark red and black ran all around the four sides. This frieze, owing to the fact that it had been glazed after painting, with a sort of native wax, is perfectly preserved, so far as colors and patterns go. It has been, however,

---

Page 213

broken in three places by fragments of the falling roof, but otherwise it is almost as legible as the day when first painted. It depicts the life of some person, evidently a shepherd, bringing him from babyhood to his death bed.

"Beneath the room I found the tomb of some one of importance, possibly of him whose life was portrayed in the frieze above. In this vault, which was only three feet in depth and lined with cement, were seventy-five pieces of bone, all that remained of a complete skeleton. One large fragment of the skull contained the blade of a hammered copper ax, which had evidently dealt death to the occupant of the tomb, and which had not been removed by his relatives or friends. The bones crumbled to the touch, so long had they been in the tomb, but there were other objects more interesting than the bones.

"One hundred and twenty-five small clay terra-cotta idols, mannikins, images and dishes of all kinds were ranged around the bottom of the tomb.

"The most wonderful and striking of these is the terra-cotta figure shown on page 214, Fig. 3. I t has the form of a man in a sitting posture; his legs are crossed Japanese fashion, and the hands on the knees.

"The type is strongly Phoenician or Semitic, while the head is hollow and movable and can be removed from the image at will, being set on the neck by means of a cleverly devised truncated tenon, which fits into a mortise at the base of the skull.

"One must remember that the examination of this room is but a step on the edge of the mystery of this great ruin 200 square miles in area, and reveals nothing of the

RELICS FROM NIVEN'S LOWEST CITY
1. Egyptian head. 2. Ancient Grecian vase. 3. A toy. 4. Little Chinaman

Page 214

Page 215

history of this wonderful people who have been completely lost to the knowledge of mankind.

"Less than three miles from this locality which I have just described I found an ancient river bed now dry, in the sands and gravel of which were thousands of terra-cotta and clay figures having faces representing all of the races of southern Asia.

"The pottery and figures found at a depth, the lowest eighteen feet below the surface, are the best, and it is reasonable to suppose that a people of such culture and of such manifold numbers had imposing temples and governmental edifices comparable with those of Mitla, Palenque and Chichen Itza; if so, when they are uncovered by future generations of archaeologists, the ashes which overlie this vast city will have preserved every ruin as perfectly as they did Pompeii and Herculaneum.

"To my mind here will be found data that will prove the Aztecs the least important of the races which have peopled Mexico, and quite probably the latest to enter Mexican boundaries in that wonderful emigration that peopled North America in forgotten ages."

Subsequent to the publication of the foregoing, Niven wrote further on the subject of the buried cities. Following are notes from this second publication:

THE LITTLE CHINAMAN

"This image proves with indisputable evidence that the people who lived ages ago in the Valley of Mexico knew and were familiar with the Mongolian type. The ruin in which I found the Chinese image was in the remains of the third or lowest civilization thirty feet down from the

---

Page 216

surface in the pit which I had dug at San Miguel Amanda, near Haluepantla, nineteen miles from the national palace in Mexico City. The first (upper) civilization, marked by a cement floor, and walls of a concrete building I found at a depth of eight feet. Eleven feet below this was the second (middle) civilization of about the same grade of development as the first, and 30 feet 3 inches from the surface of the ground I came on a bed chamber, or tomb, I do not know which, in the third stratum of ruins, which contain the finest artefacts I have ever seen in Mexico. I am inclined to think the room was thirty feet square, its walls were made of concrete and crushed down to within a foot of their bases. Below was a tomb. In the center, on a raised rectangular platform, also of concrete, lay the skull and some of the bones of a man who could not have been more than five feet in height. His arms were very long, reaching almost to the knees, and his skull was decidedly of a Mongolian type. Around his neck had been a string of green jade beads. Green jade is not a Mexican mineral.

"Lying beside the body was a string of 597 pieces of shell. I say string, but the buckskin thong which had once born them was long since rotted to dust, and the wampum, or money, lay as if it had fallen from a string. With this money lay the greatest find of all - the little Chinaman.

"It is the first of its kind ever found in Mexico, though Mongoloid types persist in sufficient numbers among the Indians of all Mexico to convince anyone that the Indian blood of the country originally came from Asia.

"His oblique eye-slits, padded coat, flowing trousers and slippers make him a present-day Chinaman in all respects, except for the queue which is lacking. The Chinese did not, however, adopt the queue until they had been conquered by the Tartar hordes from the north.

"The little statuette is about 7 inches high, and where the arms are broken off, the clay of which the image is made shows red and friable in the center; outside, however, the clay has metamorphosed into stone, so that it can be chipped with the hammer only with the greatest difficulty. It is about 3 1/2 inches in width across the chest and 1 1/2 inches in thickness through the abdomen. In the ears are huge rings similar to those worn by the Chinese today, on the head is a skull cap with a tiny button in the center, almost exactly like the caps of the mandarins of the Empire, which has now become a republic. The coat, which is loose and of a type still worn by the Chinese, is shown fastened with a frog and a button, while on the breast is a circular plate or ornament, evidently covered with a layer of beaten gold, but worn bare by contact with the earth of unknown ages. Each arm is broken off at the shoulder, and the opening of the entire tomb has failed to disclose the missing hands. This Chinese image was not made by Aztecs. It had been buried in the earth in the Valley of Mexico' for thousands of years before the Aztecs set foot on the plateau. The Aztecs were newcomers in Mexican history, the blood-thirsty conquerors of the great civilized and organized races of Mexico, who ravaged with fire and sword the cities built by the Toltecs, Ohmecs and Mayas. The Aztecs did not build; they took buildings from the builders by force of arms.

"The little Chinaman furnishes exactly the link for which we have been searching. He says without speaking

that the most ancient tribes of Mexico were offshoots of the Mongoloid.

"Near the skeleton, but off the platform, lay a flower vase about 15 inches high, undoubtedly filled with Xochitl, the yellow sacred flower of practically all of the ancient races of this country."

I will now review Niven's report of his discovery of the remains of three prehistoric civilizations, where one is buried underneath the other.

Geologically it is shown that Niven's discovery is the discovery of the most ancient works of man that have yet been found. The youngest, or upper civilization, dates far back into the Pliocene Period, Tertiary Era.

The character of the buildings and other evidence show that the oldest of the three civilizations was a highly civilized people. Geologically, it is shown that they lived tens of thousands of years before the European Pleistocene degenerates lived.

Niven notes that he found iron oxide in use in casting ornaments out of precious metals. This is the oldest record of the use of iron ever found and antedates the bronze age by tens of thousands of years.

Niven says that the characters on the gold and silver ornaments are different from either those of Mitla or Palenque. Le Plongeon (2) has called attention in his works to the fact that the characters found at Palenque, Mitla and Copan are different from and totally unlike the Maya.

Niven found that the life of the man who was buried in the vault below was depicted on the walls in the chamber above in frescos and paintings. When Prince Coh of the Can Dynasty of Mayax was buried 16,000 years ago, his

Page 219

life was depicted in frescos on the walls of his mausoleum. Thousands of years later we find the same custom followed in the burial chambers of the Egyptian kings. So that we find this custom among the first prehistoric people yet known. Niven mentions that the copper ax he found in the skull of the man was very highly tempered, so that this now lost art dates back far into the Tertiary Era.

In the second vault Niven opened he found an immense number of articles which had been placed around the corpse--mannikins, statuettes, etc. I find this a custom among all the ancients and it is still practised by some peoples.

Niven appears astonished that he found images of all the southern Asiatic races. It would have been a greater astonishment if he had not, because the people of southern Asia and the people who built these now buried cities both came from the same Motherland.

Niven notes that he found green jade beads and that green jade was not a Mexican mineral. Le Plongeon discovered in the tomb of Queen Moo of Mayax a green jade ornament which he called "Queen Moo's Talisman." I have examined this ornament and can safely say it is not New Zealand jade, so that the green jade found in Mexico must have either come there from China or the Motherland. (3)

Niven, like the rest of the scientists, for want of a more plausible explanation, has fallen back on the old threadbare theory that the first men to come to America came from Asia. His statement that "the most ancient tribes of Mexico were offshoots of the Mongoloids" needs qualification. (4)

Page 220

Along the shores of the Caribbean Sea, the original settlers appear to have been mixed, with Mongoloids predominating. Through Yucatan and the inland parts of Central America a white race predominated. They were called Mayas, and the white races of Europe, Asia Minor and northern Africa are easily traced from them. North of the peninsula of Yucatan every record and detail points to the fact that the great bulk of the original settlers were Mongoloids, and possibly in these northern regions all were Mongoloids. Eventually, however, the northern hordes of Mongols overran and conquered the whole of Mexico and Central America. They put the men to the sword and made slaves of the women, so that now, as Niven says, Mongol blood is traceable in all of the Mexican Indians.

Niven notes that yellow flowers were found in the second tomb and states that this was a custom among all the ancient races of Mexico. Yellow has ever been the sacred color. It was so among the most ancient peoples and is today among certain peoples.

Continuing his work among these most extraordinary ruins, Niven has been further rewarded by finding other treasures, including written tablets, probably the most valuable works of man from 35,000 to 40,000 years ago that have ever been brought to light. Through the great courtesy and kindness of the *Dearborn Independent*, Dearborn, Michigan, who have supplied me with cuts of these tablets, I am enabled to give what I believe to be some very valuable information about early man in North America. These tablets are in two forms of writing: pictures composed of symbols, and some Uighur-Maya hier-

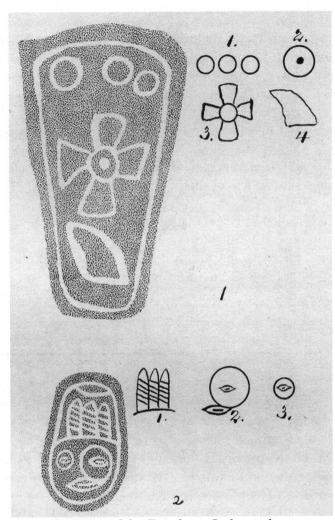

Courtesy of the Dearborn Independent
TABLETS FROM NIVEN'S MEXICAN BURIED CITIES. SECOND CITY (5)

Page 221

Courtesy of the Dearborn Independent
TABLETS FROM NIVEN'S MEXICAN BURIED CITIES. SECOND CITY (6)

Page 222

Page 223

atic sentences. The Uighur-Maya hieratic alphabet came out of that of the Motherland and includes many of the Motherland's letters without change.

The tablets were found in the remains of the second city and are made of volcanic rock and lined in red.

TABLET 1.-FIGS. 1,2,3 and 4

This tablet refers to one of Mu's colonies. It does not give the name of the colony, only its shape.

Fig. 1 is three circles, a very common way of writing "Mu" with the ancients. It gives the symbolic numeral three, so that to start with on the top we read "Mu."

Fig. 2 is the central figure and reads, "Ahau, the King of Kings." Here we find the monarch using his symbol of the Motherland.

Fig. 3. The foregoing is here confirmed by eight conventional rays emanating from a sun, as the eight rays symbolize the eight cardinal points, and the eight cardinal points form a circle. It says that this king is the ruler of the whole earth.

Fig. 4. This is a symbol of an area of land, either a colony or colonial empire, and of a somewhat triangular shape.

TABLET 2. - FIGs. 1, 2 and 3

This little tablet is an exceedingly interesting one and is a picture of the hieratic head of Mu. The temple was called the Temple of Truth and dedicated to the sun.

On his head he wears the crown of the King of Kings, showing him to be the Supreme High Priest. Adorning the crown in the front are three feathers.

Fig. 1. The feather was the symbol of truth, and being

Page 224

three, it again gives Mu's name by numeral, so that this tells us he is the king high priest of Mu.

Fig. 2. Around his left eye and connecting with his mouth is a circle, a picture of the sun, and symbol of the Deity, thus symbolizing that the eye of the Deity sees truth and from his mouth issues truth.

Fig. 3. Around the right eye is a circle. This symbolizes the moon, thus saying that both by day and night the eyes of God are ever on us.

TABLET 3.-FIGs. 1,2,3,4,5 and 6

At the top of this tablet is a face with the two hands outspread in benediction and blessing. This represents the hieratic head of Mu.

Fig. 1. Beneath the right hand is seen the symbol Ahau, King of Kings.

Fig. 2. Beneath the left hand is the symbol of the sun, therefore the King of Kings of the Empire of the Sun. Thus the top of this tablet reads, "Benedictions and blessings on your temple and people from Ra Mu, the king high priest of the Empire of the Sun."

Fig. 3. This is a compound Uighur symbol and appears in the holy of holies of the temple. It reads, "A temple of truth, dedicated to the Sun and under the jurisdiction of the Motherland."

Fig. 4. In this cartouche is shown a colony of Mu. At the top and at the bottom a colony with the word, I think, "Max," but I am not sure about one of the letters.

Fig. 5. This is the symbol of a pillar, reading "In strength."

Fig. 6. This is the symbol of another pillar, reading

Page 225

"To establish." These evidently compare with the Tat Pillars of temples of later date.

TABLET 4·-FIGs. 1, 2,3, 4, 5 and 6

This is by far the most interesting tablet of all. It depicts colonizers leaving Mu, the Motherland, to go to Mexico, there to join a colony already established, and to make their settlement to the north of the present settlement.

Fig. 1. This is the letter m in Mu's hieratic alphabet and is the alphabetical symbol of Mu.

Fig. 2. Beneath Mu, on which she is resting, is a circle with seven dots, symbolizing the creation and advent of man in Mu.

Fig. 3· To the right (east) is placed a bird flying to the east. A flying bird and a jumping fish were the two symbols of colonists leaving the Motherland.

Fig. 4. This symbol says that the colonists came from each of the three lands of M u in three different lines.

Fig. 5. Is a symbol of the colony already established and shows that they also came by three routes.

Fig. 6. This symbol shows where the colonists are going to settle, and-

These tablets were found at the place indicated by Tablet 4.

When prehistoric cities are found buried one underneath the other, archaeologists use the terms first, second and third civilization to designate the order in which they are found. This is apt to be misleading to the layman, for he might assume that the first is last, and the last is the oldest. They are numbered from the surface down; thus,

Page 226

the first one found, the one nearest to the surface of the earth, is the youngest civilization, and the one deepest down is the oldest civilization. Again the word "civilization" is out of place, for the layman might assume that there have been several civilizations, whereas there have been only two since man first appeared on earth. These two will hereafter be designated "The First and the Present Great Civilizations." The better word to have used would be: Colonization or settlement, such as the first, second and third settlement of the land.

Generally speaking, buried cities are prehistoric. The prehistoric cities belong to the First Great Civilization. Niven's "Buried Mexican Cities" and Schliemann's (7) "Ancient Troys" are examples of prehistoric cities, while Pompeii and Herculaneum are the exceptions. Although Pompeii and Herculaneum are buried, their histories are known, therefore they are not prehistoric. Again, while many cities of the First Civilization lie buried beneath the ground, there are remains of others which lie about the ground, but heaps of ruins: Baalbek in Asia Minor and the old Maya ruins in Yucatan are such examples, also the old ruins on the Polynesian and other South Sea Islands.

Niven's prehistoric cities all belong to the First Civilization and lie close to Mexico City, which was built during the Present Civilization.

During the First Civilization, Niven's prehistoric city was thrice built. I wish this carefully noted, because hereafter I shall quote records stating that another prehistoric city only a few miles away was also "thrice built." These records state why and how the destruction of this last city

Page 227

occurred. One geologically shows us the cause. The other states it in records, but both agree in every detail. The altitude of the present City of Mexico is 7400 feet above sea level, therefore the present altitude of Niven's cities is the same. As a geological problem, an extraordinary field has been opened up by Niven's wonderful discovery.

One has only to look at the following facts to see that a great part of our geological teachings must be rewritten:

1. A prehistoric city lies 7400 feet above sea level.
2. The city lies 30 feet below the surface of the ground.
3· A layer of volcanic ash covers the city.
4· The city is on a plain surrounded by mountains.
5· The mountains are many miles distant.
6. Above the remains of this city are the remains of another.
7· Over both cities are deposits of boulders, gravel and sand.
8. Above these cities are the remains of a third-
9· Also covered with boulders, gravel and sand.

At the present time the remains of Niven's cities are 7400 feet above sea level. Niven reports that the lowest city is covered with volcanic ash, but does not record the presence of lava in any form, so it is presumable that the lava from the volcano did not reach the lowest city. That the volcano or volcanoes were near is self-evident, from the fact that their ashes fell in sufficient quantities to bury the city. This being the case, it shows that then, as now, the land was a plain around about. Being a plain, this volcano, like all ancient volcanoes, piled up around the craters and formed cones, similar to those seen in South Africa and among the South Sea Islands today. Again there is

Page 228

the possibility that very little lava was ejected. This was the case with many of the ancient volcanoes.

Ashes alone would not cause such destruction as Niven depicts, so we must look for some other agent as being the force which caused the walls to crumble and the roofs to fall. One of the probable causes was earthquake shocks, preceding and accompanying the outburst of the volcano, which caused the land to rock, rise and fall until the structures came crashing down.

The Troano Manuscript, (8) describing the earthquakes in a later period of the earth's history, says: "Being constantly shaken by the fires of the underneath, and confined, these caused the land to sink and to rise several times."

The Codex Cortesianus (9) says: "The land trembled and shook like the leaves of a tree in a storm." The Lhasa Record (10) repeats the same.

I will now pass up to the second city 14 to 16 feet under the surface of the earth. Over this city there is a layer of boulders, rocks, pebbles, gravel and sand of from four to six feet in thickness.

In his report Niven does not state whether the lowest city, in addition to the volcanic ash, was also covered with boulders, gravel and sand. Volcanoes do not pile up layers of boulders, gravel and sand, so I must refer to geology to find out what agent does. We must ascertain the known agent that forms strata of boulders, gravel and sand.

Geologically, it is known that deposits of boulders, gravel and sand are the works of water-huge tidal or cataclysmic waves, which gather up the stones along their paths, and roll and tumble them along until the force of

Page 229

the water can carry them no further. Then they settle and form a deposit-the biggest and heaviest dropping first and then gradually diminishing in size until sand only is carried in the dying wave. The strata of boulders, pebbles and sand which cover the first and second cities was therefore brought in by tidal waves or cataclysms-from the ocean.

The waves which brought in these deposits certainly came from an ocean; now we find the cities 7,000 feet above the level of the ocean, with mountains thousands of feet higher surrounding the plain in which they have been found.

No tidal waves or cataclysms could assume a height that would reach the plateau forming the Valley of Mexico, much less pass over the mountains surrounding the valley. Such a wave or waves would destroy the whole earth; not a vestige of life would be left upon it. It would be impossible to form a wave even 200 feet high from volcanic workings.

As we proceed, the situation becomes more complex. I should say that tidal waves or cataclysms from oceans swept over and overwhelmed the Valley of Mexico at least twice if not three times.

It is distinctly shown that two great overwhelming waves from an ocean swept over this land at varying intervals, possibly, and probably, thousands of years apart, but each time destroying all life on the land.

I doubt if any trace of the volcano which destroyed the lowest city with its ashes can be found today except by an accident. The crater no doubt was filled in and obliterated by the two cataclysms that followed.

Page 230

Let us for a moment consider the loss of life when the first city was destroyed, a city of 200 square miles. Millions must have perished in the city alone, without taking into consideration other cities and the surrounding country destroyed by the cataclysm. The earth's greatest tragedies have never been recorded.

The cataclysmic waves which overran cities one and two started a long distance away and had lost much of their force when they had arrived at the cities. This is demonstrated by the size of the boulders, which Niven says are small. The boulders are corroborated by the thickness of the deposit. It must be remembered, however, that what is found covering the cities is not all that the waves carried on their errands of destruction; all large boulders had been dropped before arriving at the cities, and much was carried on beyond them. The deposits over these cities show only what was dropped en route.

These deposits of boulders, rocks, gravel and sand absolutely and most conclusively prove that at the time they were made the land was only a few feet above the ocean's level.

During the time that these cities were in existence there were no mountains or mountain ranges between Mexico City and the oceans, and the plateau on which Mexico City stands had not at that time been raised to its present altitude of 7,400 feet above the level of the sea.

The probability is that all Mexico, at the time of these cities, was flat land less than 100 feet above sea level.

Had the present mountains existed then, or had the Valley of Mexico been at its present level or elevation, it would have been impossible for any tidal wave or cata-

Page 231

clysm to have reached the doomed cities, much less carry along boulders with which to bury them.

The foregoing is one of the many examples that verify my contention that:

Mountains and mountain ranges are of comparatively recent origin in the history of the earth because the mountain ranges were formed by the gas belts. That up to the time the earth went into final magnetic balance at the end of the Pliocene, the gases were not controlled, and until they were controlled, mountains could not be raised. Thus, up to the beginning of the Pleistocene no mountains or mountain ranges existed on the earth's surface.

I notice from various publications that the European geologists are wavering in their opinions regarding the age of mountains.

As these ancient Mexican cities existed before the mountains were raised, it is clear that they antedate the Pleistocene Period. Therefore they are Tertiary Era cities. If the last one, the upper one, was built and destroyed before the Pleistocene dawned, according to geological calculations, which, as I have pointed out, are absurd, the upper city must be over 200,000 years old. If the upper city is over 200,000 years old, what must be the age of the third or lowest? All three cities date back to the Tertiary Era. I think the lowest city is at least 50,000 years old.

It is impossible to say what volcanic workings took place in this vicinity before gas belts were formed, but judging from geological phenomena (corroborated by old Maya traditions) they must have been very violent. Mexico, Central America· and the West Indies have one of the greatest gas belt junctions that have been formed within

---

Page 232

the earth's crust. Here various belts not only join each other, but some pass over and under others. It is one of 'the earth's greatest volcanic danger spots. Anything may happen in this vicinity if one or more of the belts become choked.

The volcanic workings in this area during the formation of the gas belts were extremely violent. Violent upheaval of lands both above and below the waters took place. The raising of submarine lands naturally caused tidal waves, through the displacement of the waters. Parts of all the principal gas belts are underneath the beds of the ocean.

There is no saying how much land was submerged or how much land was emerged by these volcanic workings. Four continental stretches we know were submerged. The raising of the ocean bed displaced the waters above. These displaced waters took the shape of great waves, which rolled in over adjacent low-lying lands, destroying everything that lay in their paths. The size and height of the wave and its power of destruction would naturally be governed by the area and height of the submarine land raised. As soon as the gas belts were formed and the mountains raised, such destructive cataclysms were prevented.

It is geologically admitted, as we have previously pointed out, that the European ape-like beings-the Piltdown man, the Heidelberg man and the Neanderthal man-lived some time during the early Pleistocene, or after the date of Niven's upper city. Thus Niven's discoveries emphatically show that man was in America in a highly civilized and cultured state tens of thousands of years before the European ape-like men lived, and proves beyond question that they were individuals and not types.

Page 233

Niven, while showing, and distinctly stating, that two of the cities were overrun and destroyed by cataclysms, apparently does not take into consideration that cataclysmic waves can come only from oceans, and that ocean waves could not possibly reach the Mexican Valley.

The two concrete pavements above the lowest city show the handiwork of two subsequent colonizations. These two colonizations were destroyed by cataclysms. As boulders, pebbles and sand are the covering, it shows that the volcanic workings, the result of which destroyed these cities, were underneath the ocean far away.

An exceptionally great geological value is attachable to this discovery from the fact that the phenomenon is twice repeated.

The thickness of the deposits of boulders, gravel and sand does not in any way intimate the time that elapsed between the building of the cities. It only intimates the size and scope of the waves that brought in the material. I have received information that it has been determined that the boulders which cover the upper and second city originated on the Pacific coast of Mexico.

What happened between this ancient civilization and our own that only the merest fragments of the great past remain? I have already answered this question in previous chapters. Niven's discoveries merely prove that my answer is the correct one.

Chapter 11: Niven's Mexican Buried Cities Notes

(1) William Niven is discussed in the Persons of Interest Appendix beginning on page A1--33. Most of the material contained in this chapter is from an article contained in James Churchward's scrapbook entitled, "Niven's Buried Cities." The text is reproduced below.
An American Pompeii
By Prof. William Niven
C.E.M.A., Member New York Academy of Sciences, Mineralogist of Mexico

Over an area of about 2,000 square miles in the Valley of Mexico, from Texcoco to Tlalnepantla, there are hundreds, yes, thousands, of clay pits, from which the material for the native adobe firebrick is taken. In the fields surrounding these pits firebricks and tile have been made since the Spanish Conquest, and probably long before, though there remains no written record of those ancient times.

After serving the City of Mexico as sources of building material for more than three hundred years, these pits have enabled me to make an extensive examination of a vast ruin which is probably as old as Thebes, and whose civilization was comparable with that of Babylon and Nineveh.(lined out section)

Recently my efforts have been rewarded with some rather remarkable and startling discoveries, which seem to open a new field for archaeological research on this continent. My operations have been confined to an area some twenty by ten miles in area in the northwestern portion of the great valley. There I have found traces of two civilizations and three well-preserved concrete floors or pavements, each one of which at some time underlay a large city. These pavements are at depths from six to twenty-five feet from the surface.

Above the first there is a deposit of pebbles, sand and small boulders, covered wit a foot-thick coating of the rich soil of the valley. The great age of this upper and youngest floor must be plain when even the layman stops to consider the number of years required to deposit on foot of earth on a level plain.
Everywhere in the deposit above this first floor I found fragments of broken pottery, sall clay figures, diorite beads, spear and arrowheads, spindle whorls and other artefacts, mostly broken and mostly comparatively modern.

The second concrete pavement is from four to six feet below the first, the difference in distance between the two being accounted for by the broken condition of the lower pavement, due probably to seismic disturbances. In the intervening space between pavements one and two I failed to find a single trace of pottery or any other trace to indicate that a people had once dwelt there. Evidently this second pavement was covered with a deposit which required centuries of silence and solitude to lay.

Underneath this second pavement, however, came the great find of my many years of work in Mexican archaeology. First I came on a well-defined layer of ashes, from two inches to three feet in thickness, and since proved by analysis in the Government laboratories here to be volcanic in origin. Just below these ashes I found traces of innumerable buildings, large but regular in size, and [apparently uniformly in more than one] hundred clay pits which I have examined and photographed during my recent investigations.

All these houses are badly ruined, crushed, filled with ashes and detritus, and it would cost at least $1,000,000 to open this portion of the vast ruin, but fortunately, in the past week's work I found a wooden door, the wood of which had petrified to stone. Analysis in the laboratories of the Mexican National Museum proved this. The door was arched with a semi-circular lintel, made by bending the trunk of a tree about five inches in thickness. This is the first curved arch ever found in the ruins of Mexico, and as the wall of the house was of laid stone, bound together with h white cement, harder than the stone itself, this wooden arch must have been put in as an ornament. Then during thousands of years - the petrified forest of Arizona is known to be more than 50,000 years old - it turned to stone and became an integral part of the stone and concrete wall surrounding it.

Cutting through this door, I came into a room about thirty feet square, filled with almost pure volcanic ashes, apparently about the only room strong enough to withstand the terrible weight of soil, ashes and stone above it. The roof, which had been of concrete and stone and flat, had caved in, but around the lower edges of the room great flat fragments of this roof had formed arches, little caves in the ashes in which were preserved many of the artefacts shown in the accompanying illustrations.

Here was another Herculaneum, another Pompeii, wiped from the face of the earth by an outburst of one or both of two white-capped volcanoes. Popocatepetl and Ixtaccihuatl, far to the south. With the artefacts of the dead races were bones, numberless bones of human beings, which crumbled to the touch like slaked lime. Above their tomb the waters of a great flood had roared, wiping out another civilization, but the flood and the crashing boulders had not disturbed the sleep of this mighty race, which died when Atlantis was a reality and when my ancestors ran naked over northern Europe.

The doorway was over six feet deep, and on the floor thirteen feet from the doorsill, I came on a complete goldsmith's outfit. It consists of a terra cotta chimney, twenty-five inches in height, tapered upward from a round furnace, fifteen inches in diameter. On the floor around the furnace, to which still adhered bits of pure gold, I found more than two hundred models, which had once been baked clay, but which I found later in the same house. Evidently this had been the home of a popular goldsmith and jeweller of the better class in this ruined city. Some of these models or patterns were less than one-twenty-fifth of an inch inn thickness and were used for the manufacture of gold, silver and copper dress, head, breast, arm and ankle ornaments which the statuettes show the people to have worn in those days.

Each model was thickly coated with iron oxide, bright red and yellow, probably put on to prevent the molten metals adhering to the patterns while in the casting pot. Later on a thin gold plate, made for the breast and ornamented with characters unlike any found at Palenque or at Mitla, rewarded my search, and I have since found several of these results of the labors of the goldsmith. The work is fine, beautifully polished and shows a height of civilization fully as great, if not greater, than that possessed by the Aztecs when the Spaniards, under Hernando Cortez, first invaded Mexico.

But what struck me as the most remarkable feature of the room was the mural decoration. Evidently there had been a slight partition through the centre, while from the rear wall the dim outline of a door appears to lead into another room, which is now so completely a ruin that I doubt if anything other than bones will be found in it. In the front part of the preserved room, however, the goldsmith evidently had his workshop, while the back was the entrance hall to his residence. Here are wall paintings, done in red, blue, yellow, green and black, which compare favorably with the best photographs I have ever seen of Greek, Etruscans or Egyptians works of the same sort.

The ground color of the wall was a pale blue, while about six inches down from the fourteen food ceiling a frieze, painted in dark red and black, ran all around the four sides.

This frieze, owing to the fact that it had been glazed after painting with some sort of native wax, is perfectly preserved so far as colors go. It has been broken in three places by fragments of the falling roof, but otherwise is almost as legible as the day first painted. It depicts the life of some person, evidently a shepherd, bringing him from babyhood to his death bed.

Beneath this room I found the tomb of some person of importance, possibly of him whose life was portrayed in the frieze above.

In this vault, which was only about three feet in depth and line with cement, were seventy-five pieces of bone, all that remained of a complete skeleton. One large fragment of the skull contained the blade of a hammered copper axe, which had evidently dealt death to the occupant of the tomb, and which had not been removed by his relatives or friends. The bones crumbled to the touch, so long had they had been in the tomb, but there were other objects even more interesting than the bones. The copper axe, for instance, though green with age, was as hard as when made, and I have since proved its temper by grinding it to an edge almost razor-like on an emery wheel.

One hundred and twenty-five small clay and terra cotta idols, manikins, images and dishes of all kinds were ranged around the bottom of the tomb. The most striking and wonderful of these is the terra cotta figure shown in one of the accompanying photos. It has the form of a man in sitting posture, the legs crossed Japanese fashion and the hands on the knees. The type is strongly Phoenician or Semetic, while the head is hollow and movable and can be removed from the image at will, being set on the neck by means of a cleverly devised truncated tenon, which fits into a mortise in the base of the skull.

One must remember that the examination of this room is but a step on the edge of the mystery of this great ruin two hundred square miles in area, and reveals nothing of the history of this wonderful people who have been completely lost to the knowledge of mankind. Less than three miles from the locality I have just described I found an ancient river bed, now dry, I the sand and gravel of which were thousands of clay and terra cotta figures having faces representing all the races of southern Asia. I have specimens from this locality which are unmistakably Chinese, Japanese, Bornese, Hindustanee, and one which shows the hairy face of the Ainu. Others present strong negroid features, and still others are undoubtedly Arabian in style.

When I showed this locality and these finds to Dr. Edward Seller, of Berlin, who is now connected wit the National School of Archaeology and Ethnology in Mexico, he said:

"This river flowed thousands of years before the lakes covered the Valley of Mexico; this buried city stood on the banks of this river and was wiped out at the same time that the river's flow was forever choked by the torrent of ashes and sand from yonder white crowned volcanoes. It is the most important ruin I have ever seen.(lined out section)

The pottery and figures found at the lowest depth, about eighteen feet from its surface, are the best, and it is reasonable to suppose that a people of such culture and such manifest numbers had imposing temples and edifices of government comparable to those which stand on the surface of Mexico at Mitla, Palenque and Chichen-Itza. If so, when they are uncovered by future generations of archaeologists the ashes which overlie the vast city probably will have preserved every ruin as perfectly as they did the hoes of the people who lived in Herculaneum and Pompeii. To my mind, and I have studied the matter carefully, here will be found data which will prove the Aztecs the least important of the races who peopled Mexico, and quite probably the latest to enter Mexico's boundaries in that wonderful migration which peopled North America in a forgotten age.

Part Two
Mexico Aug. 16.

An image of an unmistakable Chinaman moulded in clay , has been found at San Miguel Amantla buried beneath the ruins of three Mexican civilizations.

This discovery is believed by high archaeological authorities to prove the interesting theory that the ancient civilization of Mexico preceding that of the Aztecs was of Chinese or Mongolian origin. This explanation would unravel the mystery of the wonderful Maya ruins of Yucatan and other parts of Mexico.(lined out section)

The clay Chinaman, with oblique eye-slits, padded coat, flowing trousers and slippers Ð a Chinaman in everything except the queue which is lacking. The Chinese, it must be remembered, did not adopt the queue until they had been conquered by the Tartar horde from the north. Thirty feet under the ground, at San Miguel Amantla, nineteen miles from the city of Mexico, the image was uncovered in the ruins of a buried tomb by Professor William Niven, of Mexico City.

It is about seven inches in length, and where the arms are broken the clay of which the image was made shows red and friable in the centre. Outside, however, this clay has metamorphosed to stone so that it can be chipped with a hammer only with great difficulty. It is about three and one-half inches in width across the chest and one and one-half inches through the abdomen. In the ears are huge rings, similar to those worn by the Chinese to this day, and on the head is a skull cap, with a tiny button in the centre, almost exactly like the caps of the Mandarins of the empire which has so lately become a republic.

The coat, which is loose and of the type still worn by the Chinese is shown fastened with a frog and a button, while on the breast is a circular plate or ornament, evidently once covered with a thin layer of beaten gold, but worn bare by contact with the earth for unknown centuries. Each arm is broken off close to the shoulder, and the opening of the entire tomb, or room, nearly thirty feet square, in which the image was found, has failed to discover the missing hands.

This Chinese image was not made by the Aztecs. It had been buried in the earth of the Valley of Mexico a thousand years before the Aztecs set foot on the plateau. The Aztecs were newcomers in Mexico's history, the bloodthirsty conquerors of the great civilized, organized races of America's Egypt, who ravaged with fire and sword the cities built by the Toltecs, the Olmecs and the Mayas. It is probably true that the Aztecs built little, if any, of the massive ruins that mark all parts of Mexico. They took them by force of arms from the builders.

When Hernan Cortez asked of Montezuma, his captive, "Who built that huge temple?" Montezuma replied "Las Toltecas," and Bernal Diaz, historian of the conquest, named the tribe which had preceded the Aztecs in the Valley of Mexico, the Toltecs. But, in the Nahuatl tongue, which is the language of the Aztecs and which is still spoken in some of the villages of remote Mexico, "tolteca" means a builder, a mason, nothing more, and Montezuma knew as little of the race which made the Calendar Stone, which worked out its own system of astronomy and time, and which moved twenty-ton blocks of stone to build its temples as did the Spanish invaders Ð and archaeologists of today knew very little more until Professor Niven uncovered the Chinaman.

Mr. Niven who has been delving in the buried tombs and temples of Mexico for thirty years, declares that the first people of Mexico came from China, by way of the Behring Straits. Ramon Mena, the foremost living archaeologist of Mexico, who has spent twenty years in the ruins of Mexico's dead races, supports him without qualification. There is another school of archaeology, whose members insist that the aborigines of Mexico came from the east, by way of a land connection across the lower end of the Gulf of Mexico, to what is now the northward-pointing peninsula of Yucatan.

Now comes the curious Chinaman. Buried for at least fifteen hundred years, possibly more, to prove to the world that the Mongol was known in Mexico when the Wise Men followed the star to Bethlehem. The image is not an idol; nine-tenths of the figurines which are called idols in Mexico were, indeed, never intended as objects of worship. It is an ornament for the house of some prehistoric noble, probably the same man whose crumbling skull, shell money, jade ornaments and flower vase were found scattered round the Chinese images.(lined through on original)

"This image," says Professor Niven, "proves with indisputable evidence that the people who lived in the Valley of Mexico ten or fifteen centuries ago knew and were familiar with the Mongol type. The ruin in which I found it was in the remains of the third civilization in the pit which I had dug at San Miguel Amantla, near Tlalnepantla, nineteen miles from the National Palace in Mexico City. The first civilization, marked by a cement floor and the walls of a concrete buildings, I found at a depth of eight feet. Eleven feet below it was the second civilization, of about the same grade of development as the first, and, thirty feet and three inches from the surface of the ground I came upon a bedchamber, or tomb, I do not know which, in a third stratum of ruins, which contained the finest artefacts I have ever seen in Mexico.

"I am inclined to think the room, which was thirty feet square, its walls made of concrete and crushed down to within about a foot of their bases was a tomb. In the centre on a raised, rectangular platform, also of concrete, lay the skull and some bones of the skeleton of a man, who could not have been more than five feet height. His arms were very long, reaching almost to his knees, and his skull was of a decidedly Mongoloid type. Around his neck had been a string of green jade beads, another link which binds Mexico to China, for real jade has never been found in Mexico in a natural state.

"Lying beside the body was a string of five hundred and ninety-seven pieces of shell. I say string, but the buckskin thong which had once borne them was long since rotted to dust, and the wampum, or money, lay as it had fallen from the string. With this money lay the greatest find of all - the little Chinaman. It is the first find of the kind ever found in Mexico, though Mongolid types persist in sufficient numbers among the Indians of all Mexico to convince anyone, it seems to me, that the Indian blood of the country came originally from Asia.

"Near the skeleton, but off the platform, lay a flower vase, about fifteen inches in height, undoubtedly filled with xochitl, the yellow sacred flower of practically all the ancient races of this country. Undoubtedly the tomb, or room, is a part of the ruin of the ruin of a large city, and I have secured the aid of the National Museum, to who the Chinese image will be presented, to clear away the thirty feet of earth a sufficient distance around the shaft I have dug to show what lies beneath.

"It must be remembered that this was not a god, nor an idol, but an ornament, the image of some person, his portrait done in clay by some prehistoric sculptor. Thousands of images of men, women and animals, and a very few children, are found in all ancient graves in this country. They were made for preservation in houses, and to be buried with the dead, and I believe this was the image of the man whose skeleton lay on the platform in this buried room. How long was he buried? How long is required for the elements to deposit thirty feet of earth on a level surface? Making a rough guess, without figuring the rates of different classes of earth which make up this blanket, I should say not less than fifteen centuries, possibly more.

"San Miguel Amantla, where I found three buried cities, is a level plain thirty miles long by ten miles wide. There is no trace of any cataclysm which might have buried the cities deeply and suddenly. Earth was deposited slowly over the first city; then the second was built on top of that ten or eleven feet of earth. Then came another period of centuries of deposition and the third city was built. Above this upper ruin Nature laid another blanket of earth, and on the surface to-day cattle graze, while miserable brush huts dot the fields above buried palaces of stone and concrete.

The little stone Chinaman furnishes exactly the link for which we have been searching. He says without speaking that the most ancient tribes of Mexico were offshoots of the Mongoloid.

(2) Le Plongeon, Augustus is discussed in the Persons of Interest Appendix beginning on page A1—22.

(3) Jade and Jadeitite can also be found in Guatemala, British Columbia, and Alaska, in addition to Burma, China and New Zealand.

(4) An article entitled, "Central Americans of Asiatic Origin" from the Cedar Rapids Evening Gazette & Republican dated March 28, 1929 is contained in James Churchward's scrapbooks. James wrote an article entitled "Synopsis of the Earliest History of Central America and Yucatan" also contained in his scrapbooks, but undated and not sourced. The text is reproduced below:

From James Churchward

Gives Synopsis of Earlier History of Central American and Yucatan

Editor Argus: - We constantly see a great deal written about the ruins of Yucatan and Central America. These writings appear to be exclusively guess work. Herewith is a short synopsis of the history of Yucatan, based on Maya writings, Maya inscriptions, Hindu records, Egyptian records, and Greek writings, and geological phenomena.

James Churchward

Synopsis of the Earliest History of Central America and Yucatan

According to traditions, the first people who inhabited Central America and Mexico were a white race.

Their last king was named Quetzal, sometimes he was called Quetzalcoatl, also Cucumatz.

How long this white race had been in America up to the time of Zuetxal (Quetzal?) has not been revealed. The end of this white race was: they were conquered by a people of darker skins called Maya who took and settled on the land. The Mayas were composed of several distinct tribes among them being various tribes of Mongols and Semitics.

When conquered, King Quetzal refused to surrender to become a slave to the conquerors, saying, "he would die in captivity." So he, with a remnant of his white people took their ships and sailed to a far off land beyond the setting sun, i.e., to the east of America. Quetzal and his people arrived safely at that far off land where they settled and became great again.

The people of this Quetzal settlement were the forefathers of the white races of Europe, except the Latin races, the Greeks, the Semitics and the Egyptians.

All these came to Europe later in the history of man's colonization of the earth.

The American Mayas, the conquerors of Quetzal and the white race, were composed of Mongols and Semitics but dominated as a whole by another white race of a more swarthy complexion than the original white race. According to written history, they called the conquered lands Mayasc, from which the name Mexico of today came. Mayasc was the original name of Mexico, but Mayasc included Central America as well.

According to Maya and Hindoo records the Maya dominated this land for 18,000 years, during which time there were eleven separate dynasties of emperors or kings. The last dynasty was called the Cau dynasty and the preceeding one the PPeu Dynasty.

Each king or emperor assumed the title "son of the sun" to show that he came from the royal family of the earth's first empire, "The Empire of the Sun." The title "son of the sun" was the patent showing his royal descent.

During the time of the Mayas, the great structures, whose ruins we now find in Central America, Yucatan and Mexico, were erected. There were no distinctive people called Toltecs. Toltec means builder, therefore the Mayas were the Toltecs because they were the builders. The last dynasty was called the Cau dynasty. Cau was the family name of the royal family and Cau means serpent. When the Cau family became the royal family and its head the emperor, he adopted as his emblem, the great symbolical feathered serpent of creation. In these ancient days it was usual to carve in various places and to adorn all temples, palaces and the various governmental buildings with the symbol of the reigning family, - thus all such buildings having the feathered serpent carved upon them, show that they were either built by or during the reign of the Cau emperors. Maya history tells us most of the structures of Clucheu (Chichen ?) Itza, Uxmal and other cities in Yucatan were re-built by the last king Cau and for this reason we find the bulk of the ancient buildings in Yucatan adorned with carvings of the feathered serpent. Maya history does not supply us with the reason that these cities were built, but Egyptian temple histories do. They had been shaken down into ruins by earthquakes. Some few structures still remain that were built during the PPeu Dynasty. These are known by the carvings of elephants' heads on them. The elephant was the royal symbol of the PPeus. The last reigning monarch of the Cau dynasty was Queen Moo, who died 16,000 years ago on her return from a visit to the new Maya colony on the banks of the Nile Delta, at Sais.

Civil wars and internal strife sapped the vitals of the Mayax empire, so that surrounding peoples found them an easy prey, and thus virtually ended the old Mayax empire; it became split up into small kingdoms. During the Maya ascendancy in America they pushed colonies eastward first to Atlantis then to southern Europe, Northern Africa and Asia Minor.

The Latin races, the Greeks, the Semitic races and the Egyptians are all descended from this migration. From the end of the Cau dynasty down to the invasion by the Spaniards under Cortez, but little is known of what took place in Central America and Yucatan. Wars and invasions were constant. History records one prominent invasion by a people who came from the south, called Nahuates. Whether they were Mongol or not, we cannot say, but they were, without doubt a very highly enlightened people as they understood the origin and workings of the great forces far better than scientists of today. The date of this invasion is wrapped in mystery, Somewhere between 14,000 BC and 2,000 BC, a great cataclyom (cataclysm?) swept over the whole land, wiping out all life and destroying the edifices. We get this from the Egyptian temple history. So that, today, there is not a single one of the ancient Mayas in existence in Central America and Yucatan. When the country became habitable again, races from surrounding lands drifted in and repopulated the land. Then our next bit of history is where the blood-thirsty Aztecs from the north swept down over the land, putting the men to the sword and taking the women into slavery. The Aztecs introduced the human sacrifice; before the time of the Aztecs offerings consisted of fruits and flowers, which was laid on an altar having the taw "T" associated with it. The taw is the symbol for resurrection and a picture of the constellation of the Southern Cross. When the Southern Cross appears over Central America and Yucatan, it brings the rain. Seeds spring forth from the ground, trees yield flowers and fruit, and al nature is again resurrected and brought into life. After reading the Egyptian tale of the Yucatan cataclyom (cataclysm?). We asked some geologists who were going to Yucatan to examine the ground around some of the ruins and see if anything showing geologically of the flood. We got back the information from them that not only are the marks of a flood found around the Yucatan structures, but appears also around the Central American structures and monoliths, in very distinctive form.

We think we have perfect records of Central America and Mexico having been peopled by a very highly enlightened and cultured people, more than 35,000 years ago, and we have incontrovertible records and proof that the first people in Europe and Asia Minor came from America.
James Churchward

(5-6) Figures are contained in the scrapbook with the article from footnote #1. See image on next page.

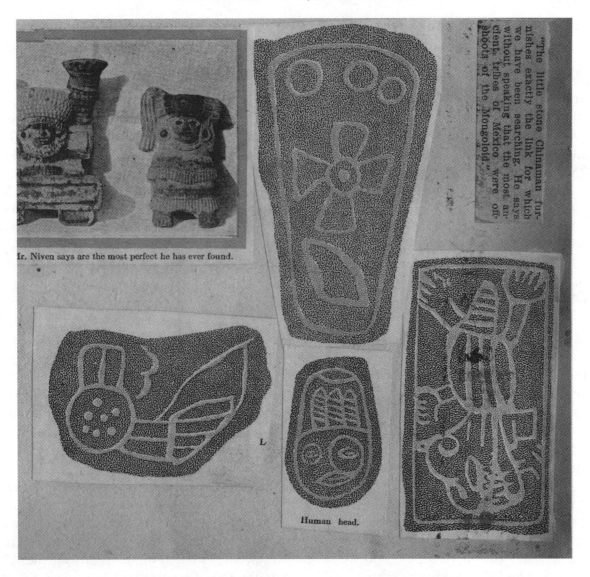

Ir. Niven says are the most perfect he has ever found.

L

Human head.

"The little stone Chinaman furnishes exactly the link for which we have been searching. He says without speaking that the most ancient tribes of Mexico were offshoots of the Mongoloid."

(7) Reference to Schliemann is to Heinrich Schliemann. Heinrich is discussed in the Persons of Interest Appendix beginning on page A1—45.

(8) The *Troano Manuscript* is discussed in the Written Works Appendix beginning on page A2—34.

(9) The *Codex Cortesianus* is discussed in the Written Works Appendix beginning on page A2—7.

(10) The Lhasa record is discussed in the Written Works Appendix beginning on page A2—16.

Page 234

ON leaving Mexico City with Niven's treasures, I shall proceed to that part of Mexico called Yucatan.

Yucatan is situated in the southeastern part of Mexico and forms a peninsula stretching out from the mainland in an easterly direction. It is bounded on the north by the Gulf of Mexico and on the east and southeast by the Caribbean Sea.

Yucatan is literally filled with the remains of ancient civilizations, although none are as old as Niven's buried cities. Central America and Yucatan formed one of the first colonies established from the Motherland. Eventually it became an empire and was called Mayax.

What are thought to be the most ancient of these ruins I shall deal with first. They consist of temples, tombs and governmental buildings all of stone, and are either partially or completely covered with earth. Next I shall take the structures completely above the ground, the ages of which have been variously estimated to be from 2,000 to 15,000 years. Quotings from ancient writings would seem to show that the youngest of these structures is at least

Page 235

15,000 years old, and there is every reason to believe that most of them are more than 15,000 years old; some of them, I am sure, are.

I think my readers will agree with me that it was not the hand of man that caused the walls of these massive buildings to crack and split and the stones to fall. It was the result of volcanic workings when the great central gas belt was forging its way under Yucatan. Up to that time, these buildings stood intact.

As a guide, every building that has carvings on it of the feathered serpent (Kukul Khan) is 15,000 or more years old. These buildings were erected during the Can (serpent) Dynasty. The Can Dynasty ended with Queen Moo. Queen Moo lived during the first century of Egyptian history.

The late Dr. Le Plongeon (1) and his wife, Alice D. Le Plongeon, very dear friends of the writer, were the first archaeological explorers to delve among the buried parts of Yucatan ruins. Their works which have been published give many interesting details of their discoveries:

Not one-half of their discoveries, however, were published. Before the death of Dr. Le Plongeon, he gave the writer his unpublished notes and translations for copy; so that what I say about Yucatan comes principally from the result of Dr. Le Plongeon's twelve years among the ruins, much of which, however, I have corroborated by a personal examination.

My first notes on Yucatan remains will concern some archaeological records unearthed by Le Plongeon.

AN OLD MAYA TEMPLE IN YUCATAN, RICH IN INSCRIPTIONS AND SYMBOLS

Page 236

THE TEMPLE OF SACRED MYSTERIES

At Uxmal there is an ancient Maya temple which Le Plongeon has called in his works, "The Temple of Sacred Mysteries."

The inscriptions on the walls, combined with the profusion of sacred symbols carved thereon, are themselves a chapter of prehistoric history. They connect very ancient man with the early history of Babylonia and Egypt.

This building, which is an emblem of the Lands of the West, is composed of three compartments. The door of the central chamber, the holy of holies, faced west, in the direction where once the Motherland stood; in this respect, corresponding to the temples and statuary found at Angkor, Cambodia, which all face east, towards the vanished land. From the central chamber a small stairway led to a terrace formed by this sanctuary. The doors of the other two rooms faced east.

The ceilings formed a triangular arch. Inside the triangle formed at each end of the two rooms facing east, by the converging lines of the arch, are semispheres. Those of the north room, three in number, form a triangle, as shown in Chapter 8, Page 127, Fig. 7. Those in the south room consisted of five, as shown on Page 127, Fig. 8. A few centimeters above the lintel of the entrance to the sanctuary is a cornice that surrounds the whole edifice. On it are sculptured and many times repeated a skeleton with cross-bones shown in Chapter 8, Page 134, Fig. II.

The most remarkable of all the symbols found in the Temple of Sacred Mysteries is the cosmogonic diagram of Mu (Chapter 9, Page 141, Fig. 1), the diagram of

---

man's first religion, which I have already shown. The Temple of Sacred Mysteries is more than 11,500 years old, and this age is verified by the following: Plutarch (2) relates that the priests of Egypt told Solon (3) that communications with the Lands of the West had been interrupted 9,000 years before, in consequence of the sinking of Atlantis, which made the Atlantic impassable on account of the mud and seaweed *and the destruction of the country beyond by overwhelming cataclysms.*

Solon visited Egypt 600 B. C. Atlantis sank 9,000 years previous to this. Thus, by adding A. D. 2000 to 600, plus 9,000, we get a date of 11,600 years ago.

Further proofs of this destructive cataclysm are given in the writings of the Spanish historian, Dr. Aguilar, (4) who relates: "In a book which I took from the idolaters there was an account of an inundation to which they gave the name *Unuycit* (flooding)," and this is geologically further confirmed by the strata around the bases of these old structures.

How long the Temple of Sacred Mysteries had been standing beyond the period I have assigned to it no one can say, but certainly not very long, because this temple was a memorial commemorating the loss of the Lands of the West and they disappeared only a short time before the disappearance of Atlantis. Le Plongeon found an inscription on the temple walls, which reads as follows:

"This edifice is a memorial commemorating the destruction of Mu, the Lands of the West, whence came our sacred mysteries."

This inscription I had verified by a native gentleman who thoroughly understood the Maya writings.

Page 239

Being a memorial, emblem or monument to the Lands of the West, it follows that this temple was erected after the Lands of the West had disappeared.

Le Plongeon also found an inscription on one of the buildings saying that "Uxmal had been destroyed by earthquakes three times and had been three times rebuilt." It is today known among the educated natives as the "Thrice Built City."

Niven's (5) Mexican buried cities are, comparatively speaking, only a few miles away from Uxmal, so that there remains the possibility that the disturbances which caused the ruin of Niven's upper cities might, and probably did, extend as far as Uxmal.

Some of our scientists who have been picnicking at Chichen Itza come back with the tale that these old structures were built only 1,500 years ago.

As a matter of fact, most of them were standing 11,500 years ago and some of them are certainly older than that. I refer to those built during the PPeu dynasty, which immediately preceded the Can dynasty.

One great authority on the antiquity of the Yucatan-Maya ruins was Bishop Landa, (6) who accompanied the Spanish under Cortez in the sixteenth century. Bishop Landa, in his work, "Relacion de las Cosas," (7) page 328, written 400 years ago, says:

"The ancient buildings of the Mayas at the time of the arrival of the Spaniards were already heaps of ruins, objects of awe and veneration to the aborigines who lived in their neighborhood.

"They had lost the memory of who built them and the object for which they were created.

Page 240

"The Maya priests wrote books about their sciences and imparted their knowledge to others whom they considered worthy of enlightenment.

"They had books containing the early history of their own nation and that of other people with whom they had friendly intercourse or war.

"In these volumes there were complete records of what had taken place in different epochs, of the various wars, inundations, epidemics, plagues, famines and every important event."

Landa burnt thousands of these books and twenty-seven large manuscripts on parchment. He destroyed 5,000 statues and 197 vases.

Cogolludo, (8) in "Historia de Yucathan," (9) Book IV, Chap. III, p. 177, says:

"Of the people who first settled in this Kingdom of Yucathan, or their ancient history, I have been unable to obtain any other data than those which follow:

"The Spanish chronicles do not give one reliable word about the manners and customs of the builders of the grand antique edifices that were objects of admiration to them, as they are now to modern travelers.

"The only answer of the natives to the inquiries of the Spaniards as to who the builders were invariably was, 'We do not know.' It is not known who the builders were and the Indians themselves have no traditions on the subject."

Lizana (10) ("Historia de Nuestra Senora de Ytzamal," (11) Chap. II): "When the Spaniards came to this country, notwithstanding that some of the monuments appeared new, as if they had been built only twenty years, the Indians did not live in them, but used them as temples and

Page 241

sanctuaries, offering in them sacrifices sometimes of men, women and children, and that their construction dates back to great antiquity."

Le Plongeon says: "These buildings were neither constructed by the present race nor their ancestors."

Pedro Beltram **(12)** ("Arte del Idioma Maya") **(13)**: "In the Maya sculptures, particularly on the trunks of the mastodon heads that adorn the most ancient buildings, the name is written 'that which is necessary.' "

Le Plongeon: "Among the symbols sculptured on the mastodons' trunks that at a very remote period in Maya history embellished the facades of all sacred and public edifices, these signs are occasionally seen: [Figs. 1,2 and 3]. Taken collectively they read, *Chaac* ('Thunder')."

The great Maya edifices did not totter and fall from age and decay, nor was their ruin wrought by the hand of man. Their destruction was first due to volcanic workings and completed by water.

During the forging of the great central gas belt under Central America and Yucatan 11,500 years ago, huge cataclysmic waves were formed. These rolled in over the land. All during the time of the splitting and rending of

A VOLCANIC CATACLYSM
Such as completed the destruction of the Maya edifices in Yucatan, after the earthquakes had shaken them to their foundations. The Yucatan Mayas – the builders – were virtually wiped out, 9,500 B.C.

Page 242

Page 243

the rocks in forming the belt, "earthquakes shook the land like the leaves of a tree in a storm," the "land rose and rolled like ocean waves." The shocks and rolls from the quakes shook the Maya structures into ruins. The great waves of water following blotted out all life (including the white Mayas of Yucatan). Thus not only were the structures destroyed, but the builders as well.

On the opposite page I have made a sketch showing one of the waves overwhelming a city.

The work of these cataclysmic waves is to be seen today in the form of sand, gravel, and small boulders around and against the old ruins, and in some cases, where the buildings were completely shaken down, this specialized stratum covers them.

Some old Egyptian Papyri refer to these cataclysms, which are confirmed by the Greek philosophers, Plato **(14)** and Plutarch (Plutarch's Life of Solon) **(15)**.

After these cataclysms had passed over Central America and Yucatan, wrecking the structures and wiping out the whole population, the country for a long time was uninhabitable. As soon as the land became fit for man again, surrounding peoples drifted in and took possession of it. These were brown races speaking the Maya language. These brown races were not a part of the white Mayas. Although they spoke the Maya tongue, they were totally different, and without doubt came from a long way off. They were a new set of colonizers. This would account for there being no traditions found among them at the time the Spaniards conquered the country.

These newcomers were neither Nahuatls nor Aztecs. The Nahuatls came from the south and conquered them.

Page 244

The Aztecs also came from the south and in turn conquered the country.

The brown races of Central America and Yucatan of today are the descendants of these various peoples, a mixture of the three tribes, mostly Mongol.

The forefathers of the present people who call themselves Mayas were not the builders of the old Yucatan structures.

The principal structures at Chichen Itza are still standing, but in ruins. These were built during the Can dynasty and the PPeu dynasty. The structures of the PPeu dynasty are easily recognizable by their having in some prominent position the PPeu totem, which was an elephant, or, as shown on the structures, the head of an elephant.

Pedro Beltram ("Arte del Idioma Maya"): "In the Maya sculpture, particularly on the trunks of the mastodon heads that adorn *the most ancient buildings.*"

On all buildings erected during the Can dynasty their emblem, the feathered serpent, was many times carved upon its stones. This accounts for the numberless feathered serpents found on the buildings at Chichen Itza.

In battle and on state occasions the feathered serpent appeared on the royal banner. As an example, on page 245 is a drawing of Prince Coh, the youngest son of the last King Can, in battle, with the royal emblem surrounding and protecting him.

This is one of the murals in Prince Coh's funeral chamber, Memorial Hall, Chichen Itza. In this chamber the life of Prince Coh is shown in pictures from his boyhood days to the day of his death.

PRINCE COH IN BATTLE, SURROUNDED AND PROTECTED BY THE FEATHERED SERPENT (16)
From a mural in his burial chamber, Yucatan

Page 245

Page 246

Here in Yucatan, tens of thousands of years afterwards, we find a custom retained which was observed in Niven's lowest buried city, described by him as the life of a "shepherd."

Wherever the feathered serpent is seen carved or painted, it will always be found to be in some way connected with the royal family of Can. The Can Dynasty was the last reigning line of Maya monarchs of Mayax. The last of the dynasty was Queen Moo. She visited the Maya Nile colony in Egypt during the first century of its existence, 16,000 years ago, as related in the Troano Manuscript.

The present natives of Yucatan are not pure-blooded.

What remained of the Maya stock after the great cataclysm had destroyed the country were conquered by a Mongol race. The men were put to the sword and the women enslaved, and the forced marriages that followed introduced the Mongol blood in their veins. Thus when the land was again settled, after the cataclysm, it was by races that knew nothing of the builders of the vast structures which lay all about. This is verified by the fact that when Cortez invaded Yucatan, Bishop Landa, who accompanied him, asked the natives, "Who built the old ruins?" The answer he received was, "The Toltecs." *Toltec* is a Maya word meaning "builder." Therefore their answer was "the builders." But who the builders were they knew not, as Landa has stated in his writings. It will be interesting to note here that the word *Toltec* means not a race, but a builder.

In Mexico there is a very ancient Aztec tradition which says that "the first settlers in Mexico were a white race."

Page 247

The tradition continues, saying: "This white race was conquered by a race with darker skins, and the darker skinned race drove the white race from the land. The white people then took their ships and sailed to a far-off land in the East, towards the rising sun, and there settled."

A prophesy accompanies the tradition, which is: "At some future time this white race will return and claim and reconquer the land."

Rider Haggard **(17)** must have found this same tradition, for in his work, "Montezuma's Daughter," **(18)** he says:

"Quetzal, or more properly, Quetzalcoatl, was the divinity who is fabled to have taught the natives of Anahuac all the useful arts, including those of government and policy. He was white-skinned and light-haired. Finally he sailed from the shores of Anahuac for the fabulous country of Hapallan in a bark of serpent skins."

The Guatemalan tradition about the blond-white race, the first inhabitants of America, is without doubt the clearest of all, because in Guatemala was Quetzal's capital city. The Guatemalan tradition is as follows:

"When King Quetzalcoatl, with the very white race, was conquered by the invading darker race, he refused to surrender, saying that he could not live in captivity; he could not survive. He then, with as many of his people as his ships could carry, sailed to a far-off land in the direction of the rising sun. He reached, with his people, this far-off land, and there settled. They prospered and became a great people.

"During the great battle many escaped and fled into the forests and were never heard of again. The rest were taken prisoners and enslaved by the conquerors."

Page 248

The Quetzal today is the national bird of Guatemala.

The name Quetzal was given to it in memory of their last white king, Quetzalcoatl. This bird was selected because, like King Quetzal, it cannot be made to survive in captivity.

The wonderful old sacred book of the Quiches, the Popol Yuh, was written in Guatemala.

The Aztec tradition about the white race, like all Aztec traditions, is very much garbled and filled in with priestly myths and inventions. I will point out a few prominent inventions and additions. I say they are inventions and additions because they do not appear in any of the other, dozen at least, traditions. All, with this exception, agree with each other in all material points.

These Aztec changes have been the cause of leading some of our prominent archaeologists away from the straight and narrow path of truth and reason.

The Aztecs began to drift into the Mexican Valley about A. D. 1090, but it was not until about the year A. D. 1216 that they made an actual settlement in the valley.

The Aztecs originally formed a part of the Empire of Mayax and Kukul Khan, the feathered serpent, was their symbol for the Deity. It was also the symbol of the Quiches, who were their neighbors.

The exact date of Quetzal's reign is unknown, because he was driven out by the darker people, whom we know as Mayas. Evidences seem to show that he lived more than 34,000 years ago. Again, other evidences would seem to point him out as belonging to one of the eleven dynasties. Whichever way it is taken, it answers my purpose, as it

---

Page 249

shows Quetzal to have lived far back beyond 16,000 years ago.

One of the Aztec changes was made in their southern home, before they settled in the Mexican Valley. They abandoned a symbol used for the Deity and adopted the great white King Quetzel as their god. They then invented a son for him, which they called Tescat.

The said Tescat was then made to escape with his father, Quetzal. The next step was to invent a prophesy, so the prophesy was invented which ran: "Tescat's spirit will return in the body of a white man with many soldiers. He will conquer and retake the country, putting the men to the sword and enslaving the women." With this they proceeded to awe the people from the king down. Constant sacrifices were demanded to propitiate Tescat; human sacrifices commenced, then the priestly power was complete-priesthood was in absolute control.

The people lived in dread, for anyone might be the next one called upon to stretch upon the bloody stone.

At the time Cortez invaded Mexico, the Aztec human sacrifices were going on at the rate of from 30,000 to 40,000 a year, if we can believe Spanish writers.

This spark of savagery flew to all parts of the world - Egypt, India, Phoenicia, etc.

Our archaeologists have apparently found something Aztec dating 1100-1200 A. D. (the period during which Quetzal was made the god of the Aztecs), and have published the erroneous statement that Quetzal lived only a few hundreds of years ago.

The name Quetzal is very much intertwined with the very ancient history of Mexico and Central America. It

Page 250

even extends to our southwestern states, Arizona and New Mexico, for there the Pueblo Indians used in their religious rites and ceremonies the feathered or bearded serpent and called it Quetzalcoatl.

Joining and comparing the various traditions, it would appear that far back there was a white race dominating Mexico and Central America; that they formed a kingdom and the name of their last king was Quetzal. Why Quetzalcoatl was used in their religious ceremonies and rites, the Pueblo Indians of today apparently cannot tell. Each one has a different tale. The true import has been lost, it is now solely traditional.

The Empire of Mayax was made up of at least seven distinct peoples, all coming from the Motherland and apparently all speaking the Maya tongue. All the kings and queens of Mayax during the twelve dynasties were of the white race.

The last white race was the forerunner of the Latins.

The forefathers of the white Polynesians of today, the forefathers of the white Mayas of Yucatan and the forefathers of all our white races were one and the same.

OWL VASE FROM THE "TREASURES OF PRIAM"
The inscription reads: *From the King Chronos of Atlantis*
After Schliemann **(19)**

A HAWK-HEADED SPHINX
A relic from Atlantis discovered by Schliemann **(20)** among the "Treasures of Priam." Ancient Troy.

Page 251

Chapter 12: Yucatan's Place Among the Ancient Civilizations Notes

(1) Le Plongeon, Augustus is discussed in the Persons of Interest Appendix beginning on page A1—22.

(2) Plutarch is discussed in the Persons of Interest Appendix beginning on page A1—27.

(3) Solon is discussed in the Persons of Interest Appendix beginning on page A1—46.

(4) Sanchez de Aguilar, Pedro (1555-1640) was born in the Yucatan, rose to become a Bishop of Yucatan and later was appointed a Judge of the Inquisition in Lima.

(5) William Niven is discussed in the Persons of Interest Appendix beginning on page A1—33.

(6) Bishop Landa [De Landa Calderon, Diego (1524-1579)] was a Bishop of Yucatan and leaves a mixed legacy with regards to the Yucatan. On one hand he destroyed most of the printed works that fell under his control, but due to his efforts to catalog the Mayan alphabet, the meaning was finally deciphered. Augustus Le Plongeon, "Queen Moo and the Egyptian Sphinx" (1896) Appendix 1 Note i contains a biography of Diego de Landa

(7) *Relacion de las Cosas*, a book that catalogues the Maya language, religion, culture and writing system was written about 1566, by Bishop Diego De Landa Calderon.

(8) Lopez de Cogolludo, Diego is discussed in the Persons of Interest Appendix beginning on page A1—25.

(9) *Historia de Yucathan* is discussed in the Written Works Appendix beginning on page A2—15.

(10) de Lizana, Bernardo is discussed in the Persons of Interest Appendix beginning on page A1—9.

(11) *Historia de Nuestra Senora de Ytzamal* is discussed in the Written Works Appendix beginning on page A2—15.

(12) Beltran de Santa Rosa Maria, Pedro was a friar that wrote a lexicon of Mayan words. No other information has been discovered.

(13) *Arte del Idioma Maya*, (English, *Art of the Mayan Language*) written in 1745.

(14) Plato is discussed in the Persons of Interest Appendix beginning on page A1—41.

(15) *Plutarch's Life of Solon* is discussed in the Written Works Appendix beginning on page A2—19.

(16) Similar to drawing on page 136 of "*Queen Moo & The Egyptian Sphinx*"; Le Plongeon, Augustus; 1896; Similar to drawing on page 81 of "*Sacred Mysteries Among the Mayas and the Quiches*"; Le Plongeon, Augustus; 1886.

(17) Haggard, Sir Henry Rider is discussed in the Persons of Interest Appendix beginning on page A1—15.

(18) *Montezuma's Daughter* is discussed in the Written Works Appendix beginning on page A2—21.

(19) Schliemann, Paul is discussed in the Persons of Interest Appendix beginning on page A1—45.

(20) Schliemann, Heinrich is discussed in the Persons of Interest Appendix beginning on page A1—45.

13
The Geological History of Mu

Page 252

AFTER having read thus far, it will be of interest to learn the geological history of Mu and to know the scientific cause of her destruction.

I have already shown how the subterranean foundation of this vast continent was undermined by the volcanic gases. (1) Granite, the primary rock in the formation of the earth's crust, appears to have been honeycombed with huge chambers and cavities and these were filled with highly explosive volcanic gases. When these chambers were emptied of their gases the supporting roofs caved in and the submersion of the land above logically followed.

My investigations have proved that the calamity that overtook this early civilization was due to the emptying of a series of isolated upper gas chambers that were upholding the land and which were probably connected with each other by cracks and fissures.

In order to make clear to the reader what I mean when referring to upper, middle and lower chambers and isolated chambers, I have made a sketch of groups of Archaean gas chambers, together with an explanation. I have inten-

Fig. A. CONDITIONS OF THE EARTH BEFORE LAND APPEARED

FIG. B. THE PROBABLE CONDITION UNDERLYING MU BEFORE HER SUBMERSION tionally drawn the chambers higher than was actually the case in order to emphasize them.

SKETCH OF ARCHAEAN GAS CHAMBERS

Fig. A. I here give the upper and part of the second series, each division showing groups of chambers at varying depths from the earth's surface. This sketch depicts a somewhat similar condition to that which existed below the surface of Mu before that ill-fated continent vanished forever beneath the waters of the Pacific. The upper series is given as being fifteen miles in depth, the middle series will be from fifteen to thirty miles and the lower series from thirty miles to the earth's molten center.

The upper series is arranged in three divisions (O, X and W). Division O runs from the earth's surface down to a depth of five miles. All chambers in this division are represented as being of the isolated variety. By "isolated" I mean that they have no connections with the chambers below, or with the earth's center, from which they might obtain additional gases that would overcompress and blow them out. As they stand, no new gases can be driven into them, and, unless additional gases are forced into them, they will stand as they are through all eternity.

Division X runs from five to ten miles below the earth's surface. These are live chambers, constantly receiving fresh gases from Division W, which passes from chamber to chamber through cracks and fissures.

To drive additional gases into the isolated chambers of Division O, volcanic workings must first open cracks and fissures from Chambers X to O^1 and then from O^1 to O^2. Gases coming from the chambers of Division W, which

are in communication with the earth's center, must first flow into Chambers X and overcompress them. This would necessitate the raising of the roofs of these chambers to make room for the new gases.

In raising the roofs, the rocks forming them would be split and fractured, forming passageways for gases from Chambers X into Chambers O^1 In time Group O^1 would become overcompressed. This would necessitate the raising of their roofs. Then the roofs of Chambers O^2 would have to be raised to accommodate the ever increasing pressure from new gases. Their roofs would go up, split and be punctured by the gases, which in the form of volcanoes would empty the chambers down to a point where the bolstering gases could no longer uphold the roof. What would be the result? Their roofs would crash down to their floors, the remaining gases would assume the form of huge flames and envelop the land as it went down. The surrounding waters would flow into the enormous hole and the land would be submerged.

Gas belts run at irregular depths below the earth's surface. From various observations of certain phenomena covering a period of over fifty years, I have come to the conclusion that, generally, the great gas belts have been forged along the upper half of the middle series and the lower parts of the upper series. Gas belts do not run at regular distances below the earth's surface, as I have indicated, but vary considerably. A section may run through Division W. The next section may be through Division X and then back again into Section W. In short stretches they come to within a mile or two of the earth's surface. This happens most often when they are approach-

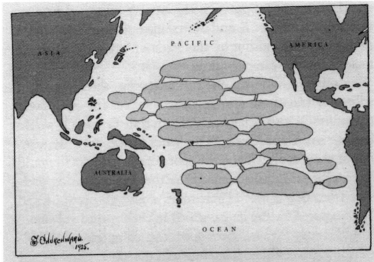

FIG. C. PROBABLE POSITION OF GAS CHAMBERS UNDERLYING MU BEFORE HER SUBMERSION

FIG. D. PRESENT GAS BELTS ACROSS AND AROUND THE PACIFIC OCEAN
1. Great central gas belt. 2. South Pacific cross belts. 3. Japanese-Ladrone belt. 4. Great Pacific circuit belt.

Page 257

ing their safety valves, the volcanoes (2), as may be noted in Hawaii, Ecuador, Central America, and several other locations. It is safe to say that no belt runs below twenty miles from the earth's surface, usually much less. My observations lead me to believe that their average depth is from fifteen to eighteen miles below the earth's surface, except when they are approaching their volcanoes.

Fig. B. This shows the probable condition that underlay Mu before her submersion. A series of isolated chambers lay very near the surface of Mu and their bolstering gases were upholding her. The next line of chambers were many miles below.

Fig. C. shows a series of chambers, O^2 corresponding with O^2 in Cuts A and B. These are connected with each other by fissures and passageways.

Fig. D. shows the principal gas belts that now run under and around the Pacific Ocean.

During the forging of the belts, Chambers I0, Fig. B, became overcompressed, causing cracks and fissures in the rocks above. Then the gases entered Chambers O^1 where the same situation developed, and from there they escaped into Chambers O^2. When this happened, the roofs of Chambers O^2 were punctured, the gases escaped, the land crashed down to the floors of the chambers, the waters of the Pacific flowed in over and Mu was no more.

It is my belief that the supporting chambers which upheld Mu were *very near* to the surface of the land. I base this opinion on the depths of the Pacific Ocean, the Troano Manuscript, the Codex Cortesianus and the Lhasa Record. None of these records speaks of the land having been raised to any great height before sinking into the Pacific.

Page 258

They do say, however, that "the land was rended and torn to pieces;" "quivering like the leaves of a tree in a storm;" "rising and falling like the waves of the ocean," and "during the night went down." All of which would indicate that no great elevation of land took place, which would have been the case had the sustaining chambers been deep down. From the fact that the records say that Mu was "twice upheaved," "twice kicked from her foundations," it may be taken for granted that another or second series of isolated chambers lay below those supporting Mu, as shown in O^1 and O^2. The first upheaval was when the gases entered O^1 from IO and the second was when O^1 broke into O^2.

That the chambers sustaining Mu were near the surface and not deep down is proven by the fact that had they been deep down, the land would have been sufficiently thick to form retaining angles to uphold it after it had been raised like our mountain ranges.

Lands and continents have thus been submerged since the beginning of time. We have instances of this through the pre-Cambrian Time, the Paleozoic Time, the Mesozoic and Cenozoic Times, through the Pleistocene Period, and down, in fact, to the very edge of history. This elimination of gas chambers and the resultant submersion of lands went on until a sufficient thickness of the primary rock was effected to permit of the rocks forming retaining angles when they were lifted, thus opening huge tunnels between continuous chambers and forming belts. When these gas belts were formed and completed it practically put an end to this destructive submersion of land.

It is geologically certain that the gas chambers which

Page 259

upheld Mu were eliminated during the forging of the Pacific division of the great central gas belt and the Pacific cross belts with their many ramifications. From the presence of certain geological phenomena I have thus come to the conclusion that it was a *series* of chambers that underlay and upheld Mu, and not one huge chamber, as was the case with Atlantis. I base this belief on the following evidence:

1. The difference in the depths of the Pacific Ocean between the various groups of islands shows that with each varying depth there was a different chamber, or one chamber under another that was eliminated. Had there been only one chamber the bottom of the Pacific Ocean would be comparatively level.

2. We find that certain islands were once parts of the continent. Had there been only one chamber these could not have remained above water.

3. These islands layover the passageways *between* the chambers and not over the chambers themselves. As there was no chamber beneath them they did not go down.

4. That the chambers were connected is shown by the islands, revealing volcanic workings. The gases worked under them from chamber to chamber. This naturally changed their contour and they became mountainous and jagged.

My remarks on this subject are based upon careful investigations and observations on volcanic disturbances reported in the Pacific during the last fifty years. The islands and their characteristics have also been taken into consideration. There appear to be two main belts with many cross belts and ramifications. It is not only possible

---

Page 260

but probable that other ramifications exist which I have not shown. In fact, I believe there are, but I have never been able to define them.

But how, will probably be asked, does this affect the story of Mu? If the reader will go back he will recall that, in a previous chapter describing the destruction of Mu, it was shown how these treacherous gas belts were the direct cause of the submersion which sent the Motherland of Man down in an abyss of scorching flames and rushing waters. There is no question in my mind but that the land of Mu was upheld by a series of upper isolated gas chambers, marked in the diagrams O^2. These gas chambers were the final assassins of Mu.

The exact location, area and height of each chamber is unknown. On surmise, based upon the positions of the islands, I have given the location of several of these chambers. I do not presume to say that they are absolutely correct in all minute details, but they do show the honeycombed condition of the rocks directly under Mu and the shallow depths of many parts of the Pacific Ocean show that they were near the surface.

As a geological proposition, my next step will be to note a few of the many large extinct volcanoes that are to be found among the Polynesian Islands. Up to the present time, nowhere upon the face of the earth are to be found evidences of volcanic outbursts equal to those found in Polynesia. These tremendous gaping mouths bear evidence of the compressed forces deep down within the earth's core that finally became unleashed and burst forth with a fury of destruction unequaled in the history of the world.

Kilauea is an extinct volcano on one of the Hawaiian Islands, the crater of which measures *three miles in diameter.* Imagine a mouth of this size taxed to the fullest capacity suddenly vomiting forth its destructive fire, smoke and lava! A flood of fire, smoke and lava three miles in diameter! To what height did it ascend? Without doubt, *thousands of feet,* when we take into consideration the tremendous motive power behind it.

Awe-inspiring as Kilauea was, nevertheless there were undoubtedly others still larger. This appears to be a certainty when the following facts are considered: The size of the chamber that was being emptied of gases, the immeasurable quantities of gases in the chamber, the force exerted by the overcompressed gases forming the belt, and the weight of the land above that rested on them and which finally forced them through the craters and released the demons of destruction that sprang at the throat of Mu and throttled her.

Taking these facts into consideration, there is little cause for astonishment at the size of these extinct craters of Polynesia. The only astonishment is that there are any craters at all. With such forces working underneath the land, the wonder is that the earth was not hurled into the sky by one mighty blast and dissolved like mist instead of being punctured and checker-boarded with volcanoes.

When the northern main division of the great central gas belt was completed through the Pacific, a safety valve was formed to take care of future accumulations of the belt in this section. A new crater was pierced through the center of Kilauea. This new crater is only *300 yards in diameter* and is called Halemaumau. While Halemaumau

is only one-eighteenth of the diameter of Kilauea, it nevertheless ranks among the largest craters of today and gives an idea, by comparison, of the enormity of its predecessor.

The northern main Pacific division of the great central gas belt runs directly under the Hawaiian Islands. At the Hawaiian Islands it is nearer to the surface than at any other point along its whole course, which encircles the central part of the earth.

The Niuafou Crater is another famous crater that is of interest to the archaeologist. Niuafou is a small island to the northeast of the Fiji Islands, nearly midway between Fiji and Samoa. The Niuafou extinct crater is *two miles in diameter.* Since the time it helped in the work of submerging the land of Mu it has filled up with water and now forms a lake.

The foregoing are only conspicuous examples of the many immense extinct volcanoes that are to be found among the Polynesian Islands. We doubt if anything in the nature of volcanic disturbances has ever before or since in the earth's history happened that would compare in horror to the appalling cataclysm that befell the race of man when these volcanic workings blew off the lid of the earth and destroyed the land of Mu some twelve or thirteen thousands of years ago.

Geology tells us that the western shores of North America were once *raised.* Geology has ever been guilty of putting the cart before the horse and this is only one more instance. Instead of the western shores of North America having been raised and the shore line thus extended, it was, as a matter of fact, *the lowering of the level of the Pacific Ocean that extended the shore lines.*

Page 263

The land of Mu was an immense continent covering nearly one-half of the Pacific Ocean. In some places the ocean went down thousands of feet. In order to fill up this vast hole, which was from 5,000 to 6,000 miles long and at least 2,000 or 3,000 miles broad, to the present depths of the ocean, the surrounding waters had to be drawn upon. To have maintained the original level of the Pacific Ocean after Mu went down, twice as much water would have been required as was then contained in the whole of the ocean. This could not be possible except by drawing the waters from surrounding areas and shores, and when this was done there was still not enough water to bring the ocean up to its original level. Mu was not the only land that went down into the Pacific Ocean. An immense northern area was also submerged, and also a smaller area to the west.

It may be asked: How did it happen that the waters of the Atlantic Ocean did not flow around Cape Horn into the Pacific Ocean and thus level off the waters again without drawing them away from surrounding shores? In answer to this I will say that the Atlantic Ocean had its own troubles to attend to during this period of the earth's history, as the following list of submerged lands will show:

The land of Mu in the Pacific Ocean, which was several thousands of miles long and thousands of miles wide.

The Bering land bridge in the north Pacific Ocean, connecting America with Asia. This bridge was not the narrow strip of land assigned to it by geology. Its southern shore line ran from Alaska to Kamchatka by way of the

Page 264

Aleutian Islands. Its northern shore I am unable to trace, but it was in the Arctic Ocean.

This submerged land has furnished scientists with a scapegoat to account for all the unaccountable things in America. Whenever anything has come up that could not be understood by the scientists, and that is quite frequent, it was always agreeably settled among themselves that it undoubtedly came to America from Asia by way of the Bering land bridge. Why Asia should have been selected to account for what is unaccountable I cannot imagine except that, as nothing is known about eastern Asia, there was no fear of contradiction.

Then there are the Pacific minor submersions. A stretch of land running down from California to the northwest corner of Colombia went down. This, apparently, was a narrow strip. Land was also submerged where the Malay Archipelago now stands, but the extent of this land is not known.

Atlantis was situated in the center of the Atlantic Ocean. It was an immense continental island, and at the time of its submersion it was the center of the earth's civilization.

Then there was the overland route to Europe, in the north Atlantic Ocean. This was land between America and Greenland, and Greenland and Norway, together with a great, triangular piece whose western line ran from Iceland to Cape Finisterre in the northwest corner of France.

A small area of land also went down off the coasts of Central America, which before submersion was a part of the mainland.

All of these submersions were caused by the volcanic

workings during the forging of the gas belts. The great central belt submerged Mu and Atlantis. The Pacific circuit belt submerged the Bering land bridge. The Appalachian-Iceland-Scandinavian belt submerged the overland route to Europe.

By the lowering of the levels of the ocean, many lands emerged from the water, and the shore lines of remaining lands were extended.

Apparently all of these great areas of land were thickly peopled, so that the loss of life was appalling. Without doubt hundreds of millions perished miserably. Mu, alone, accounted for 64,000,000.

This geological cycle is a complete confirmation of all the data previously furnished about the land of Mu. It provides the connection that might be termed a missing link. Geologically, it proves beyond question the existence of a great prehistoric continent of land in the Pacific Ocean.

Much of the present elevation of the islands of the Pacific Ocean is due to the lowering of the ocean's level.

I have made a somewhat rough calculation as to how much the earth's diameter has been reduced by the blowing out of gas chambers and the compacting of the rocks, and find that it totals between 17 and 21 miles.

Chapter 13: The Geological History of Mu Notes

(1) A theory proposed in by Dr. Thomas Gold in 1992 in an article entitled "The deep, hot biosphere", in the 'Proceedings of the National Academy of Sciences" discusses theories about gas belts/pockets. In 1999, Dr Gold published a book "The Deep Hot Biosphere" on the same subject.

(2) Many articles concerning volcanoes and earthquakes were collected by James Churchward and placed in his scrapbook.

14
The Origin of Savagery

Page 266

IN the chapter on the destruction of Mu I showed how the first savagery originated upon earth. Man was created a civilized being, and the destruction of the Motherland affected only those who survived the catastrophe and made their homes on the barren islands which were left out of the water after the proud cities and buildings had vanished forever.

A nation loses the place which it once held in the worlds' history when money becomes more precious to the souls of its people than honesty and honor. A universal, widespread greed of gain is the forewarning of some great upheaval and disaster. Civilizations have been born and completed and then forgotten again and again. There is nothing new under the sun. What is, has been. All that we learn and discover has existed before; our inventions and discoveries are but re-inventions, re-discoveries.

The orthodox theory among scientists of today is that man came up from a brute beast to a savage, and from savagery traveled on by degrees until he reached civilization.

Page 267

I do not stand alone when I say that savagery came out of civilization, not civilization out of savagery. It is only those who know nothing of savages who maintain that civilization emerged from savagery.

Baron Von Humboldt **(1)**, in speaking of the wretched groups of Indians he met along the Amazon and Orinoco Rivers, naively remarks:

"They are not the crude material of humanity; nor from this state have we arisen. These hapless beings are the last degraded remnants of some dying race which has fallen to this state. Man in a state of nature is a doomed being, doomed to death."

A savage, left to himself, does *not rise*. He has fallen to where he is and is still going down. It is only when he is brought into contact with civilization that an upward change in him becomes possible. The savage when brought into contact with civilization does one of two things: he either absorbs civilization and rises, or he absorbs only the vices of civilization, adds them to his own savage vices, becomes more brute-like and falls still lower. Such are doomed to early extinction.

There have been two causes that have evolved savagery among various peoples, and both were due to geological phenomena.

At the end of the geological Tertiary Era, the earth's crust had been cleared of old Archaean gas chambers to a sufficient depth for the gases to form belts and to raise mountains. The foregoing is explained in my geological work. Before this time there were no mountains or even high hills. The habitable earth consisted of immense fertile plains thickly populated. In forming the gas belts,

Page 268

the land above was lifted into mountain ranges. A belt passing under a thickly populated plain in lifting the land fractured it and broke it up, killing most of the people. A few, however, survived among the broken-up mountains. Those which were left on the plains, on the land which had not been raised, suffered a worse fate, for all were destroyed by great cataclysmic waves which rolled in over the plains from the oceans. This not only destroyed all life, but for a time the productiveness of the land as well.

These survivors could not return to the plains, for there all was desolation. There was nothing to eat, and so great became their sufferings that they ate one another, and thus, through one of the two geological changes-mountain raising-cannibalism was born into the world. In some instances when the mountains went up, large flat areas were carried up with them, and on this land lived the men and women who had once known all of the luxuries of a great civilization. In time, they lost all knowledge of the higher arts and sciences. They became savages and lived as such.

The most conspicuous instance of this sort was the great Uighur Empire (2) of central Asia. The eastern half was destroyed by the waters of the biblical "Flood" and all thereon perished. Afterwards the western half went up, forming the Himalaya and other central Asiatic mountains. Among these mountains were many plateaus, where the people survived and finally worked their way back into various flat countries. Those of the Uighurs who survived were the forefathers of the Aryan races. Both in India and China there are traditions relating to the raising of these mountains, the great loss of life that ensued and the

Page 269

survival of many who lived in the mountains following the great upheaval.

Among the Zulus of South Africa there are traditions that their forefathers were a company who survived during the raising of the mountains in the north.

In South America the whole city of Tiahuanaco went up with the great plateau that now exists between the two ranges of the Andes. This is told by the inscription on the great door that is so well known to archaeologists, on the shores of Lake Titicaca.

In most mountainous countries there are traditions concerning the raising of the mountains. The raising of mountains is referred to in the Bible, (3) in one of the psalms of David, called the Song of Moses (Psalms xc: 2).

Scientists of today, in judging the character and advancement of a civilization, lay great stress on flint arrow and spear heads. Thus they say that, because the arrow and spear heads of Neolithic Times were of a higher type of manufacture than these same articles during Paleolithic Times, the Neolithic men were more civilized than the Paleolithic men.

I do not say that our scientists are wrong: but this evidence does not appeal to me as showing the state of a civilization, except in the reverse way, namely: the Paleolithic men were more civilized than the Neolithic men, and there are many opposing *facts* arrayed against the scientists' *theory*.

It is quite within the realms of reason to believe also that, at the time the flint arrow and spear heads were being fashioned, conditions were somewhat similar to those of today in this respect, that all individuals were not equally expert in manufacture. A trained mechanic turns out a perfect article, a novice, an inferior and crudely formed one. The men of the Paleolithic times were novices, but were they less civilized? Personally I think not. These novices were the remnants of highly civilized people, suddenly thrown on their beam-ends by one of the many convulsions of the earth during what is called Paleolithic Times.

The assertion that the more crude and primitive a stone arrow or spear head is, the more highly civilized were the people who made them, may seem illogical on its face; but think-carry your mind back to ancient times, and see how man repeatedly was robbed of everything except his bare hands, and thrown entirely on nature's resources. Tools and everything else were gone; absolutely nothing was left except their brains and their fingers. Without the slightest knowledge of mechanics, these remnants had to commence making tools out of nothing but the stones at their feet. Could anything but the crudest forms be fashioned by them without experience and without knowledge? I think not. To me, these crude arrow and spear heads do not show savagery or a low civilization. They show a high civilization passing down into savagery. Thus the scientist's Paleolithic men were of a higher civilization than the Neolithic men who followed them, and as the manufacture improved these human beings went down.

AFTER THE SUBMERSION OF MU

Page 271

Chapter 14: The Origin of Savagery Notes

(1) Baron Von Humboldt (1769-1859) was described by Charles Darwin as "the greatest scientific traveler who ever lived." His formal training was in geology and his travels experiments and knowledge transformed western science in the 19th century.

(2) Uighur Empire, see numbers 13 & 16 in Chapter 5 Notes.

(3) The Bible is discussed in the Written Works Appendix beginning on page A2—4.

15
Ancient Religious Conceptions

Page 272

MAX MULLER (1) says: "Religion is a mental faculty which, independent of, nay, in spite of sense and reason, enables man to apprehend the Infinite under different names and under different disguises. Without that faculty no religion, not even the lowest worship of idols and fetishes, would be possible; and yet if we will but listen attentively we can hear in all religions a groaning of the spirit, a struggle to conceive the inconceivable, to utter the unutterable, a longing after the Infinite, a love of God.

"The intention of religion, wherever found or wherever we meet it, is always holy. However imperfect, however childish a religion may be, it always places the human soul in the presence of God; and however imperfect, however childish the conception of God may be, it always expresses the highest ideal of perfection which the human soul, for the time being, can reach and grasp.

"Every mythology appears as the result of the earliest efforts of the human mind to explain the mysteries of the Universe: the sky-the sun-the planets; the winds and the clouds, the summer and winter, the dawn and dark-

Page 273

ness, and the varied elemental phenomena which are of supernatural significance to the simple fancies of uncultured people."

A myth starts from a conception, an idea. The mind invents facts to embody and present it. Myths are the expression of the way primitive man represented things to himself under the influence of naturalism.

Muller in "Early Religions" (2) says:

"In one sense every religion has been a true religion at the start; they were the only religions that were possible at the time, which were compatible with the language, the thoughts, and the sentiments of each generation, which were appropriate to the age of the world. We ought therefore to put the most charitable interpretation on the apparent absurdities, the follies and the errors of ancient religions. As soon as we know anything of the thoughts and feelings of man, we find him in possession of a religion, a religion of faith or worship, of morality or ecstatic vision, a religion of fear and hope, or surmise, a reverence of the so-called gods.

"In order to approach the religion of primitive peoples we must, so to speak, get at its heart, and feel its life currents. We must place ourselves in sympathy with these ancient peoples, listen to their hymns and prayers, and witness their rites and ceremonies; we must endeavor to know their religious ideals. When Thales declared all things were full of gods, and when Buddha (3) denied that there were any other gods except the Supreme Being, both were stating their religious convictions.

"The external aspect of a religion as presented to strangers is not one often to be trusted. In the earliest and

---

Page 274

purest days of Christianity, if we were to believe the most enlightened of the heathen writers, the Christian religion consisted of the worship of animals. This idea possibly arose from the fact that the earliest pictures of Mary nursing Christ (4) show the cow's horns of the Egyptian goddess Sati on her head, and sometimes the horns of Hathor."

From the Book of the Dead: *Hathor* in Egyptian means "the house of horns." Hathor is frequently represented with the attributes of Isis. Hathor symbolizes and personifies not only all that is beautiful, but also all that is true. Isis was the personification of the female or creative attribute of the Deity.

Sati had the same attributes as Hathor. She wears the crown of Upper Egypt with cow's horns, and symbolizes motherhood.

Muller, in "Ancestral Worship," (5) says: "Ancestral worship sprang out of the universal faith of primitive peoples in the persistence of human responsibility after death. This form of worship seems to have been almost universal among mankind during a certain stage of development. Traces of it are found in all parts of the earth. The religious ideas of the Hebrews present traces of ancestral worship. The indication is strong that the special God of the Hebrew patriarch, the family God of Abraham, with whom he conversed and held personal relations, represented an ancestral divinity."

From the reading of a number of ancient writings I have come to the conclusion that ancestral worship originated through the destruction of Mu. Ancestral worship or the reverence shown to forefathers appears very prominently in the Egyptian sacred rites and ceremonies, where

Page 275

their forefathers of the land of Mu furnish the principal theme.

It is also reflected in the inscriptions on some of the Maya monuments; also in the Greek alphabet.

Muller, in "Origin of Religious Laws," (6) says: "The belief that the religious law-giver enjoyed some closer intimacy with the Deity than ordinary mortals pervades the ancient traditions of many nations. According to a well known passage in Diodorus Siculus, the Egyptians believed their laws to have been communicated to Mnevis by Hermes. The Cretans held that Minos received the laws from Zeus. The Lacedaemonians held that Lykurgus received his laws from Appolon. The Aryans believed that Zathraustes received them from the Good Spirit. According to Gatel, Zamolscis received his laws from the goddess Hestia, and according to the Jews, Moses received his laws from the God Iao.**32**"

"There was a primitive Aryan religion, a primitive Semitic religion, and a primitive Turanian religion, before each of these primeval races was broken up and became separate in language, worship and national sentiment. The highest God received the same name in the ancient mythology of India, Greece, Italy and Germany, and had retained that name whether worshipped in the Himalayan mountains, or among the oaks of Dodona, on the Capital or in the forests of Germany. He shows that his name was Dyaus in Sanskrit, Zeus in Greek, Jovis in Latin and Tiu in German.

"They bring before us with all the vividness of an event

32. Unquestionably the Seven Sacred *Inspired* Writings of the Moth-land are the foundation of this universal belief

---

Page 276

which we witnessed ourselves but yesterday, the ancestors of the whole Aryan race, thousands of years it may be before Homer and the Veda, worshipping an unseen being under the same name, the best, the most exalted name they could find in their vocabulary - under the name Light and Sky. Let us not turn away and say that this after all was nature worship and idolatry. No, it was not meant for that, although it may have been degenerated into that in later times.

"Dyaus did not mean the blue sky, nor was it the sky personified; it was meant for something else. We have in the Veda the invocation Dyaus Pitar, the Greek Zeus Pater and the Latin Jupiter, and that means in all these languages what it meant before these languages were torn asunder. It means 'Heaven Father,' or 'Heavenly Father.'"

Owen, (7) writing on the ancient religion of China, says:

"The oldest classics in China, going back to the time of Abraham, show a wonderful knowledge of God. There are passages in these classics about God worthy to stand side by side with kindred passages in the Bible. God was omnipotent, omniscient, and omnipresent; the moral governor of the world and the impartial judge of men."

Man's first religion was a simple, pure worship of the Deity. The extravagances which later crept into and disfigured the records of man's first religion were the results of that inevitable degradation which priesthood always inflicts upon great ideas committed to its charge. The original religion became discordant in many particulars, and sorely overlaid by corruptions, inventions and misconceptions.

Page 277

Manetho, **(8)** the Egyptian historian, tells us that "animal worship was introduced into Egypt in the reign of the second king of the Eleventh Dynasty."

In all my Egyptian research work I have been unable to find any traces of animal worship during the early dynasties, and it is rarely ever referred to between the age of Kufu and the reign of Rameses II. What is shown, however, is that quite early the Egyptians apparently began to worship the symbols instead of what they represented, which was the first step that led to animal worship.

Manetho says: "It was not until the Eighteenth Dynasty that animal forms of gods were depicted in the memorial chambers of the departed. Under Thotmes III these figures are constantly met with, having the head of the symbolic animal that was embalmed. After the reign of Rameses, the worship of animals grew and expanded greatly."

Here is an example of an unscrupulous priesthood, craving for power and control of wealth, degrading the pure, simple, beautiful Osirian religion, as taught by Thoth **(9)** at Sais, to accomplish their ends.

From ancient records it would appear that, about 2000 B. C., religions all over the world became degraded, dropping in many places to fiendish human sacrifices. Only Moses stood up against it and kept his people in the true road. They have been called "God's favored people." They were favored when they were selected to retain and carry on the worship of the Deity; they were called upon and were not found wanting.

The creation of the world and man has ever held a prominent place in the mind of man; for as soon as we

Page 278

know anything about the thoughts of man we find he has a conception about Creation.

It matters not whether it is the conception of the prehistoric sages, the more modern philosopher, or the present-day cannibalistic savages-all conceptions of the Creation are substantially the same. They may vary a little in phraseology, and do; but the main points are identically the same, showing that they all have a common origin.

This subject, the Creation, permeates the writings and traditions of prehistoric and ancient peoples. These traditions have been handed down to us and have been accepted by us, because science and geology prove them to be correct.

All of the prehistoric writings are written in symbolic phrases, and symbols are used in place of the names of the actual objects. Knowing the import of these symbols, however, makes reading of them very easy, so that we arrive at their true meanings and they become perfectly intelligible and understandable.

Throughout all ancient traditions, even down to the time of Moses, we see "*water* above the firmament and *waters* below," a distinction being thus made by pluralizing. Water in all these cases refers to the ether which fills space beyond atmosphere.

There can be no question about it; all traditions of the Creation, wherever found, came of a common origin. It matters not whether it is our biblical traditions, the traditions of the Hindus, Chaldeans, Egyptians, Mayas, Polynesians or others; their original source was the same and dates back to very early man, tens of thousands of years ago, and maybe even more.

Page 279

A dissection of all of the traditions brings some astonishing facts before the eyes of the reader. Probably the most astounding of all is the fact that the Polynesians, who have been shut in from the rest of the world for over 12,000 years, should have among themselves traditions of the Creation identically like the biblical account, such as the names of the first man and woman; and that the first woman was made out of man's bones; that man was a special creation of God. The Marquesans and other Polynesians could not possibly have got these traditions from the outside world. The traditions of the Polynesians start from 12,000 years back, and how much more no one can surmise. The biblical tradition started with Moses some three thousand years ago, which proves that it was handed down to Moses in some form. The Naacal and Egyptian show us in what form it was handed down and from whom.

Plato (10) amusingly recounts a legend telling how the human race became divided into man and woman.

Human beings, according to Plato's story, were originally created with the man and woman combined in one body. Each body had four arms and four legs. The bodies were round, and they rolled over and over, using the arms and legs to move them. By and by they began to treat the gods badly. They stopped their sacrifices and even threatened to roll up Mount Olympus to attack and overthrow the gods.

One god said, "Let us kill them all. They are dangerous."

Another said, "No, I have a better idea. We will cut them in half. Then they will only have two arms and two legs; they won't be round. They won't be able to roll.

Page 280

Being multiplied by two, they will offer twice as many sacrifices, and what is the most important, each half will be so busy looking for the other half that they will not have time to bother us."

The second god was the wise one. His theory turned out well. Each human half, male or female, has been so busy looking for the other half that it has neglected other things.

From the most remote times, the Serpent has been held by every people in the greatest veneration, as the embodiment of divine wisdom.

In my research work I have invariably found that all myths have a foundation, and that the foundation is some legend or tradition. The myths, inventions, legends and traditions about the Serpent are exceedingly numerous. The fact that it is conceded by all that the Serpent was held in great veneration by the ancients at once shows that there is some legend, or some foundation for it.

Let us now see the result of a little research. Eusebius (11) tells us that the Egyptians called the Creator Kneph, who was symbolized by a serpent. Here at once we see why the Serpent was held in such high veneration by the ancients-the Serpent was their symbol for the Creator.

The Mayas in their sculptures represented the Creator of all things as being protected within the coils of a serpent.

Much is to be learnt from the Hindu on the subject.

Manava Dharma Sastra (12), a Hindu book, refers to the Serpent as the Creator.

In Aytareya Bhramana, (13) a Hindu book, we find: "Sarpa Rajni, the Queen of the Serpents, the mother of all that

Page 281

moves." And again: "Caisha, the Seven-headed Serpent, the Creator."

The Mayas of America symbolized the Creator with *Ah-ac-chapat* **(14)**, the Seven-Headed Serpent.

In Popol Vuh, **(15)** the Quiche sacred book, we have: "The Creator, the Maker, the Dominator, the Serpent covered with feathers."

After many years of research, including an examination of what has been written about the Serpent by modern writers, the perusal of many ancient writings and inscriptions, considering legends, traditions and myths, and noting where and how the ancient carvings of the Serpent have been placed and used, the following are my deductions:

1. Much of what has been written in old works about the Serpent consists of myths growing out of legends and traditions. Much of what has been written by our present-day scientists and authors is worse than mythical, because there is not a particle of foundation for it. It is pure speculation, fiction and invention.

2. The Serpent adorned, as with feathers, wings or a plurality of heads, is a symbol only of the Creator and Creation;

3. The Serpent unadorned was the symbol of the waters.

4. The circular Serpent was one of the symbols used for the Universe.

Now let us see what grounds there are for my various deductions:

1. *The Serpent Adorned.*-This has been shown to be

Page 282

the symbol of the Creator among the Mayas, Hindus and Egyptians.

2. *The Serpent Unadorned* is the ancient symbol for the waters. From the Maya we find that it was selected because the movements of its body were a duplication of the ocean's roll. It originated in the Motherland, and from there was carried to Burma, India and Babylonia-and from the Motherland to Yucatan, to Central America, Greece, Asia Minor and Egypt.

The Serpent being the symbol of the waters, and the waters being the mother of nature's life, the Serpent naturally in the ancient mind was associated with Creation. The ancients, however, appear to have been very careful to differentiate between the Deity and Nature's Creative Forces by adorning the Serpent that symbolizes the Great Creator.

In all the ancient writings the Sun is always symbolically shown as fighting and overcoming the serpent of the waters-the single-headed one.

In dealing with this symbolism, many writers have erred; they have failed to differentiate between the symbol of the waters and the symbol of the Creator, both being serpents. The Sun is not fighting the Creator; as a matter of fact, he is not symbolized as fighting at all. The spear is a symbol of the Sun's Forces penetrating the waters and bringing into life the cosmic eggs that are contained therein.

In Egypt we find Horus the Sun piercing the head of the serpent Aphophis-the waters-with a spear.

In Greece Apollo, the Sun, overcomes Python the Serpent, symbol of the waters.

Page 283

In India Vishnu, the Sun, overcomes Anatha the Serpent, the symbol of the waters.

The Christians in some way received this conception, for to this day the Church of Rome pictures the Virgin Mary with a serpent at her feet.

3. *The Serpent Circular.*-A circular serpent having its tail in its mouth is one of the oldest symbols for the Universe. I found it in Naacal pictures. The Egyptians adopted it as a part of the head-dress of their symbols for the Deity.

The Seven-headed Serpent, the symbol of the Creator and Creation, has already been fully explained.

One of the reasons why the ancients assigned so many symbols to the Deity was because they thought themselves unworthy to mention His name, and always referred to Him as "The Nameless." The various symbols represented his various attributes.

We now come to a subject that has generally been placed before the public in a manner that has caused false impressions to be entertained-ancient religious rites and ceremonies. Whether the writers have been incapable of translating correctly, or because of their ignorance of the subject, I am not prepared to say, nor does it interest me; but the writings on these subjects that have found their way into print have generally attempted to cast a blot on ancient religions in the minds of the readers instead of reverence for our forefathers who so faithfully tried to apprehend the Deity. It is the true understanding of the ancients that makes Max Muller's writings so fascinating and charming. I most envy his power of concentration and his ability of allowing his soul to carry back his mind,

Page 284

and to mentally associate with and live in the hearts of the people he is writing about.

All rites and ceremonies practised in the ancient temples were symbolical-not literal, as is generally thought by writers on this subject. They were symbolical of the life a man must lead to attain perfection, so that in the end, when the time came for him to pass into the Great Beyond, he would do so with a clear conscience and without trepidation. They tried to symbolize to him what Heaven was, what God was, and the glory that awaited him if he was not found wanting.

Many of their conceptions would appear ridiculous to us today, were it not for the fact that we can mentally place ourselves beside them, appreciate their untutored mentality and realize that at that time the teachings, and the mode of teaching, were as complex as could be comprehended.

When one comes across any literary matter referring to the bat as a Maya symbol, we invariably find it stated that the Mayas looked upon the bat as a god and worshipped it as such. The Mayas *did not* look upon the bat *as a god, nor did they worship it.* This is so clearly shown in the Seventh Trial, the House of the Bat, that it is beyond controversy. How can it be called bat worship when it is distinctly stated: "The Lord comes down from on high to see and to finally pass the candidate."

The whole ceremony is a symbolical one, showing the candidate how he must be prepared to meet the end when it comes.

Max Muller was absolutely correct when he wrote:

"One should never judge any of the ancient religions from

Page 285

appearances." We must first remember that all we see is symbolical and not literal.

A great blot, however, came upon and disfigured the escutcheon of ancient religions. The Mayas, Egyptians, Phoenicians, and other of the ancients, about 3,000 years ago, turned the pure worship of God into horrible forms of idolatry. They were taught by the unscrupulous priesthood to worship first the symbols, then fetishes of wood and stone and finally - the crowning horror and disgrace - human sacrifice.

It is known that the early books of our Old Testament (16) were written by Moses (17) from Egyptian Temple records. Hieroglyphics and symbols were the common form of writing in ancient times. A hieroglyphic or a symbol is an emblem of something, and therefore must not be taken literally. They must be taken as *representing* something, but *not* as that something itself. The failure to differentiate between the symbol and what it represents has caused many decipherings and translations to be erroneous, and often, in religious matters, leaves the impression of idolatry where there is a profound reverence for, and a worship of, the Deity. This has been especially prominent in deciphering and translating records relating to the Osirian religion. By Osirian religion I mean that taught by Thoth (18) at Sais, at the commencement of Egyptian history, and not as it was preached and taught and practiced by the unscrupulous Egyptian priesthood of a later period, which commenced during the reign of the second king of the Eleventh Dynasty and reached its climax during the Eighteenth Dynasty.

According to the Old Testament, Moses wrote that man

Page 286

was a special creation and made his advent on earth in the Garden of Eden. Where was the Garden of Eden? The biblical boundaries of the Garden of Eden are geographically impossible, as anyone can see by consulting an atlas and tracing them. Rivers are made to run over mountains and across oceans. Here is a biblical error; how did it occur? Moses was a Master-he had attained the highest degrees in religion and learning. It would have been impossible for him to have suggested such impossibilities; so that we must look elsewhere to find the origin of the many biblical errors.

What Moses wrote, without doubt, were plain facts, in symbolical language-a symbolically written history, true in all respects. Subsequent translations perverted his writings.

The writings of Moses were in Egyptian hieroglyphics and hieratic characters. I have been informed by Hebrew scientists that some were on clay tablets, others on papyrus: this point I pass on as I received it.

Eight hundred years after the Israelitish Exodus from Egypt, Ezra (19), with a body of co-workers, collected all the tablets and writings of all descriptions which were connected with the family history of the Israelites, and put them into book form, which became the Bible.

Those written by Moses were in Egyptian hieroglyphics. Is it any wonder that so many mistranslations were made by Ezra and his associates, when none of them were capable of thoroughly understanding the Egyptian writings of Moses? Only a Master could understand them, and neither Ezra nor any of his associates were Masters. Their incapability is clearly shown by comparing their

Page 287

translations with the original records which we find in the Egyptian, Chaldean, Hindu and Maya. Moses wrote sense; his translators made nonsense out of many of his passages. Moses wrote in the symbolical style of his day and his translators tried to translate literally. In this they only half succeeded, and when they came across a set of hieroglyphics they did not understand, they added a myth to sound history. The boundaries of the Garden of Eden is one of their myths.

From incontrovertible evidences gained through my research work it is shown that Moses wrote the first books of the Bible from the temple records brought to Egypt from the Motherland by the Naacals via Burma and India; and that these Egyptian temple records were copies of the "Seven Sacred Inspired Writings" of the Motherland Mu. These were written on clay tablets and referred to the Creation. The legends of the Garden of Eden, the "Flood," the last magnetic cataclysm, and the raising of the mountains, are records of later date.

Moses could have made no mistake in copying these writings, so they undoubtedly left his hands perfect copies of the originals. Eight hundred years after, an attempt was made to translate them into Hebrew by men who did not understand the old Egyptian esoteric temple writings, hence the difference between what was produced and the original.

So little did Ezra and his associates understand these writings that I doubt if there is a single Hebrew today who knows the meaning of the burnt sacrifice and what it symbolized.

Before the submersion of Mu, the word sacrifice was

Page 288

unknown in any language. It was coined to describe the way in which Mu was destroyed; and a fire upon an altar symbolizes the remembrance of the beloved Motherland.

ANCESTRAL WORSHIP

The worship of ancestors, or ancestral worship, is so universally acknowledged to be of common origin that I think it unnecessary to prove it here; so I shall confine myself to showing what land it was that first fathered this custom. In order to do this, I shall quote from records of many countries.

EGYPT. *Papyrus* IV **(20)** ˜ (Boulak Museum).-"Bring offerings to thy father and to thy mother, who rest in the valley of tombs; for he who gives these offerings is as acceptable to the gods as if they were brought to themselves. Often visit the dead, so that what thou doest for them they may do for thee."

INDIA. *The Dharma Lastra* **(21)** .-"The ceremony in honor of the Manes is superior, for the Brahmins, to the worship of the gods; and the offerings to the gods that take place before the offerings to the Manes have been declared to increase their merit."

CHINA. Confucius **(22)** in *Khoung Tsen* **(23)**.-The whole of Chapter XIX is dedicated to the description of the ceremony in honor of ancestors, as practised twice a year-in the spring and in the autumn.

In *Lun Yu* **(24)** Confucius says: "It is necessary to sacrifice to the ancestors as if they were present."

JAPAN.-On the fifteenth day of the Japanese seventh month, a festival is held in honor of their ancestors, when a repast of fruit and vegetables is placed before the Itays,

Page 289

on wooden tables of peculiar shape, on which are written inscriptions commemorative of the dead. (25)

PERU. "*Fables and Rites of the Incas.*" (26) (Pages 36 to 50).-"These festivities were established to commemorate deceased friends and relatives. They were celebrated with tears, mournful song, plaintive music, and by visiting the tombs of the dear departed, whose provision of corn and chicaha they received through openings arranged on purpose from the exterior of the tomb to vessels placed near the body. The Peruvians had great festivals in honor of the dead in the month of Aya-Marca."

Le Plongeon (27), in his book, "Central America," (28) says:

"Even today the aborigines of Yucatan, Petan and other countries of Central America, where the Maya language is spoken, are wont, at the beginning of November, to hang from the branches of certain trees in clearings of the forests, at cross roads, and in isolated nooks, cakes made of the best corn and meal they can procure. These are for the souls of the departed."

R. G. Haliburton, (29) who is considered one of our best authorities on ancestral worship, in writing of the "Festival of Ancestors," (30) says:

"It is now, as it was 'formerly, held at or near the beginning of November, by the Peruvians, the Hindus, the Pacific Islanders, the people of the Tonga Islands, the Australians, the ancient Persians, the ancient Egyptians and the northern nations of Europe, and continues for three days among the Japanese, the Hindus, the Australians, the ancient Romans and the ancient Egyptians."

This startling fact at once drew my attention to the question: How was this uniformity in the time of ob-

Page 290

servance preserved, not only in far distant quarters of the globe, but also through that vast lapse of time since the Peruvians and Indo-Chinese first inherited this primeval festival from a common source?

Between the columns in the Temple of Sacred Mysteries at Uxmal there was a grand altar, and on this altar, placed at the door of the inner chamber, they were wont to make offerings to their Manes.

This decides the land of common origin. The offerings to ancestors was a sacred rite and was practised in the Temple of Sacred Mysteries. It has already been shown that the sacred rites and ceremonies practised in this temple came from the Motherland. Therefore the land of Mu originated ancestral worship.

The custom remains dear to us today, though in a modified form; for do we not visit and place flowers on the graves of our dear departed ones? Little do those who thus place flowers on graves know that the ceremony originated more than 12,000 years ago, and that they are practising a very ancient ceremony.

LANGUAGE

Language is admitted to be the most accurate guide in tracing the family relations of various peoples, even when inhabiting countries which are separated by vast expanses of water and extents of land.

A startling fact is that we find Maya words in every language of the world. In Japan, one-half of their language is Kara Maya. In India, a very large proportion of the languages spoken came, without a doubt, from the Naga-Maya. The proportion, however, varies in each language.

Page 291

The Kandian Cingalese is full of the original Maya words, and all of the European languages are permeated with them, especially the Greek, whose alphabet is composed of Kara Maya vocables. Fully fifty per cent. of the Mexican Indian language is Kara Maya. A Mexican Indian and a Japanese can converse intelligibly without the aid of an interpreter, so many words are common to both languages. The same may be said of the Incas. The old Akkadian and Chaldean languages were largely Naga-Maya; also the Egyptian. One might, with research, go on indefinitely to prove the common origin.

Naturally time has made many changes in words. This is inevitable, of course, but the root still remains in many of these changes. For instance, in Greek we often find the letter *g* replacing the Maya *k*. D often replaces the Maya *t*, and *r* often replaces the Maya *l*. This last replacement, by the way, occurs in many languages.

In all words where the letter *c* is sounded *k*, the word will be found to come out of the Maya. The greatest changes in language, however, are found where the art of writing is unknown, and where the grammar has been lost or is unknown.

Max Muller says: "There was an original language."

This statement is confirmed wherever a study of language and its origin is made.

In all languages are to be found some words, roots of words, and vocables, which are identically the same; and in all instances they are found to convey substantially the same meanings, thus proving a common origin.

In "Six Thousand Years of History" **(31)** we find this statement: "The comparison of words in Sanskrit, the ancient

Page 292

language of the Hindu; Zend, the old speech of Persia; Greek, Latin, English and other tongues, has shown that all these languages came from a distant common original, spoken by some race yet unparted by migration. In all, or nearly all of these tongues, the names of common things and persons, the words expressing simple instruments and actions, the words for family relations, such as father, brother, daughter and son, the earlier numerals, the pronouns, the very endings of nouns and verbs, are substantially the same. Accident could not have caused this phenomenon, and, since many of the nations speaking thus have for long ages been parted from each other by vast stretches of the earth's broad surface, they could not learn them in historic times from one another. Borrowing and imitation being thus excluded, the only possible account is that these words and forms were carried with them by the migratory Aryan tribes as part of the possession once shared by all in their original home."

Each of these universal words may be traced back to the ancient mother Maya language. The natural deduction, therefore, is that the Maya tongue was the mother tongue, or one of the very earliest offshoots from it.

It must be understood that the present Maya language is no more like the Maya language of five or ten thousand years ago than the English of today is like that of five hundred years ago. The Maya language of today is, very much like the English language, made up of various other languages that are intertwined with the original, these changes being brought about by conquests. Much Aztec and Nahuatl has been added to the original Maya.

The original language was, without doubt, very con-

Page 293

tracted and short of words, so that one word had many meanings. As far as I have been able to decipher ancient writings, I should say that the meaning of a word would somewhat depend on its position in a sentence and how the word was accented when it consisted of more than one syllable.

For instance, the Maya word *ma* means "mother, earth" and "country." In the Egyptian, the word *ma* also means "mother, earth" and "country"; but when prefixed to nouns, verbs or adjectives, it is the sign of negation. This also occurs in the Greek and Cingalese languages.

To show how the ancient Maya words had more than one meaning, I have selected a few from Brasseur's translations:

NAGA-MAYA   ENGLISH

Be, to go, to leave, to walk, to move, to progress.
Chi, a mouth, an opening, a border, an edging.
Ka, the soul, barriers, sediments, anything ejected.
Kaachac, exceedingly, abundant, plentiful.
Kab, a hand, an arm, a branch, anything extending.
Kak, to finish, a fire, to burn, to destroy.
Kut, to worship, the seal, the rump.
Lal, to empty, to take away, to dispose of.
Ni, a point, a ridge, a summit, a mountain.
On, circular.
On-onx, circular, whirling, whirlpool, a tornado.
Paa, a break, an opening, to open.
Ta, where, a place, smooth, ground, level ground.
Tan, towards, near, before, in the center.
Tet, deep, depth, bottom, abyss.

Page 294

Zi cold, frozen, vapor, smoke.
Ra, water, moisture.
Pe, come, from, out.

On account of the ancient words having so many meanings, it becomes an exceedingly difficult task to translate the ancient writings and inscriptions so as to convey in modern language the thoughts of the ancients. Although the *general* meaning may be set forth, I doubt whether the *exact meaning in all details* is ever obtained.

Translations are, to a great extent, dependent upon the temperament of the translator. If, for instance, he has an Oriental mind, his translations will be figurative, flowery and often exaggerated; whereas, if the translator be of a phlegmatic nature, his translations are apt to be of a cold, blunt, abrupt, curtailed nature.

THE FOUR GENII

"The Four Genii" is another very ancient conception.

We find it associated with all histories and traditions of the Creation. I say, without reservation, that they were purely symbolical. The oldest account of them we find among the Mayas of Yucatan, and it came there from the Motherland.

The ancient symbol for the earth was a four-sided square. The four-sided square has four corners or points the cardinal points: North, South, East and West. The Maya interpretation is that "Heaven is sustained on four pillars, placed one on each corner of the earth." Each pillar had a keeper. The Maya keepers were their Four Genii:

Kan-Bacab the Yellow Bacab, placed in the South

Page 295

Chac-Bacab, the Red Bacab, placed in the East

Zac-Bacab, the White Bacab, placed in the North

Ek-Bacab, the Black Bacab, placed in the West.

EGYPTIAN.-According to the Egyptians there were four Genii of Amenti, one placed at each of the cardinal points:

Amset, the genius at the cardinal point in the East

Hapu, in the West

Tesautmutf, in the North

Quabsenuf, in the South.

CHALDEAN.-The Four Protecting Genii of the human race, as believed in by the Chaldeans, were:

Sed-Alap, or Kirub, represented as a bull with a human face

Lamas, or Nigal, represented as a lion with a man's head

Ustar, after the human likeness

Nattig, represented with the head of an eagle.

HINDU.-Four gods or genii who presided at the four cardinal points:

Indra, the King of Heaven, placed in the East

Rouvera, the God of Wealth, placed in the North

Varouna, the God of the Waters, placed in the West

Yama, the Judge of the Dead, placed in the South.

CHINESE.-The four mountains, Tse-Yo, of the Chinese four quarters of the globe (as they were wont to designate their country) are:

Tai-Tsong, being the Yo of the East

Saing-fou, being the Yo of the West.

How-Kowang, being the Yo of the South.

Chen-si, being the Yo of the North. (32)

Page 296

ISRAELITES.- The conception of the four gods, pillars or genii, or whatever they may be termed, was not entirely rejected by the Jews. Although there is no mention of them in the books written by Moses, that is no criterion, because some of the books written by Moses are lost, and the reference to the four cardinal points may have been in one of these lost books. Later we see the conception among the Jews in Ezekiel, (33) I :10--"They four had the face of a man, the face of a lion, the face of an ox and the face of an eagle." And in X:14-"The first face was that of a cherub, the second that of a man, the third that of a lion and the fourth that of an eagle."

The foregoing is given as a vision of Ezekiel. (34) At the time he wrote these lines he was a captive among the Chaldeans. Let us compare his vision with the then Chaldean creed, which had been in existence for thousands of years, because these conceptions came from the Motherland through the Caucasian colony, or through the Naacals, who came to Babylonia from India.

Chaldean-Four Genii. Human face, bull, lion, eagle.

Ezekiel-Four beasts. Man, ox, lion, eagle.

If Ezekiel's vision was not an embellishment of the Chaldean creed we should like to know what it was. Four of these very beasts are now in the British Museum, having been brought there from the ruins of Nineveh. Ezekiel was without question familiar with them, as among the common architectural embellishments of buildings.

THE TRIUNE GODHEAD

The conception of a Trinity or Triune Godhead has been handed down to us from the beginning of man. It

Page 297

was preserved in the works of the philosophers, and is still held sacred by many today, among them being the Christians and the Brahmins.

The ancient symbol for the Trinity was one of the oldest of the sacred symbols-the Equilateral Triangle. Whenever or wherever this symbol is found, in any form of record or inscription, it is either in reference to, or represents, the ancient Trinity and Heaven.

MAYA.-The equilateral triangle representing the Trinity is constantly found among the temple carvings of Yucatan. I have, however, been unable to satisfactorily determine the original names of the Maya Triune Godhead. Le Plongeon and others have given sets of three, and even five, which form the full Godhead, but to me all of them appear incorrect from the fact that names are given of people who lived tens of thousands of years after the Triune Godhead was conceived.

GUATEMALA. *Popol Vuh.*-"All that exists is the work of Tzkol the Creator, who, by his will, caused the universe to spring into existence; and whose names are Bitol the maker; Alom the engenderer and Quhalom, he who gives being." Tzkol is shown as the collective God.

PERU.-"The Incas of Peru worshipped a mighty unseen Being who they believed had created all things, for which reason they called him Pacha-Camac - he being incomprehensible. They did not present Him under any shape or name.

"Pacha-Camac stood at the head of a trinity composed of Himself, Pacha-Camac, Con and Uiracocha." (35)

HINDU.-In the *Sri Santara* (36) of the Hindus the Great

Page 298

Aum, the "nameless," is figured as a trinity by the equilateral triangle.

In the Hindu book *Niroukta* **(37)** it is three times affirmed that "there are three gods only, and that these three gods designate one Sole Deity."

"The Gods are three only."

"Pradjapati, or, as He is sometimes called, Mahatma, the Lord of all Creatures, is the collective God."

CHALDEAN.-The Chaldeans symbolized "Ensoph the Great Light" as a trinity, by the equilateral triangle. **(38)**

EGYPTIAN.-The Triune Godhead of the Egyptians consisted of "Shu, Set and Horus."

GREEK.-*Plato* and *Orpheus* **(39)** refer to the trinity as three kings-"Phanes, Ouranos and Kronos."

Proclus **(40)** asserts that "the Demiurgos or Creator is triple.

The three component parts of the Deity are three intellects or kings-He who exists, He who possesses, and He who beholds."

Pythagoras **(41)** taught his disciples that God was "numbers and harmony." He caused them to honor numbers and the equilateral triangle with the name of God.

CHRISTIAN CHURCHES.-We see in the ancient Catholic churches, over the main altar, an equilateral triangle, and within it an eye. The addition of the eye to the triangle originated in Egypt-"the all seeing eye of Osiris." **(42)**

For many years I searched in India, trying to find out what the origin of the conception of the Trinity was. I traced it back to the Motherland-without finding its origin. One day, talking about it with my old Hindu friend, he said: "There is a legend about it; it may be truth or it may be a myth; I cannot say. The legend tells

---

Page 299

that the Motherland consisted of three lands, that each land was raised by a separate god, so that it took three gods to raise the whole continent; but that the three gods were only one after all, all being joined together like the sides of a triangle."

I will say to you as my dear old friend said to me - "It may be the truth, or it may be a myth; I cannot say."

Chapter 15: Ancient Religious Conceptions Notes

(1) Max Muller is discussed in the Persons of Interest Appendix beginning on page A1—31.

(2) "*Early Religions*" is discussed in the Written Works Appendix beginning on page A2—9.

(3) Buddha (Sidhartha Gautama) is the central figure of the Buddhist philosophy/religion. The quote, although from a recognized expert is inaccurate, as Buddhists do not believe in a 'Supreme Being' as other religions conceptualize.

(4) Jesus Christ is discussed in the Persons of Interest Appendix beginning on page A1—5.

(5) "*Ancestor Worship*" is discussed in the Written Works Appendix beginning on page A2—3.

(6) "*Origin of Religious Laws*" is discussed in the Written Works Appendix beginning on page A2—27.

(7) The 'Owen' discussed in this passage remains unidentified.

(8) Manetho of Sebennytos (3rd century BCE) Egyptian Priest Historian.

(9) Thoth is discussed in the Persons of Interest Appendix beginning on page A1—51.

(10) Plato is discussed in the Persons of Interest Appendix beginning on page A1—41.

(11) Eusebius is discussed in the Persons of Interest Appendix beginning on page A1—9.

(12) "*Manava Dharma Sastra*" is discussed in the Written Works Appendix beginning on page A2—20.

(13) "*Aytareya Bhramana*" is discussed in the Written Works Appendix beginning on page A2—3.

(14) Ah-ac-chapat is discussed on page 66 of "*Sacred Mysteries Among the Mayas and the Quiches*"; Le Plongeon, Augustus; 1886.

(15) "*Popol Vuh*" is discussed in the Written Works Appendix beginning on page A2—28.

(16) The Bible is discussed in the Written Works Appendix beginning on page A2—4.

(17) Moses is discussed in the Persons of Interest Appendix beginning on page A1—28.

(18) Thoth is discussed in the Persons of Interest Appendix beginning on page A1—51.

(19) Ezra is discussed in the Persons of Interest Appendix beginning on page A1—11.

(20) "*Papyrus IV (Boulak Museum)*" is discussed in the Written Works Appendix beginning on page A2—28.

(21) "*Manava Dharma Sastra (Dharma Lastra)*" is discussed in the Written Works Appendix beginning on page A2—20.

(22) Confucius is discussed in the Persons of Interest Appendix beginning on page A1—7.

(23) "*Khoung Tsen*" is discussed in the Written Works Appendix beginning on page A2—16.

(24) "*Lun Yu*" is discussed in the Written Works Appendix beginning on page A2—19.

(25) Similar to passage on page 9 of "*Queen Moo & The Egyptian Sphinx*"; Le Plongeon, Augustus; 1896

(26) "*Fables and Rites of the Incas*" is discussed in the Written Works Appendix beginning on page A2—14.

(27) Le Plongeon is discussed in the Persons of Interest Appendix beginning on page A1—22.

(28) "*Central America*" by Augustus Le Plongeon does not exist, but an excerpt from "Queen Moo and the Egyptian Sphinx" (1896) provides this text:

> Even to-day the aborigines of Yucatan, Peten, and other countries in Central America where the Maya language is spoken, as if in obedience to this affirmation of the Hindoo legislator… are wont, at the beginning of November, to hang from the branches of certain trees in the clearings of the forests, at cross-roads, in isolated nook, cakes made of the best corn and meat they can procure. These are for the souls of the departed to partake of, as their name hanal pixan ("foot of the souls") clearly indicates.
> Augustus Le Plongeon, "Queen Moo and the Egyptian Sphinx" (1896), Page 10

(29) R.G. Haliburton is discussed in the Persons of Interest Appendix beginning on page A1—17.

(30) Festival of Ancestors is discussed in the Written Works Appendix beginning on page A2—14.

(31) "*Six Thousand Years of History*" is discussed in the Written Works Appendix beginning on page A2—30.

(32) Similar to content on pages 315-319 of "*The Signs and Symbols of Primordial Man, being an explanation of the Evolution of Religious Doctrines from the Eschatology of the Ancient Egyptians*", Albert Churchward, 1910.

(33) The Bible (Ezekial) is discussed in the Written Works Appendix beginning on page A2—4.

(34) Ezekial is discussed in the Persons of Interest Appendix beginning on page A1—10.

(35) Similar to content on page 56 of "*Sacred Mysteries Among the Mayas and the Quiches*"; Le Plongeon, Augustus; 1886.

(36) "*Sri Santara*" is discussed in the Written Works Appendix beginning on page A2—31.

(37) "*Niroukta*" is discussed in Written Works Appendix beginning on page A2—26.

(38) Similar to content on page 60 of "*Sacred Mysteries Among the Mayas and the Quiches*"; Le Plongeon, Augustus; 1886.

(39) Orpheus is discussed in the Persons of Interest Appendix beginning on page A1—41.

(40) Proclus is discussed in the Persons of Interest Appendix beginning on page A1—44.

(41) Pythagoras is discussed in the Persons of Interest Appendix beginning on page A1—44.

(42) Similar to content on page 61 of "*Sacred Mysteries Among the Mayas and the Quiches*"; Le Plongeon, Augustus; 1886.

16
Ancient Sacred Mysteries, Rites and Ceremonies

Page 300

By the aid of the Popol Yuh and the decipherings of the writings within the Great Pyramid at Cairo I am enabled to describe some of the ancient mysteries, rites and ceremonies. Le Plongeon translated the Popol Yuh into English from Brasseur's French translation, checking it himself with the original Maya. This copy he kindly lent me to make notes from. The following from the Popol Yuh therefore comes through Le Plongeon.

In Guatemala the Quiche Mayas disclosed their sacred mysteries to the applicants in seven steps or degrees. After the first step or initiatory degree, the balance were conducted in six chambers or houses.

Some of these trials or degrees are exceedingly interesting, as we find them practiced later by the Egyptians and reflected all through the Old Testament.

FIRST INITIATORY STEP.-In this step the applicants for initiation to the Sacred Mysteries were made to cross two rivers, one of mud, the other of blood, before they reached the four roads which led to the place where the priests were awaiting them. The crossing of these rivers

Page 301

was full of dangers that were to be avoided. Then they had to journey along four roads-the white, the red, the green, and the black-that led to where the Council, composed of twelve priests, veiled, and a wooden statue dressed and wearing the ornaments of a priest, awaited. **(1)**

While in the presence of the Council the initiates were told to salute the King, pointing to the wooden statue. This was to try their discernment. Then they had to salute each individual, giving his name or title without being told, after which they were invited to sit down on a certain seat. If, forgetting the respect due to the august assembly, they sat as invited, they soon had reason to regret their want of breeding and proper *preparation*, for the seat, made of stone, was burning hot. Having modestly declined the invitation, they were led to the *Second Trial.* **(2)**

THE DARK HOUSE.-In the Dark House they had to pass the night and submit to the Second Trial. Guards were placed all around to prevent the candidates from holding intercourse with the outer world. Then a lighted torch of pinewood and a cigar were given to each. These were not to be extinguished, still they had to be returned whole at sunrise, when the officers in charge of the house came to demand them. Woe to him who allowed his cigar and his torch to be consumed! Terrible chastisement, even death, awaited him.

Having passed through this second trial successfully, the *Third Trial* was to be suffered in-**(3)**

THE HOUSE OF SPEARS-In the House of Spears they had to produce four pots of certain rare flowers, without communicating with anyone outside, or bringing them at the time of coming. They had also to defend themselves

Page 302

against the attacks of the best spearmen, selected for the purpose, one for each candidate. Coming out victorious at dawn they were judged worthy of the *Fourth Trial.* This consisted in being shut up a whole night in- **(4)**

THE ICE HOUSE.- In the Ice House the cold was intense. They had to prevent themselves from being overcome by the cold and frozen to death. Their *Fifth Trial* then took place.

THE TIGER HOUSE. - In the Tiger House they were exposed to the danger of being torn to pieces or devoured alive by ferocious animals. Emerging safely from the den of tigers, they were ready to sumbit to the *Sixth Trial.* **(5)**

THE FIERY HOUSE.-This was a burning fiery furnace where they had to remain from sunset to sunrise. Coming out unscorched, they were deemed worthy to undergo the *Seventh* and *Final Trial,* the most severe of all-

THE HOUSE OF THE BAT.-This was the House of Camazotz, the God of the Bats, and was full of death· dealing weapons. Here *the God himself, coming from on high,* appeared to the candidates, and beheaded them *if found off their guard.*33

The foregoing is a synopsis of Le Plongeon's translations. He says these rites were practised at Xibalba, a place in the heart of the Guatemala mountains.

I am afraid Le Plongeon has failed to give the correct impressions as regards these trials. He should have told his readers that they were all symbolical; whereas he has tried to leave the impression that they were literal, thereby

33. Do not these initiations vividly recall to mind what Henoch said he saw in his vision? "That blazing house of Creptal, burning hot and icy cold. The habitation where one appeared in great glory sitting upon the orb of the sun." **(6)**

Page 303

attempting to produce a blood-curdling, awe-inspiring, supernatural mystery. Le Plongeon, however, forgot himself on one occasion; for he states in the First Trial that the candidate is *prepared* beforehand, therefore knowing what to say, what to do, and how to act. In other words, the candidate has been previously taught his lessons, and these trials were examinations to ascertain whether he knew them.

The aforesaid is fully borne out by what is found on the walls of the temple within the Great Pyramid at Cairo. Here it is stated that the candidate is *prepared beforehand* and that a friendly spirit (an *instructor*) accompanies him and guides him through all his trials.

When one comes across any literary matter referring to the bat as a Maya symbol, it is found invariably that the writer says the Mayas looked upon the bat as a god and worshipped it as such. The Mayas did not look upon the bat as a god, nor did they worship it. This is so clearly shown in the Seventh Trial-"the House of the Bat" that it is beyond controversy. How can it be called bat worship when it is distinctly stated that "*The Lord* comes down from on high to see and to finally pass the candidate" '?

The whole ceremony is a symbolical one, showing the candidate how he must be prepared to meet the end when it comes.

THE PYRAMID TEMPLE

I will now compare the ancient Egyptian Sacred Mysteries, as disclosed by the temple within the Great Pyramid near Cairo, Egypt, with those of the Mayas as disclosed in the Popol Yuh.

Page 304

The entrance door was placed in the north, and was a single stone in the form of an equilateral triangle surmounting a square and revolved on a pivot or apex. This was symbolical of Heaven and Earth. Through these the postulant must pass, for they symbolized the passage from this to the future life. There were twelve entrances to pass through before attaining the Grand Orient, with secrets and trials restricted to each.

The first could not be seen; it was apparently a blank and was guarded by Horus. It was a blank or nothingness because the postulant was blind and bereft of his senses except motion. This portal had to be passed through with the aid of a friendly spirit.

Having passed through the portal, he was conducted down these passages by a friendly spirit that he could not see, and was taken to the place of initiation, where his Manes were regenerated by the descent of the Soul to the expecting postulants. He was then conducted to the chamber of Central Fire, which he extinguished.

Book of the Dead, **(7)** *Chapter XXII.*-"I come; I do that which my heart wishes on the day of the Fire, when I extinguish the flames as soon as they appear." And *Chapter XXV.*-"I make the man remember his name in the Great House. I make him remember his name in the House of Flame." References to the Tank of Fire are constantly met with throughout the Book of the Dead and are generally accompanied by the foregoing glyph or vignette.

From the Chamber of Central Fire (the Tank of Fire) the postulant was conducted up the grand Horizon of Heaven, and came to a portal. Questions were asked, which he answered, and then he passed through and was

Page 305

able to see-light was given to him, and he then saw his guide and friend who conducted him. He was next conducted into the Chamber of the Shadow, Judgment of the Justified, Truth and Darkness, the Seven Halls of Death.

Here he had to pass an examination, and words were given to him which he had to remember before he was led on to the second portal, where he had to give answers before he was permitted to enter.

Having passed through the second stage, the adept was allowed to enter the hall called the Tenth Hall of Truth, or Trial Scene, which was depicted in a black-and-white tessellated pavement-Right and Wrong, Truth or Falsehood.

From this hall he was conducted to the Chamber of New Birth, or place of coming forth with regeneration of soul. In this chamber were found the emblems of mortality with the sarcophagus empty. A small opening admits the light of the bright morning star Sothis into this chamber. All of the rest of the chamber reminded the adept of what he passed through. He now emerged from the tomb.

Next he was taken to the Throne of Regeneration of the Soul, and Investiture of Illumination took place. Then he passed through more ordeals to attain to the Chamber of the Orient, to the Throne of Ra, to become a Master. The uncreated light, from which was pointed out the whole happiness of the future, he could see for himself in the distance. After passing through another portal where he had to bend, he was conducted to the Chamber of the Grand Orient.

The initiate had to pass through the fiery ordeal to be

Page 306

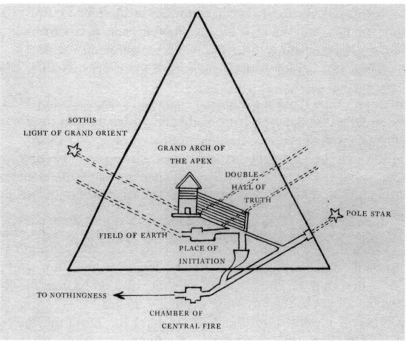

INTERIOR OF THE GREAT PYRAMID, EGYPT,
SHOWING CONSTRUCTION OF THE TEMPLE (8)

Page 307

approved as an adept. The adept had to become justified. The justified must then become illuminate. The illuminate must then be consummated Master before he could obtain the innermost mansion of the Divine House.

Comparing the Egyptian with the Maya: In the Pyramid Temple34 there were twelve rooms or portals-in the Maya seven houses. The Egyptian had a Dark Room, so also the Maya. The Egyptian had a Tank of Fire-the Maya a Fiery House. The Egyptian had Seven Halls of Death-the Maya House of the Bat corresponded with them.

After Mu was destroyed, the peoples of the earth symbolized in some way her destruction, so that "her memory should not be forgotten among coming generations."
The Mayas of Yucatan erected a pyramid as a monument for her, which stands to this day. They also erected temples to her memory.

The Quiche Mayas introduced it into their religious ceremonies in the form of a symbolical "Fiery House."

The Greeks symbolized it by forming a Maya epic, which forms their alphabet today. This epic describes the manner of her destruction.

The Egyptians, like the Quiche Mayas, symbolized the destruction in their religious ceremonies. As the initiate advanced in religious mysteries he symbolically passed through the scene of the destruction of his Motherland - thus, through life, to keep her in memory.

Moses in a very abstruse manner symbolized it in his writings, as we find in our Bible today.

34. Much of the detail concerning the Pyramid Temple comes from Dr. A. Churchward's (9) work.

Chapter 16: Ancient Sacred Mysteries, Rites and Ceremonies Notes

(1) Similar to content on page 42 of "*Sacred Mysteries Among the Mayas and the Quiches*"; Le Plongeon, Augustus; 1886.

(2) Ibid; pages 42-43

(3) Ibid; page 43

(4) Ibid; page 43

(5) Ibid; page 44

(6) Ibid; page 44

(7) "*Book of the Dead*" is discussed in the Written Works Appendix beginning on page A2—10.

(8) Similar to figure 166 on page 429 of "*The Signs and Symbols of Primordial Man, being an explanation of the Evolution of Religious Doctrines from the Eschatology of the Ancient Egyptians*", Albert Churchward, 1910.

(9) Albert Churchward, James' younger brother, surgeon and author is discussed in the Persons of Interest Appendix beginning on page A1—6.

17
Omega- The Coping Stone

Page 308

IF the question is asked, "How long ago was it that man first appeared on Earth?" My answer would be-"Without question, in the Tertiary Era."

I cannot state the number of years; no one can. Man today has no more conception of how many years ago the Pleistocene commenced, or the length in years of any geological time, era or period, than the ancient fossil on my library table.

Under the great law of Creation, there must first come a *condition*, and, with it, *a suitable life to live in it*. A condition has always been subject to the workings of *the Earth's Primary Force*.

Throughout the history of the earth this has been so, and at no time do we find the new Creation behind the condition, because the condition is the parent of the Creation or development.

When was the condition for man's appearance on earth perfected? The condition for the welfare of man was far advanced at the end of the Oligocene, and was well ad-

Page 309

vanced if not absolutely perfected during the later half of the Miocene or the beginning of the Pliocene.

This was long before the great gas belts were formed, long before the mountains were raised, and long before the geological Glacial Period. I have placed before my readers such reasonable proofs that it is clearly shown that-

First: At one time in the earth's history there was a great continent of land in the Pacific Ocean where now we find only water and groups of small islands.

Second: This land in ancient times had two names, a geographical and a hieratical. The hieratical name was Mu; the geographical the Lands of the West.

Third: In this land man made his advent on earth.

Fourth: Man was a special creation and not of nature's making. He came fully developed in form, but required education and mental development.

Now what is man'?

The late James D. Dana **(1)** says: "Man is not of nature's making; he is a special act of the Infinite Being, whose image he bears."

I cordially agree with Dana, but by an irresistible force I am compelled to go further.

All endeavors to determine when man first appeared on earth must be futile. It has always been a veiled secret, and always must remain so, because man's first home on earth, with this secret, now forms the bottom of the Pacific Ocean. We can, however, hope, through geological and archaeological research, some day to be able to get to a point that is near the date of his first appearance on earth.

Many scientists have declared their belief to be that they are descended from some forest beast, some monkey of

---

Page 310

prehistoric origin. Their contention must therefore be that man, having descended from a monkey, is a monkey still, in a developed state.

I have shown that man was on earth and in a high state of civilization during the later part of the Tertiary Era, from the quality and perfection of his works. It is shown that he must have been in existence an immensely long time before the end of the Tertiary Era. This would certainly carry him back contemporary with the first apes who resembled men.

If evolution were possible-which the old Naacal Tablets show it is not-the reverse would have occurred; that is, monkeys would have come out of man, and I am not at all certain that some men are not making monkeys out of themselves today. This tendency of some men is very strongly pointed out in the Maya, Hindu and Egyptian writings, so that it is nothing new. Man, *the most complex* of all forms of life, and *the most perfect form of life*, was created for a special purpose, as pointed out in the Naacal Tablets.

Man is an animal of the order of mammals, distinct and different from all other animals, due to the fact that he has associated with his body a *force* or *soul*, for the purpose of ruling the earth. This great gift has been bestowed on no other form of life, which proves conclusively that man is a separate and distinct creation, possessing a divine force. It is impossible that he can have come out of, or evolved from some animal *not having* that force.

Man with this force has been given the power, *when he learns how to use his force*, to place himself next to the

Page 311

Infinite Being, a part of which he has within himself. Man is therefore a son of God.

Like all other creatures, man was started at the foot of the ladder; but, unlike all other creatures, he was given the power to rise. Man has always been surrounded by influences striving against each other for good and for evil. Man's actions are governed by these influences. For easy explanation I will call them *affinities*. The soul's affinities can only suggest that which is good. Evil suggestions come from the material affinities or elementary parts. Material suggestions are not all evil-only some. The material affinities *can* suggest evil-the soul's affinities *cannot*.

The soul and its affinities suggest to the mind; the material affinities also suggest to the mind. The mind determines for the body which suggestions shall be followed. Conscience is the mouthpiece of the soul to the mind. Bodily actions and words from the mouth are the indications of the powers or influences that are controlling the mind. The material interests or affinities may control the mind of man for a time, but before the earth can end her existence Man's Soul must reign supreme over his mind and body.

At the commencement of man's existence the material affinities were very powerful, owing to the lack of experience, so that advancement was necessarily slow. Time went on, one generation followed another, and man began to rise step by step towards his preordained goal, the ascendency of the soul's affinities over the material affinities. The time must come when all of men's actions and thoughts will be governed solely by the dictation of the

---

Page 312

soul. This was the task given to the soul to perform when it was placed within man's body at his Creation-"To govern this earth."

By the advancement of man as indicated by science and learning, he is now only approaching the threshold of knowledge. When knowledge is complete - which can only be when man understands and can control certain earthly forces which will enable him to understand his own greater force-then, the works of man will be beyond our present comprehension. With his soul force thoroughly understood by himself, man will be incapable of evil thoughts or actions. Man will then be able to accomplish anything that may be dictated by his soul, because the soul will have no influences working against it. Then the works of man will be good, because his soul will be incapable of evil. We have as yet been looking only at man's past; let us for a brief moment look into his future and see what destiny holds in store for him. All things point to a time when man will have perfect control over all of the earth's elements and many of her forces; a state to which he is now advancing. The power of his soul force is only now beginning to dawn on *present* man.

There are many strange phenomena, or apparently so, where objective points are reached through working the soul force. And yet, the one accomplishing them is not aware that he is doing so by the aid of a force. He discovers he has a *power*, but does not know *what* that power is; *he only knows the results*. In some way he has been advanced far enough to work his soul force in a limited direction, yet does not understand it. The great mysteries of the Hindus, Polynesians, Egyptians and biblical mira-

Page 313

cles are and were the results of working the soul force. Both the Hindu and Polynesian knowledge are peculiar. They appear to be somewhat proficient along certain lines, but extremely inefficient in others. It would seem they have no conception that the force they are using can be used in any other direction except along certain lines.

Christ was the perfect example of the soul force being in perfect control over the mind and body. He appeared on earth as others did before him, in fulfillment of the Great Divine Law. Man's mind had arrived at the *condition*. Christ (2) was placed on earth as an example for man - to teach and to show what man eventually must become. The *development* is now going on; man must become perfect, otherwise the Great Divine Law will have miscarried. As the law is divine, it cannot miscarry.

It is regrettable, yet a notable fact, that many of our greatest scientists became atheists, and have been, as a rule, advocates of the theory of evolution; and the fact remains that a *true* evolutionist cannot be anything but an atheist. It is yet more regrettable that they became atheists, when they were struggling in the opposite direction; for, science, fully understood, cannot but impress the student with the power and mystery of the Great Supreme-- the Deity.

Science is the twin sister of religion. Science properly studied cannot help making man a better being; for, it teaches him that he himself is a higher and a grander creation than he has ever before appreciated; it gives an impetus and determination to his soul force to gain its preordained ascendency over the mind and the body's material affinities. It teaches him that within his house of clay

Page 314

there is an everlasting life, at every step the hand of God is revealed; and, above all, it teaches him that by following the suggestions of his soul everlasting glory and happiness await him.

The rock on which many scientists have wrecked their ships is *materialism*. In their studies they have eliminated forces and their workings, saying, "A force is the result of atomic movements." True-all forces are- *except the force which* FIRST *starts atomic movements.*

This is the force the atheist has never found, consequently he built his structure without considering it. He found only the minor forces originating from atomic movements; he never came in direct touch with God.

The movements of atoms are cogwheels in a piece of machinery. One turns the one it is meshed into, this one in turn turns others, and so on ad infinitum. But - *what turned the first wheel?* Not any other wheel, because *it* was the first. Therefore there must be something at the back of it. What is it'? A force independent of all atoms.

The universe is a set of atomic cogwheels. What turns the first wheel in the universe'? A force-the Great Primary Force, the Great Infinite Force-God. The atheist has never discovered that God is the Great Primary Force, working all things through subsidiary forces, and that the atomic forces are only subsidiary forces to the Supreme Force.

Thus the atheist has only studied the material side. His deductions would therefore naturally be: Elements govern forces, because without the elements the forces could not exist. This being so, forces are cast aside as being immaterial, and are virtually obliterated from consideration.

Page 315

The rudder is taken from his ship, and she is cast on the rocks.

Throughout all of the deductions and conceptions of the atheist his mind has been governed absolutely by his material affinities. His material affinities have persuaded his mind that they are the all-powerful. Nothing now remains in the mind of the atheist, except that he is a mere chemical compound of elements--no soul, no God--chaos!

Had the atheist given as careful study to forces as he did to elements, constantly working back and back, following one force back to another, he would have eventually come to the origin of movement. It would then have been disclosed to him that he himself contained a force other than physical, and that that force was a living soul. With this knowledge he would realize what he is: not the poor brute beast he is trying to make himself out to be, but one who has within himself an actual part of the Supreme, and is therefore a son of God-just as the leaf of a tree is a part of the tree itself.

Both Christ (2) and Gautama (3) declared they were "only what other men might become."

By his chemical knowledge of elements the scientist appreciates that the chemical elementary compound of his body must eventually decompose, and that this decomposition must release the soul. As he knows the ultimate finality of his elements, he knows that the soul, like the elements, cannot die. All must continue on forever; for elements decomposed pass on into other forms.

It is pre-ordained that all chemical elementary compounds must eventually decompose, separate, return to original form, and go back whence they came. The ele-

Page 316

ments having released the soul from its bondage, the soul--being governed by the same Divine Law as the elements--must also return whence it came. Coming from "The Great Source" the glorious triumphant end of man's soul must be--*its return to God.*

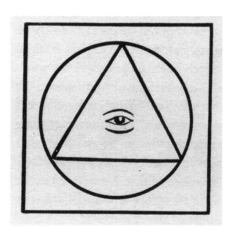

Chapter 17: Omega—The Coping Stone Notes

(1) James D. Dana (1813-1895) was an American geologist, mineralogist, and zoologist. He was a professor at Yale University and prolific author. He conducted important studies of volcanic action and the formation of continents. His quote bears no relation to his field of study.

(2) Jesus Christ is discussed in the Persons of Interest Appendix beginning on page A1—5.

(3) Buddha (Sidhartha Gautama) is the central figure of the Buddhist philosophy/religion.

Appendix 1

Persons of Interest
Referenced in the

"Lost Continent of Mu, the Motherland of Men"

The 'Persons of Interest' Appendix was created to collect information on persons (real or mythological) that have an impact on the "Lost Continent of Mu Motherland of Men." A further qualification for inclusion was the availability of information and/or amplifying data on the subject.

The creation of this appendix is intended to serve as an aid in the continuing research on James Churchward and his theories. Much like doors in a long passageway, these references will provide further pathways of discussion and research. This appendix will also allow the reader to reach his or her own sense of the validity of James Churchward's work and serve as a spring board for further studies.

The inclusion of a particular person or amplifying data should not be construed as an endorsement of that person or theories. Likewise, not including a particular person should not be construed as an attempt to discredit or denounce any person or their theories.

Appendix 1: Persons of Interest
Table of Contents

Anana (Anani) (13th Century B.C.E.)

Egyptian Scribe. Wrote the Papyrus Anani (see entry). Please note that in the 1931, *Lost Continent of Mu*, the portion quoting Anani (see pages 157-158) has been changed to read Anana.

I am unable to find copies of this papyrus that quote this exact passage, however I have found references to other portions of the text. Nothing exists to rule out the possibility that this is a mixed-up reference to the *Papyrus of Ani* (see entry.)

Side note: Seti II lived from 1199 – 1193 BCE during the 19th Dynasty.

Lost Continent of Mu, Motherland of Men
Page 128:

> *Egyptian Papyrus Anana.*- Here is an interesting quotation from the Egyptian papyrus, Anana, which is dated 1320 B. C:
> "Eternity has no end, therefore no beginning; consequently eternity is a *circle*.
> "If we live on we must continue forever, and if we continue forever, like the circle and eternity, man had no beginning.
> "Man comes into being many times, yet knows nothing of his past lives; except occasionally some day-dream or a thought carries him back to some circumstance of a previous incarnation. He cannot, however, determine in his mind when or where the circumstance occurred, only that it is something familiar. In the end, however, all of his various pasts will reveal themselves.
> "The spirits or souls of one incarnation possibly may meet again in another incarnation, and may be drawn together as if by a magnet, but for what cause neither knows."

Lost Continent of Mu, Motherland of Men
Page 157-158:

> Anani, the king's scribe and companion of Seti II, in one of his beautifully illustrated papyri, gives the following reason why the Egyptians selected the scarab to symbolize the Creative God:
> "The scarab rolls up little balls of mud with its feet and in these balls deposits its eggs, there to hatch out. The Egyptians think this a perfect example of *the Creator rolling the world around and causing it to produce life.*"
> ...
> Anani carries us back 3,500 years only, but the carvings on this knife's scabbard will carry us back to a time before the Egyptians came to Egypt.

List of publications:
• Egyptian Book of the Dead
Other references:
See online versions of the *Papyus of Ani*:
   Sacred Text Archive: http://www.sacred-texts.com/egy/ebod/index.htm
   UPenn: http://www.africa.upenn.edu/Books/Papyrus_Ani.html

Ani (15th Century B.C.E.)
Egyptian Scribe of Thebes.

Lost Continent of Mu, Motherland of Men
Page 159-160:

[Illustration with following caption:]
TAT PILLAR
Papyrus Ani B.C. 1500. British Museum

In Egyptian mythology, pillars were placed at the entrance to Amenti. Above on this page I give a cut taken from the Papyrus of Ani, showing one of the two pillars at the entrance to Amenti. The Egyptians called them Tat Pillars, but they are more commonly known throughout the world as Totem Pillars.

List of publications:
 • Egyptian Book of the Dead
Other references:
See online versions of the *Papyus of Ani*:
    Sacred Text Archive: http://www.sacred-texts.com/egy/ebod/index.htm
    UPenn: http://www.africa.upenn.edu/Books/Papyrus_Ani.html

---

Berosus (born 260 B.C.E.)
Author, Chaldean historian. The complete text of his "History of Babylonia" has been lost but portions of his writings exist as either fragments of his words or as referenced in the writings of other authors.

Lost Continent of Mu, Motherland of Men
Page 157:
    Berosus, the ancient Chaldean priest and historian, spoke of the Akkad-Mayas as being half fish and half man.

Excerpt from "FRAGMENTS OF CHALDAEN HISTORY, BEROSSUS: FROM ALEXANDER POLYHISTOR" (1832) provides this text:
    "At Babylon there was (in these times) a great resort of people of various nations, who inhabited Chaldæa, and lived in a lawless manner like the beasts of the field. In the first year there appeared, from that part of the Erythræan sea which borders upon Babylonia, an animal destitute of reason, by name Oannes, whose whole body (according to the account of Apollodorus) was that of a fish; that under the fish's head he had another head, with feet also below, similar to those of a man, subjoined to the fish's tail. His voice too, and language, was articulate and human; and a representation of him is preserved even to this day."
    I.P. Cory; "Ancient Fragments" (1832); downloaded 06-21-2008, Sacred-Texts.com; <http://www.sacred-texts.com/cla/af/af02.htm>

Excerpt from "Queen Moo and the Egyptian Sphinx" (1896) provides this text:
    "Berosus, the Chaldean historian, tells us that civilization was brought to Mesopotamia by Oannes and six other beings, half man, half fish, who came from the Persian Gulf;"
    Augustus Le Plongeon, "Queen Moo and the Egyptian Sphinx" (1896), Introduction page 26

Excerpt from "The Origin and Evolution of the Human Race" (1921) provides this text:
    "According to the legend related by Berosos a divine fish-man, Oan or Oannes, who dwelt in the Persian Gulf, came from thence to teach the Chaldeans all that they ever knew …"
    Albert Churchward, "The Origin and Evolution of the Human Race" (1921), page 362

Excerpt from "The Origin and Evolution of the Human Race" (1921) provides this text:

"Berosus tells us, speaking of the ancient days of Chaldea, "In the first year there appeared, from that part of the Erythræan Sea which borders upon Babylonia, an animal endowed with reason, by name Oannes, whose whole body (according to the account of Apollodorus) was that of a fish; that under the fish's head he had another head, with feet also below, similar to those of a man, subjoined to the fish's tail. His voice too and language was articulate and human, and a representation of him is preserved even unto this day. …"

Donnelly, Ignatius, "ATLANTIS THE ANTEDILUVIAN WORLD"; (1882), page 162

List of publications:

"History of Babylonia" circa 290-278 B.C.E.

Other references:

See online reference: FRAGMENTS OF CHALDAEN HISTORY, BEROSSUS: FROM ALEXANDER POLYHISTOR. [http://www.sacred-texts.com/cla/af/af02.htm]

Christ [Jesus (the) Christ (0 – 33 AD)]

Jesus (8–2 B.C./B.C.E. — 29–36 A.D./C.E.), also known as Jesus of Nazareth, and Jesus the Christ.

Jesus is the central figure of the Christian religion and also has a role in Islam.

Lost Continent of Mu, Motherland of Men
Page 100:

> The Upper Egyptians were *not* sun-worshippers, as stated by Mackenzie. Ra, the sun, was their collective symbol for the Deity. Temples were dedicated to Ra as *representing* the Divinity, just as the cross today represents Christ.

Lost Continent of Mu, Motherland of Men
Page 124:

> Christ's teachings were always in parables. He distinctly stated that he preached in parables because it was the only way the people could be brought to understand. Parables are phraseological symbols.

Lost Continent of Mu, Motherland of Men
Page 128:

> Christ said: "Except ye be born again ye cannot enter the kingdom of heaven."

From the King James version of the Bible (John 3:1-8):

> 1 Now there was a man of the Pharisees, named Nicode'mus, a ruler of the Jews. 2 This man came to Jesus by night and said to him, "Rabbi, we know that you are a teacher come from God; for no one can do these signs that you do, unless God is with him." 3 Jesus answered him, "Truly, truly, I say to you, unless one is born anew, he cannot see the kingdom of God." 4 Nicode'mus said to him, "How can a man be born when he is old? Can he enter a second time into his mother's womb and be born?" 5 Jesus answered, "Truly, truly, I say to you, unless one is born of water and the Spirit, he cannot enter the kingdom of God. 6 That which is born of the flesh is flesh, and that which is born of the Spirit is spirit. 7 Do not marvel that I said to you, 'You must be born anew.' 8 The wind blows where it wills, and you hear the sound of it, but you do not know whence it comes or whither it goes; so it is with every one who is born of the Spirit."

Lost Continent of Mu, Motherland of Men
Page 273-274:

"The external aspect of a religion as presented to strangers is not one often to be trusted. In the earliest and purest days of Christianity, if we were to believe the most enlightened of the heathen writers, the Christian religion consisted of the worship of animals. This idea possibly arose from the fact that the earliest pictures of Mary nursing Christ show the cow's horns of the Egyptian goddess Sati on her head, and sometimes the horns of Hathor."

This quotation is from the book *Early Religions* by Frederick Max Mueller.

Lost Continent of Mu, Motherland of Men
Page 313:

Christ was the perfect example of the soul force being in perfect control over the mind and body. He appeared on earth as others did before him, in fulfillment of the Great Divine Law. Man's mind had arrived at the *condition*. Christ was placed on earth as an example for man - to teach and to show what man eventually must become. The *development* is now going on; man must become perfect, otherwise the Great Divine Law will have miscarried. As the law is divine, it cannot miscarry.

Lost Continent of Mu, Motherland of Men
Page 315:

Both Christ and Gautama declared they were "only what other men might become."

Albert Churchward [Churchward, Albert (1852-1925)]

Younger brother of James Churchward.

From an obituary:

Bro. Dr. Albert Churchward, who received a sudden summons to attend the Grand Lodge Above on Friday, 4th inst. (the day after he had celebrated his seventy-third birthday), was known to all Masonic students by his writings, but to very few personally, for he was not a frequent visitor at Masonic gatherings. He was the senior P.M. of the Hornsey Lodge, No. 890, in which he was initiated in 1878, as he was of the South Norwood Lodge, No. 1139, while he was also the senior Past First Principal of the Hornsey Chapter. He was a P.M.W.S. of the Alleyn Chapter, No. 139, of the A. and A. Rite, and a member of the 30th Degree. He received his medical education at Guy's Hospital and Brussels, receiving his doctorate from the latter University in 1876, the same year in which he gained the M.R.C.P. at Edinburgh, having qualified as M. R.C.S. London two years previously. It is said that he was aware that his death might take place at any moment, and that his life could not be prolonged, and he freely discussed the subject with his friends. His sudden death occurred in the way he had expected. Bro. Churchward was the inventor of a hygienic bicycle saddle, improved cycle pedals, and a new process of hardening and toughening steel and armor plates.

His principal bent, however, was towards anthropology, and in his book, "The Origin and Evolution of the Human Race," published in 1921, Bro. Churchward advanced the theory that man arose in the neighborhood of the great equatorial lakes of Africa, and swarmed thence in successive migrations. These various swarms, he contended, carried with them distinctive cultures, the higher culture having been gradually evolved in the primeval "home." This theory is not accepted by anthropologists and ethnologists, for whose opinions Dr. Churchward did not conceal his contempt. In "The Origin and Evolution of Religion," published last year, Dr. Churchward proceeded on the idea that the truth of religion may be reached by deciphering the signs and symbols found all over the world, particularly the persistent ritual of Egypt. Thus, he discovered in Christianity the cult of Horus, misinterpreted. Dr. Churchward's tendency was, as a writer in the "Times" points out, to be carried away by theories which possessed the charm of simplicity, while largely ignoring the great mass of knowledge accumulated by previous workers in the same fields. It was, perhaps, this tendency to dogmatize and reject the theories and conclusions of other writers in the same field, Sir Oliver Lodge included, that made him less respected than he otherwise would have been by students. He was, however, a man of earnest spirit and of

indefatigable industry, and an undoubted searcher after truth. He had travelled extensively in Africa and other countries in pursuit of those branches of human learning and research in which he was mainly interested, and the result of his mission provoked a strengthening rather than a weakening of his faith in the Divine control of the universe.
[Obituary appearing in the "Freemason" on September 12, 1925]

Lost Continent of Mu, Motherland of Men
Page 307:
> (footnote) 34. Much of the detail concerning the Pyramid Temple comes from Dr. A. Churchward's work

List of publications:
- "The Signs and Symbols of Primordial Man, being an explanation of the Evolution of Religious Doctrines from the Eschatology of the Ancient Egyptians" (1910)
- "The Arcana of Freemasonry" (1915)
- "Origin and Evolution of the Human Race" (1921)
- "The Origin and Evolution of Religion" (1924)

Confucius (551-479 B.C.E)

Confucius was a famous Chinese philosopher. His teachings emphasize the responsibility that each person has to his family and country before oneself. His philosophy has formed the basis of Chinese thought until recent times.

Lost Continent of Mu, Motherland of Men
Page 136:
> The Chinese at the time of Confucius had "The Great Term," "The Great Unit," the great "Y." "The Y has neither body nor shape, all that has a body and shape was made by that which has no shape. The Great Term or The Great Unit comprehends Three: One is three and three are one."

Lost Continent of Mu, Motherland of Men
Page 288:
> CHINA. Confucius in *Khoung Tsen*.-The whole of Chapter XIX is dedicated to the description of the ceremony in honor of ancestors, as practised twice a year-in the spring and in the autumn.
> In *Lun Yu* Confucius says: "It is necessary to sacrifice to the ancestors as if they were present."

Excerpt from "Queen Moo and the Egyptian Sphinx" (1896) provides this text:
> Confucius in his book "Khoung-Tseu" dedicates a whole chapter to the description of the ceremony in honor of ancestors as practised twice a year, in spring and autumn, 2 and in his book "Lun-yu" he instructs his disciples that "it is necessary to sacrifice to the ancestors as though they were present."3
> 2. Confucius, Khong-Tseu, Tchoung-Young, chap. xix.
> 3. Idid., Lun-yu, chap. Iii., Sloka 12
> Augustus Le Plongeon, "Queen Moo and the Egyptian Sphinx" (1896), Page 9

List of publications:
- The Analects

Lieutenant Cushing [Cushing, Frank Hamilton (1857-1900)]

Frank Hamilton Cushing, former curator of the ethnological department of the National Museum in Washington, D.C., is best known for the years (1879-1882) that he studied the native American Zuni tribe while living with them. He is known as an innovator because of his participation in the culture under study (Zuni) as opposed to studying it as an outside observer.

Lost Continent of Mu, Motherland of Men
Page 189-191:

> Lieutenant Cushing lived among the Hopi Indians for a long time while he translated what has been called the Zuñi Myths, which are myths only because the people into whose hands they have passed have failed to understand them. These Pueblo traditions have been handed down orally from father to son for thousands of years, but a tradition is actual history, not a myth.
>
> I will take some extracts from Lieutenant Cushing's translations, which, added to my own personal knowledge of the Pueblos, makes interesting reading.
>
> For example, a Zuñi tradition says: "Once the earth was covered with water, no land appeared anywhere." Is this a myth? Not at all, for it has been corroborated by the sacred writings of the Motherland and by geology.

Excerpt from "Creation and the Origin of Corn"; (1884) provides the following text:

"First, there was sublime darkness, which vanished not until came the Ancient Father of the Sun, revealing universal waters. These were, save him, all that were."
From From "Zuñi Breadstuff," Millstone 9, no. 1 (1884): 1-3.

Continuing Lost Continent of Mu, Motherland of Men
Page 189-191:

Another Zuñi tradition says: "Just before man appeared upon the earth, the ground was so soft and watery man could not have walked upon it, his feet would sink into the ground, therefore he could not live upon it." A description of what sort of footwear a man must have had to enable him to pass over the soft, watery ground without sinking into it, is very amusing.

…

Another so-called Zuñi myth-The ancient Zuñis, thousands upon thousands of years ago, had a perfect knowledge of the great reptilian monstrosities that frequented the earth from the Carboniferous Age down to the end of the Cretaceous Period. These traditions say:

> "They were monsters and animals of prey; they were provided with claws and terrible teeth. A mountain lion is but a mole in comparison to them. Then Those Above said to these animals: 'Ye shall all be changed into stone, that ye be not evil to men, but that ye may be a great good to them. Thus have we changed ye into everlasting stone."
>
> "Thus was the surface of the earth hardened and many of all sorts of beasts turned into stone. Thus, too, it happens *that we find them throughout the world*. Their forms are sometimes large (in shape), like themselves; sometimes they are shriveled and distorted out of shape, and we often see among the rocks many beasts that no longer live, which show us that all was different in the days of the new."
>
> I think Cushing hardly caught the exact translations in the words I have italicized. My changes, however, in no way alter the meanings.

List of publications:
- Zuñi fetiches(1883) Second Annual Report of the Bureau of American Ethnology, 1880-1881 (Washington, D.C., 1883), pp. 9-15, 30-31

- Corn Raising: The Decay of the Seed; From "Zuñi Breadstuff," Millstone 9, no. 5 (1884) 75-78.
- Corn Raising: The Regeneration of the Seed; From "Zuñi Breadstuff," Millstone 9, no. 6 (1884): 93-95.
- Creation and the Origin of Corn; Millstone 9, no. 1 (1884): 1-3
- Clowns, Priests, and Festivals of the Kâ'-kâ; From "Zuñi Breadstuff", Millstone 10, no. 8 (1885): 141-44.
- A Study of Pueblo Pottery as Illustrative of Zuñi Culture Growth. Fourth Annual Report of the Bureau of Ethnology to the Secretary of the Smithsonian Institution(1886)
- Outlines of Zuñi creation myths (1896) Thirteenth Annual Report of the Bureau of American Ethnology, 1891-1892 (Washington, D.C., 1896), pp. 367-73.
- Relation of the pentagonal dodecahedron found near Marietta, Ohio. to Shamanism(1897)
- A chant, a myth, a prayer: Pai-ya-tu-ma, god of dew and the dawn. Outlines of Zuñi creation myths. (?)
- ZUÑI FOLK TALES [1901]
- Exploration of ancient key-dweller remains on the gulf coast of Florida (?)

Other references:
See online versions of F.H. Cushing's books at <http://sacred-texts.com/nam/zuni/index.htm> and Project Gutenberg <http://www.gutenberg.org/author/cushing>

Lizana [de Lizana Bernardo (?)]
Franciscan missionary and historian.

Lost Continent of Mu, Motherland of Men
Page 240-241:
> Lizana ("Historia de Nuestra Senora de Ytzamal," Chap. II): "When the Spaniards came to this country, notwithstanding that some of the monuments appeared new, as if they had been built only twenty years, the Indians did not live in them, but used them as temples and sanctuaries, offering in them sacrifices sometimes of men, women and children, and that their construction dates back to great antiquity.".

Excerpt from "Queen Moo and the Egyptian Sphinx" (1896) provides this text:
> "unmindful, likewise, of these words of Lizana: "That when the Spaniards came to this country, notwithstanding that that some of the monuments appeared new, as if they had been built only twenty years, the Indians did not live in them, but used them as temples and sanctuaries, offering in the sacrifices, sometimes of men, women, and children; and that their construction dated back to a very high antiquity"
> Augustus Le Plongeon, "Queen Moo and the Egyptian Sphinx" (1896), Introduction page xxxiii

List of publications:
- "Historia de Nuestra Señora de Izamal, de la Provincia de Yucatan" (Valladolid, 1633)

Other references:
- "Queen Moo and the Egyptian Sphinx" (1896) Appendix 1 Note v contains a biography of Bernardo Lizana

Eusebius (275-339)
Early Christian church leader based on his scholarship and knowledge. Eusebius was also a historian.

Lost Continent of Mu, Motherland of Men
Page 280:

Let us now see the result of a little research. Eusebius tells us that the Egyptians called the Creator Kneph, who was symbolized by a serpent. Here at once we see why the Serpent was held in such high veneration by the ancients-the Serpent was their symbol for the Creator.

Excerpt from "Sacred Mysteries Among the Maya and Quiches" (1886) provides this text:
> ... and Eusebius asserts, "That they represented Kneph, or the Efficient cause, as a man of blue color, with a girdle round his loins, a scepter in his hand, a crown on his head, adorned with a plume of feathers; and that emblematically they figured him under the form of a serpent."
> Augustus Le Plongeon, "Sacred Mysteries Among the Maya and Quiches" (1886), page 74
> See also pages, 99 & 109.

List of publications:
- Chronicle of Eusebius (325)
- Church History (326)
- Life of Constantine (unfinished)

Ezekiel (?)
Ezekial was a prophet to the Hebrew people that lived in the 6th century BCE. He is credited with writing the book in the Bible that bears his name.

Lost Continent of Mu, Motherland of Men
Page 296:
> ISRAELITES.- The conception of the four gods, pillars or genii, or whatever they may be termed, was not entirely rejected by the Jews. Although there is no mention of them in the books written by Moses, that is no criterion, because some of the books written by Moses are lost, and the reference to the four cardinal points may have been in one of these lost books. Later we see the conception among the Jews in Ezekiel, I :10--"They four had the face of a man, the face of a lion, the face of an ox and the face of an eagle." And in X:14-"The first face was that of a cherub, the second that of a man, the third that of a lion and the fourth that of an eagle."
> The foregoing is given as a vision of Ezekiel. At the time he wrote these lines he was a captive among the Chaldeans. Let us -compare his vision with the then Chaldean creed, which had been in existence for thousands of years, because these conceptions came from the Motherland through the Caucasian colony, or through the Naacals, who came to Babylonia from India.

King James Version; Ezekiel 1:4-10
> "4 As I looked, behold, a stormy wind came out of the north, and a great cloud, with brightness round about it, and fire flashing forth continually, and in the midst of the fire, as it were gleaming bronze. 5 And from the midst of it came the likeness of four living creatures. And this was their appearance: they had the form of men, 6 but each had four faces, and each of them had four wings. 7 Their legs were straight, and the soles of their feet were like the sole of a calf's foot; and they sparkled like burnished bronze. 8 Under their wings on their four sides they had human hands. And the four had their faces and their wings thus: 9 their wings touched one another; they went every one straight forward, without turning as they went. 10 As for the likeness of their faces, each had the face of a man in front; the four had the face of a lion on the right side, the four had the face of an ox on the left side, and the four had the face of an eagle at the back."

King James Version; Ezekiel 10:9-15

9 And when I looked, behold the four wheels by the cherubims, one wheel by one cherub, and another wheel by another cherub: and the appearance of the wheels was as the color of a beryl stone. 10 And as for their appearances, they four had one likeness, as if a wheel had been in the midst of a wheel. 11 When they went, they went upon their four sides; they turned not as they went, but to the place whither the head looked they followed it; they turned not as they went. 12 And their whole body, and their backs, and their hands, and their wings, and the wheels, were full of eyes round about, even the wheels that they four had. 13 As for the wheels, it was cried unto them in my hearing, O wheel. 14 And every one had four faces: the first face was the face of a cherub, and the second face was the face of a man, and the third the face of a lion, and the fourth the face of an eagle. 15 And the cherubims were lifted up. This is the living creature that I saw by the river of Chebar.

List of publications:
Book of Ezekiel – Old Testament

Ezra (4th Century B.C.)

Ezra was the leader of the Hebrew people that brought the people from Babylon in the 5th century BCE. He is credited with writing the Book of Ezra and the I Chronicles.

Lost Continent of Mu, Motherland of Men
Page 6:

> I have traced this same story from Mu to India, where colonizers from the vanished continent had settled; from India into Egypt; from Egypt to the temple of Sanai, where Moses copied it; and from Moses to the faulty translations of Ezra 800 years later. The plausibility of this will be apparent even to those who have not studied the subject carefully, when they see the close resemblance between the story of the creation as we know it and the tradition that originated in Mu.

Lost Continent of Mu, Motherland of Men
Page 286-287:

> Eight hundred years after the Israelitish Exodus from Egypt, Ezra, with a body of co-workers, collected all the tablets and writings of all descriptions which were connected with the family history of the Israelites, and put them into book form, which became the Bible.
>
> Those written by Moses were in Egyptian hieroglyphics. Is it any wonder that so many mistranslations were made by Ezra and his associates, when none of them were capable of thoroughly understanding the Egyptian writings of Moses? Only a Master could understand them, and neither Ezra nor any of his associates were Masters. Their incapability is clearly shown by comparing their translations with the original records which we find in the Egyptian, Chaldean, Hindu and Maya. Moses wrote sense; his translators made nonsense out of many of his passages. Moses wrote in the symbolical style of his day and his translators tried to translate literally. In this they only half succeeded, and when they came across a set of hieroglyphics they did not understand, they added a myth to sound history. The boundaries of the Garden of Eden is one of their myths.
>
> From incontrovertible evidences gained through my research work it is shown that Moses wrote the first books of the Bible from the temple records brought to Egypt from the Motherland by the Naacals via Burma and India; and that these Egyptian temple records were copies of the "Seven Sacred Inspired Writings" of the Motherland Mu. These were written on clay tablets and referred to the Creation. The legends of the Garden of Eden, the "Flood," the last magnetic cataclysm, and the raising of the mountains, are records of later date.
>
> Moses could have made no mistake in copying these writings, so they undoubtedly left his hands perfect copies of the originals. Eight hundred years after, an attempt was made to translate them into Hebrew by

men who did not understand the old Egyptian esoteric temple writings, hence the difference between what was produced and the original.

So little did Ezra and his associates understand these writings that I doubt if there is a single Hebrew today who knows the meaning of the burnt sacrifice and what it symbolized.

List of publications:
Book of Ezra
1 Chronicles

Forbes [Forbes, Henry Ogg (1851-1932)]

Explorer and Natural history collector. Director of Canterbury Museum in New Zealand (1890-1893) and Consulting Director to Liverpool Museums (1911-1932)

Lost Continent of Mu, Motherland of Men
Page 161:

Java is one of the large islands of the Malay Archipelago, and in writing of it, Forbes says:

"In Java is a tribe called the Karangs, supposed to be descendants of the aborigines of the island, whose old men and youths, four times a year, repair secretly in procession to a sacred grove in a dense forest, the old men to worship, the youths to see and learn the mysteries of their forefathers. In this grove are the ruins of terraces laid out in quadrilateral enclosures, the boundaries of which are marked by blocks of stone, or fixed in the ground. Here and there on the terraces are prominent monuments, *erect pillars*, and, especially noteworthy, a pillar *erect within a square*. Here these despised and secluded people follow the rites and customs that have been handed down to them through their forefathers from vastly remote ages (12,000 to 13,000 years), repeating with superstitious awe a litany which they do not understand or comprehend, This very litany is found in the Egyptian Book of the Dead."

Excerpt from "Signs and Symbols of Primordial Man" (1912) provides this text:

Forbes mentions that in Java is a tribe called the Karangs, supposed to be descendants of the aborigines of the island, whose old men and youths, four times a year, repair secretly in procession, by paths known only to themselves, to a sacred grove in the dense forest: the old men to worship, the youths to see and learn the mysterious litany of their fathers.

In this grove are the ruins of terraces, laid out in quadrilateral enclosures, the boundaries of which are marked by blocks of stone laid or fixed in the ground. Here and there on the terraces are more prominent monuments, erect pillars, etc., and, especially noteworthy, a pillar erect within a square. Here these despised and secluded people follow the rites and customs that have descended to them through their forefathers from vastly remote antiquity, repeating with a superstitious awe a litany which they do not comprehend, the origins and purpose of which are lost in their traditions, but which may be found in the Egyptian Papyrus (Papyrus of Leyden) and the "Ritual or Book of the Dead."
Albert Churchward, "Signs and Symbols of Primordial Man" (1912), page 17, 21

List of publications:
* A naturalist's wanderings in the Eastern archipelago : a narrative of travel and exploration from 1878 to 1883 (1885)

Professor R.W. Gilder [Gilder, Robert Fletcher (1856-1940)]

The reference to R.W. Gilder appears to be an error. Professor R.F. (Robert Fletcher) Guider did have a brother, R.W. (Richard Watson) Gilder that was a New York publisher and held parties at his residence that James may have attended.

Robert was trained as an artist and was employed as a printer for several Omaha newspapers. Later in life he became the chief archaeologist for the University of Nebraska Museum for twelve years and continued painting.

Lost Continent of Mu, Motherland of Men
Page 197:

> NEBRASKA. - Professor R. W. Gilder of Omaha, Nebraska, has made one of the most remarkable and one of the most valuable archaeological discoveries ever made in any part of the world. His discovery shows uncontrovertibly that man was living in North America, in a highly civilized state, back in the Tertiary Era.
> Gilder has discovered a civilization that was wiped out by the waters of the last magnetic cataclysm, which was the biblical "Flood" and the geological Glacial Period.

From Scrapbook #1, Sheet 31, article entitled "Den Men of Nebraska"

> Americans who lived in Underground Prairie Homes
> Professor Robert W. Gilder, archaeologist for the University of Nebraska, has made the curious discovery that the familiar "buffalo wallows" of the West were never made by buffaloes. They are, instead, the ruins of underground dwellings in which thousands of years ago lived a race which vanished other thousands of years ago.

Lost Continent of Mu, Motherland of Men
Page 198:

> Illustration captioned as follows:
> GILDER'S DISCOVERIES, NEBRASKA
> 1. Pipe – glazed clay; 2. Fishhook – bone; 3. Clay head; 4. Pink soapstone head;
> 5. Ornamental shell; 6. Comb – elk-horn

Lost Continent of Mu, Motherland of Men
Page 199-200:

> Gilder reports that: "the familiar buffalo wallows of the west were never made by buffaloes; they are, instead, the entrances to ruins of underground dwellings, in which, thousands of years ago, lived a race which has vanished from the earth. There is no indication of who the people were or *how they were wiped out.*"

From Scrapbook #1, Sheet 31, article entitled "Den Men of Nebraska":

> Americans who lived in Underground Prairie Homes
> Professor Robert W. Gilder, archaeologist for the University of Nebraska, has made the curious discovery that the familiar "buffalo wallows" of the West were never made by buffaloes. They are, instead, the ruins of underground dwellings in which thousands of years ago lived a race which vanished other thousands of years ago.

The "wallows" were thought to be what their name indicates even by the Indians, thus proving that the red men themselves knew nothing of the race that made the dens.

The modern Indian were just as much surprised as the whites when they discovered what Professor Gilder was taking out of the old indentations. The archaeologist would point to one of the wallows and then tell his little audience just what he would find in it. This he was enabled to do so by reason of the curious similarity in the arrangement of and the things found in the dens. The Indians were appalled, however, by what they thought his uncanny foresight, and now they call him "Man-Who-Sees-Through-the-Ground."

…

This mysterious people dwelt by the millions on the prairies. Professor Gilder has uncovered near the west bank of the Missouri River, near Omaha, what appears to have been a metropolis of the race. Ethnologists who have examined the relics have found no resemblance with either the pre-Columbian Indians or with the mound builders.

There is no clue to indicate who these people were or how they were wiped out. Nor is it clear what conditions forced a whole race to live in burrows beneath the ground.

Lost Continent of Mu, Motherland of Men
Page 199-200 (continued):
Among the ruins of these long-filled burrows Gilder has found various works of art of the vanished race.
Fig. 1. Is a glazed clay pipe.
Fig. 2. Is a fish-hook made of bone.
Fig. 3. Is a clay face with prominently sloping eyes.
Fig. 4. Is a small pink soapstone head. Gilder says of this: "The pink head is Egyptian in every feature. It is delicately carved and highly polished. It is Egyptian in head-dress, having even the rectangular ear-guards worn by the Egyptians. It is more than Egyptian; it resembles the face of Rameses II himself, if the marble busts in Oriental museums today are images of the Egyptian king."
Fig. 5. Is an ornament made of shell.
Fig. 6. Is a comb made of elk-horn.

From Scrapbook #1, Sheet 31, article entitled "Den Men of Nebraska":
However, among the ruins, of the long-filled burrows Professor Gilder has found a little carved head of pink soapstone.

The little pink head is Egyptian in every feature. It is delicately carved and highly polished. It is Egyptian in headdress, having even the rectangular ear guard worn by the Egyptians. It is more than Egyptian. It resembles the face of Rameses II himself. If the marble busts in Oriental museums to-day are images of the Egyptian king and the mummy unearthed I the sands of Egypt in 1881 and now reposing in the Boulak Museum in Cairo is really his corpse.

Another clay image has the pronouncedly sloping eyes peculiar to Chinese.

Lost Continent of Mu, Motherland of Men
Page 199-200 (continued):
"The floors of these underground burrows are strewn with charred sticks, reeds, coarse grasses and corncobs. In the floor of every cave is found a cache, where most of the domestic utensils and other valuables were kept hidden. Sometimes there are several in the same cave. The mouths of the caches are always found plugged with layers of burnt clay. On top of this is a layer of ashes. Beneath all, the cavity widens like a jug or bottle, often the size of a hogshead."
These artificial caves were filled in with the soil and drift torn up by the waves of the cataclysm as they rolled down over the plains. In time this filling packed and left a hollow at the entrance, which has been called a "buffalo wallow."
Gilder's civilization was wiped out by the last magnetic cataclysm. Therefore it was a *Tertiary Era civilization.*

KENTUCKY.-In Kentucky are found the remains of a civilization that was contemporaneous with Gilder's Nebraska civilization.

From Scrapbook #1, Sheet 31, article entitled "Den Men of Nebraska":
Geologists have furnished some assistance to the archaeologists in determining the probable age of the ruins. It takes years for black soil to accumulate where it is not washed in. This soil accumulates from decaying grasses. Darwin once made an experiment in the accretion of soil, and computed that but little over an inch collected in a hundred years.

How many centuries, then, may have gone while these two or three feet of black soil have gathered on the sunken roofs of the fallen cave homes!

At least a thousand years before Christ, say the geologists, our cavemen dropped into oblivion and their homes had begun to decay.

In uncovering something over thirty of these homes professor Gilda has established the general character of the caves and their contents. The floor is strewn with charred sticks, reeds, coarse grasses and charred corncobs. In the floor of every cave is found a cache where most of the domestic utensils and the other valuables are hidden. It is this cache that the archaeologist always seeks. Sometimes there are several in the same cave. The mouth of the cache is always found plugged with a layer of burnt clay. On top of this is a layer of ashes. Beneath all, the cavity widens like a jug or a bottle, often to the size of a hogshead.

Scrapbook references:
Scrapbook 1, Sheet 31; article entitled: "Den Men of Nebraska" (Note that no pictures were included with the text of the article.)

List of publications:
- Recent Excavations at Long's Hill, Nebraska. American Anthropologist January, 1908 Vol 10(1):60-73.
- Excavation of Earth-Lodge Ruins in Eastern Nebraska. American Anthropologist, 1909 Vol. 11:56-84
- The Nebraska culture man (1926)

Rider Haggard [Sir Henry Rider Haggard (1865-1925)]
Sir Henry was a prolific author and best known for his book, *King Solomon's Mines*. He traveled extensively throughout the world.

Lost Continent of Mu, Motherland of Men
Page 247:
Rider Haggard must have found this same tradition, for in his work, "Montezuma's Daughter," he says: "Quetzal, or more properly, Quetzalcoatl, was the divinity who is fabled to have taught the natives of Anahuac all the useful arts, including those of government and policy. He was white-skinned and light-haired. Finally he sailed from the shores of Anahuac for the fabulous country of Hapallan in a bark of serpent skins."

From Montezuma's Daughter (1893)
* Quetzal, or more properly Quetzalcoatl, was the divinity who is fabled to have taught the natives of Anahuac all the useful arts, including those of government and policy, he was white-skinned and dark-haired. Finally he sailed from the shores of Anahuac for the fabulous country of Tlapallan in a bark of serpents' skins.

List of publications:
- Dawn (1884)
- The Witch's Tale (1884)
- King Solomon's Mines (1885)
- She (1887)
- Jess (1887)
- Allan Quatermain (1887)
- A Tale of Three Lions (1887)
- Mr. Meeson's Will (1888)
- Maiwa's Revenge (1888)
- My Fellow Laborer and the Wreck of the Copeland (1888)
- Colonel Quaritch, V.C. (1888)
- Cleopatra (1889)
- Allan's Wife (1889)
- Beatrice (1890)
- The World's Desire (1890) (co-written with Andrew Lang)
- Eric Brighteyes (1891)
- Nada the Lily (1892)
- Montezuma's Daughter (1893)
- The People of the Mist (1894)
- Joan Haste (1895)
- Heart of the World (1895)
- Church and State (1895)
- The Wizard (1896)
- Dr. Therne (1898)
- Swallow (1898)
- A Farmer's Year (1899)
- The Last Boer War (1899)
- The Spring of Lion (1899)
- Montezuma's Daughter (1899)
- Black Heart, White Heart (1900)
- The New South Africa (1900)
- A Winter Pilgrimage (1901)
- Lysbeth (1901)
- Rural England (1902)
- Pearl Maiden (1903)
- Stella Fregelius (1904)
- The Brethren (1904)
- The Poor and the Land (1905)
- Ayesha (1905)
- A Gardener's Year (1905)
- Report of Salvation Army Colonies (1905)

- The Way of the Spirit (1906)
- Benita (1906)
- Fair Margaret (1907)
- The Ghost Kings (1908)
- The Yellow God (1908)
- The Lady of Blossholme (1909)
- Queen Sheba's Ring (1910)
- Regeneration: An account of the social work of the Salvation Army (1910)
- Morning Star (1910)
- Red Eve (1911)
- The Mahatma and the Hare (1911)
- Rural Denmark (1911)
- Marie (1912)
- Child of Storm (1913)
- The Wanderer's Necklace (1914)
- A call to Arms (1914)
- The Holy Flower (1915)
- After the War Settlement and Employment of Ex-Service Men (1916)
- The Ivory Child (1916)
- Finished (1917)
- Love Eternal (1918)
- Moon of Israel (1918)
- When the World Shook (1919)
- The Ancient Allan (1920)
- Smith and the Pharaohs (1920)
- She and Allan (1921)
- The Virgin of the Sun (1922)
- Wisdom's Daughter (1923)
- Heu-Heu (1924)
- Queen of the Dawn (1925)
- The Days of my Life: An autobiography of Sir H. Rider Haggard (1926)
- Treasure of the Lake (1926)
- Allan and the Ice Gods (1927)
- Mary of Marion Isle (1929)
- Belshazzar (1930)

R. G. Haliburton [Haliburton, Robert Grant (1831-1901)]
Canadian lawyer and ethnologist.

Lost Continent of Mu, Motherland of Men
Page 289:

> R. G. Haliburton, who is considered one of our best authorities on ancestral worship, in writing of the "Festival of Ancestors," says:
> "It is now, as it was 'formerly, held at or near the beginning of November, by the Peruvians, the Hindus, the Pacific Islanders, the people of the Tonga Islands, the Australians, the ancient Persians, the ancient

Egyptians and the northern nations of Europe, and continues for three days among the Japanese, the Hindus, the Australians, the ancient Romans and the ancient Egyptians."

Excerpt from "Queen Moo and the Egyptian Sphinx" (1896) provides this text:

Mr. R.G. Haliburton, of Boston, Mass., in a very learned and most interesting paper1 on the "Festival of Ancestors," or the feast of the dead so prevalent among all nations of the earth, speaking of the singularity of its being observed everywhere at precisely the same epoch of the year, says: "It is now, as it was formerly, observed at or near the beginning of November by the Peruvians, the Hindoos, the Pacific Islanders, the people of the Tonga Islands, the Australians, the ancient Persians, the ancient Egyptians, and the northern nations of Europe, and continued for three days among the Japanese, the Hindoos, the Australians, the ancient Romans, and the ancient Egyptians…

1. R.G. Haliburton, Festival of Ancestors," *Ethnological Researches Bearing on the Year of the Pleiades.*

Augustus Le Plongeon, "Queen Moo and the Egyptian Sphinx" (1896), Page 11

List of publications:
- "Festival of Ancestors, Ethnological Researches Bearing on the Year of the Pleiades."
- New materials for the history of man, derived from a comparison of the calendars and festivals of nations. (1863)
- How a race of pygmies was found in North Africa and Spain (1897)
- Intercolonial trade our only safeguard against disunion (1892)
- Crown colonies of Great Britain (1885)
- A sketch of the life and times of Judge Haliburton (1897)

Professor Hewitt [Hewett, Edgar Lee (1865-1946)]
Archaeologist, Director of American Archaeology at the Archaeological Institute of America in Santa Fe, New Mexico, and founder of the Museum of New Mexico in 1909.

Lost Continent of Mu, Motherland of Men
Page 197:

In confirmation of the foregoing, Professor E. L. Hewitt of the Las Vegas University reports that he has found in the homes of an ancient people, fossil remains of the mastodon and sabre-tooth tiger; also utensils made out of *live*, not fossil ivory, thus corroborating the Hava Supai Canyon picture.

List of publications:
- Government supervision of historic and prehistoric ruins. (1904)
- Circular relating to historic and prehistoric ruins of the Southwest and their preservation. (1904)
- Antiquities of the Southwest and their preservation. (1905)
- Ethnic factors in education, by Edgar L. Hewett. (1905)
- Antiquities of the Jemez Plateau, New Mexico; (1906)
- Groundwork of American archaeology, (1908)
- Excavations at Tyuonyi, (1909)
- Pajaritan culture, by Edgar L. Hewett. (1909)
- Excavation at Puye, New Mexico, (1909)
- Ancient ruins of the Southwest, by Edgar L. Hewett... (1909)
- Excavations at El Rito de los Frijoles in 1909, (1909)
- Two seasons' work in Guatemala (illustrated), by Edgar L. Hewett. (1911)

- Third season's work in Guatemala (illustrated) by Edgar L. Hewett. (1912)
- Physiography of the Rio Grande valley, New Mexico, in relation to Pueblo culture; by Edgar Lee Hewett, Junius Henderson, and Wilfred Robbins. (1913)
- Proposed "National park of the cliff cities," (1916)
- Architecture of the Exposition, by Edgar L. Hewett and Wm. Templeton Johnson. (1916)
- Our native architecture in its relation to Santa Fe, (1917)
- Southwest: yesterday and tomorrow, (1921)
- Proposed Indian theater in Santa Fé, by Edgar L. Hewett. (1925)
- Letters on the Pueblo Indian situation, by Edgar L. Hewett. (1925)
- Ancient life in American Southwest, with an introduction on the general history of the American race, (1930)
- Sciences of man in the program of research; an address by Edgar L. Hewett; delivered at the University of New Mexico, Albuquerque ... June 4, l934. (1934)
- Ancient life in Mexico and Central America, by Edgar L. Hewett. (1936)
- Chaco Canyon and its monuments, by Edgar L. Hewett. Publication of the University of New Mexico and the School of American Research. (1936)
- Indians of the Rio Grande Valley, by Adolph F. Bandelier and Edgar L. Hewett. Publication of the University of New Mexico and the School of American Research. (1937)
- Hispanic monuments, by Edgar L. Hewett. (1938)
- Pajarito plateau and its ancient people, by Edgar L. Hewett. (1938)
- Ancient Andean life, by Edgar L. Hewett ... (1939)
- Representative art and artists of New Mexico. (1940)
- Landmarks of New Mexico, by Edgar L. Hewett and Wayne L. Mauzy. Publication of the University of New Mexico and the School of American research. (1940)
- What is man? (1942)
- From culture to civilization, by Edgar L. Hewett. (1942)
- Limits of idealism, by Edgar L. Hewett. (1942)
- From cave dwelling to Mount Olympus, (1943)
- ...Mission monuments of New Mexico, by Edgar L. Hewett and Reginald G. Fisher. Publication of the University of New Mexico and the School of American research. (1943)
- Man and culture. (1944)
- Man and the state, by Edgar L. Hewett ... (1944)
- Fray Bernardino de Sahagun and the great Florentine codex, by Edgar L. Hewett. (1944)
- Campfire and trail, (1943) Pueblo Indian world; studies on the natural history of the Rio Grande valley in relation to Pueblo Indian culture, edited, adapted, and amplified by Edgar L. Hewett and Bertha P. Dutton; with appendices: The southwest Indian languages and The sounds and s (1945)
- Two score years, by Edgar L. Hewett. (1946)

Dr. Walter Hough (1859-1935)

Walter Hough, Ph.D. (1859-1935) was an American ethnologist from Morgantown, West Virginia. He was employed at the United States National Museum as an assistant curator of ethnology and as curator. He was a member of Dr. J. Walter Fewkes expedition to Arizona (1896-97.)

Lost Continent of Mu, Motherland of Men
Page 186-187:

ARIZONA. -Dr. Walter Hough of the Smithsonian Institution made an examination of the petrified forests of Arizona and reported that he had found the remains of four distinct peoples there. This find corresponds with my own discoveries in our western and southwestern states, as well as Mexico. Three of Hough's civilizations existed before the mountains were raised.

List of publications:
- Ancient Central and South American pottery in the Columbian Historical Exposition at Madrid in 1892. (1892)
- Bernadou, Allen, and Jouy Korean collections, in the U.S. National Museum. (1892)
- Environmental interrelations in Arizona;(1898)
- Early West Virginia pottery(1901)
- Collection of Hopi ceremonial pigments.(1902)
- Archeological field work in northeastern Arizona. The Museum-Gates expedition of 1901.(1903)
- Antiquities of the upper Gila and Salt River valleys in Arizona and New Mexico (1907)
- Censers and incense of Mexico and Central America. (1912)
- Culture of the ancient Pueblos of the upper Gila River region, New Mexico and Arizona(1914)
- Exploration of a pit house village at Luna, New Mexico.(1920)
- Fire origin myths of the New World(1924)
- Fire as an agent in human culture, (1926)
- Collection of heating and lighting utensils in the United States National museum(1928)
- Fire-making apparatus in the United States National museum(1929)
- Exploration of ruins in the White mountain Apache Indian reservation, Arizona,(1931)
- Ancient seating furniture in the collections of the United States National museum (1931)
- Buffalo motive in middle Celebes decorative design (1932)
- Cache of basket maker baskets from New Mexico(1933)
- Decorative designs on Elden pueblo pottery(1933)

Professor Kozloff [Kozlov, Piotr Kumich (1863-1935)]
was a Russian explorer who continued the studies of Nikolai Przhevalsky in Mongolia and Tibet.

Although prepared by his parents for military career, Kozlov chose to join Przhevalsky's expedition and continued traveling in Asia with his successors, Pevtsov and Roborovsky. In 1895, he took general command of the expedition from ailing Roborovsky. From 1899 to 1901 he explored and later described in a book the upper reaches of Huang He, Yangtze, and Mekong rivers.

During the expedition of 1907–1909, Kozlov explored the Gobi Desert and discovered remains of Khara-Khoto, a Tangut city. It took him several years to excavate the site and bring to St. Petersburg no less than 2,000 books in Tangut language he uncovered there. Kozlov described his findings in a bulky volume entitled Mongolia and Amdo and the Dead City of Khara-Khoto (1923).

His last expedition to Mongolia and Tibet (1923-1926) resulted in discovery of an unprecedented number of Xiongnu royal burials. After bringing to St. Petersburg some amazing samples of 2000-year-old Bactrian textiles, Kozlov retired from scientific work and settled in a village near Novgorod.

Lost Continent of Mu, Motherland of Men
Page 107:
> Professor Kozloff unearthed a tomb 50 feet below the surface at Khara Khoto and in it found wonderful treasures, which he photographed, not being allowed to disturb or take anything away. Through the

courtesy and kindness of the *Sunday American* I have obtained the loan of some of these pictures, two of which I here reproduce with their decipherings.

From Scrapbook #1 page 38:

> …
>
> Digging down through half-a-hundred feet of shifting sand, Professor Kozloff has unearthed there the tombs of what appear to be the legendary Seven Kings of ancient Tartary - certainly the oldest kings that ever ruled any civilization. At this depth the tools of his men struck brick and fossilized black wood. Cutting through this an opening large enough to let a man go through, they lowered Kozloff into the black depths.
>
> As the explorer reached the bottom of the secret chamber his flash revealed one of the most astonishing sites ever seen by an archaeologist - stranger than the scene that met the eyes of the finders of old Pharaoh Titankhamen's tomb.
>
> He was in a great vaulted chamber. In the center of the chamber was a long table of fossilized wood.
>
> …

Lost Continent of Mu, Motherland of Men
Page 109-110:

> Kozloff had pictures of various scepters. This illustration is of a different pattern to the one held in the queen's hand, and of later date, but symbolically reads the same, the ends being divided into three giving the numeral of the Motherland.

From Scrapbook #1 page 39:

There are two pictures (reproduced below,) and it appears that the article that the information was copied from had other pictures.

A Painting of a Goddess of the Vanished Race, Photographed by Professor Kozloff in the Tomb of the Seven Kings.

A Golden Scepter of One of the Ancient Kings Found in the Secret Tomb.

Reproduction of pictures from Scrapbook #1 page 39

Scrapbook references:
Scrapbook 1 pages 38-39

List of publications:
- Mongolia and Amdo and the Dead City of Khara-Khoto (1923)
- THE SCIENTIFIC RESULTS OF THE RUSSIAN EXPEDITION TO KHAM (1905)
- The Mongolia-Szechuan expedition of the Imperial Russian Geographical Society (1909)
- Through Eastern Tibet and Kam (1908)

LePlongeon [LePlongeon, Augustus (1825-1908)]
was a photographer, antiquarian and amateur archaeologist who made the first attempted excavations and photographic records of the ruins of Chichen Itza, a site of the pre-Columbian Maya civilization on the northern Yucatán peninsula, Central America.

Lost Continent of Mu, Motherland of Men
Page 40:

"Le Plongeon advanced the theory that Central America was the Lands of the West and therefore the land of Mu, basing his deductions on the contour of the land around the Caribbean Sea, but forgetting entirely that all records establish the fact that the Lands of the West were destroyed and submerged, while Central America to this day is, of course, unsubmerged."

Lost Continent of Mu, Motherland of Men
Page 57:

Le Plongeon found records in Yucatan stating that "the Hieratic head of the Land of Mu prophesied its destruction, and that some, heeding the prophesy, left and went to the colonies where they were saved."

Lost Continent of Mu, Motherland of Men
Page 58:

Le Plongeon's death occurred many years before Schliemann published the Lhasa Record.
[Augustus LePlongeon died in 1908, Schliemann's article was not published until 1912]

Lost Continent of Mu, Motherland of Men
Page 118:

Le Plongeon found in the center of the mausoleum of Cay, the high priest and eldest son of King Can, at Chichen Itza, Yucatan, a carving of a serpent having twelve heads, with an inscription saying that this serpent was a symbol of the twelve Maya dynasties that had reigned over Mayax previous to the Can dynasty, and that their combined reigns covered a period of 18,000 years.

Lost Continent of Mu, Motherland of Men
Page 218:

Niven says that the characters on the gold and silver ornaments are different from either those of Mitla or Palenque. Le Plongeon has called attention in his works to the fact that the characters found at Palenque, Mitla and Copan are different from and totally unlike the Maya.

Lost Continent of Mu, Motherland of Men
Page 219:

Le Plongeon discovered in the tomb of Queen Moo of Mayax a green jade ornament which he called "Queen Moo's Talisman." I have examined this ornament and can safely say it is not New Zealand jade, so that the green jade found in Mexico must have either come there from China or the Motherland.

Lost Continent of Mu, Motherland of Men
Page 235:

The late Dr. Le Plongeon and his wife, Alice D. Le Plongeon, very dear friends of the writer, were the first archaeological explorers to delve among the buried parts of Yucatan ruins. Their works which have been published give many interesting details of their discoveries:
Not one-half of their discoveries, however, were published. Before the death of Dr. Le Plongeon, he gave the writer his unpublished notes and translations for copy; so that what I say about Yucatan comes principally from the result of Dr. Le Plongeon's twelve years among the ruins, much of which, however, I have corroborated by a personal examination.

My first notes on Yucatan remains will concern some archaeological records unearthed by Le Plongeon.

Lost Continent of Mu, Motherland of Men
Page 237:

> At Uxmal there is an ancient Maya temple which Le Plongeon has called in his works, "The Temple of Sacred Mysteries. "

Lost Continent of Mu, Motherland of Men
Page 238:

> How long the Temple of Sacred Mysteries had been standing beyond the period I have assigned to it no one can say, but certainly not very long, because this temple was a memorial commemorating the loss of the Lands of the West and they disappeared only a short time before the disappearance of Atlantis. Le Plongeon found an inscription on the temple walls, which reads as follows:
> "This edifice is a memorial commemorating the destruction of Mu, the Lands of the West, whence came our sacred mysteries."

Lost Continent of Mu, Motherland of Men
Page 239:

> Le Plongeon also found an inscription on one of the buildings saying that "Uxmal had been destroyed by earthquakes three times and had been three times rebuilt."

Lost Continent of Mu, Motherland of Men
Page 241:

> Le Plongeon says: "These buildings were neither constructed by the present race nor their ancestors."
> …
> Le Plongeon: "Among the symbols sculptured on the mastodons' trunks that at a very remote period in Maya history embellished the facades of all sacred and public edifices, these signs are occasionally seen: [Figs. 1,2 and 3]. Taken collectively they read, *Chaac* ('Thunder')."

Lost Continent of Mu, Motherland of Men
Page 289:

> Le Plongeon, in his book, "Central America," says:
> "Even today the aborigines of Yucatan, Petan and other countries of Central America, where the Maya language is spoken, are wont, at the beginning of November, to hang from the branches of certain trees in clearings of the forests, at cross roads, and in isolated nooks, cakes made of the best com and meal they can procure. These are for the souls of the departed."

Excerpt from "Queen Moo and the Egyptian Sphinx" (1896) provides this text:

> Even to-day the aborigines of Yucatan, Peten, and other countries in Central America where the Maya language is spoken, as if in obedience to this affirmation of the Hindoo legislator... are wont, at the beginning of November, to hang from the branches of certain trees in the clearings of the forests, at cross-roads, in isolated nook, cakes made of the best corn and meat they can procure. These are for the souls of the departed to partake of, as their name hanal pixan ("foot of the souls") clearly indicates.
> Augustus Le Plongeon, "Queen Moo and the Egyptian Sphinx" (1896), Page 10

Lost Continent of Mu, Motherland of Men
Page 297:

> The equilateral triangle representing the Trinity is constantly found among the temple carvings of Yucatan. I have, however, been unable to satisfactorily determine the original names of the Maya Triune

Godhead. Le Plongeon and others have given sets of three, and even five, which form the full Godhead, but to me all of them appear incorrect from the fact that names are given of people who lived tens of thousands of years after the Triune Godhead was conceived.

Lost Continent of Mu, Motherland of Men
Page 300:

Le Plongeon translated the Popol Yuh into English from Brasseur's French translation, checking it himself with the original Maya. This copy he kindly lent me to make notes from. The following from the Popol Yuh therefore comes through Le Plongeon.

Lost Continent of Mu, Motherland of Men
Page 302-303:

The foregoing is a synopsis of Le Plongeon's translations. He says these rites were practiced at Xibalba, a place in the heart of the Guatemala mountains.

I am afraid Le Plongeon has failed to give the correct impressions as regards these trials. He should have told his readers that they were all symbolical; whereas he has tried to leave the impression that they were literal, thereby attempting to produce a blood-curdling, awe-inspiring, supernatural mystery. Le Plongeon, however, forgot himself on one occasion; for he states in the First Trial that the candidate is *prepared* beforehand, therefore knowing what to say, what to do, and how to act. In other words, the candidate has been previously taught his lessons, and these trials were examinations to ascertain whether he knew them.

Lost Continent of Mu, Motherland of Men
Page 303:

Le Plongeon, however, forgot himself on one occasion; for he states in the First Trial that the candidate is *prepared* beforehand, therefore knowing what to say, what to do, and how to act. In other words, the candidate has been previously taught his lessons, and these trials were examinations to ascertain whether he knew them.

List of publications:
    "Queen Moo and the Egyptian Sphinx" (1896)
    "Sacred Mysteries Among the Mayas and the Quiches" (1886)
    "The Monuments of Mayach and Their Historical Teachings" (unpublished)

Cogolludo [Lopez de Cogolludo, Diego (1613-1665)]
Was a Franciscan monk and historian.

Lost Continent of Mu, Motherland of Men
Page 240:

Cogolludo, in "Historia de Yucathan," Book IV, Chap. III, p. 177, says:

"Of the people who first settled in this Kingdom of Yucathan, or their ancient history, I have been unable to obtain any other data than those which follow:

"The Spanish chronicles do not give one reliable word about the manners and customs of the builders of the grand antique edifices that were objects of admiration to them, as they are now to modem travelers.

"The only answer of the natives to the inquiries of the Spaniards as to who the builders were invariably was, 'We do not know.' It is not known who the builders were and the Indians themselves have no traditions on the subject."

Excerpt from "Queen Moo and the Egyptian Sphinx" (1896) provides this text:
"- regardless of Cogolludo's assertion "that it is not known who their builders were, and that the Indians themselves preserved no traditions on the subject;"...
"Of the people who first settled in this Kingdom of Yucathan," he says, "nor of their ancient history, have I been able to find any more data than those I mention here."
Augustus Le Plongeon, "Queen Moo and the Egyptian Sphinx" (1896), Introduction page xxxiii

List of publications:
- "Historia de Yucathan / compuesta por el M. R. P. Fr. Diego Lopez Cogolludo, lector jubilado, y padre perpetuo de dicha provincia ... ; sacala a luz el M. R. P. Fr. Francisco de Ayeta, predicador, ex-custodio del Nuevo Mexico, comissario general del Santo" (1688)

Other references:
"Queen Moo and the Egyptian Sphinx" (1896) Appendix 1 Note ii contains a biography of Diego Cogolludo.

***

Donald A. Mackenzie (1873-1936)
Author, collector of myths and legends.

Lost Continent of Mu, Motherland of Men
Page 99-100:
Donald A. Mackenzie: "The fusion of the two ancient Egyptian cults, that of Osiris, which originally believed in a paradise in the *west* and that of the *sun-worshippers* who believed in a celestial paradise in the east.
"Osiris, an ancient deified *king* was identified with the gods of the *western* cult."
"The early conflict between the two cults is echoed in the mortuary texts, dating back till about 2700 B. C."
Like all Egyptologists, Mackenzie is sadly deficient in symbololology. All fail to differentiate between the symbol and what it represents. They fail to remember that the ancients used a special symbol for every attribute of the Deity, and that the sun was the collective symbol of all the attributes of the Deity, and therefore represented the Diety Himself.
The Upper Egyptians were *not* sun-worshippers, as stated by Mackenzie. Ra, the sun, was their collective symbol for the Deity. Temples were dedicated to Ra as *representing* the Divinity, just as the cross today represents Christ.
A symbol is an intimate reminder, mentally concentrating and bringing in closer touch with the eyes of the mind, bringing in closer touch and mental view the object addressed. With the use of symbols many encroaching outside thoughts are driven away. A symbol permits of greater concentration.
Mackenzie asserts that Osiris was an ancient king. What people he reigned over Mackenzie does not say, but by inference it would be the Egyptians; if so, he is wrong again, because when Thoth started the first Lower Egyptian colony at Sais, he taught the Osirian religion, as various papyri show, and that was 16,000 years ago. From two different sources I find it stated that Osiris lived in Atlantis 18,000 or 20,000 years ago, and that he was a great religious teacher—a master.

The two Egyptian cults form another convincing proof that the advent of man on earth was on Mu, and that Mu was situated in the Pacific. The geographical position is thus positively established as east of Burma and west of May ax and therefore in the Pacific Ocean.

List of publications:
- Elves and Heroes (1909)
- Khalifate of the West, being a general description of Morocco, by Donald Mackenzie. (1911)
- Migration of symbols and their relations to beliefs and customs, by Donald A. Mackenzie.(1926)
- Scottish folk-lore and folk life; studies in race, culture and tradition, by Donald A. Mackenzie.(1911)
- Teutonic myth and legend, by Donald A. Mackenzie; an introduction to the Eddas & sagas, Beowulf, the Nibelungenlied, etc. (1912)
- Egyptian myth and legend, by Donald A. Mackenzie, with historical narrative, notes on race problems, comparative beliefs, etc. (1913)
- Indian myth and legend [by] Donald A. Mackenzie. With illus. in color by Warwick Goble and numerous monochrome plates.(1913)
- Indian fairy stories, by Donald A. Mackenzie ... With illustrations by Maxwell Armfield. (1915)
- Stories of Russian folk-life. (1916)
- Wonder tales from Scottish myth & legend, by Donald A. Mackenzie. With illustrations by John Duncan. (1917)
- Myths Of Crete And Pre-Hellenic Europe (1917)
- From all the fronts, by Donald A. Mackenzie ... (1918)
- Ancient man in Britain, by Donald A. Mackenzie ... with a foreword by G. Elliot Smith, F.R.S. (1922)
- Myths of China and Japan, (1923)
- Wonder tales of the East (1923)
- Myths of pre-Columbian America by Donald A. Mackenzie. (1924)
- Tales from northern sagas, by Donald A. Mackenzie ... with illustrations by A. E. Haswell Miller ... (1926)
- Story of ancient Egypt, (1927)
- Footprints of early man, by Donald A. Mackenzie ... (1927)
- Ancient civilizations from the earliest times to the birth of Christ, by Donald A. Mackenzie. (1927)
- Buddhism in pre-Christian Britain, by Donald A. Mackenzie. (1928)
- Rome through five centuries; an historical survey from early times to the beginning of the Christian era, by Donald A. Mackenzie. (1928)
- Myths of Babylonia and Assyria (193?)
- Scotland: the ancient kingdom, by Donald A. Mackenzie... (1930)
- Myths and traditions of the South sea islands, by Donald A. Mackenzie. (1930)
- Myths from Melanesia and Indonesia, by Donald A. Mackenzie. (1930)
- Tales from the moors and the mountains, by Donald A. Mackenzie. (1931)

Mestrius Plutarchus [Plutarch (46 – 127)]
was a Greek historian, biographer, and essayist

Lost Continent of Mu, Motherland of Men
Page 60:

Plutarch. *Life of Solon.*—"Sanches, the High Priest of Sai's, told Solon [600 B. C.], also Psenophis, a priest of Heliopolis, that 9,000 years before, the relations of the Egyptians with the inhabitants of the *Lands of the West* had been interrupted because of cataclysms destroying the *intervening* country, *and—* the mud that had made the sea impassable since the *destruction of Atlantis by earthquakes and submersion.*"

Excerpt from "Queen Moo and the Egyptian Sphinx" (1896) provides this text:
> Plutarch, in his "Life of Solon," says that when the famed Greek legislator visited Egypt (600 years before the Chritiam era), Sonchis, a priest of Sais, also Psenophis, a priest of Heliopolis, told him that 9,000 years since, the relations of the Egyptians with the inhabitants of the "lands of the West" had been interrupted because of the mud that had made the sea impassable after the destruction of Atlantis by earthquakes.
> Augustus Le Plongeon, "Queen Moo and the Egyptian Sphinx" (1896), Preface page xi

Lost Continent of Mu, Motherland of Men
Page 238:
> The Temple of Sacred Mysteries is more than 11,500 years old, and this age is verified by the following: Plutarch relates that the priests of Egypt told Solon that _communications with the Lands of the West had been interrupted 9,000 years before, in consequence of the sinking of Atlantis, which made the Atlantic impassable on account of the mud and seaweed *and the destruction of the country beyond by overwhelming cataclysms.*

Lost Continent of Mu, Motherland of Men
Page 243:
> Some old Egyptian Papyri refer to these cataclysms, which are confirmed by the Greek philosophers, Plato and Plutarch (Plutarch's Life of Solon).

List of publications:
- Lives of the Noble Grecians and Romans
- Symposiacs
- Sentiments concerning nature
- Essays and Miscellanies

Moses, (?)

Moses is credited with being a leader of the Hebrew people and an author of the first five books of the Bible.

Lost Continent of Mu, Motherland of Men
Page 6:
> I have traced this same story from Mu to India, where colonizers from the vanished continent had settled; from India into Egypt; from Egypt to the temple of Sanai, where Moses copied it; and from Moses to the faulty translations of Ezra 800 years later. The plausibility of this will be apparent even to those who have not studied the subject carefully, when they see the close resemblance between the story of the creation as we know it and the tradition that originated in Mu.

Lost Continent of Mu, Motherland of Men
Page 19:

It is a certainty that the Egyptian legend of the creation, from which Moses wrote the biblical account, came from India when the Naacals went to Egypt as missionaries to teach the seven sacred inspired writings, religion and the sciences.

Lost Continent of Mu, Motherland of Men
Page 124:

Moses fathered the doctrine of monotheism, as an outgrowth of the Osirian religion, yet he continued the use of many of the original symbols in his teachings. In fact, some of these symbols are to be seen today in Jewish synagogues.

Lost Continent of Mu, Motherland of Men
Page 269:

In most mountainous countries there are traditions concerning the raising of the mountains. The raising of mountains is referred to in the Bible, in one of the psalms of David, called the Song of Moses (Psalms xc: 2).

Lost Continent of Mu, Motherland of Men
Page 275:

Muller, in "Origin of Religious Laws," says: "The belief that the religious law-giver enjoyed some closer intimacy with the Deity than ordinary mortals pervades the ancient traditions of many nations. According to a well known passage in Diodorus Siculus, the Egyptians believed their laws to have been communicated to Mnevis by Hermes. The Cretans held that Minos received the laws from Zeus. The Lacedaemonians held that Lykurgus received his laws from Appolon. The Aryans believed that Zathraustes received them from the Good Spirit. According to Gatel, Zamolscis received his laws from the goddess Hestia, and according to the Jews, Moses received his laws from the God Iao.[32]"

Lost Continent of Mu, Motherland of Men
Page 277:

From ancient records it would appear that, about 2000 B. C., religions all over the world became degraded, dropping in many places to fiendish human sacrifices. Only Moses stood up against it and kept his people in the true road. They have been called "God's favored people." They were favored when they were selected to retain and carry on the worship of the Deity; they were called upon and were not found wanting.

Lost Continent of Mu, Motherland of Men
Page 278:

Throughout all ancient traditions, even down to the time of Moses, we see "*water* above the firmament and *waters* below," a distinction being thus made by pluralizing. Water in all these cases refers to the ether which fills space beyond atmosphere.

Lost Continent of Mu, Motherland of Men
Page 279:

A dissection of all of the traditions brings some astonishing facts before the eyes of the reader. Probably the most astounding of all is the fact that the Polynesians, who have been shut in from the rest of the world for over 12,000 years, should have among themselves traditions of the Creation identically like the biblical account, such as the names of the first man and woman; and that the first woman was made out of man's bones; that man was a special creation of God. The Marquesans and other Polynesians could not possibly have got these traditions from the outside world. The traditions of the Polynesians start from 12,000 years back, and how much more no one can surmise. The biblical tradition started with Moses some three thousand years ago, which proves that it was handed down to Moses in some form. The Naacal and Egyptian show us in what form it was handed down and from whom.

Lost Continent of Mu, Motherland of Men
Page 285-287:

It is known that the early books of our Old Testament were written by Moses from Egyptian Temple records. Hieroglyphics and symbols were the common form of writing in ancient times. A hieroglyphic or a symbol is an emblem of something, and therefore must not be taken literally. They must be taken as *representing* something, but *not* as that something itself. The failure to differentiate between the symbol and what it represents has caused many decipherings and translations to be erroneous, and often, in religious matters, leaves the impression of idolatry where there is a profound reverence for, and a worship of, the Deity. This has been especially prominent in deciphering and translating records relating to the Osirian religion. By Osirian religion I mean that taught by Thoth at Sais, at the commencement of Egyptian history, and not as it was preached and taught and practiced by the unscrupulous Egyptian priesthood of a later period, which commenced during the reign of the second king of the Eleventh Dynasty and reached its climax during the Eighteenth Dynasty.

According to the Old Testament, Moses wrote that man was a special creation and made his advent on earth in the Garden of Eden. Where was the Garden of Eden? The biblical boundaries of the Garden of Eden are geographically impossible, as anyone can see by consulting an atlas and tracing them. Rivers are made to run over mountains and across oceans. Here is a biblical error; how did it occur? Moses was a Master-he had attained the highest degrees in religion and learning. It would have been impossible for him to have suggested such impossibilities; so that we must look elsewhere to find the origin of the many biblical errors.

What Moses wrote, without doubt, were plain facts, in symbolical language-a symbolically written history, true in all respects. Subsequent translations perverted his writings.

The writings of Moses were in Egyptian hieroglyphics and hieratic characters. I have been informed by Hebrew scientists that some were on clay tablets, others on papyrus: this point I pass on as I received it.

Eight hundred years after the Israelitish Exodus from Egypt, Ezra, with a body of co-workers, collected all the tablets and writings of all descriptions which were connected with the family history of the Israelites, and put them into book form, which became the Bible.

Those written by Moses were in Egyptian hieroglyphics. Is it any wonder that so many mistranslations were made by Ezra and his associates, when none of them were capable of thoroughly understanding the Egyptian writings of Moses? Only a Master could understand them, and neither Ezra nor any of his associates were Masters. Their incapability is clearly shown by comparing their translations with the original records which we find in the Egyptian, Chaldean, Hindu and Maya. Moses wrote sense; his translators made nonsense out of many of his passages. Moses wrote in the symbolical style of his day and his translators tried to translate literally. In this they only half succeeded, and when they came across a set of hieroglyphics they did not understand, they added a myth to sound history. The boundaries of the Garden of Eden is one of their myths.

From incontrovertible evidences gained through my research work it is shown that Moses wrote the first books of the Bible from the temple records brought to Egypt from the Motherland by the Naacals via Burma and India; and that these Egyptian temple records were copies of the "Seven Sacred Inspired Writings" of the Motherland Mu. These were written on clay tablets and referred to the Creation. The legends of the Garden of Eden, the "Flood," the last magnetic cataclysm, and the raising of the mountains, are records of later date.

Moses could have made no mistake in copying these writings, so they undoubtedly left his hands perfect copies of the originals. Eight hundred years after, an attempt was made to translate them into Hebrew by men who did not understand the old Egyptian esoteric temple writings, hence the difference between what was produced and the original.

So little did Ezra and his associates understand these writings that I doubt if there is a single Hebrew today who knows the meaning of the burnt sacrifice and what it symbolized.

Lost Continent of Mu, Motherland of Men
Page 296:

ISRAELITES.- The conception of the four gods, pillars or genii, or whatever they may be termed, was not entirely rejected by the Jews. Although there is no mention of them in the books written by Moses, that is no criterion, because some of the books written by Moses are lost, and the reference to the four cardinal points may have been in one of these lost books.

Lost Continent of Mu, Motherland of Men
Page 307:

Moses in a very abstruse manner symbolized it in his writings, as we find in our Bible today.

Scrapbook references:
- Scrapbook 1 page 12 clip 1 – has a drawing a tablet with primitive Hebrew writing and suggests that the author was Moses. A handwritten note points to the tablet and reads "Fake".
- Scrapbook 1 page 12 clip 2 – October 20, 1925 article that states Sir Flinders Petrie disputes the translation on a tablet purported by Dr. Grimme to be the work of Moses.

List of publications:
- Genesis
- Exodus
- Leviticus
- Numbers
- Deuteronomy

Max Muller [Muller, Frederick Max (1823-1900)]

Was a German-born British Philologist and Orientalist and one of the founders of Indian studies in the West.

Lost Continent of Mu, Motherland of Men
Page 124:

Max Muller writes: "As soon as we know aught of the thoughts and feelings of primitive man, we find him in possession of a religion. A religion of faith or worship, of morality or ecstatic vision; a religion of fear and hope, or of surmise, or reverence of the Great God through *various symbols*."

Lost Continent of Mu, Motherland of Men
Page 272-275:

MAX MULLER says: "Religion is a mental faculty which, independent of, nay, in spite of sense and reason, enables man to apprehend the Infinite under different names and under different disguises. Without that faculty no religion, not even the lowest worship of idols and fetishes, would be possible; and yet if we will but listen attentively we can hear in all religions a groaning of the spirit, a struggle to conceive the inconceivable, to utter the unutterable, a longing after the Infinite, a love of God.

"The intention of religion, wherever found or wherever we meet it, is always holy. However imperfect, however childish a religion may be, it always places the human soul in the presence of God; and however imperfect, however childish the conception of God may be, it always expresses the highest ideal of perfection which the human soul, for the time being, can reach and grasp.

"Every mythology appears as the result of the earliest efforts of the human mind to explain the mysteries of the Universe: the sky-the sun-the planets; the winds and the clouds, the summer and winter, the dawn and darkness, and the varied elemental phenomena which are of supernatural significance to the simple fancies of uncultured people."

...

Muller in "Early Religions" says:

"In one sense every religion has been a true religion at the start; they were the only religions that were possible at the time, which were compatible with the language, the thoughts, and the sentiments of each generation, which were appropriate to the age of the world. We ought therefore to put the most charitable interpretation on the apparent absurdities, the follies and the errors of ancient religions. As soon as we know anything of the thoughts and feelings of man, we find him in possession of a religion, a religion of faith or worship, of morality or ecstatic vision, a religion of fear and hope, or surmise, a reverence of the so-called gods.

"In order to approach the religion of primitive peoples we must, so to speak, get at its heart, and feel its life currents. We must place ourselves in sympathy with these ancient peoples, listen to their hymns and prayers, and witness their rites and ceremonies; we must endeavor to know their religious ideals. When Thales declared all things were full of gods, and when Buddha denied that there were any other gods except the Supreme Being, both were stating their religious convictions.

"The external aspect of a religion as presented to strangers is not one often to be trusted. In the earliest and purest days of Christianity, if we were to believe the most enlightened of the heathen writers, the Christian religion consisted of the worship of animals. This idea possibly arose from the fact that the earliest pictures of Mary nursing Christ show the cow's horns of the Egyptian goddess Sati on her head, and sometimes the horns of Hathor."

...

Muller, in "Ancestral Worship," says: "Ancestral worship sprang out of the universal faith of primitive peoples in the persistence of human responsibility after death. This form of worship seems to have been almost universal among mankind during a certain stage of development. Traces of it are found in all parts of the earth. The religious ideas of the Hebrews present traces of ancestral worship. The indication is strong that the special God of the Hebrew patriarch, the family God of Abraham, with whom he conversed and held personal relations, represented an ancestral divinity."

From the reading of a number of ancient writings I have come to the conclusion that ancestral worship originated through the destruction of Mu. Ancestral worship or the reverence shown to forefathers appears very prominently in the Egyptian sacred rites and ceremonies, where their forefathers of the land of Mu furnish the principal theme.

...

Muller, in "Origin of Religious Laws," says: "The belief that the religious law-giver enjoyed some closer intimacy with the Deity than ordinary mortals pervades the ancient traditions of many nations. According to a well known passage in Diodorus Siculus, the Egyptians believed their laws to have been communicated to Mnevis by Hermes. The Cretans held that Minos received the laws from Zeus. The Lacedaemonians held that Lykurgus received his laws from Appolon. The Aryans believed that Zathraustes received them from the Good Spirit. According to Gatel, Zamolscis received his laws from the goddess Hestia, and according to the Jews, Moses received his laws from the God Iao.[32]"

"There was a primitive Aryan religion, a primitive Semitic religion, and a primitive Turanian religion, before each of these primeval races was broken up and became separate in language, worship and national sentiment. The highest God received the same name in the ancient mythology of India, Greece, Italy and Germany, and had retained that name whether worshipped in the Himalayan mountains, or among the oaks of Dodona, on the Capital or in the forests of Germany. He shows that his name was Dyaus in Sanskrit, Zeus in Greek, Jovis in Latin and Tiu in German.

"They bring before us with all the vividness of an event which we witnessed ourselves but yesterday, the ancestors of the whole Aryan race, thousands of years it may be before Homer and the Veda, worshipping an unseen being under the same name, the best, the most exalted name they could find in their vocabulary - under the name Light and Sky. Let us not turn away and say that this after all was nature worship and idolatry. No, it was not meant for that, although it may have been degenerated into that in later times.

"Dyaus did not mean the blue sky, nor was it the sky personified; it was meant for something else. We have in the Veda the invocation Dyaus Pitar, the Greek Zeus Pater and the Latin Jupiter, and that means in all these languages what it meant before these languages were torn asunder. It means 'Heaven Father,' or 'Heavenly Father.' "

List of publications:
- A History of Ancient Sanskrit Literature So Far As It Illustrates the Primitive Religion of the Brahmans (1859), 1859
- Lectures on the Science of Language (1864, 2 vols.), 1866
- Chips from a German Workshop (1867-75, 4 vols.)
- Introduction to the Science of Religion (1873)
- India, What can it Teach Us? (1883)
- Biographical Essays (1884)
- The Science of Thought (1887)
- Six Systems of Hindu Philosophy (1899)
- Gifford Lectures of 1888–92 (Collected Works, vols. 1-4)
- Natural Religion (1889), Vol. 1, Vol. 2
- Physical Religion (1891), [1]
- Anthropological Religion (1892), [2]
- Theosophy, or Psychological Religion (1893), [3]
- Auld Lang Syne (1898), a memoir
- My Autobiography: A Fragment (1901)
- The Life and Letters of the Right Honourable Friedrich Max Müller (1902, 2 vols.)

Niven [Niven, William (1850-1937)]
Was a Scottish born archaeologist and mineralogist that explored the American Southwest and Mexico.

Chapter 11 ("NIVEN'S MEXICAN BURIED CITIES") is taken from an article contained in one of James' scrapbooks. The entire article has been transcribed and is contained in the notes for Chapter 11.

As documented in his biography, "Buried Cities Forgotten Gods: William Niven's Life of Discovery and Revolution in Mexico and the American Southwest," the first correspondence between William Niven and James Churchward was after the publication in 1926 of "The Lost Continent of Mu Motherland of Men." [August 1927] The same source indicates that William and James continued their correspondence for a number of years, although probably not as cordial in 1932 after the incident with the altar when it abruptly ended.

The 1931 publication of the "Lost Continent of Mu" was dedicated to William Niven.

Lost Continent of Mu, Motherland of Men
Page 43:

Niven's upper city was built before the mountains were raised at the beginning of the Pleistocene; his lowest city was built tens of thousands of years before this and goes far back into the Tertiary Era. (Page 122.)

Lost Continent of Mu, Motherland of Men
Page 102:

On page 174 I will show symbols among the Nevada cliff writings that referred to Mu, also in New Mexico, and again in Niven's "Mexican Buried Cities," page 208 and in "Yucatan," page 237.

Lost Continent of Mu, Motherland of Men
Page 120-121:

Twenty-nine miles north of Mexico City, Niven has discovered three civilizations, buried one beneath the other, with strata of sand, gravel and boulders between each. These cities are more than 1,000 feet above sea level, with mountains of from 1,000 to 15,000 feet in altitude intervening between them and the sea.

Lost Continent of Mu, Motherland of Men
Page 159:

Pillars in ancient times were placed in the porches or entrances to temples. The oldest record of their use as such comes from Niven's "Mexican Buried Cities."

Lost Continent of Mu, Motherland of Men
Page 206-233:

Chapter is entitled "Niven's Mexican Buried Cities" and contains most of an article published concerning Niven's work. A copy of the article was kept in James' scrapbook and is reproduced in the Chapter 11 Notes.

Lost Continent of Mu, Motherland of Men
Page 234:

ON leaving Mexico City with Niven's treasures, I shall proceed to that part of Mexico called Yucatan.

Lost Continent of Mu, Motherland of Men
Page 239:

Niven's Mexican buried cities are, comparatively speaking, only a few miles away from Uxmal, so that there remains the possibility that the disturbances which caused the ruin of Niven's upper cities might, and probably did, extend as far as Uxmal.

Lost Continent of Mu, Motherland of Men
Page 246:

Here in Yucatan, tens of thousands of years afterwards, we find a custom retained which was observed in Niven's lowest buried city, described by him as the life of a "shepherd."

Scrapbook references:
- Scrapbook #1 Sheets 28-30 Niven's Buried Cites: An American Pompeii
- Scrapbook #2 Sheet 39 Letter from William Niven to James Churchward

Other references:
- Buried Cities, Forgotten Gods: William Niven's Life of Discovery and Revolution in Mexico and the American Southwest; Robert S. Wicks and Roland H. Harrison; 1999 ; Texas Tech University Press

Frederick O'Brien [O'Brien, Frederick (1869 - 1932)]
Journalist – Published & edited Cablenews (Philipines newspaper) beginning in 1905. "White Shadows..." examines the effects of colonialization on the natives.

Lost Continent of Mu, Motherland of Men
Pages 38-39

'Frederick O'Brien, who has written most interestingly of the South Sea Islands, says:
"Darwin's theory is that these islands are the tops of a submerged continent, or land bridge, which stretches its crippled body along the floor of the Pacific Ocean for thousands of leagues. A lost land, whose epic awaits the singer; a mystery perhaps forever to be unsolved.

"There are great monuments, graven objects, hieroglyphs, customs and language; island people with suggestive legends, all perhaps remnants of a migration from Asia or Africa a hundred thousand years ago.

"Here, three centuries ago, they were discovered by the peoples of the great world, and, rudely encountering a civilization they did not build, they are dying here: with their passing vanishes the last living link with our pre-historic past, and I was to see it before it disappeared forever."

Where we find specks of land out of water with incontrovertible evidences of continental resources, we are made doubly certain that these specks are parts or remains of a continent. These bits of land are, as I have already said, little islands peopled by savages. They are thousands of miles away from any mainland, and it is therefore the strongest possible proof, stronger than any record, inscription or tradition, that back in prehistoric times there was a continent and that the continent was peopled by highly civilized human beings.

The entire unedited text is reproduced below from the Gutenberg Project ebook "White Shadows in the Pacific" from which the above text is quoted:

Darwin's theory is that these islands are the tops of a submerged continent, or land bridge, which stretches its crippled body along the floor of the Pacific for thousands of leagues. A lost land, whose epic awaits the singer; a mystery perhaps forever to be unsolved. There are great monuments, graven objects, hieroglyphics, customs and languages, island peoples with suggestive legends--all, perhaps, remnants of a migration from Asia or Africa a hundred thousand years ago.

Over this land bridge, mayhap, ventured the Caucasian people, the dominant blood in Polynesia to-day, and when the continent fell from the sight of sun and stars save in those spots now the mountainous islands like Tahiti and the Marquesas, the survivors were isolated for untold centuries.

Here in these islands the brothers of our long-forgotten ancestors have lived and bred since the Stone Age, cut off from the main stream of mankind's development. Here they have kept the childhood customs of our white race, savage and wild, amid their primitive and savage life. Here, three centuries ago, they were discovered by the peoples of the great world, and, rudely encountering a civilization they did not build, they are dying here. With their passing vanishes the last living link with our own pre-historic past. And I was to see it, before it disappears forever.

[Copied from the www from The Project Gutenberg eBook, White Shadows in the South Seas, by Frederick O'Brien, downloaded February 8, 2006]

Lost Continent of Mu, Motherland of Men
Pages 44-45:

I will quote, with his permission, some passages from Frederick O'Brien's fascinating book, "White Shadows in the South Seas." The passages referred to are as follows:

"Over this land bridge, mayhap, ventured the Caucasian people—*the dominant blood in Polynesia today*—and when the continent fell from the sight of sun and stars, save in those spots now mountainous islands like Tahiti and the Marquesas, the survivors were isolated for untold ages.

The quoted text is an excerpt from "White Shadows in the Pacific" and the text of the original was reproduced in the previous entry (entry for Pages 38-39.)

"Here in these islands the brothers of our long-forgotten ancestors have lived and bred since the Stone Age, cut off from the main stream of mankind's development. Here they have kept the childhood customs of our white race, savage and wild, amid their primitive and savage life."

The quoted text is an excerpt from "White Shadows in the Pacific" and the text of the original was reproduced in the previous entry (entry for Pages 38-39.)

It is evident from the foregoing that O'Brien based these paragraphs on the theory that the white race originated in Asia. It is an accepted theory and O'Brien cannot be blamed for the error.

On page 112 of his book, O'Brien writes:

"My savage friends with their clear features, their large, straight eyes and clear olive skins, still show the traces of their Caucasian blood. Their forefathers and mine might have hunted the great winged lizards together through primeval wilderness, until, driven by who knows what urge of wanderlust or necessity, certain tribes set out in that drive through Europe and Asia towards America, that ended at last when a continent sank beneath their feet in the South Seas."

The entire unedited text is reproduced below from the Gutenberg Project ebook "White Shadows in the Pacific" from which the above text is quoted

I seemed to see in this curious fact another proof of the ancient kinship between the first men of my own race and the prehistoric grandfathers of Malicious Gossip and Haabunai. My savage friends, with their clear features, their large straight eyes and olive skins, showed still the traces of their Caucasian blood. Their forefathers and mine may have hunted the great winged lizards together through primeval wildernesses, until, driven by who knows what urge of wanderlust or necessity, certain tribes set out in that drive through Europe and Asia toward America that ended at last, when a continent sunk beneath their feet, on these islands in the southern seas.

[Copied from the www from The Project Gutenberg eBook, White Shadows in the South Seas, by Frederick O'Brien, downloaded February 8, 2006]

Lost Continent of Mu, Motherland of Men
Pages 81-82:

I will now take extracts from O'Brien's "Mystic Isles of the South Seas," capping each legend with the corresponding biblical legend.
Page 21—"The great god Ra of the Polynesians."
In Ra we have a connecting link between the Polynesians and our known ancients. Ra was the symbol of the Sun, and the Sun was the collective symbol of the Deity among the Mayas, Quiches, Incas, Hindus, Chaldeans, Babylonians, Assyrians, Egyptians, etc.

Easter Island (Pages 64-66)—"Huge stone gods that had been thrown down. Some were 37 feet high, and had red stone crowns ten feet in diameter."

The quoted text are identified as excerpts from "Mystic Isles of the South Seas" and the original paragraphs are reproduced below:

> One morning when we were near the middle of our voyage I went on deck to see the sun rise. We were that day eighteen hundred miles from Tahiti and the same distance from San Francisco, while north and west twelve hundred miles lay Hawaii. Not nearer than there, four hundred leagues away, was succor if our vessel failed. It was the dead center of the sea. I glanced at the chart and noted the spot: Latitude 10∫ N.; Longitude 137∫ W. The great god Ra of the Polynesians had climbed above the dizzy edge of the whirling earth, and was making his gorgeous course into the higher heavens. The ocean was a glittering blue, an intense, brilliant azure, level save for the slight swaying of the surface, which every little space showed a flag of white. The evaporation caused by the blazing sun of these tropics made the water a deeper blue than in cooler latitudes, as in the Arctic and Antarctic oceans the greens are almost as vivid as the blues about the line.
> [Copied from the www from The Project Gutenberg eBook, Mystic Isles of the South Seas, by Frederick O'Brien, downloaded February 8, 2006]

> "I think the island had a superior race once. There are immense platforms of stone, like the paepaes of the Marquesas, only bigger, and the stones are all fitted together without cement. They built them on promontories facing the sea. Some are three hundred feet long, and the walls thirty feet high. On these platforms there were huge stone gods that have been thrown down; some were thirty-seven feet high, and they had redstone crowns, ten feet in diameter. There were stone houses one hundred feet long, with walls five feet thick. How they moved the stones no one knows, for, of course, these people there now were not the builders. Some race of whom they knew nothing was there before them.
> [Copied from the www from The Project Gutenberg eBook, Mystic Isles of the South Seas, by Frederick O'Brien, downloaded February 8, 2006]

Lost Continent of Mu, Motherland of Men
Page 83:

> O'Brien's deductions that they came down from the original white race seems to be more than confirmed by records and traditions found in various parts of the earth: Mexico, Central America, India and Egypt.

Lost Continent of Mu, Motherland of Men
Page 84:

> O'Brien has adorned his writings with many interesting and astounding traditions which he found among the South Sea Islanders. I will quote some of them:
> The Creation.—"The Marquesans said that in the beginning there was no light, life or sound in the world, that a boundless night called Po enveloped everything over which Tanaoa (darkness) and Mutu-hei (silence) reigned supreme.
> 'Then the god of light separated from Tanaoa (darkness), fought him and drove him away and confined him to the night. Then the god Ono (sound) was evolved from Atea (light) and banished silence. From all this struggle was born Atauana (dawn). Atea (light) married Atauana (dawn) and they created earth, animals and man."

The text above are unidentified excerpts from "Mystic Isles of the South Seas" and the original paragraphs are reproduced below:

The Marquesans said that in the beginning there was no light, life, or sound in the world; that a boundless night, Po, enveloped everything, over which Tanaoa, (Darkness), and Mutu-hei, (Silence), ruled supreme. Then the god of light separated from Tanaoa, fought him, drove him away, and confined him to night. Then the god Ono, (Sound), was evolved from Atea, (Light), and banished Silence. From all this struggle was born the Dawn, (Atanua). Atea married the Dawn, and they created earth, animals, man.

[Copied from the www from The Project Gutenberg eBook, Mystic Isles of the South Seas, by Frederick O'Brien, downloaded February 8, 2006]

Lost Continent of Mu, Motherland of Men
Page 85:

THE Flood.—O'Brien says in "Mystic Isles of the South Seas":
"In most of Polynesia there are legends of a universal flood from which but few escaped."
Adam And Eve.—"The Polynesians had very fixed ideas upon the origin of the universe and man."
In *Hawaii*: "Taaroa made man out of red earth Araea and breathed into his nostrils. He made woman from a man's bones and called her Ivi." (In the Polynesian language Ivi is pronounced Eve-y.)
Cain And Abel.—A Tonga tradition states that "the son of the first man killed his brother."
New Zealand: A tradition of the Maoris, the natives of New Zealand, states "that the son of the first man killed his brother."
Tower of Babel.—"In Fiji is still shown the site where a vast tower was built because the Fijians were curious and wanted to peep into the moon to discover if it was inhabited.
POLYNESIAN COSMOGONY.—*Tahiti*: "Taaroa, whose name was spelt differently in separate archipelagos, was the father of Tahitian cosmogony. His wife was Hina - the earth, and his son Oro was the ruler of the world, Tane the Hualine god was a brother of Oro and his equal."
This corresponds with the cosmogony of the most ancient namely a Trinity or a Triune Godhead.

The texts above are excerpts from "Mystic Isles of the South Seas" and the original paragraphs are reproduced below:

The Polynesians had very fixed ideas upon the origin of the universe and of man. In Hawaii, Taaroa made man out of red earth, araea, and breathed into his nostrils. He made woman from man's bones, and called her ivi (pronounced eve-y). At the hill of Kauwiki, on the eastern point of the island of Maui, Hawaii, the heaven was so near the earth that it could be reached by the thrust of a strong spear, and is to-day called lani haahaa.

The Marquesans said that in the beginning there was no light, life, or sound in the world; that a boundless night, Po, envelope everything, over which Tanaoa, (Darkness), and Mutu-hei, (Silence), ruled supreme. Then the god of light separated from Tanaoa, fought him, drove him away, and confined him to night. Then the god Ono, (Sound), was evolved from Atea, (Light), and banished Silence. From all this struggle was born the Dawn, (Atanua). Atea married the Dawn, and they created earth, animals, man.

In most of Polynesia there are legends of a universal flood from which few escaped. In Fiji it was said that two races were entirely wiped out, one of women, and the other of men and women with tails. A little bird sat on the top of the uncovered land and wailed the destruction. The Marquesans built a great canoe like a house, with openings for air and light, but tight against the rain. The ark was stored with provisions, and the animals of the earth were driven in two by two, fastened in couples. Then the family of four men and four women entered the ark, sacrificed a turtle to God, and retired to rest amidst the terrific din of the confined animals. The storm burst, and the waters covered the entire land. The storm ceased and a black bird was sent over the sea of Hawaii. It returned to the ark, and a wind set in from the north. Another bird was loosed, and alighted on thesea-shore. It was recalled, and a third bird brought back twigs. The ark soon grounded, and the four men and four women released the beasts, and went ashore. These repopulated the earth.

The Samoans believed that the earth was once covered with water and the sky alone was inhabited, until God sent his only begotten daughter in the form of a kuri, or snipe, to look for dry land. She found a spot, and brought down to it earth, and a creeping plant, which grew and decomposed into worms, and, lo! the worms turned into men and women.

In Hawaii Nuu was saved from a similar flood, and with him his three sons and their families. Ten generations later Kanehoalani was commanded by God to introduce circumcision. He went to a far-off country, had a son by a slave woman and one by his wife. He was then commanded, this descendant of Nuu in the tenth generation, to go up on a mountain and perform a sacrifice. He sought a mountain, but none appeared suitable; so he communed with God, who told him to travel to the east, and he would find a precipice. He departed with his son and a servant. The Hawaiians still call the mountains back of Koolau, near Honolulu, after the name of the three, and when the missionaries gave them the Jewish sacred books, were delighted to point out that long before Christ came to earth they had believed as above, and that

Abraham was the tenth from Noah, that Abraham practiced circumcision, and was father of Isaac and the illegitimate Ishmael, and that their descendant of Nuu, as Abraham, became the father of twelve children, and the founder of the Polynesian race, as Abraham had of the Jews.

One might detect some relation to the Hebraic scriptures in the legends of the Maoris of New Zealand and Tonga that the older son of the first man killed his brother, and that in Fiji one still is shown the site where a vast tower was built because the Fijians wanted to peer into the moon to discover if it was inhabited. A lofty mound was erected, and the building of timber upon it. It was already in the sky when the fastenings broke, and the workmen were precipitated over every part of Fiji.
[Copied from the www from The Project Gutenberg eBook, Mystic Isles of the South Seas, by Frederick O'Brien, downloaded February 8, 2006]

…

Taaroa, whose name was spelt differently in separated archipelagos, was the father of the Tahitian cosmogony. His wife was Hina, the earth, and his son, Oro, was ruler of the world. TanÈ, the Huahine god, was a brother of Oro, and his equal, but there were islands which disputed this equality, and shed blood to disprove it, as the sects of Christianity have since the peaceful Jesus died by the demands of the priests of his nation.
[Copied from the www from The Project Gutenberg eBook, Mystic Isles of the South Seas, by Frederick O'Brien, downloaded February 8, 2006]

Lost Continent of Mu, Motherland of Men
Page 86:

O'Brien gives a thrilling account of a Tahitian adept walking bare-footed on red-hot stones, without being burnt. The same thing has been shown in Hawaii and I have personally seen it done in the Fiji Islands.

The excerpt from "Mystic Isles of the South Seas" that describes the event above has been reproduced below:

When we approached the umu, I felt the heat fifty feet away. The pit was a mass of glowing stones, and half a dozen men whom I knew were spreading them as evenly as possible, turning them with long poles. Each, as it was moved, disclosed its lower surface crimson red and turning white. The flames leaped up from the wood between the stones.

About the oven, forty feet away, the people of the villages who had gathered, stood or squatted, and solemnly awaited the ritual. The tahua, Tufetufetu, was still in a tiny hut that had been erected for him, and at prayer. A deacon of the church went to him, and informed him that the umu was ready, and he came slowly toward us. He wore a white pareu of the ancient tapa, and a white tiputa, a poncho of the same beaten-bark fabrics. His head was crowned with ti-leaves, and in his hand he had a wand of the same. He was in the dim light a vision of the necromancer of medieval books.

He halted three steps from the fiery furnace, and chanted in Tahitian:

O spirits who put fire in the oven, slack the fire!
O worm of black earth,
O worm of bright earth, fresh water, sea water, heat of the oven, red of the oven, support the feet of the walkers, and fan away the fire!
O Cold Beings, let us pass over the middle of the oven!
O Great Woman, who puts the fire in the heavens, hold still the leaf that fans the fire!
Let thy children go on the oven for a little while!
Mother of the first footstep!
Mother of the second footstep!
Mother of the third footstep!
Mother of the fourth footstep!
Mother of the fifth footstep!
Mother of the sixth footstep!
Mother of the seventh footstep!
Mother of the eighth footstep!
Mother of the ninth footstep!
Mother of the tenth footstep!
O Great Woman, who puts the fire in the heavens, all is hidden!

Then, his body erect, his eyes toward the stars, augustly, and without hesitation or choice of footprints, the tahu walked upon the umu. His body was naked except for the tapa, which extended from his shoulders to his knees. The heat radiated from the stones, and sitting on the ground I saw the quivering of the beams just above the oven.

Tufetufetu traversed the entire length of the umu with no single flinching of his muscles or flutter of his eyelids to betray pain or fear. He raised his wand when he reached the end, and, turning slowly, retraced his steps.

The spectators, who had held their breaths, heaved deep sighs, but no word was spoken as the tahua signed all to follow him in another journey over the white-hot rocks. All but a few, their number obscured in the darkness, ranged themselves in a line behind him, and with masses of ti-leaves in their hands, and some with girdles hastily made, barefooted they marched over the path he took again. When the cortege had passed once, the priest said, "Fariu! Return!" and, their eyes fixed on vacancy, six times the throng were led by him forward and back over the umu. A woman who looked down and stumbled, left the ranks, and cried out that her leg was burned. She had an injury that was weeks in curing.

[Copied from the www from The Project Gutenberg eBook, Mystic Isles of the South Seas, by Frederick O'Brien, downloaded February 8, 2006]

List of publications:
- White Shadows in the South Seas (1919) written with Ruth Wilderlane
- Mystic Isles of the South Seas (1921)
- Atolls of the Sun (1922)

Orpheus (?)
Greek deity responsible for the arts of song and music, also must have been an author.

Lost Continent of Mu, Motherland of Men
Page 298:

GREEK.-*Plato* and *Orpheus* refer to the trinity as three kings-"Phanes, Ouranos and Kronos."

Excerpt from "Sacred Mysteries Among the Mayas and Quiches" (1886) provides this text:

These three intellects, therefore, he [ed. note Proclus] supposes to be the Demiurge; the same as the three kings of Plato, and as the three whom Orpheus celebrates under the names of Phaenes, Ouranes, and Krons, kings of the great "Saturnian continent," in the Atlantic ocean.
Augustus LePlongeon, "Sacred Mysteries Among the Mayas and Quiches" (1886), page 53

Plato (427 B.C.E – 347 B.C.E.)
was an immensely influential ancient Greek philosopher, a student of Socrates, writer of philosophical dialogues, and founder of the Academy in Athens where Aristotle studied. The Lost Continent of Atlantis is written about in his Dialogues entitled "Timaeus" and "Critias"

Lost Continent of Mu, Motherland of Men
Page 59:

In Plato's "Timeus Critias" we find this reference to the lost continent: "The Land of Mu had ten peoples."

Lost Continent of Mu, Motherland of Men
Page 161:

Plato informs us, speaking of Atlantis: "There the people gathered every fifth year and sixth year alternately, and with sacrifices of bulls, swore to observe the sacred inscriptions carved on the pillars of the temple."

Lost Continent of Mu, Motherland of Men
Page 243:

Some old Egyptian Papyri refer to these cataclysms, which are confirmed by the Greek philosophers, Plato and Plutarch (Plutarch's Life of Solon).

Lost Continent of Mu, Motherland of Men
Pages 279-280:

Plato amusingly recounts a legend telling how the human race became divided into man and woman.

Human beings, according to Plato's story, were originally created with the man and woman combined in one body. Each body had four arms and four legs. The bodies were round, and they rolled over and over, using the arms and legs to move them. By and by they began to treat the gods badly. They stopped their sacrifices and even threatened to roll up Mount Olympus to attack and overthrow the gods.

One god said, "Let us kill them all. They are dangerous."

Another said, "No, I have a better idea. We will cut them in half. Then they will only have two arms and two legs; they won't be round. They won't be able to roll.

Being multiplied by two, they will offer twice as many sacrifices, and what is the most important, each half will be so busy looking for the other half that they will not have time to bother us."

The second god was the wise one. His theory turned out well. Each human half, male or female, has been so busy looking for the other half that it has neglected other things.

Excerpt from "Clippings (Scrapbook)"; Sheet 15; *Tracing the First Love Story Back to Ancient Mexico And Revealing the Curious Symbols Which the Natives Used in Recording the Biblical Legend of Adam and Eve in New-Old North America;* dated 1931 is the following passage:

"The story has taken on many amusing forms, the most amusing, to my mind, being the Greek. It is as good an example of the distortion of truth by dressing up facts with frills and flounces, powdering their noses, and rouging their lips, as I have found. Read this, a translation coming from Plato, sent to me by a professor of the Athens Historical and Archaeological Society.

"Human beings were originally created with the man and woman combined into one body, each body having four arms and four legs. The bodies were round, and they rolled over and over, using the arms and legs to propel them. By and by they began to treat the gods badly; they stopped their sacrifices and even threatened to roll up Mount Olympus and overthrow the gods. One god said, "Let us kill them all." But another said, "No, I have a better idea. We will cut them in half. Then they will only have two arms and two legs; they won't be round, and they won't be able to roll about. Being multiplied by two, they will offer twice as many sacrifices, and what is most important – each half will be so busy looking for the other half that they will not have time to bother us."

That tale certainly doesn't coincide with the Adam and Eve story which we have been taught to believe, by the authority of the Book of Genesis in the Bible. Here is Colonel Churchward's comment on it:

"How's that for a fairy story? But it tells – only not half so clearly – exactly the same acts as the picture in the Niven tablet. Here – minus the frills and powder – is the story:

"Once, long ago, the earth was peopled by a race of divine beings, complete and perfect in every way. There was no sex. Man included in himself not only his positive attributes, but also those negative, receptive and altogether charming facilities belonging to woman.

"That man very soon became bored with this state of things is not at all surprising. He was so thoroughly, utterly bored that he went to sleep, and refused to wake up and go on with his job, which was, as you may read in Genesis, to make the earth a profitable, going concern, paying fruity dividends at regular intervals.

"But while he slept, he sent out, as the result of his boredom, what the modern psychologists would call a 'wish-fulfillment-desire' or something of the sort; those slender, cosmic wings on either side of his head.

"In other words, man prayed. And the creator, as always, heard his prayer and answered it. When the alarm clock rang, Man awoke.

"'Another day,' he grumbled, poking his nose into the nice warm pillow. 'I won't wake up. What's the use?'

"But he opened half and eye to see what sort of day it was, and in the pale, clear light of dawn he saw – Eve. He sat up feeling a little weak.

"'I have lost something!' he said, clutching his throat – not his side, as has been stated so frequently by those who know nothing of the matter.

"So, discovered in America, and set out in such simple language that any child can read it, runs the true story of the origin of woman – in other words, the first love story!"

Lost Continent of Mu, Motherland of Men
Page 298:
> GREEK.-*Plato* and *Orpheus* refer to the trinity as three kings-"Phanes, Ouranos and Kronos."

Excerpt from "Sacred Mysteries Among the Mayas and Quiches" (1886) provides this text:
> These three interllects, therefore, he [ed. note Proclus] supposes to be the Demiurge; the same as the three kings of Plato, and as the three whom Orpheus celebrates under the names of Phaenes, Ouranes, and Krons, king sof the great "Saturnian continent," in the Atlantic ocean.
> Augustus Le Plongeon, "Sacred Mysteries Among the Mayas and Quiches" (1886), page 53

List of publications:
Dialogues
Timaeus
Critias

Plutarch, See Mestrius Plutarchus

Prince Maya (?)
Author of the Sourya Siddhanta, according to James Churchward.

Lost Continent of Mu, Motherland of Men
Page 158-159:
> One very prominent figure in the Naga or Maya Empire in India was Prince Maya. The time of Prince Maya is doubtful. Although I have come across many records about him, not a single one even estimates the date when he lived; but according to traditions, and these traditions are as plentiful as leaves on a tree, Prince Maya lived 15,000 to 20,000 years ago.
>
> In Ramayana, we find this reference to him: "In olden times there was a prince of the Nagas whose name was Maya."

Prince Maya was the author of the *Sourya Siddhanta*, the most ancient treatise on astronomy in India. Its age has been variously estimated at from 10,000 to 22,000 years.

At the time of Prince Maya, the Nagas were an empire. When the handle and sheath of this knife were made, the Nagas were a colony antedating the Empire. That they were only a colony is clearly shown by the suns without rays on the horizon. This proves the extreme antiquity of the handle and sheath.

List of publications:
- Sourya Siddhanta

Other references:

Excerpt from "Queen Moo and the Egyptian Sphinx" (1896) provides this text:

"H. T. Colebrooke, "Memoirs on the Sacred Books of India," *Asiatic Researches*. Vol ii., pp. 369-476, says: "Maya is considered as the author of the Sourya-Siddhanta, the most ancient treatise on astronomy in India. He is represented as receiving his science from a partial incarnation of the Sun." This work, on which all the Indian astronomy is founded, was discovered in Benares by Sir Robert Chambers. Mr. Samuel Davis partly translated it, particularly those sections which relate to the calculation of eclipses. It is a work of very great antiquity, since it is attributed to a Maya author whose astronomical rules show that he was well acquainted with trigonometry (Asiatic Researches, vol. ii., pp. 245-249), proving that abstruse sciences were cultivated in those remote ages, before the invasion of India by the Aryans. (See Appendix, note vi.)"

Augustus Le Plongeon, "Queen Moo and the Egyptian Sphinx" (1896), Page 3 footnote

---

Proclus [Proclus Lycaeus or Proclus Diadochus (412 – 487)]
One of the last major Greek philosophers.

Lost Continent of Mu, Motherland of Men
Page 59:

Proclus wrote: "The Lands of the West had ten peoples.

Lost Continent of Mu, Motherland of Men
Page 298:

Proclus asserts that "the Demiurgos or Creator is triple.

Excerpt from "Sacred Mysteries Among the Mayas and Quiches" (1886) provides this text:

Proclus, platonic philosopher, director of the school of Athens in 450 after Christ, says: "the Demiurgos or Creator is triple, and the three intellects are the three kings, he who exists, he who processes, he who beholds.

Augustus Le Plongeon, "Sacred Mysteries Among the Mayas and Quiches" (1886), page 53

Pythagoras (582 – 507 B.C.E.)
Pythagoras was a Greek mathematician and philosopher; is known best for the Pythagorean theorem which bears his name.

Lost Continent of Mu, Motherland of Men
Page 298:

Pythagoras taught his disciples that God was "numbers and harmony." He caused them to honor numbers and the equilateral triangle with the name of God.

Excerpt from "Sacred Mysteries Among the Mayas and Quiches" (1886) provides this text:

> Pythagoras, who had received his knowledge of number and their meaning from the Egyptians, taught his disciples that God was number and harmony. He caused them to honor numbers and geometrical diagrams with names of the gods.
> Augustus Le Plongeon, "Sacred Mysteries Among the Mayas and Quiches" (1886), page 60

Schliemann [Schliemann, Dr. Peter (?)]

Schliemann, the self-proclaimed grandson of Heinrich Schliemann, the discoverer of legendary city of Troy. The sum total of Dr. Peter Schliemann's printed works were printed in the October 12, 1912 edition of the New York American. A complete copy of the document is contained in James' scrapbooks, minus the illustrations.

Lost Continent of Mu, Motherland of Men
Page 40

> "Schliemann, on apparently two records only, the Troano Manuscript and the Lhasa Record, asserts that Atlantis was the land of Mu. These records *do not* state that Mu and Atlantis were identical; it is mere surmise on the part of Schliemann. Other records which he might have consulted would have told him plainly that the land of Mu lay to the west of America and not to the east, the location of Atlantis."

Page 56-57:

> "The Lhasa Record —This record was discovered by Schliemann in the old Buddhist Temple of Lhasa, Tibet. Schliemann deciphered and translated it. It very evidently does not come from the same original record as do the Troano Manuscript and the Codex Cortesianus. It is more modern and is not written in Maya characters."

Page 58:

> "Le Plongeon's death occurred many years before Schliemann published the Lhasa Record."

Page 172:

> "As Schliemann has shown, the great civilization of Egypt declined with the loss of the support furnished by the Motherland."

Page 251:
Illustrations with the following captions:
'OWL VASE FROM THE "TREASURES OF PRIAM"
The inscription reads: *From the King Chronos of Atlantis*
After Schliemann'

'A HAWK-HEADED SPHINX
A relic from Atlantis discovered by Schliemann among the "Treasures of Priam." Ancient Troy.'

Scrapbook references:
Scrapbook 1 Sheets 33-34: Copy of original 1912 article by Peter Schliemann "How I Found the Lost Atlantis, The Source of All Civilization"

Schliemann [Schliemann, Heinrich (1822-1890)]

was a German classical archaeologist, an advocate of the historical reality of places mentioned in the works of Homer, and an important excavator of Mycenaean sites, such as Troy, Mycenae and Tiryns.

Lost Continent of Mu, Motherland of Men
Page 226

> 'Generally speaking, buried cities are prehistoric. The prehistoric cities belong to the First Great Civilization. Niven's "Buried Mexican Cities" and Schliemann's "Ancient Troys" are examples of prehistoric cities, while Pompeii and Herculaneum are the exceptions.'

Solon (638 B.C.E. – 558 B.C.E.)

According to Plutarch, Solon was told of Atlantis from the High Priest Sonchis and passed the information along to Plato and was the basis of his account of Atlantis.

Lost Continent of Mu, Motherland of Men
Page 41:

> Sanches, high priest of the temple of Sais, told Solon that Atlantis sank 11,500 years ago and that the passage-way to the Lands of the West was blocked on account of the sinking of this great country, and the destruction of the intervening country beyond Atlantis by cataclysms, which made that country impassable.

Lost Continent of Mu, Motherland of Men
Page 60:

> Plutarch. *Life of Solon.*—"Sanches, the High Priest of Sai's, told Solon [600 B. C.], also Psenophis, a priest of Heliopolis, that 9,000 years before, the relations of the Egyptians with the inhabitants of the *Lands of the West* had been interrupted because of cataclysms destroying the *intervening* country, *and—* the mud that had made the sea impassable since the *destruction of Atlantis by earthquakes and submersion.*"

Excerpt from "Queen Moo and the Egyptian Sphinx" (1896) provides this text:

> Plutarch, in his "Life of Solon," says that when the famed Greek legislator visited Egypt (600 years before the Chritiam era), Sonchis, a priest of Sais, also Psenophis, a priest of Heliopolis, told him that 9,000 years since, the relations of the Egyptians with the inhabitants of the "lands of the West" had been interrupted because of the mud that had made the sea impassable after the destruction of Atlantis by earthquakes.
> Augustus Le Plongeon, "Queen Moo and the Egyptian Sphinx" (1896), Preface page xi

Lost Continent of Mu, Motherland of Men
Page 238:

> Solon visited Egypt 600 B. C. Atlantis sank 9,000 years previous to this.

Lost Continent of Mu, Motherland of Men
Page 243:

> Some old Egyptian Papyri refer to these cataclysms, which are confirmed by the Greek philosophers, Plato and Plutarch (Plutarch's Life of Solon).

Sanches [Sonchis (?)]

According to Plutarch, Solon was told of Atlantis from the High Priest Sonchis and passed the information along to Plato and was the basis of his account.

Lost Continent of Mu, Motherland of Men
Page 41:

> Sanches, high priest of the temple of Sais, told Solon that Atlantis sank 11,500 years ago and that the passage-way to the Lands of the West was blocked on account of the sinking of this great country, and the destruction of the intervening country beyond Atlantis by cataclysms, which made that country impassable.

Lost Continent of Mu, Motherland of Men
Page 60:

> Plutarch. *Life of Solon.*—"Sanches, the High Priest of Sai's, told Solon [600 B. C.], also Psenophis, a priest of Heliopolis, that 9,000 years before, the relations of the Egyptians with the inhabitants of the *Lands of the West* had been interrupted because of cataclysms destroying the *intervening* country, and— the mud that had made the sea impassable since the *destruction of Atlantis by earthquakes and submersion.*"

Excerpt from "Queen Moo and the Egyptian Sphinx" (1896) provides this text:

> Plutarch, in his "Life of Solon," says that when the famed Greek legislator visited Egypt (600 years before the Chritiam era), Sonchis, a priest of Sais, also Psenophis, a priest of Heliopolis, told him that 9,000 years since, the relations of the Egyptians with the inhabitants of the "lands of the West" had been interrupted because of the mud that had made the sea impassable after the destruction of Atlantis by earthquakes.
>
> Augustus Le Plongeon, "Queen Moo and the Egyptian Sphinx" (1896), Preface page xi

---

Tanzer, G.L [Tanzer, George L. (1864-1927)

The book is dedicated to Doctor Tanzer and he is described in the Seattle Post Intelligencer as a "Seattle scientist." In the text of the same article "Is the Sun a Cool Body?" is the following paragraph:

> "Dr. Tanzer was recently honored by the dedication to him of a book, "The Lost Continent of Mu," by Col. James Churchward, well-known writer. In explaining his beliefs in a recent address before the Women's Progressive Thought Club of Seattle, Dr. Tanzer said in part: …"

"Col. James Churchward, widely known for his great research work, who is full accord with the assertions made in "Cosmic Reciprocity," gives the following proofs: First we took a cell filled with alum water, which allowed transmission to the LIGHT rays, and repelled the dark rays. After passing through the filter we focused the light rays on a thermometer – the temperature did not rise a degree. The optical pyrometer registered a temperature of 2,500 to 2,600 degrees Fahrenheit at the focus point. We then changed the cell, using one filled with an iodine solution, which allowed the DARK rays to pass through and repelled the light rays. The light at the focus point immediately disappeared. The optical pyrometer registered nothing, but the thermometer soon burst. Substances such as paper started burning at once at the focus point."

His obituary from an article with an unidentified source:

> February 25, 1927
> DR. TANZER DIES IN GERMANY

News of the death of Dr. G.L. Tanzer, Seattle business man, mining and chemical expert, was made public Thursday with the arrival here of a son and Dr. Tanzer's widow from abroad.

Dr. Tanzer was sixty-three years of age and at the time of his death was president and general manager of the Western Smelting and Power Company. He was also president of the Cooke Consolidated Copper Company and the Homestake Holding Company, Cooke, Mont. His visit to Germany was to see the land of his birth which he had not visited for twenty years.

In 1903 Dr. Tanzer was city chemist of Seattle, and for a time was a special chemist for the state. He was the author of numerous authoritative treatises on electrical and chemical subjects and was a thirty-third degree Mason.

In addition to his widow he leaves two sons, W.M. and Max W Tanzer, Seattle; and three daughters, Mrs. V.R. Nixon and Mrs. C.L. B. Cooke, Seattle, and Mrs. A.B. McNee, Randle.

Scrapbook references:

Scrapbook 1 page 3 – article "Is the Sun a Cool Body?" by Dr. G.L. Tanzer from the Seattle Post Intelligencer.

Scrapbook 2 page 47 – Obituary dated 25 February 1927 – "Dr. Tanzer Dies in Germany"

List of publications:

"Cosmic Reciprocity" described in an undated Seattle Post Intelligencer article as a "small booklet"

Numerous authoritative treatises on electrical and chemical subjects (per obituary)

The Old Greek Philosopher (?)

This categorization is attributed to Berosus (see separate entry) by Ignatius Donnelly (1831-1901) in "Atlantis: The Antediluvian World (1882.)

Lost Continent of Mu, Motherland of Men

Page 41:

> This would be in keeping with the reference to Atlantis made by the old Greek philosopher: "The Land beyond the Sea—the Saturnian Continent."

W.J. Thomson [Thomson, William Judah (1841-1909)]

U.S. Navy Paymaster, member of the crew of the USS Mohican. Authored the book/article: "Te Pito Te Henua or Easter Island" in 1891.

Lost Continent of Mu, Motherland of Men

Page 64:

> W. J. Thomson, whom I believe to be the best authority on what is found on Easter Island, says:
>> "The largest image is in one of the quarries in an unfinished condition and measures 70 feet in height; the smallest was one found in a cave, and was about 3 feet long. The majority of them are from 15 to 18 feet high. It is supposed these images represent distinguished personages, and are intended as monuments to their memory."

From "Te Pito Te Henua, or Easter Island" William J. Thompson (1891) page 497

> The largest image is in one of the workshops in an unfinished state and measures 70 feet in length; the smallest was found in one of the caves and is a little short of 3 feet in length.…
>
> The images were designed as effigies of distinguished persons and intended as monuments to perpetuate their memory. They were never regarded as idols, and were not venerated or worshiped in any manner.

Lost Continent of Mu, Motherland of Men
Page 66-70:

> *W. J. Thomson*: "There are in existence about 7 tablets, all that are left of a vast number, bearing the written story of Easter Island."

Does not appear in "Te Pito Te Henua, or Easter Island"

Thomson, with the aid of an old native, the only one on the island that knew the meaning of the glyphs on these tablets, deciphered and translated some of them. Herewith is Thomson's translation of two:

Tablet l. "When this island was first created and became known to our forefathers, the land was crossed with roads beautifully paved with flat stones. These stones were laid together so nicely that no rough edges were exposed. Coffee [mistranslation] trees were growing close together along the borders of the roads. They met overhead and their branches were laced together like muscles.

"Heke was the builder of the roads, and it was he who sat in the place of honor, where the roads branched away in every direction.

"In that happy land, that beautiful land where Romaha formerly lived with his beloved Hangarva.

"Turaki used to listen to the voices of the birds and feed them.

"In that beautiful land governed the gods from Heaven, who lived in the waters when it was cold.

"There the black and white pointed spider would have mounted to heaven, but he was held back by the bitterness of the cold."

From "Te Pito Te Henua, or Easter Island" William J. Thompson (1891) page 519

When the island was first created and became, known to our forefathers, the land was crossed with roads beautifully paved with flat stones. The stones were laid close together so artistically that no rough edges were exposed. Coffee-trees were growing close together along the borders of the road, that met overhead, and the branches were laced together like muscles. Heke was the builder of these roads, and it was he, who sat in the place of honor in the middle where the roads branched away in every direction. These roads were cunningly contrived to represent the plan of the web of the gray and black-pointed spider, and no man could discover the beginning or the end thereof.

In that happy land, that beautiful land where, Romaha formerly lived with his beloved Hangaroa, and where Turaki used to listen to the voice of the fowl, and feed them with watery food. In that beautiful land that was governed by gods from heaven, and who lived in the water when it was cold. Where the black and white-pointed spider would have mounted to heaven, hat was prevented by the bitterness of the cold.

This particular tablet is named "APAI."...

Tablet 2, entitled "The Great King": "What power has the Great King on land? He has the power to make the plants grow and to change the color of the sky.

"All hail the power of The Great King who makes us lenient to the young plants, to admire the different colors of the sky and to behold the clouds that rise.

"All hail the power of The Great King who enables us to appreciate the blessings of bright stars, the lowering clouds, the gentle dew, the falling rain and the light of the sun and the moon.

"What power has The Great King on land?

"He has the power to populate the earth to create both kings and subjects.

"All hail to the power of The Great King, who hath created the human beings, given authority to kings, and created loyal subjects.

"What power has The Great King"?

"He has the power to create the lobsters, white bait, eels, ape-fish and everything in the sea.

"What power has The Great King over the seas ?

"He hath the power to create the mighty fish that swim in deep water.

"All hail the power of The Great King who enables us to withstand the attacks of the maggots, flies, worms, fleas and all manner of insects."

From "Te Pito Te Henua, or Easter Island" William J. Thompson (1891) pages 523-524

What power has the Great King on the land?

He has power to make the plants grow and to change the sky to different colors.

All hail the power of the Great King who makes us lenient to the young plants, to admire the skies of different colors, and to behold the clouds that rise.

What power has the Great King on the land ?

He has the power to create the lobsters, white-bait, eels, ape-fish, and everything in the sea.

All hail the power of the Great King who gives us the knowledge to catch the lobsters, white-bait, eels, ape-fish, and all marine animals.

What power has the Great King on the land?

He has the power to produce the ferns, creeping plants, grass, bushes and all vegetation.

All hail the power of the Great King who has taught us to love ferns, creeping plants, and all green things.

What power has the Great King over the sea?

He has the power to create the mighty fish that swim in the deep water.

All hail the power of the Great King who has given us the strength and skill to catch the fish of the mighty deep.

What power has the Great King on the land?

He has the power to produce the yams, potatoes, and sugar-cane.

All hail the power of the Great King who enables us to use as food yams, potatoes, and sugar-cane.

What power has the Great King on the land?

He has the power to clothe the turtles in hard shell, the fish with scales, and protects every living thing.

All hail the power of the Great King who enables us to overcome the defense of the turtles, fish, and all reptiles.

What power has the Great King in the universe?

He has the power to create the stars, the clouds, the dew, the rain, the sun, and the moon.

All hail the power of the Great King who enables us to appreciate the blessings of the bright stars, the lowering clouds, the gentle dew, the falling rain, and the light of the sun and moon.

What power has the Great King upon the land?

He has the power to populate the earth, to create both kings and subjects.

All hail the power of the Great King who has created the human beings, given authority to kings, and created loyal subjects.

What power has the Great King upon the land?

He has the power to create maggots, flies, worms, fleas, and all creeping and flying insects.

All hail the power of the Great King who enables us to withstand the attacks of the maggots, flies, worms, fleas, and all manner of insects.

What power has the Great King?

All hail the unlimited power of the Great King.

This particular tablet is named "Eaha Totan Ariiki Kete", also known as "Easter Island Anthem." As indicated in the source volume.

A legend tells the following:

"This little island had once been a part of a great continent of land, crossed with many roads, beautifully paved with flat stones. The roads were cunningly constructed to represent the plan of the web of the gray and black pointed spider, and no man could discover the beginning or the end thereof."

W. J. Thomson: "At the south end of the island there are from 80 to 100 stone houses, built in a regular line against a terrace of rock or earth, which in some cases form the back walls of the building. The walls of these peculiar houses average 5' feet in thickness and 4 1/2 feet in height.
They are 4 1/2 feet broad and 13 feet long.
"The doorways are tiny affairs, not more than 20 inches high and 19 inches wide. The walls are formed by layers of irregular stones. These latter are often painted red, white and black, showing birds, faces and figures.
"Near the houses the rocks on the banks of the sea-cliff are carved in strange shapes, resembling human faces, tortoises, birds, fishes and mythical animals."

Lost Continent of Mu, Motherland of Men
Page 82:
> The Easter Island Statuary were not meant as gods. They were statues to be set up elsewhere in memory of some important personage who had passed away.
> This view is also taken by Thomson, the Easter Island authority.

From "Te Pito Te Henua, or Easter Island" William J. Thompson (1891) page 497
> The images were designed as effigies of distinguished persons and intended as monuments to perpetuate their memory. They were never regarded as idols, and were not venerated or worshiped in any manner.

Scrapbook references:
Scrapbook # 1 Sheet 37 Clip # 7. Another Easter Island tablet translation close to "The Great King"
List of publications:
- "Te Pito Te Henua or Easter Island"(1891)

Thoth [Djehuty (?)]
Thoth was an Egyptian Deity, however, James Churchward portrays him as the founder of the ancient Egyptian temple at Sais where he taught 16,000 years ago.

Lost Continent of Mu, Motherland of Men
Page 100:
> Mackenzie asserts that Osiris was an ancient king. What people he reigned over Mackenzie does not say, but by inference it would be the Egyptians; if so, he is wrong again, because when Thoth started the first Lower Egyptian colony at Sais, he taught the Osirian religion, as various papyri show, and that was 16,000 years ago.

Lost Continent of Mu, Motherland of Men
Page 164:
> THE GREAT MONOLITH AT TIAHUANACO, PERU
>
> This immense stone has been one of the great wonders and enigmas to all archaeologists who have ever looked upon it or its picture. To the archaeologist it is one of the wonders of the world. Perched up on

the shores of Lake Titicaca, 13,500 feet above the level of the Pacific Ocean, it rests as a part of a ruin of a temple.

Much has been written about this stone, and the consensus of opinion among the various writers is: "If it could only be deciphered and read, what a wonderful tale it might possibly tell about the ancient past!" This stone does tell a wonderful tale, for it takes its readers back 16,000 years, when Mu, the Motherland, still held her proud sway throughout the earth, before she sank into that fiery abyss to be mourned by mankind for many thousands of years. It tells about the times when the first settlements were being made in Egypt on the Nile Delta under Thoth - the dawn of Egyptian history.

Lost Continent of Mu, Motherland of Men
Page 167:

Queen Moo visited the Maya colony at Sais on the Nile Delta during the first century of its existence and there met Thoth, its founder, according to the Troano Manuscript. The Nile colony was started 16,000 years ago; therefore this great monolith of Tiahuanaco was carved just 16,000 years ago.

Lost Continent of Mu, Motherland of Men
Page 277:

Manetho says: "It was not until the Eighteenth Dynasty that animal forms of gods were depicted in the memorial chambers of the departed. Under Thotmes III these figures are constantly met with, having the head of the symbolic animal that was embalmed. After the reign of Rameses, the worship of animals grew and expanded greatly."
Here is an example of an unscrupulous priesthood, craving for power and control of wealth, degrading the pure, simple, beautiful Osirian religion, as taught by Thoth at Sais, to accomplish their ends.

Lost Continent of Mu, Motherland of Men
Page 285:

It is known that the early books of our Old Testament were written by Moses from Egyptian Temple records. Hieroglyphics and symbols were the common form of writing in ancient times. A hieroglyphic or a symbol is an emblem of something, and therefore must not be taken literally. They must be taken as *representing* something, but *not* as that something itself. The failure to differentiate between the symbol and what it represents has caused many decipherings and translations to be erroneous, and often, in religious matters, leaves the impression of idolatry where there is a profound reverence for, and a worship of, the Deity. This has been especially prominent in deciphering and translating records relating to the Osirian religion. By Osirian religion I mean that taught by Thoth at Sais, at the commencement of Egyptian history, and not as it was preached and taught and practiced by the unscrupulous Egyptian priesthood of a later period, which commenced during the reign of the second king of the Eleventh Dynasty and reached its climax during the Eighteenth Dynasty.

Valmiki [300 B.C.E.]
Hindu poet
According to tradition, Valmiki was the author of the Indian epic poem Ramayana ("journey of Rama"), which is thought to have been created in the third century B.C. Later he wrote the Ramayana to record the great deeds of the hero Rama, who was one of several human forms taken by the Hindu god Vishnu.

Lost Continent of Mu, Motherland of Men
Page 21:

'Valmiki mentions the Naacals as "coming to Burma from the land of their birth in the East,"'

Lost Continent of Mu, Motherland of Men
Pages 25-26:
"They were also learned architects, building great temples and palaces of stone."
See entry for Valmiki for page 61 in Lost Continent of Mu Motherland of Mankind.

Lost Continent of Mu, Motherland of Men
Pages 26-27:
"Being great navigators, their ships were constantly carrying passengers and merchandise to and from the various colonies."
See entry for Valmiki for page 61 in Lost Continent of Mu Motherland of Mankind.

Lost Continent of Mu, Motherland of Men
Pages 59-60:
"VALMIKI. *Ramayana*. Vol. I Page 342. — "The Maya adepts, the Naacals, starting from *the land of their birth in the east*, as missionaries of religion and learning went first to Burma and there taught the Nagas. From Burma they went to the Deccan in India, whence they carried their religion and learning to Babylonia and to Egypt."

Lost Continent of Mu, Motherland of Men
Page 61:
'VALMIKI. *Ramayana*. Vol. I. Page 353.— "The Mayas were mighty navigators, whose ships traveled from the Western to the Eastern oceans, and from the Southern to the Northern seas in ages so remote that the sun had not yet risen above the horizon.
"That likewise, being learned architects, they built great cities and palaces."

Excerpt from "Queen Moo and the Egyptian Sphinx" (1896) provides this text:
Valmiki, in his beautiful epic the "Ramayana," tells us that the Mayas were mighty navigators, whose ships travelled from the western to the eastern ocean, from the southern to the northern seas, in ages so remote that "the sun had not yet risen above the horizon;" that being likewise great warriors, they conquered the southern parts of the Hindostanee peninsula, and established themselves there; that being also learned architects, they built great cities and palaces.
Footnote to entry "Valmiki, Ramayana, Hippolyte Fauche's translation, vol. I., p. 353."
Augustus Le Plongeon, "Queen Moo and the Egyptian Sphinx" (1896), Page 1-2

Lost Continent of Mu, Motherland of Men
Page 74:
'Does this not entirely agree with Valmiki when he says, "The Mayas were mighty navigators, whose ships passed from the eastern to the western oceans and from the southern to northern seas"?'
See entry for Valmiki for page 61 in Lost Continent of Mu Motherland of Mankind.

Lost Continent of Mu, Motherland of Men
Page 115:
'Valmiki, the ancient Hindu historian, speaking of the works of the Mayas in India, says: "Before the sun rose above the horizon," meaning before the Hindu colony was turned into an empire.'
See entry for Valmiki for page 61 in Lost Continent of Mu Motherland of Mankind.

Lost Continent of Mu, Motherland of Men
Page 153:

'Valmiki does say, however, that it was the *First Hindu Colonial Empire* of the Motherland.'

Lost Continent of Mu, Motherland of Men
Page 169:

'Anarajapoora was not an old city, about 2,200 years only, but before it was built, Ceylon had been occupied by a warlike race for at least 10,000 years, as recorded by Valmiki, the Hindu sage and historian.'

Lost Continent of Mu, Motherland of Men
Page 171:

'From Valmiki, Druidical works, the Popol Vuh and other ancient writings we learn that such characters were driven into the forests, there to live and die like the beasts.'

Appendix 2

Written Works
Referenced in the

"Lost Continent of Mu, the Motherland of Men"

Appendix 2: Printed Works
Table of Contents

Aitareya-A'ram-'ya
Is a portion of the Upanishads.

Lost Continent of Mu, Motherland of Men
Page 17:

> *Aitareya-A'ram-'ya*, slokas 4 to 8: "Originally this universe was only a soul, nothing active or inactive existed. The thought came to Him, "I wish to create worlds," and so He created the worlds, the light, the mortal beings, *the atmosphere that contains the light*, the earth that is perishable, and the lower depths, that of the waters."

Excerpt from "Essays on the Religion and Philosophy of the Hindus"; Henry Thomas Colebrooke; 1858; page 26.

> Originally this [universe] was indeed SOUL only; nothing else whatsoever existed, active [or inactive]. HE thought, "I will create worlds:" thus HE created these [various] worlds; water, light, mortal [beings], and the waters. That 'water,' is the [region] above the heaven, which heaven upholds: the atmosphere comprises light; the earth is mortal; and the regions below are the waters.

Ancestral Worship

Full Name: *Ancestral Worship*
Author: Friedrich Max Mueller

Lost Continent of Mu, Motherland of Men
Page 274:

> Muller, in "Ancestral Worship," says: "Ancestral worship sprang out of the universal faith of primitive peoples in the persistence of human responsibility after death. This form of worship seems to have been almost universal among mankind during a certain stage of development. Traces of it are found in all parts of the earth. The religious ideas of the Hebrews present traces of ancestral worship. The indication is strong that the special God of the Hebrew patriarch, the family God of Abraham, with whom he conversed and held personal relations, represented an ancestral divinity."

Aytareya Bhramana
The Aitareya Brahmana is also known as the Ashvalayana Brahmana and is believed to have been written about 600 BCE.

Lost Continent of Mu, Motherland of Men
Page 280-281:

> In Aytareya Bhramana, a Hindu book, we find: "Sarpa Rajni, the Queen of the Serpents, the mother of all that moves." And again: "Caisha, the Seven-headed Serpent, the Creator."

Excerpt from "Sacred Mysteries Among the Maya and Quiches" (1886) provides this text:

> In the Serpent mantra, the *Aytareya Brahmana*, a passage speaks of the Earth as the *Sarpa Rajni*, the queen of the serpents, and the mother of all that moves, still worshipped by the Nayas, dwellers in the valley of Cashmere.
> Augustus Le Plongeon, "Sacred Mysteries Among the Maya and Quiches" (1886), Page 121

Excerpt from the Aitareya Brahmana of the Rigveda published 1863, 5th book, 24th chapter, page 359:

All the other priests (except the Udgutris) go from thence (the Agnidhriya fire) and proceed to the Sadat (a place in the south-east of the Uttaruvedi) all walking each in his own way, in this or that direction. But the Udgutris walk together. They chant the verses (seen) by the Queen of the Serpents (Sarpa-rajni); because the earth (iyom) is the Queen of the Serpents, for she is the queen of all that moves (Karpat).

Bible

This Bible is the book of the Christian faith, most probably used was the King James version.

Lost Continent of Mu, Motherland of Men
Page 15:

The general resemblance of the opening part of the Naacal record, as regards the story of the creation, to the account as found in the Bible is remarkable, and it is also remarkable how great the divergences thereafter are.

Lost Continent of Mu, Motherland of Men
Page 16:

The Bible uses a good symbolical example when it refers to "the breath of God." At any rate, it is clear that the meaning is *special powers received from God*, and may therefore be looked upon as a part of God, as a leaf is a part of the tree. Man came from God and must return whence he came.

Lost Continent of Mu, Motherland of Men
Page 86:

The adepts of the ancients could walk through fire without being scorched, as related in the Bible and Popol Vuh.

Lost Continent of Mu, Motherland of Men
Page 87:

The foregoing traditions and legends are astounding, and at first glance must stagger one, for here among savages who have been shut off from the outside world up to within 300 years and most of them within 200 years, we are met with the fact that they have among themselves legends and traditions about the creation and the early history of man that are identical with the legends and traditions found in the Bible.

Lost Continent of Mu, Motherland of Men
Page 142:

In Mu the novice was taught to learn this book thoroughly and to repeat it as his belief in God and the hereafter. Just as children are taught their Bibles today, so was the child of this lost continent instructed in this book in ancient times.

Lost Continent of Mu, Motherland of Men
Page 188:

Their traditions are interesting and far-reaching. An extremely fascinating tradition of theirs is about the creation of the first man and woman-the Adam and Eve of the Bible. It is most valuable by reason of the fact that the language of the Motherland is found in the esoteric meanings of some of the words.

Lost Continent of Mu, Motherland of Men
Page 269:

In South America the whole city of Tiahuanaco went up with the great plateau that now exists between the two ranges of the Andes. This is told by the inscription on the great door that is so well known to archaeologists, on the shores of Lake Titicaca.

In most mountainous countries there are traditions concerning the raising of the mountains. The raising of mountains is referred to in the Bible, in one of the psalms of David, called the Song of Moses (Psalms xc: 2).

From the King James Version of the Bible, Psalms 90:2:

"Before the mountains were brought forth, or ever thou hadst formed the earth and the world, even from everlasting to everlasting, thou art God."

Lost Continent of Mu, Motherland of Men
Page 276:

Owen, writing on the ancient religion of China, says:

"The oldest classics in China, going back to the time of Abraham, show a wonderful knowledge of God. There are passages in these classics about God worthy to stand side by side with kindred passages in the Bible. God was omnipotent, omniscient, and omnipresent; the moral governor of the world and the impartial judge of men."

Man's first religion was a simple, pure worship of the Deity. The extravagances which later crept into and disfigured the records of man's first religion were the results of that inevitable degradation which priesthood always inflicts upon great ideas committed to its charge. The original religion became discordant in many particulars, and sorely overlaid by corruptions, inventions and misconceptions.

Lost Continent of Mu, Motherland of Men
Page 286:

Eight hundred years after the Israelitish Exodus from Egypt, Ezra, with a body of co-workers, collected all the tablets and writings of all descriptions which were connected with the family history of the Israelites, and put them into book form, which became the Bible.

Lost Continent of Mu, Motherland of Men
Page 287:

From incontrovertible evidences gained through my research work it is shown that Moses wrote the first books of the Bible from the temple records brought to Egypt from the Motherland by the Naacals via Burma and India; and that these Egyptian temple records were copies of the "Seven Sacred Inspired Writings" of the Motherland Mu. These were written on clay tablets and referred to the Creation. The legends of the Garden of Eden, the "Flood," the last magnetic cataclysm, and the raising of the mountains, are records of later date.

Lost Continent of Mu, Motherland of Men
Page 307:

Moses in a very abstruse manner symbolized it in his writings, as we find in our Bible today.

1Kings, Chapter 7, 21st & 22nd verses

Lost Continent of Mu, Motherland of Men
Page 160:

In the porch, or entrance to King Solomon's Temple, two special pillars were erected (I Kings, Chapter 7, 21st and 22d verses): "And he set up the pillars in the porch of the temple; and he set up the right pillar, and called the name thereof Jachin; and he set up the left pillar, and called the name thereof Boaz."

From the King James Version, 1Kings Chapter Seven:

21 "And he set up the pillars in the porch of the temple: and he set up the right pillar, and called the name thereof Jachin: and he set up the left pillar, and called the name thereof Boaz."

22 "And upon the top of the pillars was lily work: so was the work of the pillars finished."

Ezekiel I:10 & X:14

Lost Continent of Mu, Motherland of Men

Page 296:

ISRAELITES.- The conception of the four gods, pillars or genii, or whatever they may be termed, was not entirely rejected by the Jews. Although there is no mention of them in the books written by Moses, that is no criterion, because some of the books written by Moses are lost, and the reference to the four cardinal points may have been in one of these lost books. Later we see the conception among the Jews in Ezekiel, I :10--"They four had the face of a man, the face of a lion, the face of an ox and the face of an eagle." And in X:14-"The first face was that of a cherub, the second that of a man, the third that of a lion and the fourth that of an eagle."

From the King James Version, Ezekial Chapter 1 verses 4-10:

4 As I looked, behold, a stormy wind came out of the north, and a great cloud, with brightness round about it, and fire flashing forth continually, and in the midst of the fire, as it were gleaming bronze. 5 And from the midst of it came the likeness of four living creatures. And this was their appearance: they had the form of men, 6 but each had four faces, and each of them had four wings. 7 Their legs were straight, and the soles of their feet were like the sole of a calf's foot; and they sparkled like burnished bronze. 8 Under their wings on their four sides they had human hands. And the four had their faces and their wings thus: 9 their wings touched one another; they went every one straight forward, without turning as they went. 10 As for the likeness of their faces, each had the face of a man in front; the four had the face of a lion on the right side, the four had the face of an ox on the left side, and the four had the face of an eagle at the back.

From the King James Version, Ezekial Chapter 10 verses 9-15:

9 And when I looked, behold the four wheels by the cherubims, one wheel by one cherub, and another wheel by another cherub: and the appearance of the wheels was as the color of a beryl stone. 10 And as for their appearances, they four had one likeness, as if a wheel had been in the midst of a wheel. 11 When they went, they went upon their four sides; they turned not as they went, but to the place whither the head looked they followed it; they turned not as they went. 12 And their whole body, and their backs, and their hands, and their wings, and the wheels, were full of eyes round about, even the wheels that they four had. 13 As for the wheels, it was cried unto them in my hearing, O wheel. 14 And every one had four faces: the first face was the face of a cherub, and the second face was the face of a man, and the third the face of a lion, and the fourth the face of an eagle. 15 And the cherubims were lifted up. This is the living creature that I saw by the river of Chebar.

British Museum Mayan Manuscript #9789

Lost Continent of Mu, Motherland of Men

Page 133:

This Vignette (Page 132) is from a Maya manuscript in the British Museum—No. 9789—and represents the arrival of the rain in Yucatan. The two figures are allegorical, representing the divisions of Mayax. It is also a prominent symbol in the ancient writings of the Hindus, Chinese, Chaldeans, Incas, Quiches, Egyptians and other ancient peoples.

Similar to drawing on page 134 of "Sacred Mysteries Among the Mayas and the Quiches"; Le Plongeon, Augustus; 1886. Caption reads "From a Mexican M.S, in British Museum (add. M.S. b.m. 9789)."

From "The Secret Doctrine" Vol. 2 page 36:
> "Symbols: all these are based upon and start from the figures given from the Archaic Manuscript in the proem of Book I. , the symbol of evolution and fall into generation or matter, is reflected in the old Mexican sculptures or paintings, as it is in the Kabalistic Sephiroth, and the Egyptian Tau. Examine the Mexican MSS (Add. MSS. Brit. Mus. 9789)*; you will find in it a tree whose trunk is covered with ten fruits ready to be plucked by a male and female, one on each side of it, while from the top of the trunk two branches shoot horizontally to the right and left, thus forming a perfect (tau), the ends of the two branches, moreover, each bearing a triple bunch, with a bird ˜ the bird of immortality, Atman or the divine Spirit ˜ sitting between the two, and thus making the seventh. This represents the same idea as the Sephirothal Tree, ten in all, yet, when separated from its upper triad, leaving Seven. These are the celestial fruits, the ten or 10, born out of the two invisible male and female seeds, making up the 12, or the Dodecahedron of the Universe."

Codex Cortesianus

The published work identified as the 'Codex Cortesianus' and used extensively as a reference is actually forty-two (42) pages of the Madrid Codex or Codex Tro-Cortesianus. The "Troano Manuscript/Codex" (see entry) are the other 70 pages of this 14th century Mayan book that were joined back together in 1880s. According to present-day translations of the work, the Madrid Codex is a collection of almanacs. The translations of the work used in the "Lost Continent of Mu Motherland of Men" do not match the current accepted translations of the document.

Lost Continent of Mu, Motherland of Men
Page 21:
> ... Another reference is the Codex Cortesianus, a Maya book of about the same age as the Troano Manuscript....

Lost Continent of Mu, Motherland of Men
Page 25:
> The dominant race in the land of Mu was a *white race* exceedingly handsome people, with clear white or olive skins, large, soft, dark eyes and straight black hair. Besides this white race, there were people of other races, people with yellow, brown or black skins. They, however, did not dominate.15
> Identified by footnote: #15. Troano Manuscript, Codex Cortesianus and others.

Lost Continent of Mu, Motherland of Men
Page 29:
> Many generations after this visitation, and when the phenomenon had become past history, Mu again became the victim of earthquakes. "*The whole continent* heaved and rolled like the ocean's waves. The land trembled and shook like the leaves of a tree in a storm. Temples and palaces came crashing to the ground and monuments and statues were overturned. The cities became heaps of ruins."28
> Identified by footnote: #28. Troano Manuscript, Codex Cortesianus and Lhasa Record.

Lost Continent of Mu, Motherland of Men

Page 30:
"During the night"24
Identified by footnote: #24. Codex Cortesianus and Troano Manuscript.

Lost Continent of Mu, Motherland of Men
Page 38:
Both the Troano Manuscript and the Codex Cortesianus refer to the land of Mu as the land of hills of earth or "ridges of earth." The Greek record refers to it as "plains." I feel convinced that all three of these records are correct, because up to the time that the continent vanished beneath the Pacific, there were no mountains. The volcanic workings which sent Mu down beneath the waves were preparatory to mountain raising.

Lost Continent of Mu, Motherland of Men
Page 54:
[Illustration with following caption:]Plate from the Codex Cortesianus

Lost Continent of Mu, Motherland of Men
Page 55:
[Illustration with following caption:
Plate from the Codex Cortesianus
National Museum, Madrid, Spain

Lost Continent of Mu, Motherland of Men
Page 56-57:
Codex Cortesianus.—The Codex Cortesianus is another of the old Maya books that escaped the eyes of the fanatical Bishop Landa. This book is now in the National Museum of Madrid, Spain. The characters, figures and writings would indicate that it is about the same age as the Troano Manuscript. The language of the Codex Cortesianus, however, is much more symbolical than that of the Troano Manuscript. Here are some extracts from it, bearing on our subject:
"By his strong arm Homen caused the earth to tremble after sunset and during the night *Mu, the country of the hills of earthy was submerged.*"
"Mu, the life of the basin (seas), was submerged by Homen during the night."
"The place of the dead *ruler* is now lifeless, it moves no more, after having *twice* jumped from its foundations: the king of the deep, while forcing his way out, has shaken it up and down, has killed it, has submerged it."
"Twice Mu jumped from her foundations; it was then *sacrificed by fire*. It *burst* while being shaken up and down violently by earthquakes. By kicking it, the wizard that makes all things move like a mass of worms, *sacrificed* it that very night."
It is self-evident that both the Codex Cortesianus and the Troano Manuscript were written from the same temple record. The Codex Cortesianus gives the land its hieratical name only, while the Troano Manuscript gives both its hieratical and geographical names.
The Lhasa Record —This record was discovered by Schliemann in the old Buddhist Temple of Lhasa, Tibet. Schliemann deciphered and translated it. It very evidently does not come from the same original record as do the Troano Manuscript and the Codex Cortesianus. It is more modern and is not written in Maya characters.

Lost Continent of Mu, Motherland of Men
Page 59:

Maya Beliefs.-The Mayas of Yucatan regarded the *West* as the region of darkness, the place where the souls of the dead *returned to the bosoms of their ancestors*," as shown in Codex Cortesianus.

Lost Continent of Mu, Motherland of Men
Page 112:

Thus, the Royal Escutcheon of Mu tells us that all mankind on earth was under her rule. Mu was mistress of the whole earth, and this is confirmed by the Codex Cortesianus, where Mu is referred to as *The Ruler*.

Lost Continent of Mu, Motherland of Men
Page 228:

The Codex Cortesianus says: "The land trembled and shook like the leaves of a tree in a storm." The Lhasa Record repeats the same.

Lost Continent of Mu, Motherland of Men
Page 257:

It is my belief that the supporting chambers which upheld Mu were *very near* to the surface of the land. I base this opinion on the depths of the Pacific Ocean, the Troano Manuscript, the Codex Cortesianus and the Lhasa Record. None of these records speaks of the land having been raised to any great height before sinking into the Pacific.

Early Religions

The exact title of this book has not been discovered, however a part of the passage comes from *Lectures on the Origin and Growth of Religion as Illustrated by the Religions of Asia,* (also known as the Hibbert Lectures) by Friedrich Max Mueller delivered in 1878.

Lost Continent of Mu, Motherland of Men
Page 273-274:

Muller in "Early Religions" says:

"In one sense every religion has been a true religion at the start; they were the only religions that were possible at the time, which were compatible with the language, the thoughts, and the sentiments of each generation, which were appropriate to the age of the world. We ought therefore to put the most charitable interpretation on the apparent absurdities, the follies and the errors of ancient religions. As soon as we know anything of the thoughts and feelings of man, we find him in possession of a religion, a religion of faith or worship, of morality or ecstatic vision, a religion of fear and hope, or surmise, a reverence of the so-called gods.

"In order to approach the religion of primitive peoples we must, so to speak, get at its heart, and feel its life currents. We must place ourselves in sympathy with these ancient peoples, listen to their hymns and prayers, and witness their rites and ceremonies; we must endeavor to know their religious ideals. When Thales declared all things were full of gods, and when Buddha denied that there were any other gods except the Supreme Being, both were stating their religious convictions.

"The external aspect of a religion as presented to strangers is not one often to be trusted. In the earliest and purest days of Christianity, if we were to believe the most enlightened of the heathen writers, the Christian religion consisted of the worship of animals. This idea possibly arose from the fact that the earliest pictures of Mary nursing Christ show the cow's horns of the Egyptian goddess Sati on her head, and sometimes the horns of Hathor."

Lectures on the Origin and Growth of Religion as Illustrated by the Religions of Asia

Page 13

> When Thales declared that all things were full of the gods, and when Buddha denied that there were any
> devas or gods at all, both were stating their religious convictions.

Egyptian Book of the Dead

Book of the Dead is the common name for the ancient Egyptian funerary texts. These texts were originally painted on the inside walls of the tombs and consisted of spells, charms, passwords, and the like to aid the deceased in reaching the underworld. The 'Book of the Dead' grew over time and some versions have over 190 chapters.

The Book of the Dead for Scribe Ani, The Papyrus of Ani is a papyrus from the 18th dynasty of the New Kingdom of Ancient Egypt (1540 – 1307 B.C.E.) Dating by E.A. Wallis Budge date the papyrus from 1500 to 1400 B.C.E.

It contains portions of the Book of Going Forth by Day, more commonly known as the Book of the Dead. The scroll was part of the burial of the scribe Ani of the city of Thebes. It was purchased in 1888 by Sir E. A. Wallis Budge for the collection of the British Museum where it remains today. Before shipment to England the 78 foot scroll was cut into 37 sheets of nearly equal size.

Full Name: Coming Forth By Day

Lost Continent of Mu, Motherland of Men
Page 9:

> *Vignette* 13. This vignette appears on a tablet describing the raising of the mountains and the formation of gas belts. Therefore, we see where the Egyptians obtained their symbol of fire; also the scarab. The Naacals from India carried them to Egypt. The Egyptian fire symbol is only a modification of the Naga. The Egyptians put a handle on the Naga and turned it into a sword. It is not hard to find the reason for the Egyptian change or modification. In their hieroglyphics they wanted to depict two forms of fire: the fires of the underneath and actual flames. This they did to record the destruction of the motherland, which they say "sank into a fiery abyss" and "was enveloped in flames as she went down." This symbol is shown in our chapter on the Egyptian sacred book, the Book of the Dead.

Lost Continent of Mu, Motherland of Men
Page 38:

> [Illustration with following caption:] MAP OF MU
> The Lands of the West from the Egyptian Book of the Dead

Lost Continent of Mu, Motherland of Men
Page 53:

> Sir Gardner Wilkinson, the great Egyptologist, in his book, "Manners and Customs," Volume III, page 70 says:
> "Kui-Land or the Land of Kui, according to the Maya language, was the birthplace of the goddess Maya, the mother of the gods—and of man."
> Extract 2, by the way, is corroborated many times in the Egyptian Book of the Dead.

Excerpt from "Queen Moo and the Egyptian Sphinx" (1896) provides this text:

> "Sir Gardner Wilkinson, Manners and Customs of Ancient Egyptians, vol. iii, p. 70. "Kui Land," according to the Maya language the "land of the gods," the birthplace of the Goddess Maya, "the mother of the gods" and of men, the feminine energy of Brahma by whose union with Brahma all things were produced."

Augustus Le Plongeon, "Queen Moo and the Egyptian Sphinx" (1896), Introduction page lxiv Footnote 1

Lost Continent of Mu, Motherland of Men
Page 92:

In the preceding chapter I have referred to the Egyptian Book of the Dead. It contains many records that prove that the Motherland of Men, the submerged continent of Mu, was, indeed, the original habitat of the race of men, and that other countries were merely orbits for bodies that moved about a center of attraction, which was the highly civilized continent of Mu, colonizer of the worlds that lay beyond its immediate ken; consequently it does not appear to me to be out of place to say a few words about the Book of the Dead at this point.

The Book of the Dead is the common name by which this sacred volume is known. In Egyptian hieroglyphics the name is written: *Per-m-hru*. According to Egyptologists, *per* means "coming forth," *hru* means "day" and *m* is a preposition meaning "from."

Lost Continent of Mu, Motherland of Men
Page 93:

... The Book of the Dead is a sacred commemorative memorial, dedicated to the multitudes of people who lost their lives at the destruction of Mu, the forefathers of the Egyptians and all mankind. These are the "dead" referred to. This feeling of love and devotion to the Motherland, this feeling of love and respect for forefathers is the origin of "ancestor worship," so common throughout the world in past and present ages. Have we not a reflection of it among ourselves?...

Lost Continent of Mu, Motherland of Men
Page 94-98:

At what date the Book of the Dead was first formed is unknown; apparently, however, the first copies contained only a few chapters, which were subsequently added to until it assumed the proportions in which we now find it. In this respect it has been a duplication of the Hindu book, Maha-bharatta, which commenced small and grew large with time.

Every chapter in the Book of the Dead either directly or indirectly refers to Mu, and the book is permeated with symbols which were assigned to Mu before the foot of man trod the soil of Egypt.

As already stated, Mu was first torn to pieces by earthquakes and then sank through the flames of the underneath into a fiery abyss or caldron.

I will now take a few vignettes from the Book of the Dead, decipher and translate them, to show the connection between the Book of the Dead and Mu, the Motherland.

Vignette l. This is an Egyptian compound symbol or vignette describing the destruction of Mu. Found in the Book of the Dead.
1. Is the Egyptian symbol for flames of fire?
2. Is the hieratic letter M of the Motherland and her alphabetical and geometrical symbol, and one of the most commonly used symbols for her?
3. Is an ancient symbol, depicting an abyss, a tank or a pit?
4. Is this tank or abyss filled with fire?
Thus the vignette reads: "Mu has gone down into an abyss of fire, and, as she sank, flames of fire shot up around her and enveloped her." This is told by flames being set all around Fig. 2—Mu.
One of the most prominent symbols, on account of its being so oft repeated, is a conventional altar, over which a set sun is, and above the sun a dead closed lotus.

This compound symbol is found scores of times among the vignettes of the Book of the Dead, and a notable fact is that the lotus is invariably depicted as dead and closed. Throughout the book.

I will decipher and translate this little vignette:

1. Is the Egyptian conventional form of an altar?
2. Is the sacred lotus flower, the sacred floral symbol of Mu?
3. Is the sun without rays, symbolizing that the sun has set, gone down beyond the horizon. Being placed *below* Mu, the lotus, it symbolizes that the sun has dropped below the horizon of Mu. The sun has forever set on dead Mu. All is darkness. Mu is in "the region of darkness." Before the submersion of Mu her common geographical symbol was a three-pointed figure (Fig. 4), reading, "The Lands of the West," the three areas of land which composed the Motherland.

After Mu was submerged, her geographical location was called "the region of darkness," and in this condition she was symbolized by placing a sun without rays over the center point (Fig. 6). Occasionally the center point was cut out altogether and a rayless sun substituted (Fig. 5).

THE VIGNETTE OF CHAPTER 81

In the Book of the Dead, Egyptologists have described this vignette as "a head peeping out of a lotus flower."

The last line of the eighty-first chapter reads: "I am a pure Lotus sprung out of the Field of the Sun."

The deciphering of this vignette is:

The head represents an Egyptian and Egyptians, as shown by the head-dress.

The head has arisen out of a lotus.

The lotus is shown as dead and closed.

In this vignette the lotus is dead Mu.

Translated it reads:

"The Egyptians came from Mu, a land which is dead and exists no more."

The last line is the crux of the whole chapter.

"I am a pure Lotus" means: "I am a pure descendant from the people of Mu."

"Sprung from the Field of the Sun" corroborates the lotus. 'The Field of the Sun" also means the Empire of the Sun, the imperial name of Mu.

Mu in the tongue of the Motherland meant: "mother, land, field, country, empire" and "mouth."

A free reading of this vignette would be: "I am an Egyptian of pure descent; my forefathers came from the motherland Mu, the Empire of the Sun, which is now dead and gone."

Space will not permit me to decipher more vignettes from the Book of the Dead. A large volume could be filled with them.

I will make one more note, which is all Egyptian, but only partially from the Book of the Dead.

All ancient peoples, including the Egyptians, believed in the reincarnation of the soul. Our old Oriental tablets showed us that the ancients understood the origin and the workings of all the forces: they knew that when a force had done its allotted duty, that which had been assigned to it by nature, it became exhausted, *but not dead*, force cannot die any more than an element can die. An exhausted force is drawn back to the source of generation for regeneration, then to be passed into nature's storehouse, there to await the next call from nature. This is what the old tablets tell us.

Lost Continent of Mu, Motherland of Men
Page 100-101:

The destruction of the Motherland was also commemorated in their religious ceremonies. The advancement of the novice through the second degree was by symbolically submerging him in a tank of fire to remind him of the fate that befell his forefathers in the beloved Motherland, and also to hint where his soul must go for reincarnation. This is reflected in the Book of the Dead, Chapter 22, where it says: "I come, I do that which my heart wishes on the day of the *Fire* when I extinguish the flames as soon as they appear."

Lost Continent of Mu, Motherland of Men
Page 159-160:

> [Illustration with following caption:]
> TAT PILLAR
> Papyrus Ani B.C. 1500. British Museum
>
> In Egyptian mythology, pillars were placed at the entrance to Amenti. Above on this page I give a cut taken from the Papyrus of Ani, showing one of the two pillars at the entrance to Amenti. The Egyptians called them Tat Pillars, but they are more commonly known throughout the world as Totem Pillars.

Lost Continent of Mu, Motherland of Men
Page 161:

> Java is one of the large islands of the Malay Archipelago, and in writing of it, Forbes says:
> "In Java is a tribe called the Karangs, supposed to be descendants of the aborigines of the island, whose old men and youths, four times a year, repair secretly in procession to a sacred grove in a dense forest, the old men to worship, the youths to see and learn the mysteries of their forefathers. In this grove are the ruins of terraces laid out in quadrilateral enclosures, the boundaries of which are marked by blocks of stone, or fixed in the ground. Here and there on the terraces are prominent monuments, *erect pillars*, and, especially noteworthy, a pillar *erect within a square*. Here these despised and secluded people follow the rites and customs that have been handed down to them through their forefathers from vastly remote ages (12,000 to 13,000 years), repeating with superstitious awe a litany which they do not understand or comprehend, This very litany is found in the Egyptian Book of the Dead."

Excerpt from "Signs and Symbols of Primordial Man" (1912) provides this text:

> Forbes mentions that in Java is a tribe called the Karangs, supposed to be descendants of the aborigines of the island, whose old men and youths, four times a year, repair secretly in procession, by paths known only to themselves, to a sacred grove in the dense forest: the old men to worship, the youths to see and learn the mysterious litany of their fathers.
>
> In this grove are the ruins of terraces, laid out in quadrilateral enclosures, the boundaries of which are marked by blocks of stone laid or fixed in the ground. Here and there on the terraces are more prominent monuments, erect pillars, etc., and, especially noteworthy, a pillar erect within a square. Here these despised and secluded people follow the rites and customs that have descended to them through their forefathers from vastly remote antiquity, repeating with a superstitious awe a litany which they do not comprehend, the origins and purpose of which are lost in their traditions, but which may be found in the Egyptian Papyrus (Papyrus of Leyden) and the "Ritual or Book of the Dead."
> Albert Churchward, "Signs and Symbols of Primordial Man" (1912), page 17, 21

Lost Continent of Mu, Motherland of Men
Page 274:

> From the Book of the Dead: *Hathor* in Egyptian means "the house of horns." Hathor is frequently represented with the attributes of Isis. Hathor symbolizes and personifies not only all that is beautiful, but also all that is true. Isis was the personification of the female or creative attribute of the Deity.

Fables and Rites of the Incas

The English language translation of this book is available online, however the quoted text was not found.

Full Name: *Narratives of The Fables and Rites of the Yncas*
Author: Christoval de Molina (translation by Clements R. Markham)
Date: 1570-1584 (1873)

Lost Continent of Mu, Motherland of Men
Page 289:

> PERU. "*Fables and Rites of the Incas.*" (Pages 36 to 50).-"These festivities were established to commemorate deceased friends and relatives. They were celebrated with tears, mournful song, plaintive music, and by visiting the tombs of the dear departed, whose provision of com and chicaha they received through openings arranged on purpose from the exterior of the tomb to vessels placed near the body. The Peruvians had great festivals in honor of the dead in the month of Aya-Marca."

Excerpt from "Queen Moo and the Egyptian Sphinx" (1896) provides this text:

> Great festivities were held by the Peruvians in honor of the dead in the month of *Aya-marca*, a word which means literally "carrying the corpse in arms." These festivities were established to commemorate deceased friends and relations. They were celebrated with tears, mournful songs, plaintive music, and by visiting the tombs of the dear departed, whose provision of corn and *chicha* they renewed though openings arranged on purpose from the exterior of the tomb to vessels placed near the body. 1
> 1 Christoval de Molina, *The Fables and Rites of the Yncas*. Translation by Clements R. Marjham, pp. 36-50.
> Augustus Le Plongeon, "Queen Moo and the Egyptian Sphinx" (1896), Page 9-10

Festival of Ancestors

Full Name: *Festival of Ancestors Ethnological Researches Bearing on the Year of the Pleiades*
Author: Robert Grant Haliburton

Lost Continent of Mu, Motherland of Men
Page 289:

> R. G. Haliburton, who is considered one of our best authorities on ancestral worship, in writing of the "Festival of Ancestors," says:
> "It is now, as it was 'formerly, held at or near the beginning of November, by the Peruvians, the Hindus, the Pacific Islanders, the people of the Tonga Islands, the Australians, the ancient Persians, the ancient Egyptians and the northern nations of Europe, and continues for three days among the Japanese, the Hindus, the Australians, the ancient Romans and the ancient Egyptians."

Excerpt from "Queen Moo and the Egyptian Sphinx" (1896) provides this text:

> Mr. R.G. Haliburton, of Boston, Mass., in a very learned and most interesting paper 1 on the "Festival of Ancestors," or the feast of the dead so prevalent among all nations of the earth, speaking of the singularity of its being observed everywhere at precisely the same epoch of the year, says: "It is now, as it was formerly, observed at or near the beginning of November by the Peruvians, the Hindoos, the Pacific Islanders, the people of the Tonga Islands, the Australians, the ancient Persians, the ancient Egyptians, and the northern nations of Europe, and continued for three days among the Japanese, the Hindoos, the Australians, the ancient Romans, and the ancient Egyptians…

1. R.G. Haliburton, Festival of Ancestors," *Ethnological Researches Bearing on the Year of the Pleiades.*
Augustus Le Plongeon, "Queen Moo and the Egyptian Sphinx" (1896), Page 11

Guatemala

Full Name: *Guatemala and her people of to-day : being an account of the land, its history and development; the people, their customs and characteristics; to which are added chapters on British Honduras and the republic of Honduras, with references to the other countries of Central America, Salvador, Nicaragua, and Costa Rica*
Author: Nevin Otto Winter
Date: 1909

Lost Continent of Mu, Motherland of Men
Page 91:

> Winter, in his work "Guatemala," page 15:6, says: "The mysterious symbol of the Greek cross, which has also been found on the stones of Quirigua and Copan, has been the cause of much speculation among scholars." No one, apparently, can solve this simple problem.

Historia de Nuestra Senora de Ytzamal

Full Name: *Historia de Nuestra Sefiora de Izamal, de la Provincia de Yucatan*
Author: Bernardo de Lizana
Date: 1633

Lost Continent of Mu, Motherland of Men
Page 240-241:

> Lizana ("Historia de Nuestra Senora de Ytzamal," Chap. II): "When the Spaniards came to this country, notwithstanding that some of the monuments appeared new, as if they had been built only twenty years, the Indians did not live in them, but used them as temples and sanctuaries, offering in them sacrifices sometimes of men, women and children, and that their construction dates back to great antiquity.".

Excerpt from "Queen Moo and the Egyptian Sphinx" (1896) provides this text:

> "unmindful, likewise, of these words of Lizana: "That when the Spaniards came to this country, notwithstanding that that some of the monuments appeared new, as if they had been built only twenty years, the Indians did not live in them, but used them as temples and sanctuaries, offering in the sacrifices, sometimes of men, women, and children; and that their construction dated back to a very high antiquity"

Augustus Le Plongeon, "Queen Moo and the Egyptian Sphinx" (1896), Introduction page xxxiii

Historia de Yucathan

Full Name: *Historia de Yucathan*
Author: Diego Lopez de Cogolludo
Date: 1688

Lost Continent of Mu, Motherland of Men
Page 240:

> Cogolludo, in "Historia de Yucathan," Book IV, Chap. III, p. 177, says:

"Of the people who first settled in this Kingdom of Yucathan, or their ancient history, I have been unable to obtain any other data than those which follow:

"The Spanish chronicles do not give one reliable word about the manners and customs of the builders of the grand antique edifices that were objects of admiration to them, as they are now to modern travelers.

"The only answer of the natives to the inquiries of the Spaniards as to who the builders were invariably was, 'We do not know.' It is not known who the builders were and the Indians themselves have no traditions on the subject."

Excerpt from "Queen Moo and the Egyptian Sphinx" (1896) provides this text:

"- regardless of Cogolludo's assertion "that it is not known who their builders were, and that the Indians themselves preserved no traditions on the subject;"...

"Of the people who first settled in this Kingdom of Yucathan," he says, "nor of their ancient history, have I been able to find any more data than those I mention here."

Augustus Le Plongeon, "Queen Moo and the Egyptian Sphinx" (1896), Introduction page xxxiii

---

Khoung Tsen

Author: Confucious

Lost Continent of Mu, Motherland of Men
Page 288:

CHINA. Confucius in *Khoung Tsen.*-The whole of Chapter XIX is dedicated to the description of the ceremony in honor of ancestors, as practiced twice a year-in the spring and in the autumn.

Excerpt from "Queen Moo and the Egyptian Sphinx" (1896) provides this text:

Confucius in his book "Khoung-Tseu" dedicates a whole chapter to the description of the ceremony in honor of ancestors as practiced twice a year, in spring and autumn, 2 and in his book "Lun-yu" he instructs his disciples that "it is necessary to sacrifice to the ancestors as though they were present."3
2. Confucius, Khong-Tseu, Tchoung-Young, chap. xix.
3. Idid., Lun-yu, chap. Iii., Sloka 12
Augustus Le Plongeon, "Queen Moo and the Egyptian Sphinx" (1896), Page 9

Lhasa Record

The only reference to the Lhasa Record is contained in the October 12th, 1912 edition of the New York American (newspaper). A complete copy is contained in one of James' scrapbooks, minus the illustrations.

The following represents the reference to this document in the 1912 article by Peter Schliemann:

In the records of the old Buddhistic Temple at Lhassa there is to be seen an ancient Chaldaic inscription written about 2,000 B.B. It reads:

"When the star Bal fell on the place where is now only sea and sky the Seven Cities with their Golden Gates and transparent Temples quivered and shook like the leaves of a tree in storm. And behold a flood of fire and smoke arose from the palaces. Agony and cries of the multitude filled the air. They sought refuge in their temples and citadels. And the wise Mu, the hieratic of Ra-Mu, arose and said to them: 'Did I not predict all this?' And the women and the men in their precious stones and shining garments lamented: "Mu, save us.' And Mu replied: 'You shall die together with your slaves and your riches and from your ashes will arise new nations. If they forget they are superior, not because of what they put on, but of what they put out, the same lot will befall them!" Flame and smoke choked the words of Mu. The land and its habitants were torn to pieces and swallowed by the depths in a few months."

Lost Continent of Mu, Motherland of Men
Page 21:

Second, there is confirmation of Mu in other ancient manuscripts ... Then there is the Lhasa record, with hundreds of others from Egypt, Greece, Central America, Mexico, and the cliff writings in our western states.

Lost Continent of Mu, Motherland of Men
Page 22:

"we find only water and the sky"
Identified by footnote: #1: Lhasa Record

Lost Continent of Mu, Motherland of Men
Page 24:

Many generations before, the people had selected a king and added the prefix Ra to his name. He then became the hieratical head and emperor under the name "Ra Mu."12
Identified by footnote: #12: Lhasa Record and others

Lost Continent of Mu, Motherland of Men
Page 25:

All followed the same religion, a worship of the Deity through symbols. All believed in the immortality of the soul, which soul eventually returned to the "great source" from whence it came.
Identified by footnote: #13: Lhasa Record and many others

Lost Continent of Mu, Motherland of Men
Page 26:

In the land of Mu there were *seven* great or principal cities, the seats of religion, science and learning.17
Identified by footnote: #17: Lhasa Record...

"The wealthy classes adorned themselves in fine raiment with many jewels and precious stones. They lived in imposing palaces attended by many servants. 19
Identified by footnote: #19: Lhasa Record

Lost Continent of Mu, Motherland of Men
Page 29:

"Agonizing cries of the multitude filled the air. The people sought refuge in their temples and citadels only to be driven out by fire and smoke, and the women and the men in their shining garments and precious stones cried: 'Mu save us!' "27
Identified by footnote: #27: Lhasa Record

Lost Continent of Mu, Motherland of Men
Page 40:

Schliemann, on apparently two records only, the Troano Manuscript and the Lhasa Record, asserts that Atlantis was the land of Mu. These records *do not* state that Mu and Atlantis were identical; it is mere surmise on the part of Schliemann.

Lost Continent of Mu, Motherland of Men
Page 56-57:

The Lhasa Record —this record was discovered by Schliemann in the old Buddhist Temple of Lhasa, Tibet. Schliemann deciphered and translated it. It very evidently does not come from the same original record as do the Troano Manuscript and the Codex Cortesianus. It is more modern and is not written in Maya characters.

Here is an interesting extract from the Lhasa Record:

"When the star of Bal fell on the place where now is only the sky and the sea, the seven cities with their golden gates and transparent temples, quivered and shook like the leaves in a storm; and, behold, a flood of fire and smoke arose from the palaces. Agonies and cries of the multitude filled the air. They sought refuge in their temples and citadels, and the wise Mu—*the Hieratic Ra Mu*—arose and said to them: did I not predict all this? And the women and the men in their precious stones and shining garments lamented 'Mu, save us!' and Mu replied: You shall all die together with your servants and your riches, and from your ashes new nations shall arise. If they forget they are superior not because of what they put on but what they put out the same will befall them.' Flames and smoke choked the words of Mu: the land and its inhabitants were torn to pieces and swallowed up by the depths."

Bal is a Maya word meaning "Lord of the Fields." "Transparent temples" is, without doubt, a mistranslation. These temples were not built of glass or any other transparent substance. They were *open* or *roofless* temples so constructed that the rays of Ra—the sun—could fall upon the heads of those who were in prayer and supplication within the temple, like the Parsee temples of today.

Lost Continent of Mu, Motherland of Men
Page 58:

Le Plongeon's death occurred many years before Schliemann published the Lhasa Record.

Lost Continent of Mu, Motherland of Men
Page 228:

The Codex Cortesianus says: "The land trembled and shook like the leaves of a tree in a storm." The Lhasa Record repeats the same.

Lost Continent of Mu, Motherland of Men
Page 257:

It is my belief that the supporting chambers which upheld Mu were *very near* to the surface of the land. I base this opinion on the depths of the Pacific Ocean, the Troano Manuscript, the Codex Cortesianus and the Lhasa Record. None of these records speaks of the land having been raised to any great height before sinking into the Pacific.

Scrapbook references:
Scrapbook 1 sheet 32-34. The article contained in Scrapbook #1 (3 pages,) is essentially the same as the online article at sacred-texts.com, "How I Found the Lost Atlantis, the Source of All Civilization" by Dr. Paul Schliemann. Dated October 20th, 1912 and appearing in the New York American, this article is the earliest known reference to the "Lhassa Record.

Life of Solon

Full Name: Life of Solon
Author: Plutarch (Mestrius Plutarchus)
Date: 75 C.E.

Excerpt from "Life of Solon":
His first voyage was for Egypt, and he lived, as he himself says-
"Near Nilus' mouth, by fair Canopus' shore," and spent some time in study with Psenophis of Heliopolis, and Sonchis the Saite, the most learned of all the priests; from whom, as Plato says, getting knowledge of the Atlantic story, he put it into a poem, and proposed to bring it to the knowledge of the Greeks.

Lost Continent of Mu, Motherland of Men
Page 60:
Plutarch. *Life of Solon.*—"Sanches, the High Priest of Sai's, told Solon [600 B. C.], also Psenophis, a priest of Heliopolis, that 9,000 years before, the relations of the Egyptians with the inhabitants of the *Lands of the West* had been interrupted because of cataclysms destroying the *intervening* country, *and—* the mud that had made the sea impassable since the *destruction of Atlantis by earthquakes and submersion.*"

Excerpt from "Queen Moo and the Egyptian Sphinx" (1896) provides this text:
Plutarch, in his "Life of Solon," says that when the famed Greek legislator visited Egypt (600 years before the Christian era), Sonchis, a priest of Sais, also Psenophis, a priest of Heliopolis, told him that 9,000 years since, the relations of the Egyptians with the inhabitants of the "lands of the West" had been interrupted because of the mud that had made the sea impassable after the destruction of Atlantis by earthquakes.
Augustus Le Plongeon, "Queen Moo and the Egyptian Sphinx" (1896), Preface page xi

Lost Continent of Mu, Motherland of Men
Page 243:
Some old Egyptian Papyri refer to these cataclysms, which are confirmed by the Greek philosophers, Plato and Plutarch (Plutarch's Life of Solon).

Lun Yu

Author: Confucious

Lost Continent of Mu, Motherland of Men
Page 288:
In *Lun Yu* Confucius says: "It is necessary to sacrifice to the ancestors as if they were present."

Excerpt from "Queen Moo and the Egyptian Sphinx" (1896) provides this text:
Confucius in his book "Khoung-Tseu" dedicates a whole chapter to the description of the ceremony in honor of ancestors as practiced twice a year, in spring and autumn, 2 and in his book "Lun-yu" he instructs his disciples that "it is necessary to sacrifice to the ancestors as though they were present."3
2. Confucius, Khong-Tseu, Tchoung-Young, chap. xix.
3. Idid., Lun-yu, chap. Iii., Sloka 12
Augustus Le Plongeon, "Queen Moo and the Egyptian Sphinx" (1896), Page 9

Maha-bharatta

Lost Continent of Mu, Motherland of Men
Page 94:

> At what date the Book of the Dead was first formed is unknown; apparently, however, the first copies contained only a few chapters, which were subsequently added to until it assumed the proportions in which we now find it. In this respect it has been a duplication of the Hindu book, Maha-bharatta, which commenced small and grew large with time.

Manava Dharma Sastra

Full Name:
Author:
Date:

Lost Continent of Mu, Motherland of Men
Page 17:

> HINDU : *The Manava Dharma Sastra*, Book 2, sloka 74:
> "In the beginning only existed the Infinite called Adite."
> Book l, sloka 8: "This germ became an egg."
> Book l, sloka 10: "The visible universe in the beginning was only darkness."
> Book l, sloka 9: "He first produced the waters and in them deposited an egg."

Excerpt from "Queen Moo and the Egyptian Sphinx" (1896) provides this text:

> From remote ages the Brahmins taught that in the beginning existed the Infinite. This they called the *Aditi*, "that which is above all things." …
> In this infinite dwelt AUM, whose name must proceed all prayers, all invocations.2
> …
> We read in the first chapter of the ordinances of Manu,4 that the Supreme Being produced first the waters, and in them deposited a germ, an egg, in which He himself was born again under the shape of *Brahma*, the great ancestor of all beings…
> They waters were called Nara, says Manu, 2* because they were the production of Nara the divine spirit, "the mother of truth:" …
> 2 *Manava-Dharma-Sastra*, book ii., Sloka 74
> 4 *Manava-Dharma-Sastra*, book i., Sloka 8.
> 2* *Manava-Dharma-Sastra*, book i., Sloka 10.
> Augustus Le Plongeon, "Queen Moo and the Egyptian Sphinx" (1896), Pages 22-24

Lost Continent of Mu, Motherland of Men
Page 280:

> Manava Dharma Sastra, a Hindu book, refers to the Serpent as the Creator.

Lost Continent of Mu, Motherland of Men
Page 288:

INDIA. *The Dharma Lastra.*-"The ceremony in honor of the Manes is superior, for the Brahmins, to the worship of the gods; and the offerings to the gods that take place before the offerings to the Manes have been declared to increase their merit."

Excerpt from "Queen Moo and the Egyptian Sphinx" (1896) provides this text:

If we compare this with the precepts of the "Manava-Dharma Shastra-" The ceremony in honor of the manes is superior, for the Brahmins, to the worship of the gods, and the offerings to the gods that take place before the offerings to the manes have been declared to increase their merits" " 1 – it will be easy to see that these teachings have emanated from the same school.

1 *Manava-Dharma Shastra*, lib iii., Sloka 203, also Slokas 127, 149, 207, etc, *et passim.*

Augustus Le Plongeon, "Queen Moo and the Egyptian Sphinx" (1896), Page 9

Montezuma's Daughter

Full Name: *Montezuma's Daughter*
Author: Sir Henry Rider Haggard
Date: 1892

Lost Continent of Mu, Motherland of Men
Page 247:

Rider Haggard must have found this same tradition, for in his work, "Montezuma's Daughter," he says: "Quetzal, or more properly, Quetzalcoatl, was the divinity who is fabled to have taught the natives of Anahuac all the useful arts, including those of government and policy. He was white-skinned and light-haired. Finally he sailed from the shores of Anahuac for the fabulous country of Hapallan in a bark of serpent skins."

From Montezuma's Daughter (1893)

* Quetzal, or more properly Quetzalcoatl, was the divinity who is fabled to have taught the natives of Anahuac all the useful arts, including those of government and policy, he was white-skinned and dark-haired. Finally he sailed from the shores of Anahuac for the fabulous country of Tlapallan in a bark of serpents' skins.

Mystic Isles of the South Seas

Full Name: *Mystic Isles of the South Seas*
Author: Frederick O'Brien
Date: 1921

Lost Continent of Mu, Motherland of Men
Page 81-82:

I will now take extracts from O'Brien's "Mystic Isles of the South Seas," capping each legend with the corresponding biblical legend.
Page 21—"The great god Ra of the Polynesians."
In Ra we have a connecting link between the Polynesians and our known ancients. Ra was the symbol of the Sun, and the Sun was the collective symbol of the Deity among the Mayas, Quiches, Incas, Hindus, Chaldeans, Babylonians, Assyrians, Egyptians, etc.

Easter Island (Pages 64-66)—"Huge stone gods that had been thrown down. Some were 37 feet high, and had red stone crowns ten feet in diameter."

The quoted text are identified as excerpts from "Mystic Isles of the South Seas" and the original paragraphs are reproduced below:

One morning when we were near the middle of our voyage I went on deck to see the sun rise. We were that day eighteen hundred miles from Tahiti and the same distance from San Francisco, while north and west twelve hundred miles lay Hawaii. Not nearer than there, four hundred leagues away, was succor if our vessel failed. It was the dead center of the sea. I glanced at the chart and noted the spot: Latitude 10∫ N.; Longitude 137∫ W. The great god Ra of the Polynesians had climbed above the dizzy edge of the whirling earth, and was making his gorgeous course into the higher heavens. The ocean was a glittering blue, an intense, brilliant azure, level save for the slight swaying of the surface, which every little space showed a flag of white. The evaporation caused by the blazing sun of these tropics made the water a deeper blue than in cooler latitudes, as in the Arctic and Antarctic oceans the greens are almost as vivid as the blues about the line.

"I think the island had a superior race once. There are immense platforms of stone, like the paepaes of the Marquesas, only bigger, and the stones are all fitted together without cement. They built them on promontories facing the sea. Some are three hundred feet long, and the walls thirty feet high. On these platforms there were huge stone gods that have been thrown down; some were thirty-seven feet high, and they had redstone crowns, ten feet in diameter. There were stone houses one hundred feet long, with walls five feet thick. How they moved the stones no one knows, for, of course, these people there now were not the builders. Some race of whom they knew nothing was there before them.

Lost Continent of Mu, Motherland of Men
Page 84:

O'Brien has adorned his writings with many interesting and astounding traditions which he found among the South Sea Islanders. I will quote some of them:

The Creation.—"The Marquesans said that in the beginning there was no light, life or sound in the world, that a boundless night called Po enveloped everything over which Tanaoa (darkness) and Mutu-hei (silence) reigned supreme.

'Then the god of light separated from Tanaoa (darkness), fought him and drove him away and confined him to the night. Then the god Ono (sound) was evolved from Atea (light) and banished silence. From all this struggle was bom Atauana (dawn). Atea (light) married Atauana (dawn) and they created earth, animals and man."

The text above are unidentified excerpts from "Mystic Isles of the South Seas" and the original paragraphs are reproduced below:

The Marquesans said that in the beginning there was no light, life, or sound in the world; that a boundless night, Po, enveloped everything, over which Tanaoa, (Darkness), and Mutu-hei, (Silence), ruled supreme. Then the god of light separated from Tanaoa, fought him, drove him away, and confined him to night. Then the god Ono, (Sound), was evolved from Atea, (Light), and banished Silence. From all this struggle was born the Dawn, (Atanua). Atea married the Dawn, and they created earth, animals, man.

Lost Continent of Mu, Motherland of Men
Page 85:

THE Flood.—O'Brien says in "Mystic Isles of the South Seas":
"In most of Polynesia there are legends of a universal flood from which but few escaped."
Adam And Eve.—"The Polynesians had very fixed ideas upon the origin of the universe and man."
In *Hawaii*: "Taaroa made man out of red earth Araea and breathed into his nostrils. He made woman from a man's bones and called her Ivi." (In the Polynesian language Ivi is pronounced Eve-y.)
Cain And Abel.—A Tonga tradition states that "the son of the first man killed his brother."
New Zealand: A tradition of the Maoris, the natives of New Zealand, states "that the son of the first man killed his brother."
Tower of Babel.—"In Fiji is still shown the site where a vast tower was built because the Fijians were curious and wanted to peep into the moon to discover if it was inhabited.
POLYNESIAN COSMOGONY.—*Tahiti*: "Taaroa, whose name was spelt differently in separate archipelagos, was the father of Tahitian cosmogony. His wife was Hina - the earth, and his son Oro was the ruler of the world, Tane the Hualine god was a brother of Oro and his equal."
This corresponds with the cosmogony of the most ancient namely a Trinity or a Triune Godhead.

The text above are excerpts from "Mystic Isles of the South Seas" and the original paragraphs are reproduced below:

The Polynesians had very fixed ideas upon the origin of the universe and of man. In Hawaii, Taaroa made man out of red earth, araea, and breathed into his nostrils. He made woman from man's bones, and called her ivi (pronounced eve-y). At the hill of Kauwiki, on the eastern point of the island of Maui, Hawaii, the heaven was so near the earth that it could be reached by the thrust of a strong spear, and is to-day called lani haahaa.

The Marquesans said that in the beginning there was no light, life, or sound in the world; that a boundless night, Po, envelope everything, over which Tanaoa, (Darkness), and Mutu-hei, (Silence), ruled supreme. Then the god of light separated from Tanaoa, fought him, drove him away, and confined him to night. Then the god Ono, (Sound), was evolved from Atea, (Light), and banished Silence. From all this struggle was born the Dawn, (Atanua). Atea married the Dawn, and they created earth, animals, man.

In most of Polynesia there are legends of a universal flood from which few escaped. In Fiji it was said that two races were entirely wiped out, one of women, and the other of men and women with tails. A little bird sat on the top of the uncovered land and wailed the destruction. The Marquesans built a great canoe like a house, with openings for air and light, but tight against the rain. The ark was stored with provisions, and the animals of the earth were driven in two by two, fastened in couples. Then the family of four men and four women entered the ark, sacrificed a turtle to God, and retired to rest amidst the terrific din of the confined animals. The storm burst, and the waters covered the entire land. The storm ceased and a black bird was sent over the sea of Hawaii. It returned to the ark, and a wind set in from the north. Another bird was loosed, and alighted on thesea-shore. It was recalled, and a third bird brought back twigs. The ark soon grounded, and the four men and four women released the beasts, and went ashore. These repopulated the earth.

The Samoans believed that the earth was once covered with water and the sky alone was inhabited, until God sent his only begotten daughter in the form of a kuri, or snipe, to look for dry land. She found a spot, and brought down to it earth, and a creeping plant, which grew and decomposed into worms, and, lo! the worms turned into men and women.

In Hawaii Nuu was saved from a similar flood, and with him his three sons and their families. Ten generations later Kanehoalani was commanded by God to introduce circumcision. He went to a far-off country, had a son by a slave woman and one by his wife. He was then commanded, this descendant of Nuu in the tenth generation, to go up on a mountain and perform a sacrifice. He sought a mountain, but none appeared suitable; so he communed with God, who told him to travel to the east, and he would find a precipice. He departed with his son and a servant. The Hawaiians still call the mountains back of Koolau, near Honolulu, after the name of the three, and when the missionaries gave them the Jewish sacred books, were delighted to point out that long before Christ came to earth they had believed as above, and that

Abraham was the tenth from Noah, that Abraham practiced circumcision, and was father of Isaac and the illegitimate Ishmael, and that their descendant of Nuu, as Abraham, became the father of twelve children, and the founder of the Polynesian race, as Abraham had of the Jews.

One might detect some relation to the Hebraic scriptures in the legends of the Maoris of New Zealand and Tonga that the older son of the first man killed his brother, and that in Fiji one still is shown the site where a vast tower was built because the Fijians wanted to peer into the moon to discover if it was inhabited. A lofty mound was erected, and the building of timber upon it. It was already in the sky when the fastenings broke, and the workmen were precipitated over every part of Fiji.

…

Taaroa, whose name was spelt differently in separated archipelagos, was the father of the Tahitian cosmogony. His wife was Hina, the earth, and his son, Oro, was ruler of the world. TanÈ, the Huahine god, was a brother of Oro, and his equal, but there were islands which disputed this equality, and shed blood to disprove it, as the sects of Christianity have since the peaceful Jesus died by the demands of the priests of his nation.

Lost Continent of Mu, Motherland of Men
Page 86:

O'Brien gives a thrilling account of a Tahitian adept walking bare-footed on red-hot stones, without being burnt. The same thing has been shown in Hawaii and I have personally seen it done in the Fiji Islands.

The excerpt from "Mystic Isles of the South Seas" that describes the event above has been reproduced below:

When we approached the umu, I felt the heat fifty feet away. The pit was a mass of glowing stones, and half a dozen men whom I knew were spreading them as evenly as possible, turning them with long poles. Each, as it was moved, disclosed its lower surface crimson red and turning white. The flames leaped up from the wood between the stones.

About the oven, forty feet away, the people of the villages who had gathered, stood or squatted, and solemnly awaited the ritual. The tahua, Tufetufetu, was still in a tiny hut that had been erected for him, and at prayer. A deacon of the church went to him, and informed him that the umu was ready, and he came slowly toward us. He wore a white pareu of the ancient tapa, and a white tiputa, a poncho of the same beaten-bark fabrics. His head was crowned with ti-leaves, and in his hand he had a wand of the same. He was in the dim light a vision of the necromancer of medieval books.

He halted three steps from the fiery furnace, and chanted in Tahitian:

O   spirits who put fire in the oven, slack the fire!
O   worm of black earth,
O   worm of bright earth, fresh water, sea water, heat of the oven, red of the oven, support the feet of the walkers, and fan away the fire!
O   Cold Beings, let us pass over the middle of the oven!
O   Great Woman, who puts the fire in the heavens, hold still the leaf that fans the fire!
Let thy children go on the oven for a little while!
Mother of the first footstep!
Mother of the second footstep!
Mother of the third footstep!
Mother of the fourth footstep!
Mother of the fifth footstep!
Mother of the sixth footstep!
Mother of the seventh footstep!
Mother of the eighth footstep!
Mother of the ninth footstep!
Mother of the tenth footstep!
O Great Woman, who puts the fire in the heavens, all is hidden!

Then, his body erects, his eyes toward the stars, augustly, and without hesitation or choice of footprints, the tahu walked upon the umu. His body was naked except for the tapa, which extended from his shoulders to his knees. The heat radiated from the stones, and sitting on the ground I saw the quivering of the beams just above the oven.

Tufetufetu traversed the entire length of the umu with no single flinching of his muscles or flutter of his eyelids to betray pain or fear. He raised his wand when he reached the end, and, turning slowly, retraced his steps.

The spectators, who had held their breaths, heaved deep sighs, but no word was spoken as the tahua signed all to follow him in another journey over the white-hot rocks. All but a few, their number obscured in the darkness, ranged themselves in a line behind him, and with masses of ti-leaves in their hands, and some with girdles hastily made, barefooted they marched over the path he took again. When the cortege had passed once, the priest said, "Fariu! Return!" and, their eyes fixed on vacancy, six times the throng were led by him forward and back over the umu. A woman who looked down and stumbled, left the ranks, and cried out that her leg was burned. She had an injury that was weeks in curing.

Naacal Tablets

Full Name: unknown
Author: unknown
Date: unknown

The first recorded use of the term "Naacal" is contained in Augustus Le Plongeon's work from 1896, "Queen Moo and the Egyptian Sphinx." From pages xxiii - xxiv of the preface:

> "Perhaps also will be felt the necessity of recovering the libraries of the Maya sages (hidden about the beginning of the Christian era to save them from destruction at the hands of the devastating hordes that invaded their country in those times), and to learn from their contents the wisdom of those ancient philosophers, of which that preserved in the books of the Brahmins is but the reflection. That wisdom was no doubt brought to India, and from there carried to Babylon and Egypt in very remote ages by those Maya adepts (Naacal - "the exalted"), who, starting from the land of their birth as missionaries of religion and civilization, went to Burmah, where they became known as Nagas, established themselves in the Dekkan, whence they carried their civilizing work all over the earth."

According to Augustus Le Plongeon, the Naacals were the missionaries of Mayan religion and civilization. These tablets identified by James Churchward in his books about the Lost Continent of Mu were authored by the Naacals, according to Churchward. Other than the 'Rishi', no person has seen any copies of these tablets.

Niroukta
Identified as the oldest Indian treatise on Etymology, Philology, and Semantics.

Full Name: *The Nirukta*
Author: many
Date: 800-700 BCE

Lost Continent of Mu, Motherland of Men
Page 298:

> In the Hindu book *Niroukta* it is three times affirmed that "there are three gods only, and that these three gods designate one Sole Deity."
> "The Gods are three only."
> "Pradjapati, or, as He is sometimes called, Mahatma, the Lord of all Creatures, is the collective God."

Excerpt from "Sacred Mysteries Among the Maya and Quiches" (1886) provides this text:

> The same conceptions about Deity existed in India from the remotest antiquity. H. T. Colebrooke, in his notice on "the Sacred Books of the Hindoos" says: "In the latter part of the *Niroukta*, dedicated exclusively to the divinities, it is thrice affirmed that there are only *three god*; and that these three gods designate a sole deity. The gods are three only, whose mansions are the Earth, the intermediate regions and heavens; that is the fire, the air, and the sun; but Pradjapati, the Lord of all creatures, is their collective God. In fact there is but one God, the "great soul" *Maha-atma*.
> Augustus Le Plongeon, "Sacred Mysteries Among the Maya and Quiches" (1886), Page 54-55

Origin of Religious Laws

Full Name: *Origin of Religious Laws*
Author: Friedrich Max Mueller

Lost Continent of Mu, Motherland of Men
Page 275-276:

Muller, in "Origin of Religious Laws," says: "The belief that the religious law-giver enjoyed some closer intimacy with the Deity than ordinary mortals pervades the ancient traditions of many nations. According to a well-known passage in Diodorus Siculus, the Egyptians believed their laws to have been communicated to Mnevis by Hermes. The Cretans held that Minos received the laws from Zeus. The Lacedaemonians held that Lykurgus received his laws from Appolon. The Aryans believed that Zathraustes received them from the Good Spirit. According to Gatel, Zamolscis received his laws from the goddess Hestia, and according to the Jews, Moses received his laws from the God Iao.[32]"

"There was a primitive Aryan religion, a primitive Semitic religion, and a primitive Turanian religion, before each of these primeval races was broken up and became separate in language, worship and national sentiment. The highest God received the same name in the ancient mythology of India, Greece, Italy and Germany, and had retained that name whether worshipped in the Himalayan mountains, or among the oaks of Dodona, on the Capital or in the forests of Germany. He shows that his name was Dyaus in Sanskrit, Zeus in Greek, Jovis in Latin and Tiu in German.

"They bring before us with all the vividness of an event which we witnessed ourselves but yesterday, the ancestors of the whole Aryan race, thousands of years it may be before Homer and the Veda, worshipping an unseen being under the same name, the best, the most exalted name they could find in their vocabulary - under the name Light and Sky. Let us not turn away and say that this after all was nature worship and idolatry. No, it was not meant for that, although it may have been degenerated into that in later times.

"Dyaus did not mean the blue sky, nor was it the sky personified; it was meant for something else. We have in the Veda the invocation Dyaus Pitar, the Greek Zeus Pater and the Latin Jupiter, and that means in all these languages what it meant before these languages were torn asunder. It means 'Heaven Father,' or 'Heavenly Father.' "

Papyrus Anana

Please note that in the 1931, *Lost Continent of Mu*, the portion quoting Anani (see pages 157-158) has been changed to read Anana (see biographical entry.)

I am unable to find copies of this papyrus that quote this exact passage, however I have found references to other portions of the text. Nothing exists to rule out the possibility that this is a mixed-up reference to the *Papyrus of Ani* (see entry.)

Full Name: Papyrus of Anana
Author: Anana
Date: 1320 BCE

Lost Continent of Mu, Motherland of Men
Page 128:

Egyptian Papyrus Anana - Here is an interesting quotation from the Egyptian papyrus, Anana, which is dated 1320 B. C:

"Eternity has no end, therefore no beginning; consequently eternity is a *circle*.

"If we live on we must continue forever, and if we continue forever, like the circle and eternity, man had no beginning.

"Man comes into being many times, yet knows nothing of his past lives; except occasionally some day-dream or a thought carries him back to some circumstance of a previous incarnation. He cannot, however, determine in his mind when or where the circumstance occurred, only that it is something familiar. In the end, however, all of his various pasts will reveal themselves."

"The spirits or souls of one incarnation possibly may meet again in another incarnation, and may be drawn together as if by a magnet, but for what cause neither knows."

Papyrus IV (Boulak Museum)

Full Name: *Papyrus IV* (Boulak Museum)

Lost Continent of Mu, Motherland of Men
Page 288:
> EGYPT. *Papyrus* IV~ (Boulak Museum).-"Bring offerings to thy father and to thy mother, who rest in the valley of tombs; for he who gives these offerings is as acceptable to the gods as if they were brought to themselves. Often visit the dead, so that what thou doest for them they may do for thee."

Popol Vuh

Is a Quiche manuscript from Guatemala that was transcribed in the 16th century from the oral transmission of the document. The text addresses the Quiche creation myth and is considered to be sacred to the Maya.

Full Name: *Popol Vuh*

Lost Continent of Mu, Motherland of Men
Page 86:
> The adepts of the ancients could walk through fire without being scorched, as related in the Bible and Popol Vuh.

Lost Continent of Mu, Motherland of Men
Page 171:
> In their excitement over the discovery of a few old human bones, such as the Neanderthal, Piltdown, and Heidelberg man, scientists, in both Europe and America, have completely ignored and cast aside the remains of ancient man in North America. That the European remains were those of idiots and degenerates is obvious from the abnormal shapes of their skulls. Doubtless they were outcasts from civilized communities. From Valmiki, Druidical works, the Popol Vuh and other ancient writings we learn that such characters were driven into the forests, there to live and die like the beasts. It would appear from many ancient writings that the usual method of disposing of bodies was by cremation, consequently there remained no trace of those whose bones had been consumed by fire.

Lost Continent of Mu, Motherland of Men
Page 297:
> GUATEMALA. *Popol Vuh*.-"All that exists is the work of Tzkol the Creator, who, by his will, caused the universe to spring into existence; and whose names are Bitol the maker; Alom the engenderer and Quhalom, he who gives being." Tzkol is shown as the collective God.

Lost Continent of Mu, Motherland of Men
Page 300:

>Le Plongeon translated the Popol Yuh into English from Brasseur's French translation, checking it himself with the original Maya. This copy he kindly lent me to make notes from. The following from the Popol Yuh therefore comes through Le Plongeon.

Ramayana

Full Name: *Ramayana*
Author: Valmiki
Date: ?

Lost Continent of Mu, Motherland of Men
Page 21:

>Second, there is confirmation of Mu in other ancient manuscripts, including such a classic as the Hindu epic Ramayana, written by the sage and historian, Valmiki, from the dictation of Narana, the high priest of the Rishi temple at Ayhodia, who read the ancient temple records to him.

Lost Continent of Mu, Motherland of Men
Page 59-60:

>VALMIKI. *Ramayana*. Vol. I Page 342. — "The Maya adepts, the Naacals, starting from *the land of their birth in the east*, as missionaries of religion and learning went first to Burma and there taught the Nagas. From Burma they went to the Deccan in India, whence they carried their religion and learning to Babylonia and to Egypt."

Lost Continent of Mu, Motherland of Men
Page 61:

>VALMIKI. *Ramayana*. Vol. I. Page 353.— "The Mayas were mighty navigators, whose ships traveled from the Western to the Eastern oceans, and from the Southern to the Northern seas in ages so remote that the sun had not yet risen above the horizon.
>"That likewise, being learned architects, they built great cities and palaces."

Lost Continent of Mu, Motherland of Men
Page 158:

>In Ramayana, we find this reference to him: "In olden times there was a prince of the Nagas whose name was Maya."

Rig Veda

Full Name: *Rig Veda*

Lost Continent of Mu, Motherland of Men
Page 17:

>*Rig Veda*, sec. 3, 1. 2, v. 4, pp. 316-317 (2000-2500 B.C.): "In this egg was reproduced the intellect of the Supreme Being *under the form of Buddha*, through whose union with the goddess Maya, the good mother of all the gods and man . . ." (This corresponds with Adam and Eve 1,700 years later.) Page 3: "Other than Him nothing existed; darkness there was." Page 4: "He who measures out *the light in the air*."

Lost Continent of Mu, Motherland of Men
Page 275-2766:

>Muller, in "Origin of Religious Laws," says: ...
>
>"They bring before us with all the vividness of an event which we witnessed ourselves but yesterday, the ancestors of the whole Aryan race, thousands of years it may be before Homer and the Veda, worshipping an unseen being under the same name, the best, the most exalted name they could find in their vocabulary - under the name Light and Sky..."

Six Thousand Years of History

Full Name: *Six Thousand Years of History*
Author: Sanderson, Edgar; et. al.
Date: 1899

Lost Continent of Mu, Motherland of Men
Page 291-292:

>In "Six Thousand Years of History" we find this statement: "The comparison of words in Sanskrit, the ancient language of the Hindu; Zend, the old speech of Persia; Greek, Latin, English and other tongues, has shown that all these languages came from a distant common original, spoken by some race yet unparted by migration. In all, or nearly all of these tongues, the names of common things and persons, the words expressing simple instruments and actions, the words for family relations, such as father, brother, daughter and son, the earlier numerals, the pronouns, the very endings of nouns and verbs, are substantially the same. Accident could not have caused this phenomenon, and, since many of the nations speaking thus have for long ages been parted from each other by vast stretches of the earth's broad surface, they could not learn . them in historic times from one another. Borrowing and imitation being thus excluded, the only possible account is that these words and forms were carried with them by the migratory Aryan tribes as part of the possession once shared by all in their original home."

Sourya Siddhanta

Full Name: *Sourya Siddhanta*
Author: Prince Maya

Lost Continent of Mu, Motherland of Men
Page 158-159:

>Prince Maya was the author of the *Sourya Siddhanta*, the most ancient treatise on astronomy in India. Its age has been variously estimated at from 10,000 to 22,000 years.
>
>At the time of Prince Maya, the Nagas were an empire. When the handle and sheath of this knife were made, the Nagas were a colony antedating the Empire. That they were only a colony is clearly shown by the suns without rays on the horizon. This proves the extreme antiquity of the handle and sheath.

Other references:
Excerpt from "Queen Moo and the Egyptian Sphinx" (1896) provides this text:

>"H. T. Colebrooke, "Memoirs on the Sacred Books of India," *Asiatic Researches*. Vol ii., pp. 369-476, says: "Maya is considered as the author of the Sourya-Siddhanta, the most ancient treatise on astronomy in India. He is represented as receiving his science from a partial incarnation of the Sun." This work, on which all the Indian astronomy is founded, was discovered in Benares by Sir Robert Chambers. Mr.

Samuel Davis partly translated it, particularly those sections which relate to the calculation of eclipses. It is a work of very great antiquity, since it is attributed to a **Maya** author whose astronomical rules show that he was well acquainted with trigonometry (Asiatic Researches, vol. ii., pp. 245-249), proving that abstruse sciences were cultivated in those remote ages, before the invasion of India by the Aryans. (See Appendix, note vi.)"
Augustus Le Plongeon, "Queen Moo and the Egyptian Sphinx" (1896), Page 3 footnote

Sri Santara

Full Name: *Sri Santara*

Lost Continent of Mu, Motherland of Men
Page 136:
> *Fig.* 21.—This is one of the most astounding symbols I have found among the North American Indians—two pairs of equilateral triangles interlaced, and placed one pair within the other. This is the central figure of the *Sri Santara*—the cosmic diagram of the Hindus—and conveys identically the same meaning to the Pueblo Indian as it does to the Hindu.

Lost Continent of Mu, Motherland of Men
Page 297-298:
> HINDU.-In the *Sri Santara* of the Hindus the Great Aum, the "nameless," is figured as a trinity by the equilateral triangle.

Excerpt from "Sacred Mysteries Among the Maya and Quiches" (1886) provides this text:
> The Chaldees symbolized the Eusoph or great light, by an equilateral triangle; and in the *Sri-Santara* or cosmological diagram of the Hindoos, which has served as model for many of their temples, the nameless, the great AUM that dwells in the infinite, is figured as an equilateral triangle.
> Augustus Le Plongeon, "Sacred Mysteries Among the Maya and Quiches" (1886), Page 60

Te Pito Te Henua or Easter Island

Full Name: Te Pito Te Henua or Easter Island
Author: William J. Thompson
Date: 1891

References to *Easter Island Tablet(s)* appear to reference those tablets that were reported by W.J. Thomson in his report to the National Museum in 1891.

Lost Continent of Mu, Motherland of Men
Page 23:
> It was a "beautiful"
> Identified by footnote: #2: Easter Island Tablet

Lost Continent of Mu, Motherland of Men
Page 24:
> Little feathered songsters in bush and tree vied with each other in their sweet lays.
> Identified by footnote: #7: Easter Island Tablet

Lost Continent of Mu, Motherland of Men
Page 66, 68-69:

W. J. Thomson: "There are in existence about 7 tablets all that are left of a vast number bearing the written story of Easter Island."

Thomson, with the aid of an old native, the only one on the island that knew the meaning of the glyphs on these tablets, deciphered and translated some of them. Herewith is Thomson's translation of two:

Tablet 1. "When this island was first created and became known to our forefathers, the land was crossed with roads beautifully paved with flat stones. These stones were laid together so nicely that no rough edges were exposed. Coffee [mistranslation] trees were growing close together along the borders of the roads. They met overhead and their branches were laced together like muscles.

"Heke was the builder of the roads, and it was he who sat in the place of honor, where the roads branched away in every direction.

"In that happy land, that beautiful land where Romaha formerly lived with his beloved Hangarva.

"Turaki used to listen to the voices of the birds and feed them.

"In that beautiful land governed the gods from Heaven, who lived in the waters when it was cold.

"There the black and white pointed spider would have mounted to heaven, but he was held back by the bitterness of the cold."

Remains of these roads are to be seen on Easter and many other of the South Sea Islands.

From "Te Pito Te Henua, or Easter Island" William J. Thompson (1891) page 519

When the island was first created and became, known to our forefathers, the land was crossed with roads beautifully paved with flat stones. The stones were laid close together so artistically that no rough edges were exposed. Coffee-trees were growing close together along the borders of the road, that met overhead, and the branches were laced together like muscles. Heke was the builder of these roads, and it was he, who sat in the place of honor in the middle where the roads branched away in every direction. These roads were cunningly contrived to represent the plan of the web of the gray and black-pointed spider, and no man could discover the beginning or the end thereof.

In that happy land, that beautiful land where, Romaha formerly lived with his beloved Hangaroa, and where Turaki used to listen to the voice of the fowl, and feed them with watery food. In that beautiful land that was governed by gods from heaven, and who lived in the water when it was cold. Where the black and white-pointed spider would have mounted to heaven, hat was prevented by the bitterness of the cold.

This particular tablet is named "APAI."

Tablet 2, entitled "The Great King": "What power has the Great King on land? He has the power to make the plants grow and to change the color of the sky.

"All hail the power of The Great King who makes us lenient to the young plants, to admire the different colors of the sky and to behold the clouds that rise.

"All hail the power of The Great King who enables us to appreciate the blessings of bright stars, the lowering clouds, the gentle dew, the falling rain and the light of the sun and the moon.

"What power has The Great King on land?

"He has the power to populate the earth to create both kings and subjects.

"All hail to the power of The Great King, who hath created the human beings, given authority to kings, and created loyal subjects.

"What power has The Great King"?

"He has the power to create the lobsters, white bait, eels, ape-fish and everything in the sea.

"What power has The Great King over the seas?

"He hath the power to create the mighty fish that swim in deep water.

"All hail the power of The Great King who enables us to withstand the attacks of the maggots, flies, worms, fleas and all manner of insects."

A legend tells the following:

"*This little island had once been a part of a great continent of land*, crossed with many roads, beautifully paved with flat stones. The roads were cunningly constructed to represent the plan of the web of the gray and black pointed spider, and no man could discover the beginning or the end thereof."

From "Te Pito Te Henua, or Easter Island" William J. Thompson (1891) pages 523-524

What power has the Great King on the land?

He has power to make the plants grow and to change the sky to different colors.

All hail the power of the Great King who makes us lenient to the young plants, to admire the skies of different colors, and to behold the clouds that rise.

What power has the Great King on the land?

He has the power to create the lobsters, white-bait, eels, ape-fish, and everything in the sea.

All hail the power of the Great King who gives us the knowledge to catch the lobsters, white-bait, eels, ape-fish, and all marine animals.

What power has the Great King on the land?

He has the power to produce the ferns, creeping plants, grass, bushes and all vegetation.

All hail the power of the Great King who has taught us to love ferns, creeping plants, and all green things.

What power has the Great King over the sea?

He has the power to create the mighty fish that swim in the deep water.

All hail the power of the Great King who has given us the strength and skill to catch the fish of the mighty deep.

What power has the Great King on the land?

He has the power to produce the yams, potatoes, and sugar-cane.

All hail the power of the Great King who enables us to use as food yams, potatoes, and sugar-cane.

What power has the Great King on the land?

He has the power to clothe the turtles in hard shell, the fish with scales, and protects every living thing.

All hail the power of the Great King who enables us to overcome the defense of the turtles, fish, and all reptiles.

What power has the Great King in the universe?

He has the power to create the stars, the clouds, the dew, the rain, the sun, and the moon.

All hail the power of the Great King who enables us to appreciate the blessings of the bright stars, the lowering clouds, the gentle dew, the falling rain, and the light of the sun and moon.

What power has the Great King upon the land?

He has the power to populate the earth, to create both kings and subjects.

All hail the power of the Great King who has created the human beings, given authority to kings, and created loyal subjects.

What power has the Great King upon the land?

He has the power to create maggots, flies, worms, fleas, and all creeping and flying insects.

All hail the power of the Great King who enables us to withstand the attacks of the maggots, flies, worms, fleas, and all manner of insects.

What power has the Great King?

All hail the unlimited power of the Great King.

This particular tablet is named "Eaha Totan Ariiki Kete", also known as "Easter Island Anthem." As indicated in the source volume.

Lost Continent of Mu, Motherland of Men

Page 67:

[Illustration with following caption:] Easter Island Tablet

Lost Continent of Mu, Motherland of Men

Page 70:

Raratonga Island.—On this island there is a small section of the road referred to in the Easter Island tablet and legend.

Timeus Critias

Full Name: *Timeus Critias*

Author: Plato

Date: ?

Lost Continent of Mu, Motherland of Men

Page 59:

In Plato's "Timeus Critias" we find this reference to the lost continent: "The Land of Mu had ten peoples"

Troano Manuscript

The published work identified as the 'Troano Manuscript" and used extensively as a reference is actually seventy (70) pages of the Madrid Codex or Codex Tro-Cortesianus. The "'Codex Cortesianus" (see entry) are the other 42 pages of this 14th century Mayan book that were joined back together in 1880s. According to present-day translations of the work, the Madrid Codex is a collection of almanacs. The translations of the work used in the "Lost Continent of Mu Motherland of Men" do not match the current accepted translations of the document.

Lost Continent of Mu, Motherland of Men

Page 21:

Other documents confirming the story of the sacred tablets and Valmiki are: The Troano Manuscript, now in the British Museum. This is an ancient Maya book written in Yucatan. It speaks of the "Land of Mu" using the same symbols for Mu that we find in India, Burma and Egypt.

Lost Continent of Mu, Motherland of Men

Page 23:

The valleys and plains were covered with rich grazing grasses and tilled fields, while the "low rolling "hill-lands"4

Identified by footnote: #4. Troano Manuscript

Lost Continent of Mu, Motherland of Men

Page 24:

All this great continent was teeming with gay and happy life over which "64,000,000 human beings" reigned supreme." 9

...

At the time of our narrative, the 64,000,000 people were made up of "ten tribes" or "peoples," each one distinct from the other, but all under one government." 11
Identified by footnote: #9. Troano Manuscript
Identified by footnote: #11. Troano Manuscript

Lost Continent of Mu, Motherland of Men
Page 25:

The dominant race in the land of Mu was a *white race* exceedingly handsome people, with clear white or olive skins, large, soft, dark eyes and straight black hair. Besides this white race, there were people of other races, people with yellow, brown or black skins. They, however, did not dominate.
Identified by footnote: #15. Troano Manuscript, Codex Cortesianus and others.

Lost Continent of Mu, Motherland of Men
Page 26:

According to records, inscriptions and traditions, man's advent on earth was in the land of Mu and on this account the name "land of Kui" was added to that of Mu.18
Identified by footnote: #18. Troano Manuscript and inscriptions

Lost Continent of Mu, Motherland of Men
Page 29:

Many generations after this visitation, and when the phenomenon had become past history, Mu again became the victim of earthquakes. "*The whole continent* heaved and rolled like the ocean's waves. The land trembled and shook like the leaves of a tree in a storm. Temples and palaces came crashing to the ground and monuments and statues were overturned. The cities became heaps of ruins."28
Identified by footnote: #28. Troano Manuscript, Codex Cortesianus and Lhasa Record

Lost Continent of Mu, Motherland of Men
Page 30:

"During the night"24
Identified by footnote: #24. Codex Cortesianus and Troano Manuscript

Lost Continent of Mu, Motherland of Men
Page 37:

The records and data based on the supposed age of the Troano Manuscript show that the land of Mu was in existence up to the very edge of historical times.

Lost Continent of Mu, Motherland of Men
Page 38:

Both the Troano Manuscript and the Codex Cortesianus refer to the land of Mu as the land of hills of earth or "ridges of earth."

Lost Continent of Mu, Motherland of Men
Page 40:

Schliemann, on apparently two records only, the Troano Manuscript and the Lhasa Record, asserts that Atlantis was the land of Mu. These records *do not* state that Mu and Atlantis were identical; it is mere surmise on the part of Schliemann.

White Shadows in the South Seas

Full Name: *White Shadows in the South Seas*
Author: Frederick O'Brien
Date: 1919

Lost Continent of Mu, Motherland of Men
Page 38-39:

'Frederick O'Brien, who has written most interestingly of the South Sea Islands, says:

"Darwin's theory is that these islands are the tops of a submerged continent, or land bridge, which stretches its crippled body along the floor of the Pacific Ocean for thousands of leagues. A lost land, whose epic awaits the singer; a mystery perhaps forever to be unsolved.

"There are great monuments, graven objects, hieroglyphs, customs and language; island people with suggestive legends, all perhaps remnants of a migration from Asia or Africa a hundred thousand years ago.

"Here, three centuries ago, they were discovered by the peoples of the great world, and, rudely encountering a civilization they did not build, they are dying here: with their passing vanishes the last living link with our pre-historic past, and I was to see it before it disappeared forever."

Where we find specks of land out of water with incontrovertible evidences of continental resources, we are made doubly certain that these specks are parts or remains of a continent. These bits of land are, as I have already said, little islands peopled by savages. They are thousands of miles away from any mainland, and it is therefore the strongest possible proof, stronger than any record, inscription or tradition, that back in prehistoric times there was a continent and that the continent was peopled by highly civilized human beings.

The entire unedited text is reproduced below from the Gutenberg Project ebook "White Shadows in the Pacific" from which the above text is quoted:

Darwin's theory is that these islands are the tops of a submerged continent, or land bridge, which stretches its crippled body along the floor of the Pacific for thousands of leagues. A lost land, whose epic awaits the singer; a mystery perhaps forever to be unsolved. There are great monuments, graven objects, hieroglyphics, customs and languages, island peoples with suggestive legends--all, perhaps, remnants of a migration from Asia or Africa a hundred thousand years ago.

Over this land bridge, mayhap, ventured the Caucasian people, the dominant blood in Polynesia to-day, and when the continent fell from the sight of sun and stars save in those spots now the mountainous islands like Tahiti and the Marquesas, the survivors were isolated for untold centuries.

Here in these islands the brothers of our long-forgotten ancestors have lived and bred since the Stone Age, cut off from the main stream of mankind's development. Here they have kept the childhood customs of our white race, savage and wild, amid their primitive and savage life. Here, three centuries ago, they were discovered by the peoples of the great world, and, rudely encountering a civilization they did not build, they are dying here. With their passing vanishes the last living link with our own pre-historic past. And I was to see it, before it disappears forever.

Lost Continent of Mu, Motherland of Men
Page 44-45:

I will quote, with his permission, some passages from Frederick O'Brien's fascinating book, "White Shadows in the South Seas." The passages referred to are as follows:

"Over this land bridge, mayhap, ventured the Caucasian people—*the dominant blood in Polynesia today*—and when the continent fell from the sight of sun and stars, save in those spots now mountainous islands like Tahiti and the Marquesas, the survivors were isolated for untold ages.

The quoted text is an excerpt from "White Shadows in the Pacific" and the original has been reproduced in the previous entry.

"Here in these islands the brothers of our long-forgotten ancestors have lived and bred since the Stone Age, cut off from the main stream of mankind's development. Here they have kept the childhood customs of our white race, savage and wild, amid their primitive and savage life."

The quoted text is an excerpt from "White Shadows in the Pacific" and the original has been reproduced in the previous entry.

It is evident from the foregoing that O'Brien based these paragraphs on the theory that the white race originated in Asia. It is an accepted theory and O'Brien cannot be blamed for the error.

On page 112 of his book, O'Brien writes:
"My savage friends with their clear features, their large, straight eyes and clear olive skins, still show the traces of their Caucasian blood. Their forefathers and mine might have hunted the great winged lizards together through primeval wilderness, until, driven by who knows what urge of wanderlust or necessity, certain tribes set out in that drive through Europe and Asia towards America, that ended at last when a continent sank beneath their feet in the South Seas."

The entire paragraph from "White Shadows in the Pacific" is reproduced below for the text above:

I seemed to see in this curious fact another proof of the ancient kinship between the first men of my own race and the prehistoric grandfathers of Malicious Gossip and Haabunai. My savage friends, with their clear features, their large straight eyes and olive skins, showed still the traces of their Caucasian blood. Their forefathers and mine may have hunted the great winged lizards together through primeval wildernesses, until, driven by who knows what urge of wanderlust or necessity, certain tribes set out in that drive through Europe and Asia toward America that ended at last, when a continent sunk beneath their feet, on these islands in the southern seas.

Index

Index

Index

Index

Index

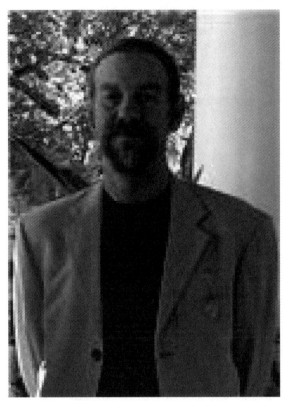

About the Author

Jack spent six years in the United States Navy and went on to earn his Bachelor of Science in Electrical Engineering from the University of South Florida. Jack has over thirty years experience in the Aerospace and Defense industry, having worked on both manned and unmanned Space programs as well as many military platforms. He is a fourth generation engineer and fourth generation patent holder and identifies himself as a Tibetan Buddhist.

Jack's research into the life and theories of his great-grandfather James Churchward, author of the series of books about the Lost Continent of Mu, is conducted using his technical expertise, unique connections, special viewpoint and access to a portion of James' original source materials. Armed with his knowledge and capabilities, Jack seeks to create a more complete understanding of James Churchward and his theories.

Jack is married with three grown children and five grandchildren and lives in Clearwater, Florida.

website: http://www.my-mu.com/
email: jack@my-mu.com

Other Books By Ozark Mountain Publishing, Inc.

Dolores Cannon
Conversations with Nostradamus,
Volume I, II, III
Jesus and the Essenes
They Walked with Jesus
Between Death and Life
A Soul Remembers Hiroshima
Keepers of the Garden.
The Legend of Starcrash
The Custodians
The Convoluted Universe - Book One,
Two, Three, Four
Five Lives Remembered
The Three Waves of Volunteers and the
New Earth
Stuart Wilson & Joanna Prentis
The Essenes - Children of the Light
Power of the Magdalene
Beyond Limitations
Atlantis and the New Consciousness
The Magdalene Version
O.T. Bonnett, M.D./Greg Satre
Reincarnation: The View from Eternity
What I Learned After Medical School
Why Healing Happens
M. Don Schorn
Elder Gods of Antiquity
Legacy of the Elder Gods
Gardens of the Elder Gods
Reincarnation...Stepping Stones of Life
Aron Abrahamsen
Holiday in Heaven
Out of the Archives – Earth Changes
Sherri Cortland
Windows of Opportunity
Raising Our Vibrations for the New Age
Michael Dennis
Morning Coffee with God
God's Many Mansions
Nikki Pattillo
Children of the Stars
A Spiritual Evolution

Rev. Grant H. Pealer
Worlds Beyond Death
A Funny Thing Happened on the Way to
Heaven
Maiya & Geoff Gray-Cobb
Angels - The Guardians of Your Destiny
Seeds of the Soul
Sture Lönnerstrand
I Have Lived Before
Arun & Sunanda Gandhi
The Forgotten Woman
Claire Doyle Beland
Luck Doesn't Happen by Chance
James H. Kent
Past Life Memories As A Confederate
Soldier
Dorothy Leon
Is Jehovah An E.T
Justine Alessi & M. E. McMillan
Rebirth of the Oracle
Donald L. Hicks
The Divinity Factor
Christine Ramos, RN
A Journey Into Being
Mary Letorney
Discover The Universe Within You
Debra Rayburn
Let's Get Natural With Herbs
Jodi Felice
The Enchanted Garden
Susan Mack & Natalia Krawetz
My Teachers Wear Fur Coats
Ronald Chapman
Seeing True
Rev. Keith Bender
The Despiritualized Church
Vara Humphreys
The Science of Knowledge
Karen Peebles
The Other Side of Suicide
Antoinette Lee Howard
Journey Through Fear
Julia Hanson
Awakening To Your Creation
Irene Lucas
Thirty Miracles in Thirty Days

Mandeep Khera
Why?
Robert Winterhalter
The Healing Christ
James Wawro
Ask Your Inner Voice
Tom Arbino
You Were Destined to be Together
Maureen McGill & Nola Davis
Live From the Other Side
Anita Holmes
TWIDDERS
Walter Pullen
Evolution of the Spirit
Cinnamon Crow
Teen Oracle
Chakra Zodiac Healing Oracle
Jack Churchward
Lifting the Veil on the Lost Continent of
Mu
Guy Needler
The History of God
Beyond the Source – Book 1
Dee Wallace/Jarrad Hewett
The Big E
Dee Wallace
Conscious Creation
Natalie Sudman
Application of Impossible Things
Henry Michaelson
And Jesus Said – A Conversation
Victoria Pendragon
SleepMagic
Riet Okken
The Liberating Power of Emotions
Janie Wells
Payment for Passage
Dennis Wheatley/ Maria Wheatley
The Essential Dowsing Guide
Dennis Milner
Kosmos
Garnet Schulhouser
Dancing on a Stamp
Julia Cannon
Soul Speak – The Language of Your
Body

For more information about any of the above titles, soon to be released titles,
or other items in our catalog, write or visit our website:
PO Box 754, Huntsville, AR 72740
www.ozarkmt.com